PATERNOSTER THEOLOGICAL MONOGRAPHS

Alvin Plantinga
and
Christian Apologetics

PATERNOSTER THEOLOGICAL MONOGRAPHS

A full listing of all titles in this series and
Paternoster Biblical Monographs appears
at the close of this book

PATERNOSTER THEOLOGICAL MONOGRAPHS

Alvin Plantinga and Christian Apologetics

Keith Mascord

Forward by Graham Cole

Wipf & Stock
PUBLISHERS
Eugene, Oregon

Wipf and Stock Publishers
199 W 8th Ave, Suite 3
Eugene, OR 97401

Alvin Plantinga and Christian Apologetics
By Mascord, Keith A.
Copyright©2006 Paternoster
ISBN 13: 978-1-55635-156-3
ISBN 10: 1-55635-156-9
Publication date 12/20/2006
Previously published by Paternoster, 2006

PATERNOSTER THEOLOGICAL MONOGRAPHS

Series Preface

In the West the churches may be declining, but theology—serious, academic (mostly doctoral level) and mainstream orthodox in evaluative commitment—shows no sign of withering on the vine. This series of *Paternoster Theological Monographs* extends the expertise of the Press especially to first-time authors whose work stands broadly within the parameters created by fidelity to Scripture and has satisfied the critical scrutiny of respected assessors in the academy. Such theology may come in several distinct intellectual disciplines—historical, dogmatic, pastoral, apologetic, missional, aesthetic and no doubt others also. The series will be particularly hospitable to promising constructive theology within an evangelical frame, for it is of this that the church's need seems to be greatest. Quality writing will be published across the confessions—Anabaptist, Episcopalian, Reformed, Arminian and Orthodox—across the ages—patristic, medieval, reformation, modern and counter-modern—and across the continents. The aim of the series is theology written in the twofold conviction that the church needs theology and theology needs the church—which in reality means theology done for the glory of God.

Series Editors

David F. Wright, Emeritus Professor of Patristic and Reformed Christianity, University of Edinburgh, Scotland, UK

Trevor A. Hart, Head of School and Principal of St Mary's College School of Divinity, University of St Andrews, Scotland, UK

Anthony N.S. Lane, Professor of Historical Theology and Director of Research, London School of Theology, UK

Anthony C. Thiselton, Emeritus Professor of Christian Theology, University of Nottingham, Research Professor in Christian Theology, University College Chester, and Canon Theologian of Leicester Cathedral and Southwell Minster, UK

Kevin J. Vanhoozer, Research Professor of Systematic Theology, Trinity Evangelical Divinity School, Deerfield, Illinois, USA

*To Judy, Damien, Jon, Daniel, Jared, Kieran
and to those many others who have walked this journey with me*

Contents

Foreword by Graham A. Cole	xi
Preface	xiii
Acknowledgements	xv

Chapter 1
Plantinga in Context 1

Chapter 2
Plantinga and Negative Apologetics:
Background Considerations 21

Chapter 3
Plantinga and Negative Apologetics:
Various Modern and Postmodern Challenges 32
3.1 Logical Positivism 33
3.2 Religious Pluralism 34
3.3 Naturalism 41
3.4 Postmodernism 47
3.5 Historical Biblical Criticism 53

Chapter 4
Plantinga and Negative Apologetics: 58
Evidentialist and *de jure* Challenges
4.1 Evidentialist Challenges 58
4.2 *De jure* Challenges 70

Chapter 5
Plantinga and Negative Apologetics: 79
Evil and Suffering
5.1 The Logical Form of the Problem of Evil 81
5.2 The Evidentialist Form of the Problem of Evil .. 95

Chapter 6
Plantinga and Positive Apologetics 110
6.1 Criticisms of Plantinga's Contribution to Positive Apologetics ... 110

6.1.1 No Intention to Contribute   111
6.1.2 A Small, but Significant Change in Attitude   111
6.1.3 Actual and Potential Contributions   119

Chapter 7
Plantinga's Theory of Theistic Belief Formation:
A Critique   **127**
7.1 Possible Instances of Basic Theistic Belief   128
7.2 Beholding the Starry Heavens   130
7.3 Other Suggested Examples of Basic Theistic Belief Formation 135
7.4 Determining the Impact of Other Beliefs   140

Chapter 8
Plantinga's Theory of Christian Belief Formation:
A Critique   **146**
8.1 The Presence and Importance of Inferences   148
8.2 The Presence and Importance of Arguments in the New Testament 154
8.3 A Warranted Trust Model of Christian Belief Formation   159
8.4 Advantages and Strengths of the Warranted Trust Model   162
8.5 Plantinga's Defence of his Supernaturalistic Model   167
8.6 Defence of the Warranted Trust Model   169

Chapter 9
Plantinga's Significance   **184**
9.1 Plantinga and Augustinianism   186
9.2 Plantinga and Thomism   190
9.3 Plantinga and the Presuppositionalist/Evidentialist Divide 202
9.4 Plantinga and Postmodernism   206
9.5 A Final Assessment   209

Bibliography   **211**

General Index   **235**

Foreword

Alvin Plantinga is one of the key players - along with Richard Swinburne - in the revival of Christians in philosophy and Christian philosophy in the late 20th century and which continues into the 21st century. In a range of books, beginning with *God and Other Minds* in 1967, through to *Warranted Christian Belief* in 2000, as well as in numerous articles, Plantinga has endeavoured to show that Christ believing can be a morally and intellectually responsible practice. I recall the excitement in my own mind when the argument of *God and Other Minds* sunk in. Christians at the time were so often called to parade a forcefulness of argument and accumulation of evidences for their beliefs when there were other beliefs of enormous existential significance, such as belief in the existence of other minds, that wouldn't have survived what T. J. Richards labels in another context 'the fallacy of unattainable standards of argument.' Christians can 'be too easily browbeaten' as C.S. Lewis said. Reading Plantinga, for me, was a therapeutic exercise.

Keith Mascord deftly expounds Plantinga's Reformed Epistemology and its implications for the practice of negative and positive apologetics. He does so with clarity, care and charity, but also with an independence of mind and judicious criticisms. This is not a work of hagiography. In it, we learn not only much of the implications of Plantinga's thought for the apologist's calling, but also about Plantinga himself. As someone who has both heard and met Plantinga - and not simply read his work - it is humbling to meet such a combination of sharp intellect, graciousness and humour. In this work, you can hear Plantinga's voice.

The task of Christian apology is all the more urgent in the post-Christendom era. Like their counterparts in the 2nd century, Christians today will need not only commend the Faith, but also to defend its truth claims. Defending those claims involves both the clarification of Christian beliefs and providing warrant for commitment to them. And so, like that century, there is a great need for a new order of Christian apologists who take seriously the challenges of naturalism, the plurality of religions, our experience of evils and the matter of epistemic responsibility. Plantinga has made a massive contribution to the task - albeit often by way of implications to be drawn from his various epistemological projects. Such a significant thinker as Plantinga deserves a significant engagement with his ideas, and Mascord supplies that engagement. In this work, the reader is well served.

Graham A. Cole
Professor of Biblical and Systematic Theology
Trinity Evangelical Divinity School

Preface

The aim of this work is to describe and assess Alvin Plantinga's contribution to Christian apologetics. Of necessity, this description and assessment will need to be provisional. Plantinga is still actively doing apologetics, as well as contributing to apologetic theory. Moreover, his thinking is still in the process of development and refinement. However, now is an appropriate time to at least begin taking stock of Plantinga's extensive and intensive involvement in apologetic theory and practice. His long time interest in the subject has culminated in the publication of *Warranted Christian Belief*, which, along with the earlier *Warrant: The Current Debate* and *Warrant and Proper Function*, represents Plantinga's mature understanding of epistemology and its relationship to theistic and Christian belief.

In chapter one, Plantinga's intellectual context, as this bears upon apologetic theory and practice, is laid out. Chapter two describes and suggests a number of reasons for Plantinga's career-long preoccupation with negative apologetics. Chapters three to five, which are largely descriptive, rather than critical, outline Plantinga's responses to various contemporary challenges to Christian faith. In the process, his own distinctive and evolving epistemology is laid out, laying the groundwork for later criticism. In chapter six, Plantinga's contribution to positive apologetics is discussed in light of criticisms that Plantinga's contribution in this area has been disappointing. In chapters seven and eight, certain aspects of Plantinga's theory are critiqued, and an alternative model of Christian belief formation proposed. In chapter nine, concluding judgements are made about the stature and significance of Plantinga's contribution to apologetics.

Acknowledgements

This book begain its life as a ThD thesis, and remains substantially unaltered. There are a number of people I would like to mention by way of acknowledgment. Special thanks are due to Dr. Graham Cole for suggesting Alvin Plantinga's writings as a subject worthy of study (he was right); to Dr. Bruce Langtry, whose insightful comments and questions were indispensably helpful in refining and tightening the arguments of this book; to Ken Perszyk for valuable comments on chapter five; to Patrick Roche for very useful suggestions on the latter chapters of the thesis; to Alvin Plantinga who has read and given valuable comments on three of the chapters, including the two most critical of his work. The opportunity to meet with Plantinga on a number of occasions, and to be the beneficiary of his generous and gracious advice were hugely appreciated. Special thanks also go to my friends, colleagues and students, particularly Jennifer Baddeley for her skilful, meticulous proof reading. I have been encouraged and helped by these and other people in more ways than I can name. Finally, I would like to thank my wife, Judy, and sons, Damien, Jon, Dan, Jared and Kieran for putting up with the eight year obsession which has been this work.

CHAPTER 1

Plantinga in Context

In order to assess the contribution of Plantinga to the enterprise of Christian apologetics, it will be helpful to place him into his intellectual and theological context. This will be done mostly in broad terms in this chapter, before moving to a more detailed description of Plantinga's theological and apologetic context in chapter two.

As a first step, it will be helpful to define what is meant by apologetics. The word apologetics is normally used with one of two meanings. It can be used to refer to what is a theoretical discipline, the primary aim of which is to explore the nature, justification and purpose of apology.[1] As a theoretical discipline, apologetics is a relatively recent phenomenon. L. Russ Bush notes that it was only after Christian theology began to be self-consciously organised into various departments, under the influence of Friedrich Schleiermacher (1768-1834), that apologetics as a systematic discipline emerged. Prior to that, apologetic studies had largely been topical, consisting of specific responses to specific challenges.[2]

The word apologetics is also used to describe the activity of defending and/or commending the faith. Understood in this way, apologetics is as old as the faith itself. Christians have consistently been required, both by circumstance and injunction, to make a defence of their faith, or hope (1 Peter 3:15). They have produced countless apologies well before the study of how one might or should apologise was formalised into a recognisable discipline.

It is worth noting, before considering Plantinga's intellectual context, that Plantinga is not primarily either an apologist or an apologetic theorist. His major area of interest is epistemology. The apologetic implications of his work, which are many, are only occasionally spelled out by him. Having said that, Plantinga has clear and developed (and developing) ideas about the role and function of apology, and therefore about apologetics understood as a theoretical discipline. He also, throughout his career, has written some form of response to every major contemporary intellectual challenge to traditional Christian faith. He has, thus, been heavily involved in apologetics, understood as an activity. In assessing Alvin Plantinga's contribution to Christian apologetics, both his

---

1   Or defence, from the Greek apologia – ἀπολογία.
2   L. Russ Bush, *Readings in Christian Apologetics* (Grand Rapids: Academie Books, 1983), 377.

theoretical and practical contributions will be considered. First, we turn to the promised intellectual and theological map.

As a result of nineteenth and twentieth century theorising about apologetics, a number of significant theoretical movements within the history of Christian thought have been identified. Two of these having particular significance for apologetics are the Augustinian and the Thomistic streams.[3]

Augustine (ca 354-430), one of the greatest of all Christian theologians, was also one of Christianity's finest apologists. His powerful engagement with the skepticism of the New Academy still stands as a masterpiece of philosophical reasoning. His defence of a Christian view of history, in the *City of God,* is a testimony to his rarely surpassed brilliance. However, in the field of apologetics, Augustine's significance lies more in the abiding impact of his epistemological approach, or at least one aspect of it: his understanding of the relationship between faith and reason.

Put simply, and with some risk of over-simplification, Augustine's position is as follows. Augustine believed that human sin, expressed especially in an unwillingness to move beyond the created order in search of God, prevented people from coming to know God. Special revelation was thus necessitated, its purpose being to humble human pride, and to move people back towards a love for God, in Christ. Faith was the necessary first step on the road to the knowledge of God. According to Augustine, there were two broad ways of knowing: knowing by seeing,[4] which Augustine refers to as understanding, and knowing by belief,[5] which is the way of faith.[6] The first, the way of understanding, was epistemologically superior to the second because it involved immediate and direct contact between the knower and known. With faith, the object of belief was known indirectly, chiefly through the testimony of others. Testimony does not irresistibly demand acceptance, and therefore an act of the will was required. A decision to trust needed to be made. Faith, which was this

---

3 Note that a distinction between Augustine and Aquinas with respect to apologetics tends to be made by Protestants, and more narrowly still by Reformed Protestants who see themselves as appropriating certain aspects of Augustine's thought. Bernard Ramm, for example, in his *Varieties of Christian Apologetics* (Grand Rapids: Baker Book House, 1973), places Augustine and Aquinas at the headwaters of two, for him, significantly different apologetic streams.

4 To know by seeing is to have immediate and personal access to the object of knowledge, such as when one perceives the truth of the principles of geometry.

5 To know by believing is to know indirectly, for example, through the testimony of others.

6 At times Augustine sharply differentiates between knowledge and belief, because of the insubstantial and inconclusive nature of belief. However, more often he would grant to belief, if properly grounded, the status of a kind of knowledge, G. O'Daly, 'Augustine', in D. Furley, (ed), *From Aristotle to Augustine* (London: Routledge, 1999), 393.

decision to trust, is essentially an act of willing assent[7] to propositions proposed for belief by an authority one has come to accept as reliable; in the case of Christian faith, by God.[8]

Because Christian faith was dependent on an act of will, Augustine insisted that personal purification was necessary for faith (and, ultimately, for sight) to be possible. Knowledge by belief can easily be ignored or resisted (evidenced in the response of sinful human beings), and thus, the Christian faith must, necessarily, be a gift which comes only after some measure of healing takes place. As Augustine puts it:

> Will you be able to lift your heart unto God? Must it not first be healed in order for you to see? Do you not show your pride when you demand "First let me see and then I will be healed"?[9]

Faith, for Augustine, was the key to understanding. Thus, his over-all approach to the knowledge of God has come to be represented in terms of Anselm's famous statement, 'faith seeking understanding' (*fides quaerens intellectum*).[10] This statement has become something of a slogan to represent Augustine's understanding of the relationship between faith and reason. Those who see themselves as appropriating this approach have tended to emphasise faith at the expense of reason, especially where reason is considered to be in any way

---

7   Augustine defined faith as 'thinking with assent'. See, for example, 'On the Predestination of the Saints', *Saint Augustine's Anti-Pelagian Works*, tr. P. Holmes, R. E. Wallis, The Nicene and Post-Nicene Fathers (Grand Rapids: Eerdmans, 1971), 2.5, 499. Both the will and thought are involved; the will because belief is not overpoweringly demanded by the evidence, the mind because one must have some understanding of what one believes, and also some reason to believe, D. X. Burt, *Augustine's World: An Introduction to His Speculative Philosophy* (Lanham, Maryland: University Press of America, 1996), 44, 45.

8   See further, Norman Kretzmann, 'Faith Seeks, Understanding Finds: Augustine's Charter for Christian Philosophy', in Thomas Flint, (ed), *Christian Philosophy* (Notre Dame: University of Notre Dame Press, 1990), 1-36.

9   'Enarrationes in Psalmos', 39, 21, *Patrologia Latina*, Vol. 34, 447; quoted in *Augustine's World*, 46.

10   This expression and way of understanding originates with Augustine. See, for example, 'Sermon 43' in John E. Rotelle, (ed), *Sermons*, The Works of Saint Augustine (Brooklyn, New York: New City Press, 1992): 'If a person says to me, "I want to understand in order that I may believe", I reply, "Believe in order that you may understand."'; also, Sermon 126, in *Sermons*; 'On Free Will', in *Earlier Writings*, J. H. S. Burleigh, (ed), The Library of Christian Classics, (Philadelphia: Westminster, 1979), II, ii, 6, 137-138; 'Tractate 27' in *Augustine: Tractates on the Gospel of John*, trans. J. W. Retting, The Fathers of the Church (Washington: The Catholic University of America Press, 1988), 9, 2, 284.

independent of faith, or of special revelation (faith's object).[11] There has also been a tendency to minimise, or even deny, the place of reason prior to faith, which, as chapter nine will demonstrate, does not truly represent Augustine's position.

The second major line of thought which has been influential in apologetic theory and practice is Thomism, the name derived from Thomas Aquinas (1225-1274). Aquinas is regarded by many as the greatest Christian apologist of all time. So successful was he in responding to the major challenge to Christian faith in his day, that his apologetic became for many centuries a dominant force in the Western Church.

In terms of religious epistemology, Aquinas is perhaps best known for his theory that there are two complementary ways in which a person can discover truth about God. The first is the way of reason, while the second is the way of faith. A classic statement of this position is found in Aquinas's *Summa Contra Gentiles:*

> There is a twofold mode of truth in what we profess about God. Some truths about God exceed all the ability of the human reason. Such is the truth that God is triune. But there are some truths which the natural reason also is able to reach. Such are that God exists, that He is one, and the like. In fact, such truths about God have been proved demonstrably by the philosophers, guided by the light of natural reason.[12]

Aquinas viewed philosophy and theology as being in a relationship of mutual support.[13] Reason (or nature) was perceived as anticipating grace (or

---

[11] R. P. Russell, for example, in 'Augustinianism' in *The New Catholic Encyclopedia*, Vol. 1 (New York: McGraw Hill, 1967), 1063, describes as Augustinian the view which excludes the possibility of a philosophy which is autonomous in its own right or completely independent of theology. According to Bernard Ramm, an Augustinian approach to apology is built upon the following convictions: (1) Divine revelation has priority over human philosophy. No philosophy is more fundamental than Holy Scripture nor has a position prior to divine revelation; (2) Human depravity affects the will of man and the passions of man making him weak in temptation and pushing him into sin. Sin affects the mind of man, especially with reference to God and the knowledge of God; (3) If man is a sinner, he needs the purification of the mind to see the truth. The gospel is received in faith. The gospel received in faith brings purification of the heart and illumination of the mind. In this sense, then, we believe in order to understand, *A Christian Appeal to Reason* (Waco: Word Books, 1972), 36, 37.
[12] *Summa Contra Gentiles,* (hereafter, *SCG*) A. C. Pegis, trans. (Notre Dame: Notre Dame Press, 1975), 1, 3, 2.
[13] Each sphere of study (philosophy and theology) was considered to be significantly independent of the other. For some of the implications of this for Thomistic scholarship see A. Plantinga, 'Augustinian Christian Philosophy', *The Monist,* Vol. 75, No. 3 (July, 1992), 312-17.

revelation),[14] and grace did not contradict nature, but perfected it.[15] Since all truth is God's truth, no ultimate conflict was possible between the true deliverances of reason and the truths of revelation.[16] In cases of apparent conflict, Aquinas gave to revealed truth the right to censor profane truth, and also to act as the ultimate criterion of truth. Reason was, in this sense, subordinate to faith.[17]

Aquinas had a high view of faith, or at least of Christian faith, the object of which is truth, and ultimately the first truth, who is God. Like Augustine, Aquinas understood faith as involving an act of the will,[18] unlike what typically happens in cases of knowledge, where the intellect is moved directly and involuntarily to assent to truth, such truth being clearly and immediately grasped. Faith is exercised in the absence of compelling evidence, and in this consists its merit, according to Aquinas. Faith is meritorious because it is not compelled either by evidence or force; it involves a free act of consenting to propositions proposed for belief by God, who also gives the grace to believe. Faith is also meritorious because it arises from a desire for God and for eternal life, the reward promised for faith.[19]

---

14 In that its conclusions were significantly the same as what is revealed in Scripture.

15 In the sense that grace provides the answers and the filled out content that reason is unable to. According to Ramm, 'this thesis (*gratia non tollit naturam sed perficit*) pervades and colors the entire Thomistic apologetic,' B. Ramm, *Varieties of Christian Apologetics* (Grand Rapids: Baker Book House, 1973), 104.

16 If there is a conflict, then a mistake has been made in one field or the other; either a theological misunderstanding or a misinterpretation of the world.

17 Aquinas was here in direct reaction to the philosophy of Averroes (1126-1198), an Islamic philosopher and theologian. Averroes sought to establish the autonomy of philosophical investigation unimpeded by religious and theological considerations. Aquinas, contrary to the opinions of those who see him as giving priority to reason, was very clear in his teaching on the subordination of reason to revelation. He was explicitly critical of those who would let reason be the arbiter of religious truth. See, for example, 'Commentary on Boethius' De Trinitate', in *The Trinity and the Unicity of the Intellect*, trans. Sister Rose Emmanuella Brennan, (St. Louis: Herder, 1946), 2, 1, obj 1, resp.; 2, 3, resp.

18 Like Augustine, he defined faith as 'thinking with assent', *The Disputed Questions on Truth*, trans. J. V. McGlynn, S. J., Chicago: Henry Regnery, 1953, XIV, 1, 207f; also *Summa Theologiae*, (hereafter *STh*) trans. Thomas Gilby et al, 61 vols, (New York: McGraw-Hill, 1964-81), II-II, q.2, art.1.

19 For a good short discussion of Aquinas's understanding of faith, see Kenneth Konyndyk, 'Faith and Evidentialism', in R. Audi and W. Wainwright, (eds), *Rationality, Religious Belief and Moral Commitment* (Ithaca: Cornell University Press, 1986), 85-89. For more detail see, Arvin Vos, *Aquinas, Calvin, and Contemporary Protestant Thought: A Critique of Protestant Views on the Thought of Thomas Aquinas* (Washington: Christian University Press, 1985).

Tied up with faith's virtue is its limitation. Faith does not quite achieve the epistemic grandeur of knowledge. Knowledge is attained by moving from what is self-evident to what can be infallibly deduced from this, resulting in certainty. The certitude of faith is the certitude of an unwavering will. The certitude of knowledge is the certitude of clear vision. The pursuit of this clear vision, which constitutes a beginning of the beatific vision, is the task of natural theology.

Natural theology, although not for every Christian, and despite its high level of difficulty, was nevertheless for Aquinas an important activity. Apart from the intrinsic and Augustinian value of converting faith to knowledge, its pursuit and outcomes were beneficial for a number of other reasons: key Christian beliefs were confirmed;[20] various errors refuted; and arguments of great power were also made available for the purpose of convincing unbelievers of the truth of Christian theism.[21]

Theologians and apologists who have objected to Thomism have tended to do so on the grounds that human reason is given too prominent a place. Not only did Aquinas have a high view of reason's ability with respect to the things of God, he also, effectively, drove a wedge between philosophy (understood as the activity of acquiring knowledge by means of independent inquiry) and theology (understood as reflection upon special revelation). Human reason is thus able to be understood as significantly independent.

It is this idea of autonomous reason which is, for many, the defining difference between Thomism and Augustinianism.[22] Whether rightly or wrongly, Aquinas is understood to have broken the nexus between revelation and reason. In the words of Francis Schaeffer, he freed philosophy 'to take

---

20 See, for example, *SCG* I, 2, 2. The proofs of natural theology have the effect of giving some credibility to the articles of faith, even though they mostly provide no direct evidence for them.

21 The apologetic use of natural theology was particularly useful with those who did not accept the Christian Scriptures. With such people, 'We must ... have recourse to the natural reason, to which all men are forced to give their assent', *SCG* I, 2, 3.

22 John Frame, in his discussion of Thomism in 'Scripture and the Apologetic Task' *The Journal of Biblical Counselling* Vol. 13, No. 2 (Winter, 1995), 9-12, notes that Aquinas differentiated between reasoning with and reasoning without the assistance of revelation. It is because of this that the Thomistic attitude to human reason is characterised as "autonomous" or "neutralist," 10. Plantinga has a similar understanding. In 'Augustinian Christian Philosophy', 324, he points out that according to the Thomistic tradition there is a clear demarcation between theology (what is known by faith) and every other science (the province of reason), so much so that it is thought illegitimate to appeal to what one knows by faith in pursuing the non-theological sciences. Plantinga is unhappy with this division, arguing that, on the contrary, 'what we need and want, in studying a given area, is the best *total* understanding we can get, using all the resources at our command.' This he identifies as the Augustinian position.

wings ... and fly off wherever it wished, without relationship to the Scriptures.'[23] Those identifying with Augustine (as over against Aquinas) have insisted on the subservience of reason to revelation, with special revelation being seen as the indispensable foundation stone in any scholarly investigation of the world. Those identifying with Aquinas have tended to have a higher view of independent reason: reason which operates both prior to and alongside of faith. They have given to natural theology an important, even foundational role within the theological and apologetic enterprise,[24] and, in many cases, have also come to believe, under pressure from Enlightenment evidentialism, that Christian theism requires the support of reasons and evidence in order to be rational.[25]

It is largely because of the felt need of (many) Thomists to provide evidential or rational support for Christian conclusions that William Dryness uses the inverse version of Anselm's slogan to characterise Thomism in contrast to Augustinianism. Summing up both, he writes: 'basically there have been two approaches to apologetics, one [the Thomistic] emphasizes that we must *understand in order to believe;* the other [the Augustinian] insists we must

---

23 Francs Schaeffer, *Escape From Reason* (Downers Grove: InterVarsity Press, 1968), 11-12.
24 Linda Zagzebski notes that Catholic scholarship has long accepted the idea that 'revealed theology rests on natural theology, which is to say, the work of philosophers, and the preeminent philosophy was that of Aquinas. This was officially recognized in the encyclical *Aeterni Patris* (1879), in which Pope Leo XIII called special attention to the importance of Thomistic philosophy and declared it to be the basis of ecclesiastical theology,' *Rational Faith: Catholic Responses to Reformed Epistemology* (Notre Dame: Notre Dame Press, 1993), 3.
25 They have thus tended to be apologetic evidentialists. For more on evidentialism, see below. Vos argues that Aquinas himself was not an evidentialist, bearing in mind that evidentialism as a morality of knowledge post-dated Aquinas. The embracing of evidentialist principles by those in the Thomistic stream is, according to Vos, a post-16th century phenomena. He suggests, following G. de Broglie ('La vraie notion thomiste des "preambula fidei",' *Gregorianum*, Vol. 34 (Roma: Piazzadella Pilotta, 1953), 341-389, that pressure from the Enlightenment's preoccupation with the subjective act of reasoning led to the development of positions which were embracive of evidentialist principles. Catholic as well as Protestant theologians began to assume that for faith to be rational both the existence of God and the fact of revelation needed to be discursively established. Natural theology thus came to assume a position of prominence that Aquinas himself had not given it, *Aquinas, Calvin and Contemporary Protestant Thought*, 92, 115. See also Nicholas Wolterstorff, 'The Migration of the Theistic Arguments: From Natural Theology to Evidentialist Apologetics, Audi, R., and Wainwright, W., (eds), *Rationality, Religious Belief and Moral Commitment* (Ithaca and London: Cornell University Press, 1986), 38f; Paul Helm, *Faith and Understanding* (Grand Rapids: Eerdmans, 1997), 33-35.

believe in order to understand.'[26] This, certainly, has been a common (and, for Plantinga, an influential) way of understanding the difference between Thomism and Augustinianism.[27] However, as will be seen in chapter nine, such an understanding needs significant modification.

The Augustinian/Thomistic divide is not the only historical factor affecting present day attitudes to apology. Of equal, if not greater importance is the impact of the Enlightenment, and, prior to that, of the ground-breaking theology of John Calvin. Any analysis of present day apologetics which neglects either of these would be seriously defective.

John Calvin (1509-1564) has had a profound impact upon apologetic theory and practice. His understanding of how human beings come to a knowledge of God has become the basis of a number of significant attempts to formulate a distinctively 'Reformed' understanding of apology. However, the precise nature of Calvin's position is the subject of ongoing controversy.

In the broadest of terms, it is generally agreed that Calvin held that a true and saving knowledge of God comes only as a result of the gracious revelation of God in the Scriptures, applied to the hearts and minds of his elect, through the working of the Holy Spirit. Calvin acknowledged that 'there is within the human mind, and indeed by natural instinct, an awareness of divinity',[28] a *sensus divinitatis*,[29] and that God has 'revealed himself and daily discloses himself in the whole workmanship of the universe [as a consequence of which] men cannot open their eyes without being compelled to see him'.[30] However, he believed that human sin was of such a character that any truth that comes as a result of nature's witness is suppressed and distorted. It is also uncontroversial that Calvin had a negative attitude towards natural theology, and therefore to the epistemological approach of Thomas Aquinas.

Beyond this, scholarly consensus is hard to find. There is, for example, on-going debate over whether any knowledge of God whatsoever is possible (or actual) through the revelation of God in nature; whether without the 'spectacles'

---

26 William Dyrness, *Christian Apologetics in a World Community* (Downers Grove: Inter-Varsity Press, 1983), 15.
27 Greg L. Bahnsen, for example, in *Van Til's Apologetic: Readings and Analysis* (Phillipsburg: P&R Publishing, 1998), describes the difference between Augustine and Aquinas in these terms: 'Simply put, Augustine argued that man's understanding and reasoning function only upon the foundation of faith in God. Reason has no self-sufficient ability to interpret experience and no true authority to judge the veracity of Christian faith. Augustine said, "I believe in order to understand." ... It could be said that Aquinas reversed this, saying that faith in God had to be founded upon the independent results of man's reasoning and understanding,' 47.
28 John Calvin, *Institutes of the Christian Religion*, The Library of Christian Classics, Vol. 20, John T. McNeill, (ed), (Philadelphia: The Westminster Press, 1960), I, iii, 1.
29 *Institutes*, I, iii, 3.
30 *Institutes*, I, v, 1.

Plantinga in Context

provided by special revelation people can, in any sense, know God.[31] There is debate over Calvin's understanding of the *sensus divinitatis*.[32] The exact character of the knowledge gained (or potentially gained) through God's revelation in nature is also debated; as is the question of whether this knowledge is an inferred knowledge, leading one back in the direction of natural theology, or a direct, even innate knowledge.[33]

Despite on-going controversy regarding the exact nature of Calvin's theology and epistemology, it is nevertheless clear that Calvin's influence has been considerable. His ideas, whether rightly understood or not, have had a shaping influence on at least one significant strand of apologetic theorising, out of which Plantinga himself has emerged. Included among insights credited to Calvin, and embraced by his followers, are the dismissal of natural theology; the (relative or absolute) depreciation of arguments designed to support Christian conclusions, an emphasis both upon the noetic effects of sin, and the Holy Spirit whose ministry is necessary for a saving knowledge, or as some would argue, for any knowledge of God.

Reformed apologists and epistemologists have also, particularly in the last hundred years or so, tended to interpret Calvin as teaching that knowledge of God is naturally or normally acquired non-inferentially; by way of some form of

---

31 John Beversluis, for example, in 'Reforming the "Reformed" Objection to Natural Theology', *Faith and Philosophy*, Vol. 12 (April, 1995) argues that 'Calvin unambiguously asserts that, in their fallen condition, human beings have no eyes to discern the revelation of God in Nature,' 194. The *sensus divinitatis* is therefore completely nonfunctional in post-lapsarian human beings. Michael Czapkay Sudduth, in 'Calvin, Plantinga, and the Natural Knowledge of God: A Response to Beversluis', *Faith and Philosophy*, Vol. 15, No. 1 (January, 1998), 92-103, argues, I think persuasively, that Calvin *does* teach that fallen, unregenerate people do hold (some) true beliefs about God, where such beliefs are among the deliverances of reason, 96. Plantinga thinks likewise: 'we human beings typically have at least some knowledge of God, and some grasp of what is required of us; and this even in the state of sin and even apart from regeneration. The condition of sin involves *damage* to the *sensus divinitatis*, but not obliteration,' *Warranted Christian Belief* (Oxford: Oxford University Press, 2000), (hereafter, *WCB*), 210. See also 214, 215.

32 For example, is this sense of divinity internal, innate and *a priori*, as was suggested in the Abridgments to *The Institutes* and in the various commentaries on the Heidelberg Catechism, or is it the result of inferential reflection upon nature, as has been suggested this century by Edward Dowey (following B. B. Warfield). Dowey draws attention to what he sees as the 'highly inductive character' of Calvin's 'natural arguments' and asserts that 'man infers certain attributes of God from nature,' *The Knowledge of God in Calvin's Theology* (New York: Columbia University Press, 1952), 77.

33 Michael Czapkay Sudduth, for example, in 'The Prospects for "Mediate" Natural Theology in John Calvin', *Religious Studies*, Vol. 31 (1995), 53-68, argues that some form of 'mediate' natural theology is at least consistent with Calvin's elaborated epistemology.

direct insight, and not as the result of reasoned argument or deliberative meditation.[34] This understanding has been a distinctive feature of Reformed or Calvinistic approaches to apology, creating perhaps *the* major area of contrast between Reformed and Thomistic approaches. Dewey J. Hoitenga argues that this understanding ultimately dates back to Plato, through Augustine,[35] which, if corrects, would locate Calvin and his followers on the Augustinian side of the Augustinian/Thomistic divide.

The impact of Calvin upon present day apologetic theory and practice, although significant, is easily surpassed by the impact of the Enlightenment. As a movement, the Enlightenment of the late seventeenth and eighteenth centuries had its earlier beginnings in the ferment of thought produced in western Europe by the translation of Arabic writings into Latin, the impact of Aristotelian philosophy, the flood of classical ideas at the time of the Renaissance, the passionate debates of the Reformation, and the beginnings of modern science in the seventeenth century. By the middle of the eighteenth

---

34 Nicholas Wolterstorff, in the Introduction to H. Hart, J. Van der Hoeven, N. Wolterstorff, (eds), *Rationality in the Calvinian Tradition* (Lanham: University Press of America, 1983), suggests 5 theses on rationality which he sees as characteristic of the Calvinist tradition. These are, in summary: (1) one can be justified as a theist even if one does not accept the crucial tenets of theism on the basis of some argument or reasons; (2) one may well be within one's rights in believing immediately that the Christian Scriptures are the revelation of God; Scripture is self-authenticating; (3) sin has darkened our capacities for acquiring justified beliefs and for acquiring knowledge; (4) scientific enterprises, although they may be intellectually and scientifically competent are nevertheless not neutral with respect to the Christian faith; (5) when a Christian engages in science, his activity ought in appropriate ways to be directed by his faith, v, vi.

35 In Dewey J. Hoitenga, Jr., *Faith and Reason from Plato to Plantinga: An Introduction to Reformed Epistemology* (Albany: State University of New York Press, 1991). Hoitenga considers Plato's theory of direct acquaintance as one of the significant epistemological sources of Reformed Epistemology. He distinguishes between two different doctrines of knowledge in Plato. The first he labels 'knowledge as acquaintance' - *viz.*, 'that which results from direct experience of an object' (p.8). This first doctrine Hoitenga believes can be found in *The Republic*, and is in contrast to that found in the *Theatetus*, which is a forerunner of the doctrine of knowledge as justified true belief, which, prior to Gettier ('Is Justified True Belief Knowledge?' *Analysis*, Vol. 23, No. 6, June, 1963, 121-123) was the dominant account of knowledge in the West. It is the former doctrine (the acquaintance doctrine) that Hoitenga identifies as that which gave rise to the tradition that undergirds Reformed epistemology. He argues that the Augustinian formula, *faith seeking understanding*, applied to the knowledge of God possible in this life, refers paradigmatically to a kind of direct seeing rather than to a rational demonstration. Not everyone, however, is persuaded by this suggestion. See, for example, chapter two of R. Douglas Geivett, *Evil and the Evidence for God* (Philadelphia: Temple University Press, 1993).

century, a new ethos dominated Western civilisation. It was characterised by a spirit of reaction against pre-modern dependence upon authority (particularly ecclesiastical authority), and by confidence in the powers of human reason to understand and master the human environment. Further, a commitment to a morality of knowledge developed in which beliefs were only accepted as knowledge if they passed certain stringent tests, including the evidentialist test.

According to this test, which began to be articulated from the time of John Locke (1632-1704), a belief was not held with greater assurance than the proofs it was built upon would warrant.[36] The evidentialist test was grounded in an evidentialist principle, one extreme example of which was the articulation by W. K. Clifford (1845-1879), the English mathematician and philosopher: 'It is wrong always, everywhere, and for anyone, to believe anything upon insufficient evidence.'[37]

The evidentialist principle (or principles)[38] became the evidentialist challenge to Christian faith.[39] Christians were faced with the apologetic task of providing reasons or evidence in support of their faith. This task, although embraced by Catholics and Protestants alike, became increasingly difficult because of the strength of Enlightenment attacks upon Christian beliefs.

Of particular early significance were the skeptical writings of David Hume (1711-1776). Nancey Murphy makes the plausible suggestion that the subsequent course of Christian theology (and therefore, by implication, of apologetics) was determined by two parallel reactions to Humean skepticism: the first by Thomas Reid (1710-1796), the second by Immanuel Kant (1724-1804).[40]

Thomas Reid is known as the originator of the Scottish 'common sense' school of philosophy, or, as it is perhaps better known, of Scottish common sense realism. Reid's major philosophical work, *Enquiry into the Human Mind*

---

36 Plantinga expounds the Lockean position in *WCB*, 71-81.
37 W. K. Clifford, 'The Ethics of Belief', in *Lectures and Essays*, Leslie Stephen and Frederick Pollock, (eds), 2nd ed. (London and New York: Macmillan, 1886), 342-46.
38 Stephen Wykstra, in 'Toward a sensible evidentialism: On the notion of needing evidence', in W. Rowe and W. Wainwright, *Philosophy of Religion* (New York: Hartcourt Brace Jovanovich, 1989), argues for a more sensible version of the evidentialist principle. The point is that there is no one evidentialist principle, but rather a number of possible formulations.
39 Michael Czapkay Sudduth spells out the evidentialist challenge with respect to belief in God in terms of the following two propositions: (1) A person S is rational in believing that Pt (where Pt = the proposition *God exists*) only if S's belief that Pt is based upon adequate reasons; and (2) There are no adequate reasons for the belief that Pt, 'Bi-level Evidentialism and Reformed Apologetics', *Faith and Philosophy*, Vol. 11, No. 3 (July, 1994), 380.
40 Nancey Murphy, *Beyond Liberalism and Fundamentalism* (Valley Forge: Trinity Press International, 1996), 4f. Murphy tracks the influence of Reid's thought through Princeton theology to fundamentalism, 5.

on the Principles of Common Sense,[41] attempted to counter the corrosive effects of Humean skepticism. Reid developed an alternative epistemology which defended the common sense view that human belief forming faculties are mostly reliable, and that these can successfully interact with mind-independent reality. Instead of employing a *guilty-until-proven-innocent* principle of rationality, which, through Descartes' influence, has become almost axiomatic in Western epistemology, Reid suggested, as a better alternative, an *innocent-until-proven-guilty* principle. Underlying Reid's approach was the belief that human belief-forming mechanisms are God-created, and are therefore likely to be reliable.[42]

Embracement of a Reidian style epistemology has implications for apology. In the American context it helped to produce generations of Christian apologists confident both in the powers of human reason and in their ability to employ reason to meet the evidentialist challenge to Christian faith. Mark Noll notes that Protestant America was able to resist the more extreme and skeptical expressions of Enlightenment thought largely because of its ready acceptance of Scottish common sense realism.[43] The most articulate spokesmen for this position were Protestant educators and ministers.[44] Summing up, Noll writes:

> The American Revolution differed from the later Revolution in France in part because of the ability of the American evangelicals to align faith in reason with faith in God. The intellectual goal of evangelicals in the struggle against the irreligion and disorder of the Revolutionary period was, in Witherspoon's [an early President of Princeton] word, 'to meet [infidels] upon their own ground, and to show them from reason itself, the fallacy of their principles.'[45]

Reidian-inspired optimism about the powers of human reason contributed to apologetic practice in America being dominated, particularly in the nineteenth century, by Thomistic style apologies. These were characterised by a ready employment of natural theological arguments, along with inductive appeals to historical and other supporting evidence for Christianity's truth.

---

41 Thomas Reid, *An Inquiry into the Human Mind on the Principles of Common Sense* (Edinburgh: Printed for A. Millar, London, and A. Kincaid and J. Bell, Edinburgh, 1764).
42 The essential difference between Reid and Descartes, who also argued to the conclusion that our belief forming mechanisms have a God-secured reliability, is that Reid began his pursuit of knowledge with trust, whereas Descartes began the same pursuit with doubt, doubt which becomes irremediably corrosive.
43 Mark A. Noll, *The Scandal of the Evangelical Mind* (Grand Rapids: William B. Eerdmans, 1994), 84f.
44 *Scandal*, 85.
45 *Scandal*, 91.

Plantinga in Context 13

For our purposes, it is interesting that Plantinga acknowledges significant indebtedness to Thomas Reid.[46] One wonders whether there are within this indebtedness seeds of possible *rapprochement* between Thomistic and Augustinian-Calvinian apologetic approaches. To this possibility we will return at a later stage.

A second historically and theologically significant reaction to Humean skepticism was the Kantian reaction, a response which was both similar and dissimilar to Reid's. Like Reid, Kant's reply to Hume involved an appeal to the way human beings are rationally constituted. Unlike Reid, Kant created a radical epistemological dualism by differentiating between reality as it is in itself (the noumenal) and our experience of reality (the phenomenal). Kant believed that theoretical reason, by which conclusions are reached about phenomenal reality, was unable to secure knowledge of noumenal or transcendent reality, including God. Ruled out in principle, therefore, was the enterprise of natural theology. God's existence or character could not be established by way of reasoning from phenomenal reality.[47] Religious truth was therefore disassociated from theoretical knowledge.

The significance of this for apologetics was enormous. In Clark Pinnock's words, 'Apologetics has never been quite the same since.'[48] With faith being significantly set adrift from rationalistic grounding, various non-cognitive alternatives came to be explored, such as conscience or feeling. Faith's lack of rationalistic grounding came even to be seen as a virtue, as in the case of Søren Kierkegaard, who described faith as a passion, a leap, a commitment which exists, and can only exist as faith, precisely because it lacks rationalistic grounding. For Kierkegaard, reason and apologetics were not only unnecessary, they were enemies of the faith.[49]

Apologetics, to exist at all within the framework of a Kantian understanding, had to be radically re-defined. One method for achieving this was the shifting of the apologetic centre of Christianity from reason to experience. This, in

---

46 See, for example, *Warrant: The Current Debate* (Oxford: Oxford University Press, 1993), (hereafter *WCD)*, viii; and *Warrant and Proper Function,* (Oxford: Oxford University Press, 1993), (hereafter, *WPF)*, x, where Plantinga describes his own externalist epistemology as 'broadly Reidian' and where he also asserts that 'the global outline of Thomas Reid's epistemology seems to me to be largely correct.' See also 'Reid, Hume and God', unpublished paper, which is substantially reproduced in *WCB,* 222-227.

47 It could, however, be established as morally necessary; as necessary to make sense of the universal human experience of moral obligation. For Kant, the existence of God, as well as of freedom and the afterlife, were postulates of practical reason.

48 Clark Pinnock, 'Cultural Apologetics: an evangelical perspective', *Bibliotheca Sacra*, Vol. 127 (January-March, 1970), 59 (fn 3).

49 J. H. Gill, 'The Possibility of Apologetics', *Scottish Journal of Theology*, Vol. 16 (1963), 137.

essence, was the approach of Friedrich Schleiermacher (1768-1834), the acknowledged father of modern liberal theology.

Schleiermacher's theology can be seen as an attempt to circumvent the problems created by Kant's philosophy for Christian faith. According to Schleiermacher, the essence of religion is not to be sought in dogma or in a commitment to certain propositional truths, but in inward experience, in man's deepest feelings or intuitions of the divine. This feeling, described by Schleiermacher as the feeling of absolute dependence, is universal to human experience, finding expression in all religions. It is by this feeling that people were convinced of the reality of God, rather than by alleged proofs of his existence. Schleiermacher did not repudiate apologetics, but rather redefined its content and purpose. Christian apology became an apology for a particular experience, exemplified most supremely in Jesus, but existing universally. It was not an apology for particular Christian doctrines or dogmas, understood as descriptions of the way things are.[50]

Schleiermacher's radical and Kantian-inspired re-interpretation of Christian theology and apology stands at the headwaters of the liberal/fundamentalist-evangelical divide in modern theology. It has become one of three quite different ways of understanding theology with consequences for apology. These are helpfully described by George Lindbeck, in *The Nature of Doctrine*.[51] The first approach to theology, which is the approach of traditional orthodoxies, 'emphasizes the cognitive aspects of religion and stresses the ways in which church doctrines function as informative propositions or truth claims about objective realities. Religions are thus thought of as similar to philosophy or science as these were classically conceived.'[52] The second approach, which is the approach of Schleiermacher and of those who have broadly followed his lead, 'focuses on ... the "experiential-expressive" dimension of religion, [interpreting] doctrines as noninformative and nondiscursive symbols of inner feelings, attitudes, or existential orientations.'[53] The third approach to religion and doctrine, with obvious indebtedness to the later Wittgenstein, is the "cultural-linguistic" theory, according to which religions resemble languages or cultures, in which schema doctrines have the function of regulating communal life and thought.

The third approach is, in some ways, a development from, or variation on, the second. Both operate with a non-cognitive understanding of the purpose of religious language and practice. One emphasises the subjective and inward, while the other the social or communitarian. Each has arisen as a post-Kantian

---

50 A. Dulles, *A History of Apologetics* (London: Hutchinson and Co Ltd, 1971), 161.
51 George Lindbeck, *The Nature of Doctrine: Religion and Theology in a Postliberal Age* (Philadelphia: Westminster Press, 1984).
52 *The Nature of Doctrine*, 16.
53 *The Nature of Doctrine*, 16.

interpretation of religion, but also under the impact of modern critical Biblical scholarship. As doubt about the historical and doctrinal accuracy of Biblical propositions mounted (whether justifiably or not), the attractiveness of non-propositional understandings of theology increased. With these new understandings of theology inevitably came new understandings of apologetics. The experiential and social aspects of Christianity were increasingly taken to be the primary 'selling points' of the faith as the perceived need for an apology diminished, leading to a decrease in the practice of apologetics.

There are, it should be said, certain inherent anti-apologetic tendencies within thinking which embraces the second and third approaches. If the cognitive or informational content of Christianity is minimised or dismissed, and replaced by an emphasis on the social, it is a short step from here to the position that religions other than Christianity should be accepted as equally legitimate forms of religion because of their similar function.[54] All religions can be (and increasingly are) seen as expressions of the same underlying religious experience or experiences; all religions have a socially regulatory function. Christian uniqueness is harder to identify in these areas than in the distinctiveness of its doctrinal statements. Once these are re-interpreted in a non-cognitive direction, the gates are opened to a pluralistic understanding of Christianity, which in turn removes the need for apologetics, understood as a defence of Christian uniqueness.

It is partly due to these inherent tendencies that those in the liberal and broadly Schleiermachian stream of theology have never been particularly interested in apologetics, and are even less so in the current pluralistic and relativistic age. Commenting on the American scene, Paul Griffiths notes that:

> In almost all mainstream institutions in which theology is taught in the USA, apologetics as an intellectual discipline does not figure prominently in the curriculum. You'll look for it in vain in the catalogues of the Divinity Schools at Harvard or Chicago. Liberal Protestants have never been wedded to the virtues of apologetics.[55]

The impact of the Enlightenment is not, however, to be restricted to non-conservative forms of Christianity. Of particular significance for understanding Plantinga are two contrasting reactions to the Enlightenment by scholars from within the conservative Reformed tradition. An influential representative of one of those reactions was Benjamin Breckinridge Warfield (1851-1921). At the

---

54 A non-cognitive interpretation of religion does not necessitate a blurring of religious differences. Schleiermacher himself believed in the superiority of Christianity over other religions.
55 Paul Griffiths, 'An Apology For Apologetics', *Faith and Philosophy*, Vol. 5, No. 4 (October, 1988), 399. Griffiths goes on to note that the Roman Catholic tradition of systematic apologetics has also suffered significantly. He describes it as being 'killed' by the Second Vatican Council and especially by *Nostra Aetate*, 399.

headwaters of the second reaction was Abraham Kuyper (1837-1920). Influenced by Kuyper, and of more contemporary relevance (with respect to the theory and practice of apologetics) was Cornelius Van Til (1895-1987). In what follows, the positions of each of these three figures will be considered, with special attention given to the nature of their reaction to the Enlightenment.

B. B. Warfield is known as Princeton Seminary's last great defender of Calvinistic orthodoxy.[56] Warfield succeeded Archibald Alexander Hodge as professor of didactic and polemic theology at Princeton in 1887. He was one of a long line of Princetonians to appropriate a Reidian response to the Enlightenment. Along with his predecessors, Warfield affirmed the basic reliability of human belief-forming mechanisms, a reliability metaphysically grounded in the character and good purposes of God.[57] Warfield, in line with his confidence in reason, developed an approach to apology which can be described as broadly Thomistic.[58]

Warfield believed that the need for apology, or for the provision of reasons for belief, was one of 'the fundamental needs of the human spirit.'[59] As a result, he believed it to be:

> incumbent on the believer to be able to give a reason for the faith that it is in him, it is impossible for him to be a believer without a reason for the faith that is in him; and it is the task of apologetics to bring this reason clearly out in his consciousness, and make its validity plain.[60]

---

56 M. A. Noll, 'Warfield, Benjamin Breckinridge', in Walter A. Elwell (ed) *Evangelical Dictionary of Theology* (Grand Rapids: Baker Book House, 1984), 1156.
57 Nineteenth century Princetonians have been accused of uncritically accepting scientific inductivism, which among Enlightenment thinkers was given a physical rather than a metaphysical base. Donald Fuller and Richard Gardiner argue persuasively that this was not the case, certainly for Charles Hodge and B. B. Warfield, 'Reformed Theology at Princeton and Amsterdam in the Late Nineteenth Century: A Reappraisal', *Presbyterion*, Vol. 21, No. 2 (1995), 89-117.
58 William Dyrness names B. B. Warfield as an American example of the Thomistic approach. Warfield's Thomism is evidenced by his relative confidence in the powers of human reason, and in his willingness to countenance natural theology as a legitimate element of a Christian apology. Both of these convictions are at odds with the thinking of Calvin himself, although they were characteristic of Protestant Scholasticism which developed in the wake of the Reformation, *Christian Apologetics*, 16.
59 B. B. Warfield, 'Apologetics', in S. M. Jackson, (ed), *The New Schaff-Herzog Encyclopedia of Religious Knowledge* (Grand Rapids: Baker Book House, 1960), 233.
60 'Apologetics', 233.

Plantinga in Context 17

Warfield here clearly accepts the validity of the evidentialist challenge to Christian faith,[61] which he believed was acknowledged by Aquinas:

> 'He who believes,' says Thomas Aquinas, in words which have become current as an axiom, 'would not believe unless he saw that what he believes is worthy of belief.' Though faith is a gift of God, it does not in the least follow that the faith which God gives is an irrational faith, that is, a faith without cognizable ground in right reason.[62]

Warfield divided the apologetic task into five divisions. In the first two, the existence of God 'as a personal spirit, the Creator, preserver, and governor of all things,'[63] as well as the human ability to access this reality, are established. In the last three, the uniquely true status of Christianity as a revealed religion is demonstrated.[64]

Although Warfield's approach to apology is Thomistic (or at least in line with the Thomistic approach of his contemporaries), it is worth noting that Warfield's approach is Augustinian in at least two respects. First, like Augustine, Warfield accepted the need for evidence or reason prior to faith.[65] Second, he emphasised the importance of faith as a prerequisite for understanding. The Christian religion could only be truly understood by the person whose mind was enlightened, whose heart was beautified, and whose life was obedient to God.[66] Warfield represented one influential response to, and outcome of, the Enlightenment.

A quite different response, at about the same time, came in the form of the thinking of Abraham Kuyper (1837-1920). Kuyper was as influenced by, and as accommodating of the Enlightenment as was Warfield, contrary to the opinion

---

61 Warfield comes close to Cliffordian evidentialism in his insistence that individual believers must, at some level of consciousness, have reasons for their beliefs. 'It is,' he writes, 'not necessary for his act of faith that all the grounds of this conviction should be drawn into full consciousness and given explicit assent to his understanding, though it is necessary for his faith that sufficient ground for his conviction be actively present and working in his spirit,' *Apologetics*, 237.
62 *Apologetics*, 236-7.
63 *Apologetics*, 236. The way in which these truths were established was by way of the traditional arguments of natural theology. The use of these arguments by Reformed thinkers significantly pre-dates Warfield. Michael Czapkay Sudduth, in 'Bi-level Evidentialism', 394, fn 10, notes that the explicit endorsement of theistic arguments (and a natural theology based on them) entered into Reformed theology with the development of Protestant Scholasticism under people such as Girolamo Zanchi (1516-90), Theodore Beza (1519-1605), and Lambert Daneau (1530-90).
64 *Apologetics*, 236.
65 This point will be elaborated on in chapter nine.
66 W. Andrew Hoffecker, 'Benjamin B. Warfield', in David. F. Wells (ed), *The Princeton Theology* (Grand Rapids: Baker Book House, 1989), 68, 69.

of some.[67] He made deliberate and approving use of the philosophy of Immanuel Kant to reshape Reformed theology, with very clear implications for apologetics. Kant's contention that theoretical reason is unable to secure knowledge of noumenal reality became for Kuyper an opportunity to exclude reason from any assessment of revelation. Since Kant had (for Kuyper at least) proved that one cannot know God by the use of natural reason, special revelation became particularly necessary, and faith, understood as 'that function of the soul by which it obtains certainty directly and immediately, without the aid of discursive demonstration',[68] became the instrument by which one gained access to the noumenal.[69]

Faith and its content (whether Scripture or God), rather than reason, became the 'first principle' of theological method. Being a first principle, it did not need to be (nor, in Kuyper's thinking, should it be)[70] established discursively.[71] It was produced supernaturally through the work of the Holy Spirit by the enlightenment of human minds to accept the truth of self-authenticating

---

67 This is the thesis argued for by Donald Fuller and Richard Gardiner. They note (and react against) the view expressed by scholars such as Cornelius Van Til, Edward Dowey, John Vander Stelt, and, more recently by George Marsden and Richard Lints that the Reformed evidentialism of the old Princeton represents an unfortunate accommodation of Christian theology and apology to Enlightenment principles, 'Reformed Theology at Princeton and Amsterdam', 89f.
68 Abraham Kuyper, *Encyclopaedie der heilige Godgeleerdheid*, 3 vols. (Amsterdam: J.A. Wormser, 1894); ET, *Principles of Sacred Theology* (1898, reprinted Grand Rapids: Baker Books, 1980), 182.
69 Prior to Kuyper, among Reformed thinkers as well as Catholic, the ontological basis for a knowing relationship between the human and the divine was located in the *imago dei*. It was believed that there existed an *analogia entis* (an analogy of being) between us and God. Charles Hodge, the Princetonian theologian, made use of the concept to affirm the knowledge of God as innate or intuitive, and as the ontological basis for the project of natural theology, 'Reformed Theology at Princeton and Amsterdam', 108, fn. 58. Kuyper, like Karl Barth after him, completely repudiated the *analogia entis*.
70 Michael Czapkay Sudduth notes that 'Reformed evidentialists (such as Jonathan Edwards, Charles Hodge, and B. B. Warfield) ... have generally not questioned the plausibility of taking theistic belief as a first principle, but they have questioned the inference from this that such principles should *never* be argued for.' Sudduth notes the recognition by writers such as these that intuitive truths can also be discursively established. It was their conviction that in apologetics one must do this, for the sake of convincing those not holding to Christian belief intuitively, 'Bi-level Evidentialism', 382.
71 Kuyper stressed the point that every system of thought rests upon presuppositions, and that every act of demonstration must terminate in first principles. Because first principles are appropriately argued from, rather than to, there is no need for Christians to argue to their first principles, that is, either to God or to Scripture.

Scripture. Apologetics, understood as the activity of arguing for faith and for the truth of Scripture, was thus unnecessary, even undesirable, given its traditional commitment to more ultimate criteria of assessment.[72] Kuyper was strongly opposed to apologetics, and this resulted in a virtual abandonment of apologetics among Reformed scholars who followed him.[73]

By way of conclusion, it is worth noting that the Augustinianism motto, 'faith seeking understanding', obviously and appropriately applies to Kuyper. Faith, very definitely, was seen by him as the starting point for all thought.[74] Whether, and to what extent, this reflects Augustine himself will be the subject of later discussion.

An important exception to the widespread Reformed rejection of apologetics was Cornelius Van Til (1895-1987). Van Til, a native of Holland, moved to Indiana, USA, at the age of 10. He subsequently attended Calvin College and Calvin Theological Seminary, both being schools of his (and Plantinga's) denomination: the Christian Reformed Church. After a year at Calvin Seminary, Van Til transferred to Princeton Theological Seminary, theological home to Warfield and Hodge. He there encountered the confident Princetonian belief that the truth of Christianity could and should be established by way of argument, and that arguments in favour of Christianity were of sufficient strength that any fair-minded person would be able to understand them, and be brought to faith accordingly.[75] Van Til, with obvious indebtedness to Kuyper, strongly reacted against this position. In the wake of a reorganisation of Princeton in a liberal direction, Van Til joined the staff of the newly established Westminster Theological Seminary, in Philadelphia, which opened in 1929. While there, he became increasingly convinced that Protestant apologists (including B. B. Warfield and both Charles and A. A. Hodge, all members of the 'Old Princeton') had sold out on the Bible, and on the Reformation, in their apologetic methods. Van Til sought to correct this fault.

Unlike Kuyper, Van Til believed in the necessity of apologetics, but sought to devise an apologetic which was consistent both with the insights of Calvin and with the truth of the Bible. With Calvin and Kuyper, Van Til insisted that unregenerate human beings actively suppress the knowledge of God, a knowledge which is continually impinging on their consciousness. Human beings are never neutral or objective in their evaluation of evidence. Rather, in every act of interpretation and understanding, they act either as servants of God or as unbelievers asserting their autonomy. It is at this point that apologetics

---

72 Such as the principles of reason.
73 *Readings in Christian Apologetics*, 381.
74 Kuyper believed that faith lay at the root of all scientific and theological endeavour.
75 James D. Bratt, 'The Dutch Schools', in David F. Wells, (ed), *Dutch Reformed Theology* (Grand Rapids: Baker Book House, 1989), 22.

functions by exposing the folly and inevitable limitations and contradictions of non-Christian (or inconsistently Christian) thought.[76]

Van Til developed a theory of apologetics known as presuppositionalism, which has been strongly influential not only among Presbyterians, but also among conservative and evangelical sections of the church, both in North America and beyond. Van Til's theories do not appear to have been greatly influential within the American Dutch community, despite Van Til's impeccable Dutch Reformed pedigree. Plantinga, for example, makes only passing reference to Van Til in his writings.[77]

Van Til is significant in that he is at least one example of a Reformed thinker who promoted apologetics as a useful, even necessary Christian activity, despite the contrary opinion of his theological 'mentor', Abraham Kuyper. He is also significant because of his groundbreaking attempts to develop a decidedly Reformed apologetic approach.

To sum up, and draw this chapter to a conclusion, we have seen that apologetic theory and practice can be roughly divided into two camps; the Augustinian and the Thomistic. The former places greater emphasis on faith as the necessary first step towards understanding. The latter gives emphasis to the place of understanding or reason prior to faith. Plantinga deliberately locates himself on the Augustinian side of this divide. Plantinga is not only avowedly Augustinian, he is also Calvinistic, identifying most strongly with the Dutch Calvinism of Abraham Kuyper. He is also at various points indebted to Thomas Reid whose Scottish common sense realism was so influential among American Calvinists such as B. B. Warfield, whose apologetic position is best located on the Thomistic side of the Augustinian/Thomistic divide. With respect to what it is that needs to be defended, Plantinga is theologically conservative, clearly located in the first of Lindbeck's three categories. Biblical doctrines are not simply a way of expressing feelings, or of regulating the life of a community of believers; they are also descriptive of the way the universe is.

Having located Plantinga into his intellectual and theological context, his contribution to apologetic theory and practice can now be considered. This will begin in chapter two with a consideration of a number of significant biographical details. These will help to locate Plantinga even more precisely against his background.

---

76 'The Dutch Schools', 23.
77 For example, in *WCB*, 217.

CHAPTER 2

Plantinga and Negative Apologetics: Background Considerations

Apologetics can roughly be divided into two sub-disciplines: negative and positive apologetics. Negative apologetics has as its concern the defence of Christian beliefs against various challenges to those beliefs. The task of the negative apologist is two-fold: (1) to fortify the Christian in the face of these challenges, and (2) to demonstrate to the unbeliever that the challenges do not constitute sufficient reason for rejecting Christian belief. Conversely, positive apologetics is concerned with the construction and use of arguments to commend Christian belief, for the benefit of believer and unbeliever. The positive apologist aims to show that there are good reasons to believe the Christian message, either as a whole or in part. In this chapter, and in the three which follow, Plantinga's contribution to negative apologetics will be considered, and, in chapter six, his contribution to positive apologetics.

In my judgement, Plantinga's scholarly contribution to negative apologetics is unsurpassed by any person in the latter part of the twentieth century. For the greater part of his adult life, Plantinga has been actively and productively engaged in the task of understanding and responding to the most serious of contemporary and perennial challenges to the Christian faith.

Plantinga's interest in, and approach to, negative apologetics has been shaped by a number of biographical factors. Plantinga was brought up in a strong Christian home. His parents were members of the Christian Reformed Church, set up in America by Dutch immigrants. His father, Cornelius, attended high school in Calvinistic Christian schools. Like his son after him, Cornelius attended Calvin College in Grand Rapids, and later returned there to teach philosophy. As a boy, Alvin was mostly unthreatened by challenges to the beliefs he had inherited from his parents and from his Christian community. It was only when he accepted a scholarship to attend Harvard, in his first year after finishing high school, that Alvin 'encountered serious non-Christian thought for the first time.'[1]

It was an experience that would be repeated in the years ahead, but with increased strength. American universities, and their philosophy departments in

---

1   A. Plantinga, 'Plantinga: A Christian Life Partly Lived', in J. C. Kelly, (ed), Philosophers Who Believe (Downers Grove: InterVarsity Press, 1993), 50.

particular, were decidedly unfriendly environments for those who, like the young Plantinga, persisted in holding traditional Christian beliefs.[2]

Rather than bowing under the pressure of opposition, Plantinga instead set out to understand and respond to the various challenges to his beliefs. While at the University of Michigan doing graduate work, he began, for the first time, to consider antitheistic claims such as: that theism is incompatible with the existence of evil; that such belief arises out of wish fulfilment (the Freudian claim); that talk about God is meaningless (the positivistic claim); and that traditional belief is an outmoded relic of a pre-scientific age (the Bultmanian claim).[3]

Plantinga's interest in negative apologetics was fuelled by his experience at Wayne State University in Detroit, where he first began to teach philosophy in the fall of 1957. It was there that he was confronted with antitheistic arguments 'of a depth and philosophical sophistication and persistence' that, to that point, he had not yet encountered.[4] In 'A Christian Life Partly Lived', Plantinga describes three members of the philosophy department, Hector Castañeda, George Nakhnikian and Edmund Gettier, who, together, provided formidable opposition to Plantinga's Christian beliefs:

> Both Gettier and Nakhnikian were sons of the clergy; both had resolutely turned their backs upon Christianity, and both attacked Christianity with great verve and power. They were joined by Castañeda, who was raised as a Catholic in Guatemala but had long since given up the religion of his youth (and indeed displayed a sort of bitter resentment against it).[5]

Plantinga benefited from the experience of being at Wayne State. It brought him into personal and friendship creating contact with unbelievers of high intellectual calibre.[6] The experience of having to wrestle with powerfully

---

2 This was especially so in the late 40's and early 50's when Plantinga began his philosophical career. Plantinga has this to say about the status of Christianity among American philosophers in those early days: 'When I left graduate school in 1957, there were few Christian philosophers willing to identify themselves as such. Had there been such a thing as the Society of Christian Philosophers, it would have had few members. Positivism was very much in the ascendancy, and the general attitude among professional philosophers was something like George Nakhnikian's: an intelligent and serious philosopher couldn't possibly be a Christian. It looked as if Christianity would have an increasingly smaller part to play in the academy generally and in philosophy specifically; perhaps it would dwindle away altogether,' 'A Christian Life', 81.
3 A. Plantinga, 'Self-Profile', in J. E. Tomberlin, P. Van Inwagen, (eds), Alvin Plantinga (Dordrecht: D. Reidel Publishing Company, 1985), 18.
4 'A Christian Life', 64.
5 'A Christian Life', 64.
6 Plantinga puts it this way: '[The] atmosphere at Wayne was in one way extremely good for me. My colleagues were people I loved and for whom I had

articulated objections to Christianity both sharpened his thinking and provided him with renewed confidence that Christianity could stand against those objections.[7] Despite these benefits, the experience was far from easy. In Plantinga's own words:

> I often felt beleaguered and, with respect only to my Christianity, alone, isolated, nonstandard, a bit peculiar or weird, a somewhat strange specimen in which my colleagues displayed an interest that was friendly, and for the most part uncensorious, but also incredulous and uncomprehending.[8]

Plantinga's early experiences of opposition to Christian belief contributed to his career-long interest in negative apologetics. For a number of reasons, Plantinga has, over the years, tended to favour negative apologetics, almost to the exclusion of positive apologetics. That was certainly the case early in his career. In *Self Profile*, written in the mid-eighties, Plantinga even defines apologetics in negative (or defensive) terms. Noting that one of his chief scholarly interests 'has been in philosophical theology and in apologetics', he defines apologetics as:

> the attempt to defend Christianity (or more broadly, theism) against the various sorts of attacks brought against it ... perhaps the main function of apologetics is to show that from a philosophical point of view, Christians and other theists have nothing whatever for which to apologize.[9]

Plantinga, even then, was aware of the existence of positive apologetics, of attempts to *commend*, rather than simply *defend* Christian faith. However, his attitude to positive apologetics was, at best, ambivalent. Plantinga had come to believe that positive apologetics, as practiced over the years, had been unsuccessful in its attempts to establish the truth of theism,[10] and of Christian theism in particular. Although arguments existed, of varying degrees of strength, none was judged strong enough to compel belief. One could still, in the face of such arguments, rationally withhold belief.

This perceived lack of success enjoyed by positive apologetics was not the only reason for Plantinga's concentration on negative apologetics. Linked with it was the influence of his Reformed background, and, more specifically, the influence of Kuyperian, Dutch Reformed thinking. Characteristic of this stream

---

enormous respect; there was among us a close and happy camaraderie unmatched in my experience of philosophy departments. It was us against the world, and the world was in real trouble. We worked closely together, forging a kind of common mind', 'A Christian Life', 64.
7   'A Christian Life', 64, 65.
8   'A Christian Life', 65.
9   'Self-Profile', 33.
10 As will be spelt out more fully in chapter four.

of Calvinistic theology has been an almost universal rejection of positive apologetics.[11] Plantinga was brought up in an environment strongly influenced by, and endorsing of, this attitude to positive apologetics. Although he has come, in recent years, to significantly different conclusions about the value of positive apology, now recognising its occasional importance,[12] he nevertheless retains important aspects of his Kuyperian heritage. He believes, for example, that it is epistemically superior to believe without the aid of arguments.[13] That being the case, the importance of positive apologetics is inevitably devalued, to some degree at least.

There is one further complementary explanation for Plantinga's tendency to devalue or neglect positive apologetics. Plantinga has had a number of significant religious experiences, the first occurring at Harvard. It is noteworthy that this first experience happened at a time when Plantinga was attempting to refute serious objections to his Christian faith, for the first time.

Plantinga's initial and understandable reaction to opposition was to *argue* to defend and commend the faith of his upbringing. His arguments, however, do not appear to have been particularly successful, either from his own perspective, or that of his opponents. Plantinga was so adversely affected by the disputes that he began to seriously question whether what he had always believed was true. It was at this point of doxastic crisis that Plantinga had the first of his experiences of God which, in his words, helped resolve the 'doubts and ambivalences' that had begun to afflict him. The experience occurred during Plantinga's second semester at Harvard, and is described by him in these terms:

> One gloomy evening (in January, perhaps) I was returning from dinner, walking past Widener Library to my fifth-floor room in Thayer Middle (there weren't any elevators, and scholarship boys occupied the cheaper rooms at the top of the building). It was dark, windy, raining, nasty. But suddenly it was as if the heavens opened; I heard, so it seemed, music of overwhelming power and grandeur and sweetness; there was light of unimaginable splendor and beauty; it seemed I could see into heaven itself; and I suddenly saw or perhaps felt with great clarity and persuasion and conviction that the Lord was really there and was all I had thought. The effects of this experience lingered for a long time; I was still caught up in arguments about the existence of God, but they often seemed to me merely academic, of little existential concern, as if one were to argue about whether there has really been a past, for example, or

---

11 Alvin Plantinga, in 'The Reformed Objection to Natural Theology', Proceedings of the American Catholic Philosophical Association, Vol. 54 (1980), points out that with a few notable exceptions, 'Reformed or Calvinist theologians have for the most part taken a dim view of [the enterprise of positive apologetics, their attitudes ranging from] indifference, through suspicion and hostility, to outright accusations of blasphemy,' 49.
12 As will be seen in chapter six.
13 See further chapter four.

whether there really were other people, as opposed to cleverly constructed robots.[14]

Plantinga goes on to comment:

> Such events have not been common subsequently, and there has been only one other occasion on which I felt the presence of God with as much immediacy and strength.[15]

This second experience occurred while Plantinga was hiking in the North Cascades. He describes it thus:

> That night, while shivering under a stunted tree in a cold mixture of snow and rain, I felt as close to God as I ever have, before or since. I wasn't clear as to his intentions for me, and I wasn't sure I approved of what I thought his intentions might be (the statistics on people lost alone in that area were not at all encouraging), but I felt very close to him; his presence was enormously palpable.

Although Plantinga has had only two such overwhelming experiences of God's presence, he notes that:

> On many other occasions I have felt the presence of God, sometimes very powerfully: in the mountains (the overwhelming grandeur of the night sky from a slope at thirteen thousand feet), at prayer, in church, when reading the Bible, listening to music, seeing the beauty of the sunshine on the leaves of a tree or on a blade of grass, being in the woods on a snowy night, and on other kinds of occasions. In particular I have often been overwhelmed with a sense of *gratitude* - sometimes for something specific like a glorious morning, but often with no particular focus.[16]

In considering Plantinga's attitude to positive apologetics, it is hard not to see these experiences, the most vivid ones, as well as the others, as particularly significant. For Plantinga, arguments have played very little role in the formation and confirmation of his beliefs. Plantinga's belief in God and in the truth of the Christian religion were inherited from his parents. He believed (in the first instance at least) because they believed. When those beliefs first came under serious threat, arguments did more to cause doubts than alleviate them. It was experience, specifically the experience of being aware of the presence of God, that brought immediate and convincing confirmation that the beliefs Plantinga had inherited were true. It is surely significant that in later years, when Plantinga began to reflect on the phenomenology of religious belief, that

---

14 'A Christian Life', 51, 52.
15 'A Christian Life', 52.
16 'A Christian Life', 52.

he developed a theory that de-emphasises argument and placed the primary stress upon experiential triggers to belief, some (or all) of which Plantinga himself had experienced.[17]

Sufficient explanation has been given as to Plantinga's tendency to neglect or devalue positive apologetics. His conviction, arrived at early in his career, that the arguments of positive apologetics were inconclusive, along with his own vivid and convincing experiences of God, certainly help to explain Plantinga's attitude to positive apologetics. There is, however, a puzzle provoked by these explanations. Why is it that, in spite of these influences, Plantinga has nevertheless consistently maintained a keen interest in negative apologetics? The very factors which led Plantinga to devalue positive apologetics could easily have also contributed to a devaluation of negative apologetics.

One (so far unstated) characteristic of the Kuyperian stream of Reformed thinking, which has been so influential in Plantinga's own thinking, has been its tendency to devalue negative as well as positive apologetics. A key reason for this has been the conviction that unbelievers do not need to have their objections refuted, nor reasons given for belief in God; they already believe, or *should* believe, because of the immediately accessible revelation of God through nature, or through Scripture. Negative apologetics, like positive apologetics, is a concession to unbelief. It represents a failure to recognise the fundamentally religious nature of all attacks upon Christian belief. Plantinga is well aware of this way of thinking, as shown by the following question, posed by him at a conference held in honour of Hermann Dooyeweerd:

> But isn't the very idea of apologetics, whether negative or positive, contrary to the basic Reformed insight of Kuyper and Dooyeweerd? If all thought has religious roots, then the thing to say about attacks on Christianity is just that they too have religious roots - *nonChristian* religious roots; thus they do not require an answer. Faith cannot reason with unbelief; it can only preach to it.[18]

One wonders why Plantinga has held back from this aspect of his Reformed heritage, particularly considering the strength of his own religious experiences. The need to defend theistic belief would seem to be no greater, from Plantinga's own perspective, than the need to find arguments supportive of such belief. A vivid and convincing experience of God is surely as powerful an answer to objections as it is a reason to believe in the truth of Christian faith. One would therefore think that Plantinga does not need, or, ideally, should not *feel* the need, to be so involved in the enterprise of negative apologetics. This is

---

17 Examples of such triggers will be discussed in chapter seven.
18 A. Plantinga, 'Christian Philosophy at the End of the 20th Century', in Sander Griffioen and Bert Balk, (eds.), Christian Philosophy at the Close of the 20th Century (Kampen: Uitgeverij Kok, 1995), 37.

especially so when one considers that Plantinga's experience of arguing for the faith has not been a particularly positive one. Why, then, this almost life long interest in negative apologetics?[19]

There are a number of possible inter-related reasons. First, Plantinga was confronted early in his career, in an experientially impressive and disturbing way, with powerful objections to Christian belief. Although some of those objections were easily refuted, others, in particular the problem of evil and suffering, cried out for the sort of response Plantinga himself attempted to provide. Plantinga simply could not dismiss the sorts of objections to his faith that people like Castañeda, Nakhnikian and Gettier propounded. His reaction was not only for their benefit, but for his as well. That Plantinga himself had a vested interest in answering these objections can be illustrated by reference to a second career and life shaping occurrence, described in 'A Christian Life Partly Lived'. For Plantinga, this second occurrence was just as significant as his earlier experience of God's presence. As with that experience, it occurred during Plantinga's second semester at Harvard.

Plantinga had returned home to Grand Rapids on a visit to his parents during the spring recess, and, while there, had the opportunity to sit in on some classes, including three by William Harry Jellema. Plantinga describes the impact of the experience in this way:

> Jellema was obviously in dead earnest about Christianity; he was also a magnificently thoughtful and reflective Christian. He was lecturing about modernity: its various departures from historic Christianity, the sorts of substitutes it proposes, how these substitutes are related to the real thing and the like. Clearly he was profoundly familiar with the doubts and objections and alternative ways of thought cast up by modernity; indeed, he seemed to me to understand them better than those who offered them. But (and this is what I found enormously impressive) he was totally unawed. What especially struck me then in what he said (partly because he put into words something I felt at Harvard but couldn't articulate) was the thought that much of the intellectual opposition to Christianity and theism was really a sort of intellectual imperialism with little real basis. We are told that humankind come of age has got beyond such primitive ways of thinking, that they are outmoded, or incompatible with a scientific mindset, or have been shown wanting by modern science, or made irrelevant by the march of history or maybe by something else lurking in the neighborhood. (In this age of the wireless, Bultmann quaintly asks, who can accept them?) But why should a Christian believe any of these things? Are they more than mere claims?
>
> I found Jellema deeply impressive - so impressive that I decided then and there to leave Harvard, return to Calvin and study philosophy with him. That was as

---

19 In 'Self-Profile', Plantinga notes that he 'can scarcely remember a time when [he] wasn't aware of and interested in objections to Christianity and arguments against it,' 33.

important a decision, and as good a decision, as I've ever made. Had I not returned to Calvin from Harvard, I doubt (humanly speaking, anyway) that I would have remained a Christian at all; certainly Christianity or theism would not have been the focal point of my adult intellectual life.[20]

A number of things stand out in this description. One is that Plantinga was impressed by Jellema's confidence in the face of objections, particularly in his not being intimidated by modernity and its doubts. A striking characteristic of Plantinga's own approach to philosophy and apologetics is this same Christian confidence and refusal to be over-awed. Plantinga has clearly followed the example of his teacher. A second feature of the account is the obvious background of concern created for Plantinga by objections to the faith. So potentially disturbing were these objections, along with the accompanying climate of disdain for Christianity in American universities at that time, that Plantinga is able to wonder, in retrospect, whether he would have remained a Christian had it not been for his meeting Jellema and coming to Calvin.

That is a very significant admission. It shows the extent to which Plantinga was upset and unsettled by objections to his faith. Not even his quite outstanding experience of God's presence was considered to be sufficient, in itself, to prevent Plantinga from losing faith. Something further was considered necessary. In Plantinga's case, this was the confident, non-defensive, intellectual Christianity of William Harry Jellema.

There is a second reason, connected to the first, for Plantinga's almost life-long interest in negative apologetics. Plantinga's own experience of feeling the need to defend his faith, of feeling pressure from an unbelieving world, and his awareness of the possible loss of his own faith, all contributed to a realistic understanding of human frailty.

It may be that in an ideal world, or, at least, ideally in a non-ideal world, there would be no need for people to seek argumentative support for their theistic beliefs. Christians would know immediately that their beliefs were true. Non-Christians would also know the truth about God, rendering non-existent the need to argue with them. In such a world, Christians would have no use for negative apologetics (either for themselves or others). In an idealised world populated by idealised types, this may be so. But the real world is not such a world, as Plantinga came to recognise:

> Perhaps in a world where the wheat and the tares were more clearly separated and more thoroughly articulated something like this would be right. But our world is not such a world. In our world there are people who are moving in opposite directions, but nevertheless occupying some of the same places. And the places they occupy are not abstract types. It is the part of Calvinism to hold that Christians are not complete; they are in process. John Calvin, himself no mean Calvinist, points out that believers are constantly beset by

---

20 'A Christian Life', 53.

doubts, disquietude, spiritual difficulty and turmoil; 'it never goes so well with us,' he says, 'that we are wholly cured of the disease of unbelief and entirely filled and possessed by faith' (1536, III, ii, par. 18). It never goes that well with us, and it often goes a good deal worse. There is an unbeliever within the breast of every Christian; in the believing mind, says Calvin, 'certainty is mixed with doubt'. (No doubt the proportions differ for different people and for the same person at different times.) But then objections brought by the atheologians - the Freud's, Marx's and Nietzsche's, the Flew's, Mackie's and Nielsen's - these objections can and do trouble the Christian community and need to be answered. And that is, in part, the function of negative apologetics: to refute such objections, thus removing one kind of obstacle to the spiritual peace and wholeness of the Christian community.[21]

There is a third and final explanation for Plantinga's keen and career-long interest in negative apologetics. It is more a rational than an experiential reason, though Plantinga's experiences are not irrelevant to it. It has to do with what Plantinga has come to see as the role of arguments and evidence in relation to beliefs which initially were formed independently of arguments or evidence.

Plantinga, in line with his Reformed heritage, believes that belief in God can be, and often is, properly basic, that is, it can quite justifiably or warrantedly be believed without needing the support of arguments or propositionally articulated evidence. An obvious question, which Plantinga himself raises in 'Reason and Belief in God', is: do arguments and evidence have *any* role to play in relation to properly basic beliefs? Thinking in terms of theistic belief, would it be proper for a person to eschew arguments altogether, not only in coming to belief, but in continuing to believe, even in the face of objections to such belief? Plantinga's answer: 'Surely not.'[22] His reason is as follows: even beliefs which are formed in a basic way may, occasionally, need to be overturned. For example, someone having a basic belief that God exists may also come to accept as basic some propositions from which, by arguments whose corresponding conditionals he accepts as basic, it follows that belief in God is false. According to Plantinga, if the person accepts these propositions more strongly than he does belief in God, then he ought to renounce belief in God.[23]

For Plantinga, the idea that theistic belief might need to be given up is hypothetical; he does not, in fact, believe there to be other properly basic propositions from which, by arguments whose corresponding conditionals he accepts as basic, it follows that theistic belief is false. Nevertheless, Plantinga

---

21 'Christian Philosophy at the End of the 20th Century', 37.
22 'Reason and Belief in God', in A. Plantinga, N. Wolterstorff, (eds), Faith and Rationality: Reason and Belief in God (Notre Dame: University of Notre Dame Press, 1983), 82.
23 'Reason and Belief in God', 82.

is unwilling to rule out this possibility. The sort of dogmatism which refuses even to consider potentially contradictory evidence or arguments is, he thinks, inconsistent with a true understanding of the epistemic status of basic beliefs. This is so because the justification conferred upon basic beliefs is very often only *prima facie*, rather than *ultima facie* justification. It can, therefore, be overridden, as for example when someone believes they are being appeared to by a tree when, in fact, their belief has been formed as a result of 'a dreaded dendrological disorder, whose victims are appeared to treely only when there are no trees present.'[24]

Theistic belief is therefore open to the possibility of defeat, a possibility which is by no means academic, as Plantinga points out:

> Many believers in God have been brought up to believe, but then encountered potential defeaters. They have read books by skeptics, been apprised of the atheological argument from evil, heard it said that theistic belief is just a matter of wish fulfilment or only a means whereby one socioeconomic class keeps another in bondage.[25]

One cannot help but perceive how autobiographically relevant this description is. This was Plantinga's own experience. What he goes on to state gives as strong an indication as any we have considered so far as to why Plantinga has been involved, and has felt obliged to be involved, in the enterprise of negative apologetics:

> These circumstances [the reading of books by skeptics etc.] constitute potential defeaters for justification in theistic belief. If the believer is to remain justified, something further is called for - something that *prima facie* defeats the defeaters. Various forms of theistic apologetics serve this function (among others).[26]

Negative apologetics serves a crucial function for the theist, and for the theistic community.[27] It has, as one of its roles, the critical task of safeguarding the justification of properly basic theistic and Christian belief. It does this in circumstances when that belief comes under threat from the sorts of *prima facie* defeaters that Plantinga himself has had to wrestle with throughout his career.[28]

Enough by now has been said to account for Plantinga's almost life-long interest in negative apologetics. In summary, we have noted various biographical factors which, it seems likely, have contributed to Plantinga's

---

24 'Reason and Belief in God', 83, 84.
25 'Reason and Belief in God', 84.
26 'Reason and Belief in God', 84.
27 'Christian Philosophy at the End of the 20th Century', 37; WCB, 438.
28 For more on Plantinga's understanding of defeaters, and their impact on Christian belief, see WCB, 357-367.

career long preoccupation with negative apologetics. These include: the impact of encountering, early in his philosophical career, serious non-Christian objections to Christian faith; the influence of his (Dutch) Reformed upbringing; the abiding impact of a number of vivid and convincing religious experiences; and his keen awareness of (his own and other's) human frailty, occasioning (in this less-than-ideal world) the need for negative apologetics. We also noted Plantinga's understanding of the Christian communities' need to respond to *prima facie* defeaters of properly basic theistic and Christian belief. Negative apologetics plays a key role in this process.

CHAPTER 3

Plantinga and Negative Apologetics: Various Modern and Postmodern Challenges

Having considered something of the history and background to Plantinga's career-long involvement in negative apologetics, I will now examine this contribution in some detail. In 'Christian Philosophy at the End of the 20th Century', Plantinga mentions what he thinks have been among the more important objections to Christian faith which have troubled thoughtful Christians during the twentieth century. These have been:

> (1) the positivistic claim that Christianity really makes no sense, (2) the argument from evil, which is a sort of perennial concern of Christian apologists, (3) the heady brew served up by Freud, Marx, Nietzsche and other masters of suspicion, and (4) pluralistic considerations: given that there are all these different religions in the world, isn't there something at least naive and probably worse, in doggedly sticking to Christianity?[1]

One could add to these a number of other challenges which have been considered significant by Plantinga, and which he has addressed: naturalism, Enlightenment evidentialism, the related charge that theistic and Christian belief is in some sense irrational or defective, postmodernism and historical Biblical criticism. In this and in the next two chapters, I will outline and comment upon Plantinga's response to each of the nine challenges mentioned.[2] Plantinga's response to Freud, Marx and Nietzsche will be included in a discussion of the rationality of theistic and Christian belief.

Some of Plantinga's responses are briefer and less developed than others, and could hardly be said to have broken new ground, or to have had widespread impact either within Christian or secular intellectual communities. Yet each does represent (or illustrate) some aspect of Plantinga's overall contribution to negative apologetics. Describing them will also provide some of the necessary background to later attempts to assess the nature and significance of Plantinga's contribution to apologetics, which is the purpose of this thesis.

---

1   'Christian Philosophy at the End of the 20th Century', 38.
2   Although not in exactly the same order as they are listed here.

3.1 Logical Positivism

The first challenge is that of logical positivism. Logical positivism, as a movement, had its origins in Austria and Germany in the 1920's. It flourished in Europe in the years 1928-34, and was influential among analytical philosophers until about 1960. Plantinga briefly articulates the positivistic challenge to theistic belief in these terms:

> ... there is the claim that as a matter of fact there is no such thing as belief in God, because the sentence "God exists" is, strictly speaking, nonsense. This is the positivists' contention that such sentences as 'God exists' are unverifiable and hence 'cognitively meaningless' (to use their charming phrase), in which case they altogether fail to express propositions. On this view those who claim to believe in God are in the pitiable position of claiming to believe a proposition that as a matter of fact does not so much as exist.[3]

Although this challenge has by now receded,[4] Plantinga mentions it in order to draw some lessons from what was, in his opinion, a sorry chapter in the history of negative apologetics. He writes:

> Positivism ... has by now crawled back into the woodwork; but I am sorry to say Christian apologetes cannot claim much of the credit. Far too many Christian philosophers were thoroughly intimidated by the positivistic onslaught, suspecting that there must be much truth to it, and suggesting various unlikely courses of action. Some thought we should just give up; others said, for example, that we should concede that Christianity is in fact nonsense, but insist that it is important nonsense; still others proposed that we continue to make characteristically Christian utterances, but mean something wholly different by them, something that would not attract the wrath of the positivists. This was not a good chapter in our history, but since positivism is no longer with us, we shall avert our eyes from the unhappy spectacle and move on.[5]

Plantinga writes as one who began his career in philosophy after the threat of positivism had begun to recede. Although he himself was quick to point out its

---

3   'Reason and Belief in God', 20, 21.
4   Although this is true, other similar challenges have persisted such as the Kantian influenced belief that human concepts and ideas do not and cannot apply to the being Christians identify as God. Plantinga has an extensive consideration of this challenge to traditional Christian belief in chapters one and two of *WCB*. Plantinga also mentions the Wittgensteinian fideism of D. Z. Phillips, which, in his words, is 'a sort of continuation of positivism by other means,' 7, fn 12.
5   'Christian Philosophy at the End of the 20th Century', 38.

fatal weaknesses,[6] the criticisms did not originate with him, nor with the Christian community. For Plantinga, educated in the confidently-Christian school of Jellema, this was a real tragedy. To be so weakly 'apologetic' (in the popular meaning of that word), in the face of the challenge of positivism, was to be needlessly defensive, capitulating too quickly, particularly when such capitulation was unnecessary. Plantinga's implicit advice, in the above quotation, is that Christians should resist being bullied into jettisoning their beliefs. They should rather question the basis, and establish the merit, of any criticism. This has been Plantinga's practice throughout the length of his career. His recurring question, when faced with challenges such as this is, 'But why should we accept such a thing? What is to be said in favor of it?'[7]

Plantinga's confident, non-defensive approach to anti-theistic challenges has certainly been a distinguishing characteristic of his practice of negative apologetics. The example he has set in this regard represents a significant contribution to the enterprise of negative apologetics. His example has encouraged others to be bolder, and less easily intimidated by anti-theistic arguments, or by the culture that so often accompanies them.

3.2 Religious Pluralism

The challenge of religious pluralism is introduced by Plantinga in these terms:

> pluralist objections [also] trouble many Christians, especially Christian academics and others who are acutely aware of some of the other major religions of the world. This is something of a new or revitalised worry for the Christian community; as a result we have just begun to work at it and think about it. But I venture to predict that these pluralist objections will loom large in the next segment of our adventure as Christians.[8]

True to Plantinga's prediction, the challenge of religious pluralism has indeed begun to loom large on the intellectual horizon, providing a significant threat to traditionally understood Christianity. It comes with special strength for those adhering to the first of Lindbeck's three models of theological understanding, that is, to those who accept traditional formulations of Christian doctrine.

---

6   For example, in 'Analytic Philosophy and Christianity', *Christianity Today*, Vol. 8 (October 25, 1963), 17-20; *God and Other Minds: a study of the rational justification of belief in God* (Ithaca: Cornell University Press, 1967), 156-183; 'Advice to Christian Philosophers', *Faith and Philosophy*, Vol. 1, No. 3 (July 1984), 256-258.
7   See, for example, 'Is Belief in God Rational', 25, *WCB*, 99.
8   'Christian Philosophy at the End of the 20th Century', 39.

Plantinga's first major response to religious pluralism is found in 'Pluralism: A Defense of Religious Exclusivism'.[9] In this article, Plantinga sets out to answer the following two questions, often posed in today's pluralistic setting: 'Isn't it somehow arbitrary, or irrational, or unjustified, or unwarranted, or even oppressive and imperialistic to endorse one [religion] as opposed to all the others?',[10] and, 'Can I [as an individual] sensibly remain an adherent to just one ... [while] rejecting the others?'[11]

Plantinga begins an answer to these questions by noting that an awareness of religious diversity has always existed throughout Christian church history. However, what is new is a more widespread and sympathetic awareness of religious differences.[12] The question of how to respond to religious diversity is therefore sharper in the present context.

One response to this diversity, which Plantinga will defend, is *exclusivism*. The exclusivist, as Plantinga understands him, 'holds that the tenets or some of the tenets of *one* religion - Christianity let's say - are in fact true; he adds naturally enough, that any propositions, including other religious beliefs, that are incompatible with those tenets are false.'[13] So as to sharpen the dilemma (or potential difficulty) created by religious plurality, Plantinga defines an exclusivist more narrowly as someone who is rather fully aware of other religions and of the apparently genuine piety and devoutness that exists within them,[14] but who nevertheless believes (without overwhelmingly strong proof[15]) that propositions such as the following are true:

(1) The world was created by God, an almighty, all-knowing, and perfectly good personal being (one that holds beliefs; has aims, plans, and intentions; and can act to accomplish these aims)

and

---

9   A. Plantinga, 'Pluralism: A Defense of Religious Exclusivism', in Thomas Senor (ed), *The Rationality of Belief and the Plurality of Faith: Essays in Honor of William P. Alston* (Ithaca, New Haven: Cornell University Press, 1995), 191-215. Plantinga reproduces this article, with modification and expansion, in *WCB*, 437-457.
10   'Pluralism', 192.
11   'Pluralism', 193.
12   'Pluralism', 194; *WCB*, 439, 440.
13   'Pluralism', 194.
14   'Pluralism', 195; *WCB*, 440. By such a narrow definition, Plantinga sets aside cases of exclusive belief which are unlikely to invite censure, such as the case of a person brought up to believe a certain way without significant exposure to alternative belief systems, or to the suggestion that believing oneself to be right is in some way morally objectionable.
15   Someone who believed there was absolutely compelling proof of his religious beliefs would not have a defeater for his beliefs in the fact of religious diversity.

(2) Human beings require salvation, and God has provided a unique way of salvation through the incarnation, life, sacrificial death, and resurrection of his divine son.[16]

It is worth noting, before considering Plantinga's defence of exclusivism, that the above description would not be considered specific enough for some who embrace the exclusivistic label. Within theological literature devoted to the issue of religious pluralism, a distinction is often made between exclusivists and inclusivists, both of whom would accept (2), but who would differ in their understanding of how God's unique way of salvation can be appropriated. An exclusivist would typically insist on adding a proposition such as the following:

(3) Only those who have been the recipients of the Biblical gospel,[17] and have responded to it in faith and obedience will be saved.[18]

An inclusivist would typically deny (3), and would leave open the possibility that among those who have not heard the Biblical gospel there will be some who will be saved.[19] Plantinga's defence of exclusivism, as we will see, leaves open the question of which version of exclusivism is being defended.

Plantinga's basic contention, with respect to exclusivism as he has defined it, is that 'exclusivism need not involve either epistemic or moral failure and that furthermore something like it is wholly unavoidable, given our human condition.'[20] He begins his case by considering the charges of oppression and intellectual arrogance. Plantinga concedes that exclusivism might *contribute* to oppression, but doubts whether exclusivism, in itself, is oppressive. The charge of arrogance may similarly be warranted. However, any reflective attitude (including non-exclusivism) runs a similar risk of being so labelled: 'These charges of arrogance are a philosophical tar baby: get close enough to them to

---

16 'Pluralism', 192; *WCB*, 438.
17 The term 'Biblical gospel' is here used to refer to the revealed content of God's saving purposes, the fulfilled content of which is the gospel about Jesus. What is assumed by (3), expressed in this way, is that people in Old Testament times such as Abraham, Moses and David can be thought of as 'saved', even though they do not have explicit faith in Jesus.
18 Sometimes this position is also referred to as 'restrictivism', because of the way it restricts salvation to only those who have heard and responded appropriately to the gospel. See, for example, Clark Pinnock, *A Wideness in God's Mercy* (Grand Rapids: Zondervan, 1992), 14, 15.
19 For a useful discussion of inclusivism and exclusivism, along with other positions including the religious pluralism of John Hick, see D. L. Okholm and T. R. Phillips, (eds), *Four Views on Salvation in a Pluralistic World* (Grand Rapids: Zondervan, 1995).
20 'Pluralism', 195.

use them against the exclusivist, and you are likely to find them stuck fast to yourself.'[21]

This arises because any critic of exclusivism will inevitably believe certain propositions (for example the negation of (1) and (2)); and will also think their position right in contrast to others. Therefore, if the Christian exclusivist is guilty of intellectual arrogance or egoism, so also is the (exclusivistic) critic of Christian exclusivism, who is thus inevitably 'hoist with his own petard.'[22] Even adopting the ploy of holding back from either affirming or denying (1) and (2) is not doing enough to avoid the charge of arrogance. In doing this, one still adopts a particular stance, which involves an implicit condemnation of other points of view. Moreover, such a refraining from making a judgement results in the forfeiture of the right to object to another person's exclusivism.

Plantinga continues by considering epistemic objections to exclusivism. He notes that the epistemic vice with which the exclusivist is most frequently charged is that she is unjustified or irrational in holding beliefs such as (1) and (2).[23] Plantinga considers the claim to be unfounded. If understood as involving a charge that one has been negligent in fulfilling one's epistemic duties, such as the duty of trying one's best to get into and stay in the right relation to the truth, then the exclusivist surely need not be in violation of this duty. As Plantinga puts it:

> isn't the exclusivist conforming to that duty if, after ... careful, indeed prayerful, consideration ... it still seems to him strongly that (1), say, is true and he accordingly still believes it?[24]

Another possible reason for the charge of irrationality is that the exclusivist is intellectually *arbitrary,* in that similar cases are not treated similarly.[25] If it is the case that the propositional evidence for a belief is on a par with the propositional evidence for a competing religious belief; if it is also the case that both beliefs have a similar phenomenology,[26] then is not the believer arbitrary in believing and holding onto her beliefs?

Plantinga responds to this possibility initially by questioning whether there genuinely is phenomenological and propositional parity between the competing beliefs. He thinks there is not. Not only is the phenomenology likely to be

---

21   'Pluralism', 197, 198.
22   'Pluralism', 200.
23   'Pluralism', 201.
24   'Pluralism', 202.
25   This is John Hick's major criticism of exclusivism. See, for example, John Hick, 'The Epistemological Challenge of Religious Pluralism', *Faith and Philosophy*, Vol. 14, No. 3 (July, 1997), 280; Alvin Plantinga, 'Ad Hick', *Faith and Philosophy*, Vol. 14, No. 3 (July, 1997), 295.
26   That is, they are formed in essentially similar ways, with similar internal (to the believer) characteristics.

different,[27] so also is the propositional support. Plantinga believes that there are arguments in support of (1), if not of (2), which are not available to its competitors.[28] However, even if phenomenological and propositional parity exists, this, in itself, does not necessitate arbitrariness. Plantinga mentions two examples where he would readily concede phenomenological and propositional parity between himself and someone disagreeing with him; that is, his (Plantinga's) reaction to Nathan's parable concerning David's adultery; and his belief in Serious Actualism. In each case, Plantinga cannot see that he is being arbitrary in continuing to believe as he does.[29] He explains his reasoning:

> And the reason here is this: in each of these cases, the believer in question doesn't really think the beliefs in question are on a relevant epistemic par. She may agree that she and those who dissent are equally convinced of the truth of their belief, and even that they are internally on a par, that the internally available markers are similar, or relevantly similar. But she must still think there is an important epistemic difference: she thinks that somehow the other person has *made a mistake*, or *has a blind spot*, or hasn't been wholly attentive, or hasn't received some grace she has, or is in some way epistemically less fortunate.[30]

Plantinga points out that the pluralist critic is in the same position with respect to her beliefs. Concluding that others are wrong is inevitable. That one might oneself be wrong is true, but that makes no difference with respect to the inevitability of having exclusive views, as Plantinga explains:

> But couldn't I be wrong? Of course I could! But I don't avoid that risk by withholding all religious (or philosophical or moral) beliefs; I can go wrong that way as well as any other, treating all religions, or all philosophical thoughts, or all moral views, as on a par. Again there is no safe haven here, no-way to avoid risk. In particular, you won't reach safe haven by trying to take the same attitude toward all the historically available patterns of belief and withholding: for in so doing, you adopt a particular pattern of belief and withholding, one incompatible with some adopted by others. You pays your

---

27 In 'Ad Hick', Plantinga elaborates in these terms: 'The exclusivist is likely to think that he has been epistemologically favored in some way; he believes what he does on the basis of something like Calvin's *sensus divinitatis*; or perhaps the Internal Witness of the Holy Spirit; or perhaps he thinks that he has been converted by divine grace, so that he now sees what before was obscure to him - a blessing not bestowed upon the dissenters,' 296.
28 'Pluralism', 203; *WCB*, 452.
29 'Pluralism', 204; *WCB*, 453.
30 'Pluralism', 205; *WCB*, 453.

money and you takes your choice, realizing that you, like everyone else, can be desperately wrong. But what else can you do?[31]

In Plantinga's considered opinion, the pluralist objection to exclusivism fails. At best, an awareness of the enormous variety of religious responses serves as an undercutting defeater of exclusivism, as opposed to a rebutting defeater.[32] Because it raises questions about the source and truthfulness of one's own belief, it reduces, or can reduce, the level of confidence one has in that belief.[33] It could also have the opposite effect of *increasing* one's appreciation for one's own religion, thus increasing the level of confidence.[34]

Plantinga's defence of religious exclusivism is, in my opinion, largely successful, as far as it goes. Plantinga has effectively demonstrated the inevitability of people being exclusivistic in one way or another. He has revealed the inadequacies of various typically urged arguments against religious exclusivism. However, there are a number of blind spots in Plantinga's defence. The first relates to Plantinga's concession that an awareness of other religions can serve as an undercutting defeater of exclusivism. Plantinga underestimates the seriousness of such a defeater. Moreover, his elaborated epistemology of theistic and Christian belief formation is, in various ways, ill-suited to meeting the challenge of this undercutting defeater, as will now be demonstrated.

In responding to the charge of arbitrariness, Plantinga suggests that a Christian exclusivist is likely to think of herself as being in an epistemologically superior position, and this because she is the beneficiary of at least two belief forming mechanisms originating with God. The first, the *sensus divinitatis*, when operating successfully, will deliver the true belief that God exists; the second, the internal witness of the Holy Spirit, will deliver true belief in the distinctives of the Christian gospel. As will be seen in chapter four, Plantinga believes that each of these beliefs is formed in a basic way, that is, without being dependent for their formation on inferences from still further beliefs. Experientially, they take the form of a conviction that the beliefs in question are true. However, other human beings of other religious and ideological persuasions also have convictions, which, for all we know, are just as profound and intense as are the convictions of Christians. This creates the

---

31 'Pluralism', 205.
32 An undercutting defeater is a reason for thinking that the ground for a belief is not a *reliable* indication of the truth of that belief. A rebutting defeater is a reason for thinking that one's original evidence for a belief is false; it gives one reason for believing the denial of the proposition defeated.
33 'Pluralism', 214. Plantinga notes that one's level of confidence could even drop sufficiently for knowledge to revert to mere belief, *WCB*, 456, 457.
34 'Pluralism', 215.

potential for serious and justifiable[35] doubts about whether Christian experience really is veridical, let alone superior.

The way in which this might work is that someone, under the impact of becoming aware of other religions, begins to lose confidence that her own Christian religion is uniquely true in its affirmations about God and the gospel. This loss of confidence represents an erosion of conviction, which, at some point, is likely to become a serious problem, particularly if conviction (about the truth of the Christian religion) is a believer's sole experiential basis for belief, as Plantinga thinks it is.[36] If all (or the most) one has is conviction, what happens when conviction is lost?

One possible answer to that question is that when conviction is under threat, one can search for collaboratory evidence to bolster, or provide confirmation, that one's convictions are well-founded. This is a typical, even natural reaction in the face of challenge.[37] However, Plantinga effectively discourages such a quest for evidence, at least with respect to distinctively Christian beliefs. Although, in his opinion, there exist good arguments in support of theism,[38] the same cannot be said for Christian theism, for beliefs such as (2) above.[39] If Plantinga is correct,[40] this is a serious and potentially destabilising fact. If the very doctrines which mark Christianity out as different from the other theistic religions of the world cannot be shown to be adequately supported by evidence, I can well imagine believers having their confidence in those doctrines further eroded, even to the point of extinction. Lost conviction is not easily retrieved.

A second blind spot in Plantinga's defence of exclusivism has to do with his failure to specify which version of exclusivism he is defending. An exclusivist who also holds to proposition (3) (above) may well be able to avoid the charge

---

35   The observation that people of other religions have apparently similar levels of convictions about the truth of their beliefs raises the legitimate question, 'Is my conviction any better grounded in reality than theirs?'
36   Plantinga believes, as will be further elaborated on in chapter four, that people come to believe in the truth of the gospel simply because it 'seems' right or true. On hearing the gospel the conviction forms within them that what they are hearing is true. Evidential considerations are all but irrelevant to this process.
37   William Hasker, in 'The Foundations of Theism: Scoring the Quinn-Plantinga Debate', *Faith and Philosophy*, Vol. 15, No. 1 (January, 1998), argues that it is, at least, to the believer's advantage to so cast around. In his words, 'Even if [a believer's] non-inferential justification for theism is sufficient to outweigh the combined force of the objections, the latter is great enough that sooner or later it is going to take its toll, creating genuine discomfort and perplexity. It seems, then, that it will be to her advantage, even if it is not absolutely essential for justified belief, to have available to her further answers which defeat the objections and contribute to an over-all case for the rationality of theistic belief,' 64.
38   For more on this, see chapter six.
39   For more on this, see the end of this chapter, and chapter four.
40   A point which I will further discuss in chapter eight.

of arbitrariness or arrogance, but will still face a sizeable ethical challenge. If it really is true that only those who have been the recipients of the Biblical gospel, and have responded to it in faith and obedience will be saved, then serious questions are raised about the scope and effectiveness of God's saving purposes, not to mention his love. In the words of John Hick,

> ... can one suppose that the Heavenly Father, who loves all human beings with an equal and unlimited love, has ordained that only those who have the good fortune to be born in certain parts of the world shall have the opportunity for salvation?[41]

Exclusivism, *per se,* is not problematic, but particular versions of exclusivism are. Doctrinally conservative Christianity, of which Plantinga himself is a defender, has traditionally, and almost universally, accepted proposition (3), or some version of it. Movements away from (3) are recent,[42] and, in my opinion, have been occasioned by difficulties associated with (3).[43] Plantinga's failure to address these difficulties limits the value of his contribution to the religious pluralism debate.

3.3 Naturalism

Plantinga's apologetic response to naturalism largely takes the form of an argument against naturalism, consisting of two arguments: a preliminary argument and a main argument.[44] Naturalism is taken by Plantinga to be 'the view that there is no such person as God, nor anyone or anything at all like

---

41   J. Hick, 'The Epistemological Challenge of Religious Pluralism', 282.
42   In private correspondence, (e-mail correspondence, 5.7.2001) Plantinga has distanced himself from (3) by suggesting, as a possibility, that 'there would have to be "something" in the life of someone who has never heard of Jesus Christ; something that consists in, or is like saying yes to God, but it wouldn't have to be explicit belief in Jesus. Perhaps it would be something like thinking God has a plan for us, together with an acceptance of that plan.' Plantinga also expressed an inclination to accept C. S. Lewis's idea that God gives human beings repeated postmortem chances to accept Him.
43   It seems to me that these difficulties can be best understood as constituting a version of the problem of evil and suffering. The omnibenevolence of God is called into question by the fact, if it is a fact, that the vast majority of the human race, past and present, have not even heard of, let alone responded to, the Biblical gospel.
44   This argument is developed by Plantinga in 'An Evolutionary Argument Against Naturalism', in E. S. Radcliffe, and C. J. White, (eds), *Faith in Theory and Practice: Essays on Justifying Religious Belief* (Chicago and La Salle: Open Court, 1993), 35-65.; in the final chapter of *WPF*; in 'Naturalism Defeated' unpublished manuscript; and in *WCB*, 227-240.

him.'[45] In developing his arguments against naturalism, Plantinga particularly targets contemporary evolutionary naturalists who, because of the availability of evolutionary theory, have certain beliefs about human ontology and origin.

In a nutshell, Plantinga's case against evolutionary naturalism is this:

> Most human beings think that at least one function or purpose of our cognitive faculties is to provide us with true beliefs; although we make mistakes, for the most part we are successful. However, naturalistic evolution, which is the conjunction of naturalism with the view that we and our cognitive faculties have arisen by way of the mechanisms proposed by contemporary evolutionary theory, gives us reason to doubt two things: (1) that a purpose of our cognitive systems is that of serving us with true beliefs, and (2) that they do, in fact, furnish us with mostly true beliefs.[46]

Plantinga cites Darwin, who expresses essentially the same uncertainty which is the basis of Plantinga's argument:

> With me, the horrid doubt always arises whether the convictions of man's mind, which has been developed from the mind of the lower animals, are of any value or at all trustworthy. Would any one trust in the convictions of a monkey's mind, if there are any convictions in such a mind?[47]

The fundamental problem with evolutionary naturalism lies in its account of how our cognitive structures evolved:

> these structures were not selected for their penchant for producing true beliefs in us; instead, they conferred an adaptive advantage or were genetically associated with something that conferred such an advantage. And the ultimate purpose or function, if any, of these belief-producing mechanisms will not be the production of true beliefs, but *survival* - of the gene, genotype, individual, species, whatever.[48]

---

45   *WCB*, 227. This is by no means an exhaustive definition of naturalism, as Plantinga himself acknowledges. Frequently also included in a definition of naturalism is the idea that all of reality can be explained, at least in principle, in naturalistic terms; that is, in terms of the natural or physical sciences. Rather than trying to achieve definitional precision, Plantinga draws attention to a number of paradigmatic cases of naturalism, such as expressed by Daniel Dennett in *Darwin's Dangerous Idea* (London: Allen Lane, 1995), and develops his argument with these examples in mind.
46   'Evolutionary Argument', 35-38.
47   'Evolutionary Argument', 38.
48   *WCB*, 228.

In the light of this problem, Plantinga develops his two arguments. The first, which has been modified over time in the face of criticism,[49] is a probabilistic argument for the falsehood of naturalism. The following letters are used to represent various of its parts:

N = metaphysical naturalism which is the view that there is no such person as God, nor anyone or anything like him.

E = the proposition that human cognitive faculties have arisen by way of mechanisms to which contemporary evolutionary thought draws our attention.

T = theism, which is the belief that there is a God.

R = the claim that our cognitive faculties are generally reliable, in the sense that they produce mostly true or verisimilitudinous beliefs in the sorts of environments that are normal for them.[50]

Plantinga argues that if evolutionary mechanisms are as they are described in contemporary evolutionary theory, the probability that the evolutionary process has produced cognitive faculties which are on the whole reliable is 'low, somewhere less than one-half.'[51] However, the same cannot be said if theism is true. Reliable cognitive faculties are what a theist could reasonably expect.[52] This being the case, if a person thinks that his cognitive faculties *do* reliably deliver true beliefs, then he has at least some reason to prefer theism to naturalism.[53] Plantinga does not think that this preliminary argument is a particularly strong one.[54] A person deciding between theism and evolutionary naturalism would need to take into account many more reasons than this to prefer one over the other. However, given that one accepts the cogency of the argument, and that one's cognitive faculties are reliable, one has at least one reason to prefer theism to evolutionary naturalism.

---

49 In *WCB*, Plantinga admits that his earlier formulation of the argument was 'straightforwardly incorrect', 229. He corrects the fault, and my representation of the argument takes this correction into account.
50 'Evolutionary Argument', 40; *WCB*, 227.
51 'Evolutionary Argument', 49. For Plantinga's argument to this conclusion, see 44-49; also *WCB*, 231-237.
52 Plantinga points out that 'according to traditional (Jewish, Christian, Muslim) theism, God created us in his image, a part of which involves our having knowledge over a wide range of topics and areas,' 'Evolutionary Argument', 51.
53 'Evolutionary Argument', 51.
54 *WCB*, 62.

In developing his main argument against naturalism, Plantinga concedes that his estimation of P(R/N & E) may well be incorrect.[55] Perhaps the probability could be high rather than low. However, without good reason to think that it is high, the best one could do is be agnostic about P(R/N & E), in which case, Plantinga's main argument works equally well. If a person isn't sure about the reliability of his belief producing faculties, he has just as much a defeater for any belief produced by them as someone who considers them unreliable.[56]

Plantinga's main argument, in summary, is that someone who accepts N & E, and also grasps the argument for a low or inscrutable value of P(R/N & E), has a *defeater* for R, and, indeed, for any belief produced by his cognitive faculties, including evolutionary naturalism itself. Thus evolutionary naturalism is self-defeating. The implication of this is that if a defeater cannot be found to overturn the judgement about the low or inscrutable value given to the probability of R/N & E, then the rational course for a devotee of N & E is to reject N & E, or at least be agnostic about it.

Plantinga believes that no attempt to argue one's way out of this unfortunate situation will work:

> .. any argument [a person] offers for R is, in this context, delicately circular or question begging. It is not *formally* circular; its conclusion does not appear among its premises. It is instead (we might say) *pragmatically* circular in that it purports to give a reason for trusting our cognitive faculties, but is itself trustworthy only if those faculties (at least the one involved in its production) are indeed trustworthy. In following this procedure and giving this argument, therefore, he subtly assumes the very proposition he proposes to argue for. Once I come to doubt the reliability of my cognitive faculties, I can't properly try to allay that doubt by producing an *argument;* for in so doing I rely on the very faculties I am doubting. Naturalistic evolution gives its adherents a reason for doubting that our beliefs are mostly true; perhaps they are mostly wildly mistaken; for the very reason for mistrusting our cognitive faculties generally will be a reason for mistrusting the faculties generating the beliefs involved in the argument.[57]

Doubt once begun becomes viscously corrosive. So corrosive is it that even an argument for the existence of a non-deceiving God comes under justifiable suspicion.[58] The same applies to any potential defeaters of the defeater provided by Plantinga's argument, with the implication that a devotee of N & E has an ultimately undefeatable reason for rejecting N & E.

---

55 'Evolutionary Argument', 51.
56 'Evolutionary Argument', 53.
57 'Evolutionary Argument', 58.
58 As Plantinga points out, any such argument will be 'under as much suspicion as its source. Here there is no argument that will help you; here salvation will have to be by grace, not by works,' 'Evolutionary Argument', 61.

Does this mean that N & E are not true, and that theism is? Plantinga answers this question in the negative as he begins to elucidate the implications of the argument:

> If you accept N&E, you have an ultimately undefeated reason for rejecting N&E. But then the rational thing to do is to reject N&E. If, furthermore, one also accepts the conditional *if N is true, then so is E*, one has an ultimately undefeated defeater for N. One who contemplates accepting N and is torn, let's say, between N and theism, should reason as follows: if I were to accept N, I would have a good and ultimately undefeated reason to be agnostic about N; so I shouldn't accept it. Unlike the preliminary argument, this is not an argument for the *falsehood* of naturalism and thus (given that naturalism and theism are the live options) for the truth of theism; for all this argument shows, naturalism might still be true. It is instead an argument for the conclusion that (for one who is aware of the present argument) accepting naturalism is irrational ... the argument isn't for the falsehood of naturalism, but for the irrationality of accepting it. The traditional theist, on the other hand, isn't forced into this appalling loop. On this point his set of beliefs is stable.[59]

What is to be said about the success and significance of this argument? Its success is yet to be determined. Plantinga himself considers the argument successful. In 'Naturalism Defeated', after responding to a range of objections to his theory,[60] he concludes that his evolutionary argument against naturalism 'emerges unscathed'.[61] In a more recent publication, he reaches the same conclusion, and even makes the claim that the various criticisms mounted against his argument have resulted in a 'strengthened version of the argument; some of the points made by the commentators suggest more subtle and nuanced ways of putting the argument.'[62]

Whether Plantinga is right in his assessment has yet to be seen. Scholars have disputed Plantinga's case at a number of points. Some have questioned Plantinga's attempt to show that the P(R/N & E) is low or inscrutable.[63]

---

59 'Evolutionary Argument', 59, 60.
60 A. Plantinga, 'Naturalism Defeated' [unpublished paper] consists in an exploration of objections to Plantinga's argument.
61 'Naturalism Defeated', 56.
62 'Reply to Beilby's Cohorts', in James Beilby, (ed), *Naturalism Defeated Essays on Plantinga's Evolutionary Argument Against Naturalism*, (Ithaca: Cornell University Press, 205.
63 See, for example, Evan Fales, 'Plantinga's case against naturalistic epistemology', *Philosophy of Science*, Vol. 63 (1996), 432-451; 'Darwin's Doubt, Calvin's Calvary' in *Metaphysical Naturalism*, page numbers undetermined; Michael Levin, 'Plantinga on Functions and the Theory of Evolution', *Australasian Journal of Philosophy*, Vol. 75, No. 1 (March, 1997), 83-98; W. J. Talbott, 'The Illusion of Defeat', in *Metaphysical Naturalism*, page numbers undetermined.

Others have suggested that beliefs other than N and E need to be taken into account in assigning a probability to R;[64] others that non-propositional evidence is also relevant;[65] still others that Plantinga's arguments are based upon assumptions, say about knowledge, that are no longer tenable.[66] Some have argued that Plantinga's own theistic beliefs have within them the raw material for a similar argument against the rationality of theistic belief.[67] The arguments continue.

More can be concluded regarding the significance of the Plantinga's evolutionary argument against naturalism. The most significant achievement of the argument is that it requires a defence from naturalists. It has normally been theists who have been put on the defensive over the last few centuries. Plantinga, by his argument, reverses the pressure. Although the argument is unlikely to result in large scale (or even any) conversions from naturalism to theism, it does, nevertheless, represent a significant reply to contemporary naturalism,[68] which, in recent years, has become increasingly strident. As Plantinga observes, philosophical naturalism has become 'much more articulate and explicit ... [and has] assumed a much higher profile in contemporary intellectual life.'[69] By his argument, and by other forays into the area of naturalistic science and Christian faith,[70] Plantinga has sought to meet this

---

64   See, for example, N. M. L. Nathan, 'Naturalism and Self-Defeat', *Religious Studies*, Vol. 33, No. 2 (June, 1997), 135-142; A. Peressini, 'Naturalism, evolution, and self-defeat', *International Journal for Philosophy of Religion*, Vol. 44 (1998), 41--51; Ric Otte, 'Conditional Probabilities in Plantinga's Argument Against Naturalism', in *Metaphysical Naturalism*, page numbers undetermined.
65   See, for example, Michael Bergmann, 'Commonsense Naturalism', in *Metaphysical Naturalism*, page numbers undetermined.
66   J. Wesley Robbins, for example, argues that those holding to a pragmatic view of truth are untouched by Plantinga's argument, 'Is Naturalism Irrational?' *Faith and Philosophy*, Vol. 11, No. 2 (April, 1994), 255-259.
67   Evan Fales, for example, in 'Darwin's Doubt, Calvin's Calvary', argues that since it is impossible (on Plantinga's own reckoning) for a theist to explain the existence of evil, she clearly does not understand God's intentions very well. Given this lack of understanding of the purposes of God, a theist is not in a position to judge the P(R/theism) as more than inscrutable. Therefore, there exists a parallel argument against the rationality of theistic belief.
68   Although not a completely novel reply. C. S. Lewis, in the first edition of *Miracles* (London: Geoffrey Bles., 1947), advanced an essentially similar argument, as has Stephen Clark, for example in *From Athens to Jerusalem* (Oxford: Clarendon Press, 1984), a fact acknowledged by Plantinga, *WPF*, 194.
69   A. Plantinga, 'Twenty Years Worth of the SCP', *Faith and Philosophy*, Vol. 15, No. 2 (April, 1998), 154.
70   See, for example, the following Plantingan articles: 'When Faith and Reason Clash: Evolution and the Bible'; 'Evolution, neutrality, and antecedent probability: a reply to McMullin and Van Till', *Christian Scholar's Review*, Vol. 21, No. 1 (1991), 80-109; 'Science: Augustinian or Duhemian?' *Faith and Philosophy*, Vol.

challenge. As always, he has managed to stay at, or somewhere near, the leading edge of the interface between Christianity and its competitors.[71]

3.4 Postmodernism

In the first of two lectures published in *The Twin Pillars of Christian Scholarship* (1990), Plantinga argues that the contemporary western intellectual world is 'a battleground or arena in which rages a battle for men's souls.'[72] He sees the battle as having three main contestants, each vying for supremacy; the first is Christian theism; the second is 'perennial naturalism', the third is 'creative anti-realism,' or 'Enlightenment subjectivism.'[73] Had Plantinga penned these words more recently, he is likely to have substituted postmodernism for creative anti-realism, postmodernism being the broader intellectual movement which includes creative anti-realism under its larger conceptual umbrella. Plantinga does discuss creative anti-realism under the heading of postmodernism in *WCB*.[74]

Understood as a broad and wide-ranging reaction to modernism, postmodernism is not necessarily an enemy of Christian belief. In fact, there are elements within it which have been welcomed by Christians, who have even participated in the repudiation of various modernist dogmas, including classical foundationalism.[75] Plantinga, in light of his own rejection of classical foundationalism (described in chapter four), could himself be described as postmodern. He certainly agrees with certain prominent postmodern themes, including:

13, No. 3 (1996), 368-94; 'Dennett's Dangerous Idea', *Books and Culture*, (May/June, 1996), 16-18, 35; 'Creation and Evolution: a Modest Proposal', given at the Eastern Division Meetings of the American Philosophical Association, Dec. 1998, unpublished manuscript.

71 Plantinga thinks that, increasingly, 'biology, including molecular biology, evolutionary biology, environmental studies, evolutionary psychology (Pinker, Dennett, Wright, etc.), sociobiology, as well as other branches of cognitive science', are where 'the action' is with respect to the interface between religion and science, 'Twenty Years Worth of the SCP', 153. It is likely that Plantinga will himself contribute to this 'action'.

72 *The Twins Pillars of Christian Scholarship*, 8.

73 *The Twins Pillars of Christian Scholarship*, 9, 10. Creative anti-realism is the name that Plantinga prefers to 'Enlightenment Subjectivism' or 'Enlightenment Humanism' which he also uses to refer to this position, 10.

74 *WCB*, 422-437. In 'Dennett's Dangerous Idea', Plantinga describes creative antirealism as associated with 'certain brands of postmodernism', 16.

75 Plantinga notes that postmodernists are joined here by 'such doughty spokespersons for Christian belief as Abraham Kuyper, William Alston, and Nicholas Wolterstorff and, for that matter, in anticipatory fashion by Augustine, Aquinas, Calvin and Edwards,' *WCB*, 423.

sympathy and compassion for the poor and oppressed, the strong sense of outrage at some of the injustices our world displays, celebration of diversity, and the "unmasking" of prejudice, oppression and power-seeking masquerading as self-evident moral principle and the dictates of sweet reason.[76]

There are, however, other aspects of postmodernism which Plantinga, as a Christian, is not so happy with.

There is opposition to 'metanarratives', there is insistence that God is dead (which is ordinarily intended to imply, I believe, that there is no such person as God), and there are patronizing references to God ... There is also a kind of exultation or apotheosis of autonomy, so that (as with Heidegger) one feels guilty for not having created the world (along with the suggestion that God should be ashamed for having the temerity to interfere with one's autonomy). There is a sort of recrudescence of the 19th century romantic exultation of the self, self-deification and its rejection of all things bourgeois.[77]

There are other ideas typically associated with postmodernism which are likely to be incompatible with traditional Christian belief,[78] such as:

the claim that there is no such thing as objectivity ... the claim that there is no such thing as truth, or that if there is, it is something totally different from what we thought (perhaps it is a social construction, or "what our peers will let us get away with saying", or something else of that sort)[79]

Plantinga, in his response to postmodernism, notes that for Christian belief to be under any real pressure of being defeated by the anti-theistic and anti-Christian claims made by postmodernists, there needs to be something said by way of argument, or, at the very least, Christians need to be put into a situation, or exposed to some experience which will (with good warrant) defeat their Christian belief.[80] It is not sufficient to simply claim that Christian faith is unacceptable, as is too often done.[81] Plantinga argues that postmodernists have neither argumentative nor non-argumentative defeaters for Christian faith, with the exception, perhaps, of evil and suffering and its impact. Plantinga sums up the problem for the Christian apologist:

---

76   *WCB*, 424.
77   *WCB*, 423.
78   Or, at least, with how this has been understood.
79   *WCB*, 422, 423.
80   *WCB*, 425.
81   As Plantinga colourfully puts it: ' ... you don't automatically produce a defeater for Christian belief just by standing on your roof and proclaiming (even loudly and slowly), 'God is dead!' (Not even if you add: 'And everybody I know says so too.') *WCB*, 425, 426.

> Postmoderns ... don't ordinarily give arguments for claims inconsistent with Christian belief. Indeed, they don't ordinarily give arguments for anything at all; perhaps because they think the whole frame of mind that makes argument seem useful is something we should 'get beyond.'[82]

Although arguments are difficult to find, Plantinga isolates two which he considers worthy of attention: the argument from historical conditionedness;[83] and the argument that human beings construct the truth.[84] The second of these two arguments, which I will consider first, is essentially the argument of creative anti-realism.

Creative anti-realism is defined by Plantinga as the view that 'things in the world owe their fundamental structure and perhaps their very existence to the noetic activity of our minds.'[85] Plantinga's first published response to creative anti-realism comes in the form of a Presidential Address to the Eighteenth Annual Western Division Meeting of the American Philosophical Association in Columbus, Ohio, in April 1982.[86] In this response, Plantinga focuses on Rorty's suggestion that truth is 'what our peers will let us get away with saying', and on Putnam's idea that what is true is what ideally meets our epistemic requirements.[87]

Much of Plantinga's address is taken up with a detailed response to the anti-realism of Putnam and Rorty. The essence of Putnam's case against realism, the 'cardinal anti-realist intuition', is that 'if the best efforts of mind can't settle the question whether a proposition is true, then there's no truth there to be known.'[88] The epistemic situation which has given strength and credibility to this intuition is described by Plantinga in the following terms:

> A striking feature of the intellectual situation is persistent *disagreement* about such matters of deep human concern as religion, morality and for that matter philosophy. Kant was appalled by the fact that after centuries of effort metaphysics had not yet attained the secure path of science; he therefore proposed that his predecessors had been confused and that what was needed was a Copernican Revolution. Indeed, ever since Descartes, modern thought has witnessed one alleged new beginning after another, each innovator declaring his predecessors utterly misguided. And this sort of disagreement is a source of wonder. It is also a source of philosophy. One sort of response it presently provokes - especially in continental thought - is anti-realism. If disagreement - about the existence of God, or human freedom, or the nature of

---

82 *WCB*, 427.
83 *WCB*, 427-429.
84 *WCB*, 429-436.
85 'How To Be An Anti-Realist', *Proceedings of the American Philosophical Association*, Vol. 56 (1982), 48.
86 Published as 'How To Be An Anti-Realist'.
87 'How To Be An Anti-Realist', 51.
88 'How To Be An Anti-Realist', 62.

substance - persists century after century despite our best efforts, perhaps the conclusion to draw is that there isn't any real truth to be grasped there.[89]

Rorty, agreeing with this conclusion, argues that the long-standing Western impulse to find a method to settle such disagreements is misguided. There is no such method. Plantinga responds to the anti-realism of Rorty and Putnam firstly by pointing out the tendency for all such views to be self-referentially incoherent. He says this of Rorty's view:

> Rorty suggests that truth is what our peers will let us get away with saying. But this suggestion immediately and obviously falls prey to self-referential difficulties. For neither his peers nor mine will let either him or me get away with saying any such thing. If it is true, therefore, it isn't true; so if it is true it both is and isn't true, in which case it isn't true. Perhaps it doesn't follow, on Rorty's view, that it is *false*; for our peers, being an irascible lot, might not let us get away with saying this or its denial. But in any event it isn't true.[90]

There are other difficulties with Rorty's position which are explored in further detail in *WCB*. If Rorty is at all serious in his definition of truth as 'what our peers will let us get away with saying,'[91] then this has the following consequences: whether there is a God depends upon the behaviour of one's peers, as do such 'realities' as AIDS, cancer, world poverty, the Tiananmen Square massacres, and the holocaust.[92] If Rorty's claim is not intended to be taken literally, then the question needs to be asked, what exactly does he mean? Plantinga considers, and rejects, Gary Gutting's attempts to interpret Rorty as simply objecting to philosophical theorizing about truth.[93] He thinks it more likely that Rorty is claiming that truth is a human construct and that claims to truth are true only in so far as they stand in a certain relationship to human society.[94] Plantinga has difficulty locating arguments to these conclusions, but does locate one in *Contingency, Irony and Solidarity*.[95] In brief, Rorty argues that without sentences there is no truth, and that since sentences are elements of human language, and human languages are human creations, then truth is a

---

89   'How To Be An Anti-Realist', 62.
90   'How To Be An Anti-Realist', 64.
91   Richard Rorty, *Philosophy and the Mirror of Nature* (Princeton: Princeton University Press, 1979), 175-76.
92   *WCB*, 430.
93   In 'Richard Rorty: the Rudiments of Pragmatic Liberalism' in G. Gutting, (ed), *Pragmatic Liberalism and the Critique of Modernity* (New York: Cambridge University Press, 1999); *WCB*, 431-433.
94   *WCB*, 433-434.
95   Richard Rorty, *Contingency, Irony and Solidarity* (New York: Cambridge University Press, 1989); *WCB*, 434.

human creation which cannot exist independently of human minds.[96] Plantinga responds to this argument by noting that sentences are not the only things that can be said to be true; the same can be said about beliefs, assertions and propositions.[97] More seriously (even fatally), even if it were true that the only things that are true (or false) are sentences, and that sentences are human creations, in that we bring them into being as a sequence of symbols, it does not follow from this that we bring it about that these sentences are either true or false, as Plantinga explains:

> We make it the case that the sequence of marks 'There once were dinosaurs' is a sentence and thus capable of being true or false. It doesn't follow that we make it true that there were once dinosaurs.[98]

Plantinga concludes that Rorty's position, however it is understood, does not constitute a serious defeater to Christian belief. Plantinga thinks that the arguments of anti-realism, in general, are 'frail reeds indeed.'[99]

Plantinga isolates a second argument which tends to be used by postmodernists, which is the argument that because our philosophical and theological views are so heavily constrained and conditioned by the societies in which we live, and have been socialised in, these views are in some way 'substandard, unwarranted, irrational, or in some other way not up to par.'[100] Plantinga finds this argument unconvincing, for two reasons. First, if beliefs were found to be defective merely because a person is unlikely to hold them in different circumstances, then belief in this objection itself is defective. It too is unlikely to be believed in every circumstance.[101] Second, the argument does not take account of the reasonable possibility of change over time. Plantinga uses the example of Albert Einstein:

> Had Einstein been born in the eighteenth century, he would not have believed special relativity; nothing follows about special relativity.[102]

Just because people in different circumstances and different times are likely to believe different things, does not mean that some views are not inferior to others, nor that some views are unable to be shown to be true, whereas others are not. The most the argument does is to draw attention to the fact that people are influenced by their social and temporal environment, and that this suggests

---

96 *WCB*, 434.
97 *WCB*, 434, 435.
98 *WCB*, 435.
99 'How To Be An Anti-Realist', 67.
100 *WCB*, 428.
101 *WCB*, 428.
102 *WCB*, 428.

human limitation. Plantinga is more than willing to admit, and lament,[103] the fact of human limitation. He considers postmodernism itself as an understandable reflection upon this limitation.[104] However, just because human beings are limited, and therefore run the risk of being wrong, even with respect to their most cherished beliefs, does not mean that true beliefs are impossible, nor that people are wrong to believe, even with great firmness,[105] that what they believe is true.

To draw this discussion to a close, a number of things can be said about the significance of Plantinga's brief treatment of issues pertaining to postmodernism. First, Plantinga has at least begun to engage postmodernism as a movement, and this by taking issue with a number of its influential spokespeople, chiefly within the United States. Second, in a way which is consistent with his career-long style, Plantinga is not disconcerted nor impressed by the skeptical and anti-Christian ethos which pervades much of the postmodern movement. As always, he insists on being given good reasons to think that his traditional Christian faith ought to feel threatened. In the absence of such good reasons, he feels entirely warranted in continuing to hold his beliefs, and encourages the Christian community to do likewise.

Third, although Plantinga has identified a number of the weaknesses that often characterise postmodern theorizing, he could, with justice, be criticised for not being completely fair in his critique of postmodernism. For example, Rorty is by no means wanting to deny the existence and causal impact of the space-time world 'out there'.[106] Nor would he think that events such as the Tiananmen Square massacre can be created (or uncreated) simply at the whim of scholarly consensus. Plantinga's criticism of Rorty falls somewhat short of engaging the implications of the valid observation that the modern quest for truth[107] has been chronically and irremediably dogged by disagreement and controversy. This is particularly the case at higher levels of abstraction and theory production, such that it makes some sense to adopt a pragmatic view of truth. Plantinga's own elaborate, and theory conditioned theorising about theistic and Christian belief formation, along with the (inconclusive) reactions it will inevitably occasion, must give at least some support to the relativising theses of postmodernism.

---

103 A. Plantinga, 'Ad de Vries', *Christian Scholar's Review*, Vol. 19 (1989), 176.
104 Plantinga represents postmodernism as an understandable failure of nerve in the face of Western attempts to discover a secure and certain foundation for knowledge, *WCB*, 436-437.
105 'Ad de Vries', 174.
106 As Rorty makes clear in the very same *Contingency, Irony and Solidarity* (eg. 5) which Plantinga draws upon in his critique of Rorty.
107 In particular, big T truth; truth understood as the ideal towards which we strive in our efforts to accurately describe Reality in language.

3.5 Historical Biblical Criticism

The final threat to traditional Christian faith to be considered in this chapter is the challenge of historical Biblical criticism. Plantinga describes historical Biblical criticism (HBC) as:

> an Enlightenment project; an effort to look at and understand biblical books from a standpoint that relies upon reason alone ... The idea is to see what can be established (or at least made plausible) using only the light of what we could call 'natural, empirical reason.' The faculties or sources of belief invoked, therefore, would be those that are employed in ordinary history: perception, testimony, reason taken in the sense of *a priori* intuition together with deductive and probabilistic reasoning, Reid's sympathy, by which we discern the thoughts and feelings of another, and so on - but bracketing any proposition one knows by faith or by way of the authority of the church.[108]

Plantinga notes that practitioners of HBC often aspire to pursue a scientific approach to Scripture, by which they mean, among other things, that theological or dogmatic assumptions are avoided. The idea, as expressed by E. P. Sanders, is that one should rely upon 'evidence on which everyone can agree.'[109] The focus of the historical Biblical critic's enquires are questions of authorship and composition: for example, questions regarding when the document was written, and by whom; the likely sources, how these were arranged; the likelihood of the details being factual.[110]

Historical Biblical critics, although similar in their commitment to proceeding on the basis of reason, without employing theological assumptions, nevertheless vary considerably when it comes to what is meant by reason, and on exactly what sort of reasoned approach one should take. Plantinga identifies three distinct positions. The first is Troeltschian HBC. Troeltschian HBC operates on the basis of four principles: the principle of criticism;[111] the principle of analogy;[112] the principle of correlation,[113] and the principle of

---

108 *WCB*, 386.
109 E. P. Sanders, *Jesus and Judaism* (Philadelphia: Fortress Press, 1985), 5; quoted in *WCB*, 388.
110 *WCB*, 389-390.
111 Which is the principle that since any conclusion is subject to revision, historical inquiry can never attain absolute certainty but only relative degrees of probability, *WCB*, 391.
112 Which is the principle that historical knowledge is possible because all events are similar in principle; therefore we must assume that the laws of nature in biblical times were the same as now, *WCB*, 391.
113 Which is the principle that the phenomena of history are inter-related and inter-dependent, with no event being able to be isolated from the sequence of historical cause and effect, *WCB*, 391.

autonomy.[114] Plantinga notes that although these principles can be given platitudinous interpretations, they are normally taken to exclude direct divine action in the world.[115]

The second broad position is Duhemian HBC. Pierre Duhem, 'both a serious Catholic and a serious scientist,'[116] believed that the proper way to pursue physical theory was to keep physical theory completely independent of religious or metaphysical views or commitments. He reasoned that, by doing this, valuable dialogue could be maintained within the scientific community which would otherwise be impossible. Plantinga applies Duhem's methodology to Scripture scholarship, defining *Duhemian* Scripture scholarship as 'scripture scholarship that doesn't involve any theological, religious or metaphysical assumptions that aren't accepted by everyone in the relevant community.'[117] Duhemian Scripture scholarship, unlike Troeltschian Scripture scholarship, does not rule out the occurrence of miracles, or the divine authorship of the Bible; it simply does not assume these things in advance.

The third position identified by Plantinga is Spinozistic HBC. Spinozistic HBC is different to Troeltschian HBC in that special acts by God in the world are not dismissed, and different to Duhemian HBC in that no deliberate attempt is made to operate on the basis of shared assumptions. As Plantinga puts it, 'you might think that, as a matter of fact, there are deliverances of reason not accepted by everyone party to the project of scripture scholarship ... Then you might yourself employ those deliverances of reason in pursuing scripture scholarship ... thereby rejecting Duhemianism.'[118]

Plantinga contrasts historical Biblical criticism of whatever variety with traditional Biblical commentary which approaches the Bible *with* various theological and doctrinal assumptions.[119] He notes, however, that in elucidating each of these four approaches, he is generalising and that not every work of Scripture scholarship falls neatly into one of the four categories he identifies.[120]

---

114 Which is the principle that neither church nor state can prescribe for the scholar which conclusions should be reached, *WCB*, 391.
115 Plantinga gives a number of examples, in *WCB*, 393-395, of what has been a widespread rejection of miraculous interventions into what is taken to be a closed continuum of cause and effect. According to Bultmann, for example, this continuum 'cannot be rent by interference of supernatural, transcendent powers,' Schubert Ogden (ed), *Existence and Faith* (New York: Meridian Books, 1960), 291-92, quoted in *WCB*, 393.
116 *WCB*, 395.
117 *WCB*, 397.
118 *WCB*, 398.
119 For Plantinga's description of traditional Biblical commentary, see *WCB*, 381-385.
120 *WCB*, 399.

In considering the challenge created by HBC for traditional Christian belief, Plantinga observes that the threat has been a serious one: the assumption of the Bible's unity has been undermined, prophecy as a supernatural gift denied; miracles rejected; the straightforward testimony of the text doubted; the resurrection explained in naturalistic terms; and the story of Jesus retold in often unrecognisable terms.[121] HBC has led its practitioners to doubt virtually every Biblical affirmation. In the words of Van Harvey, whose testimony is accepted by Plantinga: 'So far as the biblical historian is concerned ... there is scarcely a popularly held traditional belief about Jesus that is not regarded with considerable skepticism.'[122]

One would think that the effect of such radical doubt would be devastating for traditional Christian faith. However, Plantinga notes that the impact has been less than one might have thought. He quotes Van Harvey: 'Despite decades of research, the average person tends to think of the life of Jesus in much the same terms as Christians did three centuries ago.'[123] In a section entitled 'Why aren't most Christians more concerned?', Plantinga suggests some possible explanations for this: skeptical Scriptural scholars display vast disagreement among themselves; their arguments are often inconclusive; they display more confidence in their results than is warranted given the probabilities involved,[124] the methodology involved is clearly prejudicial to conservative outcomes. This is certainly the case with Troeltschian HBC, which, not surprisingly given its assumptions, reaches conclusions wildly at variance with those accepted by the traditional Christian.[125]

Plantinga concludes that HBC of any variety poses no substantial threat to traditional Christian faith, or, at least, it provides no good reason for the serious believer to jettison her beliefs. Plantinga observes, however, that HBC provides little by way of support for traditional Christian beliefs, even in its less methodologically biased versions.[126] With respect to what can be known about Jesus, for example, only a very limited number of things can be accepted as true beyond reasonable doubt. A. E. Harvey suggests the following: that Jesus 'was known in both Galilee and Jerusalem, that he was a teacher, that he carried out cures of various illnesses, particularly demon-possession, and these were widely regarded as miraculous; that he was involved in controversy with fellow Jews over questions of the law of Moses: that he was crucified in the governorship of

---

121 *WCB*, 399-401.
122 Van A. Harvey, 'New Testament Scholarship and Christian Belief' in R. Joseph Hoffman and Gerald A. Larue, (eds), *Jesus in History and Myth* (Buffalo: Prometheus Books, 1986), 193; *WCB*, 401.
123 'New Testament Scholarship', 194; *WCB*, 401.
124 *WCB*, 402.
125 *WCB*, 413.
126 *WCB*, 415.

Pontius Pilate.'[127] Not included in this list are the resurrection of Jesus and the divine authorship of Scripture. These, according to Plantinga, are not beyond reasonable doubt, if judged by the standards of HBC, even of non-Troeltschian HBC.

That HBC is not able to confirm (although it does not disconfirm) traditional Christian doctrine is not something that should concern a Christian, according to Plantinga. He reasons that the Christian has access to alternative sources of warranted belief in addition to perception, testimony, deductive and probabilistic reasoning, sympathy and the other sources of belief relied upon by the historian. The Christian believes what she does by faith, which is produced in her by the inner (and supernatural) testimony of the Holy Spirit. Her faith, in Plantinga's opinion, does not need to rest on the results of historical scholarship.[128] It is largely, although not entirely independent of such scholarship. Plantinga admits the possibility that historians (employing HBC methodology) may discover facts which could seriously threaten Christian belief:[129]

> A series of letters could be discovered, letters circulated among Peter, James, John and Paul, in which the necessity for the hoax and the means of its perpetration are carefully and seriously discussed; these letters might direct workers to archeological sites in which still more material of the same sort is discovered ...[130]

Plantinga admits that since Christian faith is an *historical faith*, in that it essentially depends upon historical events, evidence of this kind would constitute a conflict between faith and reason.[131] However, in his opinion, 'nothing at all like this has emerged from HBC.'[132] The traditional Christian is thus entirely warranted to continue believing as she does.

In later chapters I intend to take up a number of the points Plantinga makes in his discussion of HBC, and so, at this stage, will not evaluate the significance of Plantinga's efforts. Instead, I would like to progress to Plantinga's more significant and longer term contribution to negative

---

127 A. E. Harvey, *Jesus and the Constraints of History* (Philadelphia: Westminster Press, 1982), 6; quoted in *WCB*, 415. Plantinga also notes John Meier's conclusions in *A Marginal Jew: Rethinking the Historical Jesus*. 'About all that emerges from Meier's painstaking work is that Jesus was a prophet, a proclaimer of an eschatological message from God, someone who performs powerful deeds, signs and wonders, that announce God's kingdom, and also ratify his message,' *WCB*, 416.
128 *WCB*, 416, 417.
129 *WCB*, 420.
130 *WCB*, 420.
131 *WCB*, 421.
132 *WCB*, 421.

apologetics, his response to the charge that theistic and Christian belief is irrational or in some other way intellectually deficient.

CHAPTER 4

Plantinga and Negative Apologetics: Evidentialist and *de jure* Challenges

4.1 Evidentialist Challenges

In 'Self-Profile', published in 1985, Plantinga mentioned three considerations that had troubled him most deeply over the years with respect to belief in God: the first was the problem of evil; the second was the decision by people whom Plantinga respected to reject belief in God; the third was 'the fact that it [was] difficult to find much by way of noncircular argument or evidence for the existence of God.'[1]

The first of these Plantinga admitted he still found 'deeply baffling', the second 'mildly disquieting', but of the third he wrote: 'The last, I think, is least impressive and no longer disturbed me after I had worked out the main line of argument of *God and Other Minds*.'[2]

Clearly, a watershed in Plantinga's thinking occurred with the writing of *God and Other Minds*. In 'Self-Profile', Plantinga notes that when he set out to write the book, he had assumed that the proper way to approach the question of the rationality of theistic belief was in terms of argument for and against the existence of God. This, doubtless, was why Plantinga had set out to examine the leading arguments of natural theology, and of natural atheology. What happened in the process, however, was that Plantinga came to the conclusion that *neither* argumentative enterprise was successful. The arguments both for and against God's existence were inconclusive. This realisation occasioned such a significant re-assessment for Plantinga that the final section of *God and Other Minds* includes an exploration of the possibility that belief in God can be rational 'even if none of the theistic arguments work and even if there is no non-circular evidence for it.'[3]

Plantinga began to build upon the observation that there are other significant beliefs which are likely to be thought of as rational, but which also lack non-circular evidential support; belief in other minds, for example. Our belief that

---

1 'Self-Profile', 34.
2 'Self-Profile', 34.
3 'Self-Profile', 55, 56. Plantinga notes that he was anticipated in this by James Tomberlin, in his 'Is Belief in God Justified?' *Journal of Philosophy*, 67 (1970), 31-38.

we are not alone in thinking, feeling, reasoning and believing, but that others exist who do this, suffers from the same lack of non-circular argumentative support as does belief in God, but is nevertheless unlikely to be deemed irrational.

Belief in God may, of course, be significantly different to belief in other minds, so that although belief in other minds does not require evidential support, belief in God does. Plantinga explores and discards that possibility in *God and Other Minds*,[4] before tentatively concluding: 'if my belief in other minds is rational, so is my belief in God. But obviously the former is rational; so, therefore, is the latter.'[5]

Plantinga had here taken a small, but significant step toward establishing the rationality (for him at least) of theistic belief.[6] The exercise of writing *God and Other Minds* raised the question of what constitutes rational belief. It also provided Plantinga with the beginnings of a response to the evidentialist objection to theistic belief: 'the objection that theistic belief is irrational just because there is no evidence or at any rate insufficient evidence for it.'[7] Plantinga notes in 'Self-Profile' that in the 1950's and 60's he had 'heard [this challenge] a thousand times if [he] had heard it once.'[8] Responding to it would become a major preoccupation, and, in time, a major contribution by Plantinga to negative apologetics. In what follows, I will trace the development of Plantinga's thinking, from the time of writing *God and Other Minds* on, especially as it relates to Plantinga's increasingly sophisticated response to the evidentialist objection to theistic (and Christian) belief.

After writing *God and Other Minds*, Plantinga had something of a break from thinking about the rationality of theistic belief until after he had finishing writing *The Nature of Necessity*.[9] During the following year, 1974, he wrote 'Is it Rational to Believe in God',[10] in which he argued that belief in God can be 'perfectly rational even if none of the theistic arguments work and even if there is no non-circular evidence for it.'[11] His aim was to argue for the rationality of taking belief in God as basic; 'that is, to accept theistic belief without accepting it on the basis of argument or evidence from other

---

4   *God and Other Minds*, 270, 271.
5   *God and Other Minds*, 271.
6   It is worth noting that even before *God and Other Minds* was published, Plantinga had anticipated its basic thesis in 'The Skeptic's Strategy', in J. Hick (ed), *Faith and the Philosophers* (New York: St. Martin's Press, 1965), 226-227.
7   'Self-Profile', 56.
8   'Self-Profile', 56.
9   'Self-Profile', 55.
10 This paper was presented at Cornell University in the Spring of 1975, and was later published as 'Is belief in God rational?'
11 'Self-Profile', 55, 56.

propositions one believes.'[12] To achieve this, Plantinga needed to address, and in this article he did for the first time, the issue of what it means for something to be rational. Plantinga had observed that although, for many philosophers, the issue of the rationality of theistic belief is 'a central question - perhaps *the* central question - of the philosophy of religion,'[13] they had been notably silent when it came to spelling out what it means to be rational. Typically, believers would be issued with the challenge to provide evidence (or sufficient evidence) for their beliefs (evidence conceived of in propositional terms),[14] and if they could not provide such evidence they would be judged irrational. Believers, for their part, would (mostly, and mostly uncritically) accept the challenge of providing evidence. Both would 'concur in holding that belief in God is rational only if there is, on balance, a preponderance of evidence for it - or less radically, only if there is not, on balance, a preponderance of evidence against it.'[15]

In exploring the notion of rationality that underlies this challenge, Plantinga came to see two things; first, that the challenge was often, if not always, linked to a particular theory of knowledge known as foundationalism,[16] and, second, that the notion of rationality associated with this theory implied a particular morality of knowledge.

Plantinga began to explore the foundationalist-based challenge in 'Is Belief in God Rational?'. He noted that an evidentialist (such as W. K. Clifford),[17] would insist on judging the rationality of belief in God by examining its relation to other propositions, and in particular to propositions that belong to the foundations of a person's noetic structure. As Plantinga puts it:

> Suppose we say that the assemblage of beliefs a person holds, together with the various logical and epistemic relations that hold among them, constitutes that person's *noetic structure*. Now what the Cliffordian really holds is that for each person S there is a set F of beliefs such that a proposition p is rational or rationally acceptable for S only if p is evident with respect to F - only if, that is, the propositions in F constitute, on balance, evidence for p. Let us say that this set F of propositions is the *foundation of* S's *noetic structure*. On this view every noetic structure has a foundation; and a

---

12 'Self-Profile', 56.
13 'Is Belief in God Rational', 8.
14 'Is Belief in God Rational', 9.
15 'Is Belief in God Rational', 9.
16 Plantinga acknowledges the fact that an evidentialist objection could be urged by a non-foundationalist, by a coherentist, for example. For a discussion of this possibility, see 'Reason and Belief in God', 63.
17 W. K. Clifford (mentioned in chapter one of this book) is used by Plantinga as an example of a foundationalist evidentialist.

proposition is rational for S, or known by S, or certain for S, only if it stands in the appropriate relation to the foundation of S's noetic structure.[18]

The foundationalist doctrine of knowledge, as spelled out here, does not in itself entail the irrationality of theistic belief. As Plantinga points out, if belief in God is included in the foundation of one's noetic structure, then 'it will automatically be evident with respect to F [the foundation].'[19] The only way in which foundationalism could pose a threat would be if belief in God could be successfully (and with good reason) excluded from the foundations of one's noetic structure *and* it be shown that belief in God does not stand in an appropriate relation to what rightfully is within the foundations of a believer's noetic structure.

Clearly, Plantinga, at this stage of his career at least, was of the opinion that if one did accept the exclusion of belief in God from the foundations of one's noetic structure, such belief would be in danger of not standing in appropriate relation to the remaining acceptable foundational beliefs.[20] In *God and Other Minds*, Plantinga had admitted: 'I think it must be conceded that the theist has no very good answer to the request that he explain his reasons for believing the existence of God; at any rate he has no answer that need convince the skeptic.'[21]

The only option open to Plantinga, which, no doubt, he was happy to pursue, given his Reformed background, was the option of arguing that belief in God cannot successfully be excluded from the foundations of one's noetic structure.

In order to understand Plantinga's argument, the nature of the foundationalist challenge needs to be considered a little more fully. According to foundationalist doctrine (exemplified by Clifford) 'a proposition is rational for S, or known by S, or certain for S, only if it stands in the appropriate relation to the foundation of S's noetic structure.'[22] Two issues need to be clarified here: first, the issue of what constitutes a foundational belief; second, the issue of what it means for something to be in an appropriate relation to these foundational beliefs.

With respect to what is a foundational belief, Plantinga's answer is that a foundational belief is one which is properly or rationally held without needing the inferential support of still further beliefs. It lies at the foundation of a person's noetic structure, where the inferential process starts or ends.[23]

---

18 'Is Belief in God Rational', 12.
19 'Is Belief in God Rational', 13.
20 Plantinga would later be much more concessive of the value and potential success of arguments drawn from theistically independent and foundationally grounded premises to the conclusion that God exists.
21 *God and Other Minds*, 268.
22 'Is Belief in God Rational', 12.
23 'Is Belief in God Rational', 13.

Plantinga describes such beliefs as 'properly basic' beliefs. A basic belief is one that is not accepted on the basis of still further beliefs.[24] A *properly* basic belief is one that is properly, or reasonably, or justifiably, basic for a person.[25] As to which beliefs qualify as properly basic, different answers have been given. Ancient, medieval and modern foundationalists (referred to collectively as 'classical foundationalists' by Plantinga[26]) have suggested various candidates including: self-evident beliefs; beliefs about what is evident to the senses;[27] and, from the time of Descartes, incorrigible beliefs.

With respect to what it means for something to be in an appropriate relation to these foundational beliefs, the classic foundationalist position has been that non-basic beliefs:

> must be provable from what is in the foundational level of knowledge, that is, from what is self-evident or incorrigible. There may be things that I believe but can't prove; but anything I *know* is something I can prove from the foundations of knowledge.[28]

Foundationalists have differed in their understanding of what it means to 'prove' something. Various candidates have been proposed as constituting the proper basis for accepting one belief on the basis of others:

> One candidate, for example, is *entailment*; A supports B only if B is entailed by A, or perhaps is self-evidently entailed by A, or perhaps follows from A by an argument where each step is a self-evident entailment. Another and more permissive candidate is probability: perhaps A supports B if B is likely or probable with respect to A. And of course there are other candidates.[29]

Plantinga, at the time of writing *God and Other Minds*, had assumed the necessity of less permissive standards of proof. Along with 'virtually everyone else', he had believed that 'a *good* argument (either theistic or antitheistic) would have to be more or less conclusive, appealing to premises and procedures hardly any sensible person could reject.'[30] The threat posed by classical

---

24 'Rationality and Religious Belief', in S. Cahn and D. Shatz, (eds), *Contemporary Philosophy of Religion* (New York: Oxford University Press, 1982), 259.
25 'Rationality and Religious Belief', 260; 'Ad de Vries', 171.
26 The term 'classical foundationalism' was coined by Plantinga to refer to 'the disjunction of ancient and medieval with modern foundationalism,' 'The Reformed Objection to Natural Theology', *Proceedings of the American Catholic Philosophical Association*, Vol. 54 (1980), 57.
27 'Is Belief in God Rational', 13, 14.
28 'On Reformed Epistemology', *Reformed Journal*, Vol. 32 (January, 1982), 13.
29 'The Reformed Objection', 193.
30 'A Christian Life', 74.

foundationalism was understandably greater for those, such as Plantinga, who accepted more rigorous standards of proof.

The threat posed by classical foundationalism can also be construed in normative terms. As has been noted, Plantinga came to understand that the notion of rationality associated with classical foundationalism implied a particular morality of knowledge. In order to be rational in one's beliefs, one had to fulfil certain epistemological duties, the non-fulfilment of which would render a person irrational and therefore immoral.[31] The particular duty urged by the evidentialist was the duty to not believe anything without adequate evidence, or, at least, to proportion belief to the evidence.[32] Plantinga, although not denying the existence and even importance of duties such as these,[33] argues that the evidentialist challenge simply misses the mark when applied to belief in God. Belief in God, because it is properly basic, does not need the support of still further beliefs.

For the evidentialist challenge to succeed, belief in God must be excluded, and with good reason, from the foundations of a person's noetic structure. In Plantinga's opinion, such a task is not easily done, nor has it been done successfully. To argue, for example, that only self-evident and incorrigible propositions belong in the foundations of a person's noetic structure is to simply beg the question of what properly belongs there.[34] Such a narrow specification certainly cannot be established by arguments meeting the requirements of classical foundationalism.[35]

The foundationalist needs, and Plantinga himself needs, some way of determining which beliefs qualify as foundational beliefs. It may be that belief in God is difficult to exclude from the foundations of a person's noetic structure. However, this, in itself, does not mean that it should be included. There needs to be some good reason for including it. Plantinga proceeds to do this in two ways: first, by suggesting an inductive approach to determining which beliefs are properly basic, and, second, by suggesting a reason for thinking that belief in God is properly basic.

---

31 In 'The Reformed Objection to Natural Theology', Plantinga writes that 'classical foundationalism is *best construed* [my emphasis] as a thesis about *rational* noetic structures. A noetic structure is rational if it could be the noetic structure of a person who was completely rational. To be completely rational ... [is] to do the right thing with respect to one's believings ... which means to fulfil appropriate epistemic duties and responsibilities,' 55.
32 'Reason and Belief in God', 30.
33 See, for example, 'Reason and Belief in God', 30-32; WCB, 96, 97.
34 'Is Belief in God Rational', 25, 26.
35 As Plantinga points out, the proposition that *only* those propositions which are self-evident or incorrigible are properly basic for S is itself neither self-evident nor incorrigible, nor does it appear to follow from what is self-evident or incorrigible, 'Is Belief in God Rational', 25, 26.

First then, Plantinga suggests that the way (in fact, the only way) to determine which beliefs are properly basic is to employ an inductive approach. He arrives at this conclusion in the process of answering the now famous 'Great Pumpkin Objection'. The Great Pumpkin Objection, in essence, is the objection that once one accepts belief in God as properly basic the flood gates are opened to the acceptance of all sorts of other beliefs, including ones which are manifestly irrational:

> If belief in God is properly basic, why can't just any belief be properly basic? Couldn't we say the same for any bizarre aberration we can think of? What about voodoo or astrology? What about the belief that the Great Pumpkin returns every Halloween? Could I properly take *that* as basic?[36]

Plantinga's answer is: 'Certainly not.'[37] Plantinga argues that his objection to the criteria for proper basicality proposed by the classical foundationalist does not in any way commit him to accepting manifestly irrational beliefs.[38] All it does is to re-open the question of what such criteria might be. The way to develop criteria, Plantinga suggests, is to examine (potential) classes of properly basic beliefs on a case by case basis, thus determining criteria 'on the run'.[39] Plantinga points out that attempts to find criteria for proper basicality are fraught with difficulties. The problem is that any suggested criteria are likely to be universal in form, in which case they themselves will need to meet their own conditions. This has proved problematic for the modern foundationalist criterion for proper basicality. It is also likely to be a problem for any other proposal.[40]

Plantinga's reason for thinking that belief in God should be included in any list of properly basic beliefs is that God himself has designed things that way. Drawing upon his understanding of Calvin,[41] Plantinga asserts that God has created human beings with 'an innate tendency, or nisus, or disposition to believe in him'.[42] This tendency is activated in a number of widely realised circumstances, such as 'upon beholding the starry heavens, or the splendid majesty of the mountains, or the intricate, articulate beauty of a tiny flower.'[43] Belief in God thus formed is typically basic belief. It is not formed as a result

---

36 'The Reformed Objection', 58.
37 'The Reformed Objection', 58.
38 With respect to belief in the Great Pumpkin, Plantinga sensibly points out that a Christian (as would be the case for people of other world views) has ample reason to rule out belief in the Great Pumpkin, 'The Reformed Objection', 61; WCB, 412f.
39 'The Reformed Objection', 60.
40 'The Reformed Objection', 60.
41 An understanding shaped by the (Dutch) Reformed tradition of which Plantinga is a part.
42 'The Reformed Objection', 51.
43 'The Reformed Objection', 52.

of argument (such as the teleological argument for example). It is not based upon other propositions. It is formed immediately and non-inferentially. To the possible charge that beliefs formed in this way are arbitrary, because not grounded in the particular support of other beliefs, Plantinga responds by pointing out that properly basic beliefs, although they lack propositional support, are not for that reason *groundless*. They too need to meet certain conditions to be considered justified.[44]

It is this point of discussion which, arguably, was the breeding ground for Plantinga's later more developed epistemological theory. As Plantinga pursued his response to evidentialism, he also began to think more broadly about what was necessary for a belief (theistic or otherwise) to have 'positive epistemic status'.[45] This terminology came to be used by Plantinga to encompass a number of related, but distinguishable methods of evaluating the epistemic status of beliefs. Included under the banner of positive epistemic status were the concepts of justification, rationality and warrant. In order to keep these concepts conceptually separate, Plantinga used the term 'warrant' to refer to that somewhat elusive quality which, along with true belief, is able, depending upon the degree of warrant,[46] to constitute knowledge.

---

44 Included among such conditions is the having of a particular type of experience (such as being appeared to in a characteristic sort of way) which, in itself, confers some epistemological right to hold the resulting belief. See further, 'Reason and Belief in God', 79.

45 The terms 'positive epistemic status', borrowed from Roderick Chisholm, began to appear in Plantinga's writings in the mid 80s, for example, in 'Coherentism and the evidentialist objection to belief in God', in R. Audi, (ed), *Rationality, Religious Belief, and Moral Commitment: New Essays in the Philosophy of Religion* (Ithaca: Cornell University Press, 1986), 109-138, and in 'Justification and theism', *Faith and Philosophy,* Vol. 4 (October, 1987), 403-426. Note that when Plantinga first used 'positive epistemic status' he used it to refer to what he would later call warrant. And so, in 'Justification and Theism', he states, 'I shall borrow Chisholm's term "positive epistemic status" as my official name of the quality in question - the quality enough of which distinguishes mere true belief from knowledge,' 404. More recently, Plantinga appears to use positive epistemic status as a broader term which encompasses warrant, but which can also incorporate other positive epistemic conditions. See Plantinga's summary article, 'Reformed Epistemology', in Philip L. Quinn and Charles Taliaferro, (eds), *A Companion to Philosophy of Religion* (Oxford: Blackwell Publishers, 1997), 386; see also *WCB*, 241, where Plantinga identifies justification, rationality and warrant as three varieties of 'positive epistemic status'.

46 Plantinga notes that warrant comes in degrees. A true belief will only constitute knowledge if it possesses a particular degree of warrant, *WCD*, 4.

Plantinga's work on warrant has been ground-breaking. After surveying a range of contemporary understandings of warrant, both internalist and externalist,[47] Plantinga formulated his own theory, according to which:

> a belief has warrant for [a person] only if (1) it has been produced in [her] by cognitive faculties that are working properly (functioning as they ought to, subject to no cognitive dysfunction) in a cognitive environment that is appropriate for [her] kinds of cognitive faculties, (2) the segment of the design plan[48] governing the production of that belief is aimed at the production of true beliefs, and (3) there is a high statistical probability that a belief produced under those conditions will be true. Under those conditions, furthermore, the degree of warrant is an increasing function of degree of belief.[49]

Plantinga's theory is not only original, significant and promising in its own right as an analysis of knowledge, it also provides the theoretical underpinning for Plantinga's efforts to meet the evidentialist challenge to theistic belief. Evidentialism, as an epistemological ideology, has frequently assumed an internalist account of knowledge. According to this understanding, one can only say that one has achieved knowledge if one has self-consciously fulfilled certain epistemic duties, such as not believing anything more strongly than the evidence allows. Plantinga (as already stated) denies neither the existence nor the importance of epistemic duties. However, he insists that the acquisition of knowledge (as well as the achievement of rationality) does not in every case depend on a conscious fulfilment of such duties. The important thing with respect both to knowledge and rationality is that the person concerned forms their knowledge using cognitive faculties that are working properly in an appropriate cognitive environment, and so on.[50] This account leaves room for the contention of Plantinga, and of those within his particular Reformed tradition, that belief in God is formed spontaneously and non-inferentially in

---

47 In *WCD*.
48 In using the term 'design plan' Plantinga is not thereby committing himself to theism, even though the terminology fits nicely within a theistic framework. He is using it to refer to the way that particular cognitive faculties characteristically work. See *WPF*, 11-17.
49 *WPF*, 46. Since writing *WPF*, Plantinga's theory has received a number of criticisms, some of which he has accepted, resulting in a slight modification, the addition of what he calls the Resolution Condition: (RC) A belief B produced by an exercise E of cognitive powers has warrant sufficient for knowledge only if *MBE* (a mini-environment with respect to B and E) is favorable for E, *WCB*, 186; for Plantinga's discussion of the need for this modification, 156-161.
50 Plantinga's theory, importantly, does not entirely set aside internalistic considerations. One could argue, for example, that a failure to take sufficient account of evidence may, on occasion, constitute an example of cognitive faculties malfunctioning, thereby preventing knowledge.

various appropriate environments, such as on a mountaintop, or in the observation of the intricate, articulate beauty of a flower. It also provides the theoretical background for Plantinga's contention that a believer in God does not need the support of evidence, construed propositionally, to be rational in his believing. If adequate grounds for belief exist, and one has reason to think that the beliefs delivered are likely to be true (Plantinga's Calvinistic theory provides the rationale for affirming both of these possibilities), then the belief can be said to have warrant,[51] even warrant sufficient to constitute knowledge.[52]

Before bringing this section to a close, a few things need to be said regarding the significance of Plantinga's response to the evidentialist challenge. To begin, Plantinga's response is, without doubt, an impressive piece of philosophical work. It is hard to fault Plantinga's logic, particularly where he shows up the inherent inadequacies in the evidentialist dismissal of properly basic theistic belief. He certainly does enough to leave open the possibility of such belief. Whether he also does enough, positively, to establish that such belief exists is another question, one which will be taken up in chapter seven.

Plantinga is not the first person to have attacked foundationalist evidentialism. Prior to Plantinga, the American pragmatist philosopher William James (1842-1910), in a classic essay, 'The Will to Believe', sought to combat evidentialist claims by noting legitimate non-rational factors involved in the formation of beliefs.[53] Nevertheless, Plantinga has certainly

---

51 On the relationship between rationality and warrant, see below.

52 It is worth noting, at this point, that Plantinga's evolving theory of warrant allowed him to differentiate between two senses of proper basicality. According to the first sense, a belief is properly basic for a person if the person is *justified* in holding it in a basic way, which is to say, he is 'within his epistemic rights, is not irresponsible, is violating no epistemic or other duties in holding that belief in that way.' According to the second sense, a belief is properly basic for a person if the belief has warrant for that person, which would be the case if the belief was produced by cognitive faculties functioning properly in a congenial epistemic environment according to a design plan successfully aimed at truth, *WCB*, 177, 178.

53 William James, 'The Will to Believe,' in *The Will to Believe and Other Essays* (New York: Longman's and Green, 1896). Note also that there have been other philosophers such as Austin Farrer and E. L. Mascal, who have argued along similar lines to Plantinga that theistic belief is, in some sense, properly basic (although without using this terminology). Mascal, for example, argues that 'God is known primarily by intuition or "contuition" ... our knowledge of God is direct in so far as it is non-discursive, but indirect in so far as it is mediated ...' *The Openness of Being: Natural Theology Today* (London: Darton, Longman and Todd, 1971), 108, 109. Among Neo-Thomists of the 19th and 20th centuries, were some who argued, analogously, that belief in God is best understood as intuitive. See John Haldane, Thomism' in *The Routledge Encyclopedia of Philosophy*, Vol. 9, (London: Routledge, 1998), 383.

been the most prominent philosopher of his calibre in recent times to seriously question an evidentialism with respect to belief in God which had achieved an almost universal dogmatism. In *WCB*, Plantinga notes that no-one, to his knowledge, in Western philosophical circles, with the exception of William James, had called into question this dogmatism. Certainly at the time of writing *God and Other Minds*, no other scholar was raising the sorts of questions posed by Plantinga, such as the question of whether evidence needs to be in propositional form.

Outside philosophical circles, scholars from within Plantinga's Reformed tradition, from Abraham Kuyper onwards, had been resisting the imperialistic encroachments of foundationalist evidentialism. Plantinga's insights are therefore not entirely new. What is new, or at least noteworthy, is the clarity and strength of Plantinga's counter-attack. Plantinga brings to his work a sharp analytical mind. No-one, to my knowledge, has done as good a job of analysing and critiquing the evidentialist position as has Plantinga. No one has done as good a job of putting a case for properly basic theistic belief. In the words of Thomas Sullivan, Plantinga presents '... what may well be the ablest defense of unargued religious belief in this century.'[54]

Two final things to note. First, Plantinga's reply to the evidentialist challenge is one further example of his confident, non-defensive, self-consciously Christian approach to philosophical issues. Here as elsewhere, Plantinga refuses to be intimidated by contrary opinions or challenges. Rather than be on the defensive himself, he has put others on the defensive, issuing a strong counter challenge to those who would urge an evidentialist objection.

Second, and related to the previous point, Plantinga's development of an externalist account of knowledge reflects not only with Plantinga's confident style, but a more general confidence that belief systems such as Christianity can be known to be true. Linda Zagzebski, in describing Plantinga's development of an externalist account of warrant notes the significance of externalist accounts in general:

> An important motivation driving externalist theories is the desire to avoid skepticism; in fact, this is one of its most attractive features. As long as nature has insured that we respond to stimuli from the external world in a way that reliably leads to truth, our beliefs are warranted, and if they are true, as they often are, we have knowledge. Indeed, Plantinga began to develop his epistemic theory as a response to religious skepticism. His work demonstrates that the generous optimism about knowledge that we find in this

---

54 Thomas D. Sullivan, 'Adequate Evidence', in L. A. Kennedy, (ed), *Thomaistic Papers IV* (Houston, Texas: Center for Thomistic Studies, 1988), 86. Sullivan includes the work of Nicholas Wolterstorff in this assessment.

school of epistemology can be rather easily extended to religious knowledge.[55]

More could (and will in subsequent chapters) be said about the significance and success of Plantinga's response to the evidentialist challenge. However, I would like now to broaden the discussion somewhat. In the course of responding to the evidentialist challenge to theistic belief, Plantinga came to understand that challenge as part of a broader challenge to theistic and Christian belief. Unsympathetic evidentialists have tended to believe that theistic and Christian belief displays an epistemological, even a moral deficiency. Others have agreed, for different reasons. In *WCB*, Plantinga sets out to respond to this broader challenge, concentrating in this instance on Christian belief, and not simply on theistic belief. He poses the following questions, the answering of which becomes his primary objective in *WCB*:

> ... is [Christian belief] intellectually acceptable? In particular, is it intellectually acceptable for *us*, *now*? For educated and intelligent people living in the twenty-first century, with all that has happened over the last four or five hundred years? Some will concede that Christian belief was acceptable and even appropriate for our ancestors, people who knew little of other religions, who knew nothing of evolution and our animal ancestry, nothing of contemporary subatomic physics and the strange, eerie, disquieting world it postulates, nothing of those great masters of suspicion, Nietzsche, Marx and Freud, nothing of the acids of modern historical biblical criticism. But for us enlightened contemporary intellectuals (so the claim continues) things are wholly different; for people who know about those things (people of our rather impressive intellectual attainments) there is something naive and foolish, or perhaps bullheaded and irresponsible, or even vaguely pathological in holding onto such belief.[56]

In his attempt to isolate the exact nature of this objection to Christian belief, Plantinga isolates two distinct styles of objection. Included in the first are *de facto* objections: objections to the *truth* of Christian belief; included in the second are *de jure* objections, which are 'arguments or claims to the effect that Christian belief, whether or not true, is at any rate unjustifiable, or rationally unjustified, or irrational, or not intellectually respectable, or contrary to sound morality, or without sufficient evidence, or in some other way rationally unacceptable, not up to snuff from an intellectual point of view.'[57]

---

55 Linda Zagzebski, 'Religious Knowledge and the Virtues' in *Rational Faith: Catholic Responses to Reformed Epistemology* (Notre Dame: University of Notre Dame Press, 1993), 202.
56 *WCB*, vi.
57 *WCB*, vii. Note that Plantinga first uses the term *de jure* to refer to the rational acceptability of Christian belief in 'What's the Question?' *Journal of Philosophical Research*, Vol. 20 (1995), 19, 20.

4.2 *De jure* Challenges

In the preface to *WCB*, Plantinga observes that those (including evidentialists) who have accused Christians of being irrational, or unjustified, or otherwise intellectually irresponsible in their believing have seldom elucidated the exact problem.[58] Plantinga attempts in his book to discover exactly what this undefined problem might be, 'to try to find [if he can] a serious and viable *de jure* objection to Christian belief, one which could, at least plausibly, be attached to Christian belief.'[59]

In order to achieve this, Plantinga sets out to disentangle and describe the three most commonly employed categories of epistemic health or ill-health: justification, rationality and warrant. If there is a viable *de jure* objection to Christian faith, Plantinga believes that it is likely to lie in the area of one of these three categories.[60]

Justificatory language is most commonly used in a deontological sense. To be justified in one's believing means acting in accord with duty, being within one's rights and flouting no epistemological obligations. It means being responsible in one's believing.[61] The justificationist tradition dates back at least to John Locke, who insisted that people regulate their intellectual lives according to God-given reason. Plantinga does not believe that a sensible *de jure* challenge to Christian belief can be advanced in justificatory terms. Although the requirement to be responsible in the area of belief formation is a reasonable one, he thinks that a Christian, even a sophisticated and knowledgeable contemporary Christian, aware of all the major criticisms that Christian faith is subject to, can easily meet that requirement.[62] Plantinga considers it entirely possible that such a person could be conversant with the works of Freud, Marx and Nietzsche (not to mention Flew, Mackie and Nielsen) and other such critics of Christian or theistic belief, and still continue to firmly believe as she does. He thinks this is particularly the case for someone possessing 'a rich inner spiritual life'.[63] Plantinga describes the possible thinking of such a person in these terms:

> it seems to her that she is sometimes made aware, catches a glimpse, of something of the overwhelming beauty and loveliness of the Lord; she is often aware, as it strongly seems to her, of the work of the Holy Spirit in her

---

58 *WCB*, viii.
59 *WCB*, viii.
60 *WCB*, viii.
61 Plantinga sees this idea of being responsible in one's believings as 'the aboriginal and basic idea of the justificationist tradition, the palimpsest in terms of which other justificationist notions are to be understood by way of analogical extensions,' *WCB*, 87.
62 *WCB*, 100.
63 *WCB*, 100.

heart, comforting, encouraging, teaching, leading her to accept the 'great things of the gospel' (as Edwards calls them), helping her see that the magnificent scheme of salvation devised by the Lord himself is not only for others but for her as well. After long, hard, conscientious reflection, this all seems to her enormously more convincing than the complaints of the critics.[64]

Plantinga argues that such a person can hardly be said to be unjustified in her believing. She 'isn't flouting any discernible duty. She is fulfilling her epistemic responsibilities; she is doing her level best; she is justified.'[65] A number of things can be said by way of critique. However, these are best postponed until a more detailed exposition of Plantinga's position, which is yet to come.

Plantinga continues, in *WCB*, to consider (or rather reconsider[66]) the notion of rationality, to see whether a sensible *de jure* criticism of Christian faith can be mounted in rationalistic terms. Drawing on earlier work,[67] he identifies and describes five main conceptions of rationality: (1) Aristotelian rationality (in the sense of human beings being rational); (2) rationality as proper function; (3) rationality as within, or conforming to, the deliverances of reason; (4) means-ends rationality (where the question is whether a particular means someone chooses is a good means to her ends); and (5) deontological rationality, which Plantinga identifies with the justificatory tradition. Plantinga adds to this William Alston's *practical rationality*.

Without going into detail, Plantinga considers and dismisses all but one of these notions of rationality as providing promising possibilities for a sensible *de jure* criticism of Christian faith.[68] The conception of rationality containing at least some potential for such a challenge, in Plantinga's opinion, is the concept of rationality as proper function. Plantinga differentiates between two forms of this type of rationality: the first internal, the second external. Plantinga describes internal rationality as 'a matter of proper function of all belief-producing processes "downstream from experience."'[69] It involves:

---

64 *WCB*, 100, 101.
65 *WCB*, 100, 101.
66 As was seen in our consideration of the evidentialist challenge, Plantinga has had a long- standing interest in what is meant by rationality. It was consideration of this notion which led Plantinga to differentiate between justification, rationality and warrant.
67 In *WCD*.
68 In *WCB*, 108-134.
69 *WCB*, 110. Plantinga explains the expression 'downstream from experience' in terms of the individual knower's response to the various sorts of experience, phenomenal and doxastic, 110, 111.

forming or holding the appropriate beliefs in response to experience, including both phenomenal imagery and doxastic experience.[70] With respect to the first, I will form beliefs appropriate to the phenomenal imagery I enjoy ... [the second involves forming the right beliefs in response to doxastic experience].[71]

Also involved in internal rationality is achieving coherence;[72] drawing the right inferences;[73] and taking appropriate action in the light of those inferences. It involves doing 'what proper function requires with respect to such things as preferring to believe what is true, looking for further evidence when that is appropriate, and in general being epistemically responsible.'[74] This aspect of rationality clearly overlaps with, or encompasses the justificatory aspect of epistemic health (or ill-health).

External rationality requires proper function with respect to the formation of sensuous and doxastic experience. The lack of external rationality would manifest itself, for example, in all sorts of clinical psychoses.[75] Although Plantinga doubts that Christian believing can be described as irrational in terms of internal or external rationality, certainly if the claim is made that Christian believing is typically pathological, or arises from some neurosis, he does signal the possibility that a sensible *de jure* question might lie in the neighbourhood of a more subtle form of cognitive malfunction.[76]

In order to explore this possibility, Plantinga turns his attention to the notion of warrant. It is here that Plantinga thinks it most likely that a sensible *de jure* challenge to Christian belief might be found, and the most likely candidates for offering such a challenge, he suggests, are Freud, Marx 'and the whole cadre of their nineteenth and twentieth century followers.'[77] What Freud and Marx and their followers have suggested, in essence, is that religion, including the Christian religion, can be understood adequately and exhaustively in psychological or sociological terms.[78] According to Freud, the cognitive mechanism giving rise to religious belief is 'wish-fulfilment', which, although it produces beliefs which are infantile, and better discarded, at least perform the function of enabling people to remain relatively happy in a cold and heartless

---

70 Plantinga uses the term 'doxastic experience' to refer to experiences like the feeling that a particular proposition is true. Doxastic experience is the experiential dimension to belief formation, what it feels like to believe something. *WCB*, 111.
71 *WCB*, 111.
72 *WCB*, 112
73 *WCB*, 112.
74 *WCB*, 112, 113.
75 *WCB*, 112.
76 *WCB*, 113.
77 *WCB*, 136.
78 Included among those who have thought and argued this way are Jean Jacques Rousseau, David Hume, Friedrich Nietzsche, Northrop Frye and Charles Daniels.

world. Marx was more inclined to view religious belief as wholly negative, in Plantinga's terms, as an example of cognitive dysfunction, brought about by a perverted world consciousness, resulting from a perverted social order.

Plantinga suggests that these and other explanations and implied criticisms of Christian belief can best be understood in terms of proper function (which lies at the heart of Plantinga's theory of warrant). One of two things is true about Christian belief: either a person's (or community's) cognitive faculties are functioning properly, but the process involved is not designed to yield true belief, or those faculties are not functioning properly and some cognitive dysfunction is involved. In either case, the resulting belief lacks warrant. The Freudian-Marxian criticism can be thus summarised as: '[the criticism] that religious belief is not produced by cognitive faculties that are functioning properly and aimed at the truth.'[79]

Plantinga thinks that he has at last discovered a sensible *de jure* criticism, which is that: 'theistic belief and religious belief generally *lacks* warrant'.[80] He responds to the criticism in two ways: first, by suggesting a model for a way in which theistic belief may be seen to have warrant, and second, by suggesting a development of this model for application to specifically Christian beliefs.

Plantinga dubs his model the A/C model (A standing for Aquinas, C for Calvin). This, essentially, is the model which Plantinga both appealed to and developed in arguing his case for the proper basicality of belief in God. According to both Aquinas and Calvin, there is a kind of natural knowledge of God available to human beings. According to Calvin, 'there is a kind of faculty or a cognitive mechanism [the *sensus divinitatis*], which in a wide variety of circumstances produces in us beliefs about God.'[81] These beliefs, moreover, are basic, and, because they are produced in us by cognitive faculties operating (to some degree[82]) as they were designed to operate, they are properly basic. They have warrant, and very often sufficient warrant to constitute knowledge.[83]

Plantinga's A/C model is extended so as to include specifically Christian beliefs. According to the extended A/C model, human beings, despite having been made in the image of God, have fallen into sin, described as 'a calamitous condition from which we require salvation.'[84] The effects of sin are both affective and cognitive. Affectively, human affections are distorted, the human heart now being capable of harbouring deep and radical evil. Love for God is replaced by love of self. Cognitively, the once clear knowledge of God available to human beings is dimmed. The narrow image of God is destroyed, the broad

---

79 *WCB*, 152.
80 *WCB*, 153.
81 *WCB*, 172.
82 Plantinga acknowledges, as will be seen, the effects of human sin upon the operations of the *sensus divinitatis*.
83 *WCB*, 178, 179.
84 *WCB*, 205.

image distorted. The *sensus divinitatis* has been damaged and deformed, with its operations now being resisted.[85] The consequence of this is that human beings are unable, by their own efforts, to extricate themselves from this predicament. The intervention of God is necessary. Fortunately, God has provided a remedy for sin and its effects in the life, death and resurrection of his divine Son, Jesus. By his actions there has been a restoration and repair of the image of God in human beings.[86]

Plantinga outlines the more specifically cognitive side of his model in these terms:

> God needed a way in which to inform human beings of many times and places of the scheme of salvation he has graciously made available. No doubt he could have done this a thousand different ways; in fact he chose to do so in the following way. First, there is Scripture, the Bible, a collection of writings by human authors, but specially inspired by God in such a way that he can be said to be its principal author. Second, he sent his Holy Spirit, promised by Christ before his death and resurrection. A principal work of the Holy Spirit with respect to us human beings is the production in us of the gift of *faith,* that 'firm and certain knowledge of God's benevolence towards us, founded upon the truth of the freely given promise given in Christ, both revealed to our minds and sealed upon our hearts through the Holy Spirit' of which Calvin speaks. By virtue of the internal instigation of the Holy Spirit, we come to see the truth of the central Christian affirmations.[87]

Plantinga describes the internal invitation of the Holy Spirit as 'a source of belief, a cognitive process that produces in us belief in the main lines of the Christian story.'[88] It is, in Plantinga's understanding, a supernatural process used by God to bring about Christian belief. The resultant beliefs do not come 'by way of memory, perception, reason, testimony, the *sensus divinitatis*, or any other of the cognitive faculties with which we human beings were originally created; they come instead by way of the work of the Holy Spirit ... they are a supernatural gift.'[89]

As to how this supernatural process works, Plantinga believes that, as is the case with the operation of the *sensus divinitatis*, the internal instigation of the Holy Spirit (henceforth IIHS) creates beliefs which are basic. He describes the phenomenology in these terms:

> We read Scripture, or something presenting Scriptural teaching, or hear the gospel preached, or are told of it by parents, or encounter a Scriptural

---

85 *WCB*, 205.
86 *WCB*, 205.
87 *WCB*, 205, 206.
88 *WCB*, 206.
89 *WCB*, 245.

teaching as the conclusion of an argument (or conceivably even as an object of ridicule), or in some other way encounter a proclamation of the Word. What is said simply seems right; it seems compelling; one finds oneself saying, 'Yes, that's right, that's the truth of the matter; this is indeed the word of the Lord.' I read 'God was in Christ, reconciling the world to himself'; I come to think: 'Right; that's true; God really was in Christ, reconciling the world to himself!' And I may also think something a bit different, something *about* that proposition: that it is indeed a divine teaching or revelation, that in Calvin's words it is 'from God'. What one hears or reads seems clearly and obviously true, and (at any rate in paradigm cases) seems also to be something the Lord is intending to teach ... So faith may have the phenomenology that goes with suddenly seeing something to be true: 'Right! Now I see that this is indeed true and what the Lord is teaching!' Or perhaps the conviction arises slowly, and only after long and hard study, thought, discussion, prayer. Or perhaps it is a matter of a belief's having been there all along (from childhood, perhaps), but now being transformed, renewed, intensified, made vivid and alive. The process can go on in a thousand ways; in each case there is a presentation or proposal of central Christian teaching, and by way of response, the phenomenon of being convinced, coming to see, forming a conviction. There is the reading or hearing, and then there is the belief or conviction that what one reads or hears is true and a teaching of the Lord.[90]

Returning to the question of warrant, Plantinga, not surprisingly, thinks that specifically Christian beliefs formed in the manner outlined above, have warrant,[91] or, at least, are likely to have warrant given the truth of a particular metaphysical assumption, namely that God exists. The same applies for theistic belief formed in a basic way.

The role of one's metaphysical assumptions is critical. Plantinga is well aware, and indicates that his theory of warranted theistic belief rests upon the metaphysical assumption that theism is true. If theism is not true, then it is probably not the case that basic theistic belief has warrant. It certainly would not have sufficient warrant for knowledge, since the relevant beliefs would be false.[92] However, if theism is true, it is more likely than not that theistic belief has warrant. The reason for this, Plantinga argues, is that if a loving creator God does exist, it is likely that he will desire that his existence and requirements be known, and that the cognitive mechanisms involved in bringing this about will be successful in producing warranted, true belief.[93]

---

90 *WCB*, 250, 251.
91 Plantinga also argues, and, as noted above, finds it easy to argue that these beliefs are also justified in a deontological sense (see *WCB*, 252-255), as well as being internally and externally rational (see *WCB*, 255-258).
92 Although false beliefs can occasionally have some warrant, Plantinga thinks it unlikely that theistic beliefs would have warrant, if untrue, *WCB*, 186-188.
93 *WCB*, 188, 189.

Plantinga argues in a similar manner for the likely warrantedness of specifically Christian beliefs.[94]

An implication which follows from this, according to Plantinga, is that *de jure* objections to Christian faith are logically dependent upon the success of *de facto* objections. The epistemological issue of warrant is then, at root, a metaphysical or ontological issue. Those seeking to object to Christian theism in terms of warrant (which Plantinga argues is the strongest *de jure* criticism), can only be successful in their quest if they first establish the falsity of Christian theism. As Plantinga states, in this case with simple theism on view:

> a successful atheological objection will have to be to the *truth* of theism, not to its rationality, or justification, or intellectual respectability, or rational justification, or whatever. The atheologian who wishes to attack theistic belief will have to restrict herself to objections like the argument from evil, or the claim that theism is incoherent, or the idea that in some other way there is strong evidence against theistic belief. She can't any longer adopt the following stance: "Well, I certainly don't know whether theistic belief is *true* - who could know a thing like that? - but I do know this: it is irrational, or unjustified, or contrary to reason or intellectually irresponsible or. There really isn't a sensible *de jure* question or criticism that is independent of the *de facto* question. There aren't any *de jure* criticisms that are sensible when conjoined with the *truth* of theistic belief; all of them either fail right from the start (as with the claim that it is unjustified to accept theistic belief) or else really presuppose that theism is false.[95]

Plantinga has here skilfully subverted those seeking to establish the irrationality of theistic belief. He claims that his argument has also invalidated 'an enormous amount of recent and contemporary atheology', much of which is devoted to questions of the justification of theistic belief which are independent of questions of truth.[96] To the extent that Plantinga is correct in this claim, this has been an achievement of some magnitude. However, there are a number of reasons to think that Plantinga is not correct. First, Plantinga's argument depends somewhat crucially on his elaborated theory of theistic and Christian belief formation. If it is the case that theistic and Christian belief is able to acquire warrant without inferential dependence on other beliefs, then Plantinga is, at least, in a strong position to immunise theistic and Christian belief from *de jure* challenges. This is because he has ruled out the importance of arguments and evidence in establishing the rationality of such belief, and has posited the existence of two quite reliable belief forming mechanisms. However, if one is convinced, with good reason, that theistic and Christian belief *does* require inferential support, then to the extent that such support is lacking, such belief

---

94 *WCB*, 285.
95 *WCB*, 191.
96 *WCB*, 191.

will lack warrant, even before the falsity of theism and/or Christianity is established.

Second, and related, a decision about what makes a belief unjustified or unwarranted can reasonably be arrived at independently of metaphysical assumptions such as that God exists or that Christianity is true. Suppose, for example, that one has noticed that the phenomenology of religious belief formation is similar across a wide range of religious traditions, but without being productive of compatible religious beliefs. This observation would give reasonable grounds for questioning whether the mechanism(s) by which religious beliefs are produced are reliably truth producing.[97] It would also give credence to attempts by such people as Freud and Marx to account for religious experience in purely psychological or sociological terms. Considerations such as these could quite sensibly be pressed into the service of a *de jure* objection to theistic and Christian belief, even before any conclusions are reached as to the truth or falsity of such belief. One could even postulate that God does exist, and still throw doubt on the warrant enjoyed by religious belief. If it could be established that religious belief is best understood as arising from wish fulfilment, then, arguably, such belief lacks warrant, even if God does exist.

Third, and also related, there are a number of obviously *de facto* challenges to theistic and Christian belief that can also reasonably be construed in *de jure* terms, and this independently of the outcome of the *de facto* challenge. The challenge of religious plurality is one such challenge. So also is the challenge that arises from the fact and extent of evil and suffering in the world. This problem can certainly be construed in *de facto* terms, and normally is. However, a point can also be reached in one's consideration of the problem where questions begin to be raised about the rationality of continuing to believe in God. Although atheologians have been notoriously unsuccessful in proving that the God of Christian theism does not exist, the problems created by evil and suffering, as well as the history-long inability of people to adequately account for evil and suffering, provide reasonable grounds for withholding belief. At the very least, they raise to an acute level the question of how well grounded theistic and Christian belief is.

In order to develop this point a little further, imagine a person who is unsettled by pluralistic considerations, such as discussed in chapter three, as well as by her inability to adequately account for evil and suffering. Suppose that she also believes that her Christian beliefs are poorly grounded by way of arguments or evidence,[98] and that her method of coming to belief is remarkably

---

[97] Practitioners of individual religions would be faced with the difficulty of establishing exactly how other religionists have gone wrong in their believing. They may, for example, account for the religious beliefs of others in terms of wish-fulfilment, but would then need to provide a convincing alternative account of how they themselves have come to believe with warrant.

[98] Which is also what Plantinga believes, as will be seen in chapter eight.

similar to how people in other religious traditions form their beliefs. Would she be justified in continuing to believe as she did? I am not sure that she would be. Given that she has grounds for questioning the reliability of her belief forming mechanisms, given that her beliefs lack (propositional) grounding, and that very serious questions have been raised about the explanatory adequacy of her beliefs, she would seem, at the very least, to be in a vulnerable epistemological position. From the outside, looking in, Plantinga may argue that the operation of the *sensus divinitatis* and the IIHS guarantees that the person's belief continues to have warrant, so long as the person's convictions remain strong. However, from the perspective of the person concerned, severe questions of an undercutting nature have been posed, such that some diminution of confidence would seem to be reasonable; and, to the extent that confidence is undermined, so also is warrant.

In summary, it *is* possible to pose *de jure* challenges to theistic and Christian belief which are independent of *de facto* challenges. As said, this is the case with the problem of evil, to which we now turn.

CHAPTER 5

Plantinga and Negative Apologetics: Evil and Suffering

We come now to consider Plantinga's response to what he, rightly, considers to be the most serious and on-goingly disturbing challenge to theistic belief: the problem (or problems) of evil and suffering. Plantinga, who has been a major contributor in responding to this challenge, is well aware of its magnitude. Nowhere does he minimise the problem, as is exemplified in the following passage from 'Self-Profile':

> Evil comes in many kinds; and some are particularly perplexing. A young man of twenty-five, in the flood tide of vigor and full of bright promise, is killed in a senseless accident; a radiant wife and mother, loved and needed by her family, is attacked by a deadly cancer; a sparkling and lovely child is struck down by leukemia and dies a painful and lingering death: what are we to make of these things? Why does God permit them? There is also the sheer *extent* of suffering and evil in the world. Hume's catalogue of evils in Pt. X of his *Dialogues Concerning Natural Religion* is no doubt hyperbolic; nevertheless the world contains a staggering amount of evil. There are earthquakes, famines, deadly diseases. Even more disturbing is the evil resulting from human error, hatred and wrong doing. In one extended battle during the Chinese Civil War, 6,000,000 people were killed. There are Hitler and Stalin and Pol Pot and a thousand lesser villains. Why does God permit *so much* evil in his world?
>
> Sometimes evil displays a cruelly ironic twist. I recall a story in the local paper a few years ago about a man who drove a cement mixer truck. He came home one day for lunch; his three year old daughter was playing in the yard, and after lunch, when he jumped into his truck and backed out, he failed to notice that she was playing behind it; she was killed beneath the great dual wheels. One can imagine this man's broken-hearted anguish. And if he was a believer in God, he may have become furiously angry with God - who after all, could have forestalled this calamity in a thousand different ways. So why *didn't* he? And sometimes we get a sense of the demonic - of evil naked and pure. Those with power over others may derive great pleasure from devising exquisite tortures for their victims: a woman in a Nazi concentration camp is forced to choose which of her children shall be sent to the ovens and which preserved. Why does God permit all this evil, and evil of these horrifying

kinds, in his world? How can they be seen as fitting in with his loving and providential care for his creatures?[1]

Plantinga frankly and honestly admits that '[the] Christian must concede he doesn't know.'[2] At the time of writing 'Self-Profile', Plantinga was wary of attempts to explain why God allows such evil. All such attempts, referred to by him as theodicies, were, in his opinion, 'tepid, shallow and ultimately frivolous.'[3] Plantinga's own approach to the problem of evil therefore included an agnostic element. He was willing to admit that we simply do not know why God has allowed suffering on the scale he has, nor why any particular evil has been permitted. Plantinga believed that the best that a Christian could do, in the face of the problems created by evil and suffering, was to trust that God does have a good reason for allowing them, and to respond to the various atheological arguments which are designed either to discount or render improbable the existence of God.

Over time, Plantinga has had to contend with two broad versions of the problem of evil: the logical form and the evidential form. According to the logical form, there is an inconsistency between certain theistic claims about God and evil. Typically, it is argued that the following two statements[4] are inconsistent with each other:

(1) An omnipotent, omniscient and perfectly good God exists.

(2) Evil exists in the world.

Someone advancing a logical version of the problem of evil needs to demonstrate that both of these statements cannot simultaneously be true. Since (2) is manifestly true, (1) must be false. Less ambitious than the logical form of the problem of evil is the evidential form. Those advocating this form (or forms), argue not that (1) is inconsistent with (2), but that (1) is rendered *implausible* by (2). It is *unlikely* that a God with the characteristics mentioned in (1) exists. Note that the existence of evil *per se* is seldom the problem, certainly for those arguing an evidential form of the argument from evil. It is evil of a particular quality or quantity, or, more exactly, evil in the amount, kind and distribution as is found in the actual world.[5]

---

1 'Self-Profile', 34, 35.
2 'Self-Profile', 35.
3 'Self-Profile', 35.
4 Or some variation of these.
5 That Plantinga was aware of this will emerge in the discussion that follows.

5.1 The Logical Form of the Problem of Evil

In the earlier part of Plantinga's philosophical career, he was almost exclusively[6] preoccupied with the logical form of the problem of evil,[7] this because the evidential form is a more recent player in the debate, and was not then so commonly urged. Plantinga's basic approach to disarming the logical form of the problem has been, first, to highlight what is required for any prospective argument to work; second, to demonstrate the difficulty of such a project, and, third, to propose a defence in the face of suffering which shows the consistency of (1) and (2) above.[8]

For the (or a) logical form of the problem of evil to succeed, a contradiction must be shown to exist between a number of beliefs a theist holds to be true, such as (1) and (2). This is not as simple as some proponents have thought. (1) and (2) clearly are not *explicitly* contradictory.[9] Perhaps they are *implicitly* contradictory. An implicit contradiction can be shown to exist within a set of propositions when a further proposition can be deduced from one or more of the stated propositions which explicitly contradicts at least one of the others. Plantinga argues that those who want to develop a successful version of the logical argument must, at the very least, demonstrate that propositions such as (1) and (2) are implicitly contradictory. For this to be so, the propositions must fulfil the following condition:

> S is implicitly contradictory if there is some necessarily true proposition p such that by using just the laws of ordinary logic, we can deduce an explicit contradiction from p together with the members of S.[10]

In 'Self-Profile', Plantinga notes that most atheologians (to that point in time, at least) had not acknowledged the need to explicitly demonstrate the existence of contradiction. They seemed content to simply declare that a contradiction

---

6 Plantinga does briefly address the probabilistic argument in *The Nature of Necessity* (Oxford: Oxford University Press, 1974), 193-195.
7 Plantinga's response to the logical form of the problem of evil is principally worked out in 'The Free Will Defense', in M. Black, (ed), *Philosophy in America* (Ithaca, NY: Cornell University Press, 1965), 204-220; *God and Other Minds*, (1967), 115-155, *The Nature of Necessity*, (1974), 164-193, *God, Freedom, and Evil* (London: George Allen and Unwin Ltd, 1975), and 'Self-Profile', (1985). My exposition of Plantinga's position will draw on all but the earliest of these sources.
8 See, for example, 'Self-Profile', 40.
9 An explicit contradiction is a 'conjunctive proposition, one conjunct of which is the denial or negation of the other conjunct,' *God, Freedom and Evil*, 12.
10 *God, Freedom and Evil*, 16.

existed.[11] J. L. Mackie was a notable exception. In 'Evil and Omnipotence' (*Mind*, 1955),[12] he acknowledged that:

> the contradiction does not arise immediately; to show it we need some additional premises, or perhaps some quasi-logical rules connecting the terms 'good,' 'evil,' and 'omnipotent'. These additional premises are that good is opposed to evil, in such a way that a good thing always eliminates evil as far as it can, and that there are no limits to what an omnipotent thing can do.[13]

Mackie suggests two additional premises which are considered by Plantinga:

(3)[14] A good thing always eliminates evil as far as it can.

and

(4) There are no limits to what an omnipotent being can do.[15]

Plantinga points out that if Mackie means to show that (1) and (2) are implicitly contradictory, then he must hold that (3) and (4) are not merely *true* but *necessarily true*.[16] He then goes on to show that neither *is* necessarily true.[17] Plantinga's conclusion:[18]

> Even Mackie, who sees that some 'additional premises' or 'quasi-logical rules' are needed, makes scarcely a beginning towards finding some additional premises that are necessarily true and that together with the members of set A formally entail an explicit contradiction.[19]

Plantinga then goes on to make this further more sweeping claim:

---

11   'Self-Profile', 38.
12   Described by Plantinga as 'perhaps the clearest and most explicit development of the atheological claim,' 'Self-Profile', 38.
13   J. L. Mackie, 'Evil and Omnipotence', *Mind* (1955), 200, 201.
14   My numbering.
15   'Evil and Omnipotence', 201. Note that Mackie effectively modifies the second of these propositions in subsequent discussion by conceding that omnipotence might well be compatible with God not being able to do the logically impossible, 203.
16   *God, Freedom and Evil*, 17. If the propositions were only contingently true, then a possible world would exist in which these propositions are not true, thereby avoiding a contradiction.
17   *God, Freedom and Evil*, 17-18.
18   After having considered a number of alternative propositions Mackie might have used, *God, Freedom and Evil*, 18-23.
19   *God, Freedom and Evil*, 23, 24.

No atheologian has produced even a plausible candidate for this role, and it is certainly not easy to see what such a proposition might be.[20]

Plantinga, at this stage, has succeeded (to his own satisfaction at least) with respect to two of his three aims. His strategy for meeting the challenge of the logical form of the problem of evil, was, as stated, first, to spell out what was required of any such challenge; second, to indicate the difficulty faced by those attempting it, illustrated by their lack of success thus far, and third to propose a defence in the face of suffering which would make it clear that (1) and (2) are consistent. It was in pursuing this third aspect of his strategy that Plantinga developed his Free Will Defence.

In seeking to show the consistency of (1) and (2), Plantinga realised that all he needed to do was to find a proposition consistent with (1) which, in conjunction with (1), would entail (2). His task was similar to the atheolgian's, but its opposite. The atheologian needed to find a necessarily true proposition which, in conjunction with (1), would entail the negation of (2), thus showing that (1) and (2) are implicitly contradictory. Plantinga's counter was to find a proposition which would show (1) and (2) to be implicitly consistent.

Plantinga spells out the relevant procedure in the following terms:

> [To show that a set of propositions S is implicitly consistent] you think of a *possible state of affairs* (it needn't *actually obtain*) which is such that if it were actual, then all of the members of S would be true.[21]

> one way to show that p is consistent with q is to find some proposition r whose conjunction with p is possible, in the broadly logical sense, and entails q.[22]

Plantinga suggests a proposition which, in his words, 'might do the trick',[23] that is:

(5) God creates a world containing evil and has a good reason for doing so.[24]

(5) together with (1) certainly entails (2). The issue is whether (5) is consistent with (1). Plantinga identifies two possible ways in which their consistency could be established:

> On the one hand, we could try to apply the same method again. Conceive of a possible state of affairs such that, if it obtained, an omnipotent, omniscient,

---

20   *God, Freedom and Evil*, 24.
21   *God, Freedom and Evil*, 25.
22   *God, Freedom and Evil*, 25.
23   *God, Freedom and Evil*, 26.
24   *God, Freedom and Evil*, 26; my numbering.

and wholly good God would have a good reason for permitting evil. On the other hand, someone might try to specify *what God's reason is* for permitting evil and try to show, if it is not obvious, that it is a good reason.[25]

The latter of these two approaches is the approach of the theodicist.[26] It is the approach exemplified by Augustine, who argued that it was better for God to have created free creatures, even though he knew they would sin, than to not create free creatures and thereby ensure that evil would not eventuate. The former approach, preferred by Plantinga, is the way of 'defence'. Someone mounting a defence may, with Plantinga, appeal to free will. The difference is that a free will *defender* is not aiming to say 'what God's reason *is*, but at most what God's reason *might possibly be.*'[27]

Plantinga develops a defence, partly, no doubt, because of his dissatisfaction with theodicy (mentioned above), but also because a defence is all that is needed for the consistency of (1) and (5) to be established. Like the theodicist, he seeks to find a proposition *r*, which in conjunction with (1) entails (5); unlike the theodicist it is not important to him to show that *r* is true. It does not need to be true for consistency to be established.[28]

Having established his 'defensive' approach, Plantinga goes on to make a preliminary statement of the Free Will Defence as follows:

A world containing creatures who are [sometimes[29]] significantly free (and freely perform more good than evil actions) is more valuable, all else being equal, than a world containing no free creatures at all. Now God can create free creatures, but He can't *cause* or *determine* them to do only what is right. For if he does so, then they aren't significantly free after all; they do not do what is right *freely*. To create creatures capable of *moral good*, therefore, He must create creatures capable of moral evil; and He can't give these creatures the freedom to perform evil and at the same time prevent them from doing so. As it turned out, sadly enough, some of the free creatures God created went wrong in the exercise of their freedom; this is the source of moral evil. The fact that free creatures sometimes go wrong, however, counts neither against God's

---

25   *God, Freedom and Evil*, 26.
26   A theodicy is understood by Plantinga to be 'an attempt to specify God's reason for permitting evil'; 'in the words of John Milton it is an attempt to "justify the ways of God to man," to show that God is just in permitting evil,' *God, Freedom and Evil*, 27.
27   *God, Freedom and Evil*, 28.
28   'Self-Profile', 43-44; *The Nature of Necessity*, 165.
29   The word 'sometimes' is missing from this quotation in *God, Freedom and Evil*, but is there in the otherwise almost identical earlier passage from *The Nature of Necessity*, 166, 167. The addition or otherwise of the word 'sometimes' is probably not important, although its presence suggests a possibility, exploited by some, that God might have created creatures with a certain degree of freedom, but without the freedom to perform certain clearly undesirable or detrimental actions.

omnipotence nor against His goodness, for He could have forestalled the occurrence of moral evil only by removing the possibility of moral good.[30]

Plantinga considers a number of objections to his defence. One is that freedom and determinism are compatible. If so, God could have caused his free creatures to always and freely choose good. As Plantinga puts it:

> If freedom were compatible with causal determinism, then God could have his cake and eat it too: he could create significantly free persons and cause them always to do only what's right.[31]

Plantinga acknowledges that his Free Will Defence fails if compatibilism is true.[32] However, he sees no convincing reason to suppose that compatibilism *is* true. In fact, he thinks it is 'utterly implausible'.[33] Incompatibilism is not only true,[34] according to Plantinga, it also accords well with theism, with God himself being a person who 'freely performs and is responsible for actions with respect to which he is not causally determined.'[35]

---

30 *God, Freedom and Evil*, 30.
31 'Self-Profile', 45.
32 'Self-Profile', 45. It could be that Plantinga was too hasty in making this concession. Edward Wierenga, for one, thinks he was. Wierenga points out that compatibilists typically argue that an agent's desires and beliefs are the cause of particular actions which, even though caused, can be described as 'free'. He goes on to make the sensible point: 'Now the claim of the Free Will Defense that God "cannot *cause* or *determine* ... [his free creatures] to do only what is right" needn't presuppose that for an action to be right, and hence, free, there can be *no* antecedent conditions and causal laws jointly sufficient for its occurrence; all that's required is that if *God* causes someone else's actions to occur it's not free action,' Review of Alvin Plantinga, in *Faith and Philosophy*, Vol. 5, No. 2 (April, 1988), 216. For an attempt to develop a compatibilist version of the Free Will Defence, see John Bishop, 'Compatibilism and the Free Will Defence,' *Australasian Journal of Philosophy*, Vol. 71, No. 2 (June, 1993), 104-120; for a critique, see Ken Perszyk, 'Compatibilism and the Free Will Defence: A Reply to Bishop,' *Australasian Journal of Philosophy*, Vol. 77, No. 1 (March, 1999), 92-105.
33 *God, Freedom and Evil*, 32.
34 For Plantinga's understanding of libertarian freedom, see *God and Other Minds, 134*-135; *The Nature of Necessity*, 165, 166; and *God, Freedom and Evil*, where Plantinga describes libertarian freedom in these terms: 'If a person is free with respect to a given action, then he is free to perform that action and free to refrain from performing it; no antecedent conditions and/or causal laws determine that he will perform the action, or that he won't,' 29. Plantinga goes on insist that this understanding does not imply unpredictability, 29, 30.
35 'Self-Profile', 47. Plantinga believes that fundamental to this discussion is the concept of agent causation, the concept of a person as an ultimate source of action. He thinks that this concept is not only viable, but is part of the very notion of personhood.

A second more serious objection to Plantinga's Free Will Defence is that God, if he is omnipotent, could surely have actualised a world in which free creatures (free in a libertarian sense) always choose good.

J. L. Mackie, in 'Evil and Omnipotence', argues that God could have done such a thing, such a thing is logically possible, and since he has not, either he is not omnipotent, or he does not exist. In Mackie's words:

> ... if God has made men such that in their free choices they sometimes prefer what is good and sometimes what is evil, why could he not have made men such that they always freely choose the good? If there is no logical impossibility in a man's freely choosing the good on one, or on several occasions, there cannot be a logical impossibility in his freely choosing the good on every occasion. God was not, then, faced with a choice between making innocent automata and making beings who, in acting freely, would sometimes go wrong; there was open to him the obviously better possibility of making beings who would act freely but always go right. Clearly, his failure to avail himself of this possibility is inconsistent with his being omnipotent and wholly good.[36]

Plantinga responds to this argument firstly by making and supporting the claim that there are certain things even an omnipotent God cannot do. These include the actualisation of a particular outcome when God, by means of middle knowledge,[37] knows that another outcome will result. Plantinga's argument, in essence, is as follows:[38]

Imagine two possible states of affairs:

(i) If a certain set of circumstances S obtains, Adam will freely eat the fruit.

or

(ii) If a certain set of circumstances S obtains, Adam will freely *not* eat the fruit.

---

36   'Evil and Omnipotence', 209.
37   Middle knowledge is a concept developed by the 16th century Spanish Jesuit Luis de Molina, to describe God's [supposed] knowledge of what a creature would freely (in a libertarian sense) do if put into a particular circumstance. Middle knowledge is *middle* knowledge because it has an intermediate (logical or conceptual) status; it stands between God's *natural* and *free* knowledge. God's natural knowledge is knowledge of truths which are necessary and independent of his will. God's free knowledge is knowledge of truths which are contingent and dependent on his will. God's middle knowledge is knowledge of truths which are both contingent and independent of his will.
38   I have sought to simplify Plantinga's argument, more detailed versions of which can be found in *God, Freedom and Evil*, 29-49; 'Self- Profile', 48-52.

God, who is intending to actualise Adam and who has middle knowledge,[39] knows which of these two is true. Suppose, for the sake of argument, that God knows that (i) is true. He knows that if he actualises the set of circumstances S, and also actualises a free Adam, Adam will eat the fruit. Given that God knows this, he cannot then actualise the same set of circumstances and have as the outcome that Adam *does not* eat the fruit. This is the case because he knows that if he actualises circumstances S, Adam *will* freely eat the fruit. Therefore, although it is entirely possible that God could have created a world in which Adam did not eat of the fruit (that certainly was a possibility), this possibility is ruled out if God knows, by means of middle knowledge, that Adam, if actualised, will eat the fruit.

The example illustrates two things. Firstly, there are possible worlds that God, although omnipotent, is not able to actualise. Secondly, what is possible for God in any given situation, even with the possession of middle knowledge, will depend upon what humans like Adam actually choose:

> Whether or not it is within God's power to actualise a world in which Adam doesn't choose fruit at time *t* depends upon what Adam would do if he was free in that situation. It is partly up to Adam what God can and cannot do.[40]

Plantinga has so far given good reason to think that there are certain things that God, although omnipotent, cannot do.[41] However, he needs to do more for his Free Will Defence to work. He needs specifically to establish the possibility that God, although omnipotent, may not be able to create a world in which his creatures always and freely choose good; in other words, a world containing moral good but no moral evil.

Such a world is possible. The atheologian is justified in asking why God did not actualise that world. By way of response, Plantinga suggests, as a possibility, that human beings suffer from what he refers to as 'transworld depravity',[42] that is, in every world that God can actualise, each and every free

---

39 Plantinga raises the possibility of developing a Free Will Defence that does not assume middle knowledge in 'Self-Profile', 50. This possibility is explored by Ken Perszyk in 'Free will defence with and without Molinism', *International Journal for Philosophy of Religion*, Vol. 43 (1998), 29-64.
40 *God, Freedom and Evil*, 44, 45.
41 Whether omnipotence is consistent with being restricted by creaturely free choices is something which will be discussed.
42 Plantinga provides the following definition of transworld depravity in *God, Freedom and Evil*, 48: A person P suffers from transworld depravity if and only if the following holds: for every world W such that P is significantly free in W and P does only what is right in W, there is an action A and a maximal world segment S' such that:
> (1) S' includes A's being morally significant for P.

creature will do at least one wrong action. If God, by means of middle knowledge, knows that all those he creates who have (libertarian) freedom will err with respect to at least one action, then (following the logic outlined above) he cannot actualise a world in which his free creatures never do what is wrong.[43]

The possibility that all human beings suffer from transworld depravity need only be a (logical) possibility.[44] Plantinga, as stated, is developing a defence, not a theodicy. All he needs, to show the consistency of (1) and (2), is a proposition whose conjunction with (1) is possible, in the broadly logical sense, and which entails (2).

Plantinga's suggestion of transworld depravity provides the material for such a proposition. If transworld depravity does exist, affecting every free creature that God creates, or may create, then God, although omnipotent,[45] could not have created any possible worlds containing persons who always and only choose good; worlds containing moral good but no moral evil. Therefore, if transworld depravity holds, then if God wants to create a world containing moral good (and it is plausible that a world with moral good is better than one without), then the necessary price to pay is that he creates one in which there is also moral evil.[46]

Returning to Plantinga's project of establishing the consistency of (1) and (2), the following proposition now suggests itself:

(6) It was not within God's power to create a world containing moral good but no moral evil; and God has actualised a world containing moral good.

Plantinga is of the opinion that (6) fulfils the conditions of being consistent with (1), and, together with (1), entailing (2). If this is so, it achieves the goal of establishing the consistency of (1) and (2).

To lay out the argument in full:

---

(2) S' includes P's being free with respect to A.

(3) S' is included in W and includes neither P's performing A nor P's refraining from performing A.

(4) If S' were actual, P would go wrong with respect to A.

43   Note that if God does not possess middle knowledge, and libertarian freedom obtains, it may have been impossible for God to know, in advance, the exact outcome of his choice to give creatures freedom.

44   Whether transworld depravity is logically possible is a question which will be addressed later in this chapter.

45   On the issue of whether God, in a situation like this, would be genuinely omnipotent, see below.

46   *God, Freedom and Evil*, 49.

Negative Apologetics: Evil and Suffering

(1) An omnipotent, omniscient and perfectly good God exists

(2) Evil exists in the world

(6) It was not within God's power to create a world containing moral good but no moral evil; and God has actualised a world containing moral good.

(7) Every (possible) free person suffers from transworld depravity.

Note that (7) entails the first conjunct of (6). (7) and (6), both together and separately, entail (2). They are also thought by Plantinga to be consistent with (1). On the basis of these considerations, he believes that his defence is successful.[47]

Assuming that Plantinga has been successful, what exactly has his defence achieved? As it stands, not a great deal. At most, what has been shown is that (1) is consistent with *some* evil being present in the world. It does not show that (1) is consistent with any and every amount of evil that might be present, or that is present in the world, as Plantinga readily acknowledges:

> The world, after all, contains a *great deal* of moral evil; and what we have seen so far is only that God's existence is compatible with *some* evil.[48]

Plantinga needs to extend his Free Will Defence to include a response to evil not simply as an abstraction, but to evil in its concrete actuality.[49] He seeks to achieve this by arguing that although it is possible that there may be many possible worlds that are better than this one, in that they display a better balance of good and evil, it may also be the case (for all we know) that the same constraints which prevent God from producing a world without evil[50] may also prevent God from creating a world with a better balance of good and evil than obtains in the actual world. It may not have been possible for God to have instantiated a better world than this one.[51]

Plantinga's Free Will Defence, taking into account this additional development, can be represented this way:

---

47 *God, Freedom and Evil*, 55.
48 *The Nature of Necessity*, 190.
49 For this distinction helpfully explored, see Michael Tooley, 'The argument from Evil,' *Philosophical Perspectives* 5, Philosophy of Religion (1991), 91-93.
50 That is, creaturely freedom and transworld depravity.
51 For Plantinga's development of this argument, see *The Nature of Necessity*, 190-193; *God, Freedom and Evil*, 55-59. In 'Self-Profile', Plantinga states that this argument represents the 'central insight of the Free Will Defense,' 47.

God has actualized a possible world A containing significantly free creatures; some of these creatures are responsible for moral and natural evil; and it was not within God's power to create significantly free creatures with respect to whose actions there would be a better balance of good over evil than that displayed in A.[52]

Having laid out Plantinga's Defence, a number of things can now be said regarding its success and significance, particularly from an apologetic point of view. With respect to its success, one would have to say that the jury is still out. Although some have been quick to declare the Defence successful,[53] certain aspects of Plantinga's total case continue to be questioned.[54] For example, some have argued that transworld depravity, if it exists, represents a non-logical limitation on God's power, and is therefore inconsistent with God's omnipotence.[55] If this is so, (7) and (6) are not consistent with (1), and the Free Will Defence fails.[56] Others have questioned the plausibility of Plantinga's Molinist assumptions.[57] Still others have argued that if God *is*

---

52   This is a modified version of Marilyn McCord Adams' formulation of Plantinga's Free Will Defence, in *Horrendous Evils and the Goodness of God* (Carlton South: Melbourne University Press, 1999), 20.

53   Robert Adams, writing in the mid '80s, was unequivocal: 'it is fair to say that Plantinga has solved [the logical problem of evil]. That is, he has argued convincingly for the consistency of [God and evil],' 'Plantinga on the problem of evil' in J. E. Tomberlin, P. Van Inwagen, (eds), *Alvin Plantinga* (Dordrecht: D. Reidel Publishing Company), 1985, 226. William Rowe, an atheistic philosopher, put it this way a few years earlier: 'Some philosophers have contended that the existence of evil is logically inconsistent with the existence of the theistic God. No one, I think, has succeeded in establishing such an extravagant claim. Indeed, granted incompatibilism, there is a fairly compelling argument for the view that the existence of evil is logically consistent with the existence of the theistic God. (For a lucid statement of this argument, see Alvin Plantinga, *God, Freedom and Evil*), 'The Problem of Evil and Some Varieties of Atheism,' *American Philosophical Quarterly*, Vol. 16 (1979), 10, fn. 1.

54   See, for example, D. Howard-Snyder and J. O'Leary-Hawthorne, 'Transworld sanctity and Plantinga's Free Will Defense,' *International Journal for Philosophy of Religion*, Vol. 44 (1998), 1-21; M. Bergmann, 'Might-Counterfactuals, Transworld Untrustworthiness and Plantinga's Free Will Defence,' *Faith and Philosophy*, Vol. 16, No. 3 (July, 1999), 336-351.

55   Ken Perszyk, in 'Free Will Defence With and Without Molinism', 35, interprets J. L. Mackie, in *The Miracle of Theism* (Oxford: Clarendon Press, 1982), as making essentially this point. Molinists would assert that such a limitation does not represent a denial of omnipotence.

56   The Free Will Defence may still, of course, work to defend a modified version of (1). The definition of who God is would need to be modified.

57   For example, Robert Adams, 'Middle Knowledge and the Problem of Evil', *American Philosophical Quarterly*, Vol. 14, No. 2 (April, 1977), 109-117; and 'An anti-Molinist argument', in *Philosophical Perspectives*, 5, 343-353; William

armed with middle knowledge, he has the resources to significantly restrict the amount of evil in the world, even given the fact of transworld depravity.[58] If so,[59] it may still be possible to show that (1) is inconsistent with some proposition detailing the actual amount and character of evil in the world. Questions can also be raised about the logical possibility of transworld depravity. Plantinga asks his readers to accept, as logically possible, that no matter what circumstances God could actualise, no matter what disposition he created his free creatures with, no matter what character, they would still, every one of them, sin at least once. Does such a possibility exist?[60] It is on this possibility that Plantinga's Free Will Defence rests.

Debate over the success or otherwise of Plantinga's Defence will no doubt continue, but let us assume, for the present, that Plantinga has been successful in showing that (1) is consistent (or may well be consistent) with the existence

---

Hasker, 'A Refutation of Middle Knowledge', *Noûs*, Vol. 20 (Dec. 1986), 545-557. For a response to these objections, Thomas Flint, *Divine Providence: The Molinist Account* (Ithaca: Cornell University Press, 1998).

58   Even while retaining creaturely freedom and associated moral goods. Various options have been considered open to God. For example, God could have actualized only those circumstances which he knew, by means of middle knowledge, would either result in no evil, or in evil of a relatively minor nature. For a discussion of the various options open to God which, conceivably, would produce a better balance of good over evil in the world, see Evan Fales, 'Should God Not Have Created Adam?', *Faith and Philosophy*, Vol. 9, No. 2 (April, 1992), 193-209; David Lewis in 'Evil For Freedom's Sake?', *Philosophical Papers*, Vol. 22, No. 3 (1993), 153-162. Lewis admits that the hypothesis of transworld depravity could be tightened to disallow God's realisation of a better balance of good over evil, 162.

59   It does seem possible. It is not easy to imagine why God could not have actualised a world with a more favourable balance of good and evil than the present one. David O'Connor argues that God could have actualised a better world than the present one by eliminating all purely natural evil (that is, evil not caused by free human agency). This he could have done without surrendering various positive values historically associated with human freedom, *God and Inscrutable Evil: In Defence of Theism and Atheism* (London: Rowman and Littlefield, 1998), 84-91.

60   Marilyn McCord Adams suggests that Francisco Suárez (1548-1617), an early defender of middle knowledge, would have found transworld depravity impossible because of God's necessary resourcefulness, which Suárez took to have the following implication: necessarily, for any possible person and any situation in which they can exist, there are some helps of grace that would (should God supply them) win the creature over without compromising its incompatibilist freedom, 'The Problem of Evil', in *Routledge Encyclopaedia*, Vol. 3, 469. Daniel Howard-Snyder and John O'Leary-Hawthorne also mount an argument against the possibility of transworld depravity, in 'Transworld sanctity and Plantinga's Free Will Defense', which is responded to by William L. Rowe, in 'In defense of "The Free Will Defense"', *International Journal for Philosophy of Religion*, Vol. 44, No. 2 (October, 1998), 115-120.

of evil such as exists in the actual world. The nature and significance of this (assumed) achievement must be evaluated.

To establish consistency (or even the possibility of consistency) is no small achievement, particularly in an environment where it was widely assumed that (1) and (2) were incompatible. Plantinga, almost single handedly, has inverted that perception.[61] He has also been the first philosopher to attempt a resolution of the logical form of the problem of evil by way of a free will defence.[62] Plantinga undoubtedly deserves praise for such ground-breaking work. However, the magnitude of Plantinga's achievement can be over-stated. At best, Plantinga has suggested a (logically) possible reason why God may allow evil to exist. As David Lewis points out, this is not an overly difficult achievement.[63] Plantinga suggests, as possibilities, (6) and (7), but he could, as easily, have suggested:

(8) Only a fraction of the things we consider to be evil are in fact evil, and those things in the world which are evil all contribute substantially to our greater good.[64]

(8) fulfils the requirements of a defence. (8) is consistent with (1), or so one could argue, and together with (1), it entails (2). It may not be plausible. In fact, almost necessarily, it is not. We are unlikely to think that our moral intuitions are, for the most part, in error. However, (8) still more than adequately does the job of defence. This example demonstrates the severely limited nature of a defence, and, in particular, of Plantinga's Defence.

Plantinga's Defence, as it stands, is not designed to make any contribution whatsoever to the task of theodicy. Plantinga does not need to be committed to the truth of libertarian freedom, nor to the truth of transworld depravity.[65] He is

---

61 As some indication of that inversion of perception, Thomas Talbott, writing in 1990, summed up the then present situation in these words: 'As anyone familiar with recent work on the problem of evil knows, the argument that theism is self-contradictory because evil is itself inconsistent with the existence of God has been remarkably unsuccessful; no one, it seems, has managed to deduce a contradiction from doctrines essential to theism, and Alvin Plantinga's proof of consistency, whether successful in every detail or not, remains a formidable obstacle to any *deductive* argument of the relevant kind.' 'The Doctrine of Everlasting Punishment', *Faith and Philosophy*, Vol. 7, No. 1 (January, 1990), 19.
62 'Self-Profile', 41.
63 'Evil For Freedom's Sake', *152*.
64 This is a variation of an example used by David Lewis in 'Evil For Freedom's Sake', 151, 152.
65 Interestingly, Plantinga has given some signs that he does think that something like transworld depravity might be true. In private conversation with Ken Pressie, noted in 'Free will defence with and without Molinism', *International Journal for Philosophy of Religion*, Vol. 43 (1998), 61, fn. 38, Plantinga argues

simply arguing that they are possibly true. Although none of this is problematic from the point of view of Plantinga's acknowledged purpose, it may be (experientially) problematic for a theistic believer who is on-goingly troubled by the existence of evil in the world. It may be particularly disturbing to someone who has believed, as many do, that God's granting of freedom to his creatures is at least part of the reason that evil exists in the world. Plantinga's Defence does not rule out this possibility. In fact, it rules it in. However, Plantinga's Defence crucially depends on the hypothesis of transworld depravity. If this possibility is judged implausible,[66] then Plantinga's Free Will Defence is prevented from taking even a small step beyond defence towards theodicy. The effect of this frustration is to throw significant doubt on an historically influential and long-standing attempt to account for evil in God's world.[67] It is also likely to prove disappointing to those hoping for progress towards even a limited understanding of God's good reason for allowing evil and suffering.[68] Plantinga's Defence is limited because it is simply that, a defence.

Plantinga's Defence is limited in another way. It does not target or take into specific account cases of horrendous evil, examples of which are mentioned in the quotation at the beginning of this chapter. Despite mentioning such cases, Plantinga deals with evil in a global or abstract way. The balance of good over evil is considered, rather than particular, troubling instances of evil. Various questions are raised by this approach: Even given that a particular world (say ours) has the best possible overall balance of good and evil, would God, even still, be morally justified in allowing even one of his creatures to experience

---

that since human beings are made in the image of God, they will naturally be inclined to see themselves in the way that God sees himself, that is, as at the centre of all things. Hence, it is at least possible that creatures such us will go wrong at least once.

66 It *is* hard to believe that, as a contingent fact, every free creature that God has, or ever could create would do evil on at least one occasion. One wonders, for example, why God could not actualise creatures with a disposition such as people will have in heaven, where, presumably, free creatures never sin. If one responds by suggesting, as James F. Sennett does in 'Is there Freedom in Heaven?' *Faith and Philosophy*, Vol. 16, No. 1 (January, 1999), 69-82, that people in heaven no longer have libertarian freedom, but rather have compatibilist freedom, then an obvious question is, 'Is libertarian freedom necessary at any stage in God's creative work?'

67 For a contemporary attempt to utilise freedom within a more broadly ranging theodicy, see Richard Swinburne, *Providence and the Problem of Evil* (Oxford: Oxford University Press, 1998).

68 David Lewis helpfully distinguishes between 'know it all' theodicies which attempt to provide the reason or reasons for evil, and tentative, even speculative theodicies which advance plausible hypotheses to account for evil. He rightly suggests that this latter project is likely to be important for Christians, 'Evil for Freedom's Sake', 152.

such pain and horror as would unfavourably tip the balance of good and evil in their case? Could God, in a case like this, be said to genuinely love that person? Could God's omnibenevolence be preserved in such a case?[69] Questions such as these raise again the question of whether Plantinga has been truly successful in his attempted Defence.[70]

There is one further and related way in which Plantinga's Defence is limited. It mounts a defence of theism, but not necessarily of Christian theism in all of its doctrinal richness. It may be that Plantinga's defence works for theism, as defined by (1), but not for Christian theism, or for particular varieties of Christian theism. It is, for example, unusual to find someone from such a strongly Reformed background suggesting that the granting of free will might (even possibly) be a reason for God's allowance of evil. According to traditional Reformed teaching, post-lapsarian human beings are not free, and are certainly not free to successfully pursue their ultimate good.[71] Their nature is such that they persistently and predominantly choose evil over good, and are damned for these choices. Even salvation, when it comes, is not the result of human choice, but of God's choice to show mercy. If this is indeed the case, and if, as many Reformed Christians believe, a great many of the world's population, possibly the majority, will, as a result of their freedom-less choices, be spending an eternity in hell, very serious questions are raised about the goodness of a God who would actualise such a world.[72] The problem of evil

---

69   Questions such as these are skilfully proposed and examined by Marilyn McCord Adams in *Horrendous Evils and the Goodness of God*. They are not unanswerable from a Christian point of view. Issues of justice as well as of love, or of justice as a form of love, might profitably be brought into the discussion at this point.

70   Michael Tooley, in 'The Argument from Evil', 90-93, argues that concrete versions of the problem of evil, which draw attention to particular instances of evil in the world, such as innocent children suffering agonising deaths, are much more likely to achieve success than abstract versions in which the amount or balance of unspecified evil is considered as the problem facing theism. If this is so, Plantinga's Defence may have missed the point somewhat.

71   See, for example, L. Berkhof, *Systematic Theology* (London: The Banner of Truth Trust, 1939), 248.

72   On hell and other Christian doctrines as complicating factors in any theodicy, see, for example, Jerry L. Walls, 'Is Molinism As Bad As Calvinism?' *Faith and Philosophy*, Vol. 7, No. 1 (January, 1990), 85-98; Thomas Talbott, 'The Doctrine of Everlasting Punishment'; Mark Pestana, 'Radical Freedom, Radical Evil and the Possibility of Eternal Damnation,' *Faith and Philosophy*, Vol. 9, No. 4 (October, 1992), 500-507; David O'Connor, 'A Reformed Problem of Evil and the Free Will Defense', *International Journal for Philosophy of Religion*, Vol. 1 (February, 1996), 33-63; Richard Swinburne, 'A Theodicy of Heaven and Hell', in A. Freddosco, (ed), *The Existence and Nature of God*, (Notre Dame: Notre Dame Press, 1983), 37-54; Charles Seymour, *A Theodicy of Hell* (Dordrecht: Kluwer Academic Publications, 2000).

becomes increasingly more difficult to solve when certain additional Christian doctrines are added to the propositional mix.

The reason for highlighting these various limitations and complications is to make the point that although Plantinga has contributed in a ground-breaking way to meeting the challenge posed by logical forms of the problem of evil, the problem still remains as an on-goingly formidable obstacle to Christian belief, as do evidentialist forms of the argument, to which we now turn.

5.2 The Evidentialist Form of the Problem of Evil

Despite various limitations and difficulties with Plantinga's defence, it nevertheless has succeeded in helping to shift the focus of scholarly interest from logical to evidential or probabilistic forms of the argument from evil. A number of Christian philosophers apart from Plantinga, including William Alston, Peter van Inwagen and Stephen Wykstra have been involved in seeking to counter evidentialist or probabilistic forms of the problem of evil. Plantinga's own contribution (to date) consists chiefly of four articles,[73] as well as a chapter in *WCB*. In what follows, major points made by Plantinga in these five sources will be summarised.

In the first of his articles, Plantinga points out that to say that something is improbable given some other fact does not *necessarily* constitute a problem or a challenge to the first of those beliefs. Suppose, for the sake of argument, that the following proposition:

G   God exists and is omniscient, omnipotent and wholly good.
is improbable with respect to

E   There are 10^{13} turps of evil.[74]

This, in itself, does not imply that a person who believes G is irrational in his believing, or is guilty of noetic impropriety.[75] It may be, for example, that G

---

73 'The Probabilistic Argument from Evil', *Philosophical Studies*, Vol. 35 (1979), 1-53; 'Epistemic Probability and Evil', *Archivio di Filosophia*, Vol. 56, No. 1-3 (1988), 557-584; 'On Being Evidentially Challenged,' in Daniel Howard-Snyder (ed), *The Evidential Argument from Evil* (Bloomington and Indianapolis: Indiana University Press, 1996), 244-261; 'Degenerate Evidence and Rowe's New Evidential Argument from Evil', *Noûs*, Vol. 32, No. 4 (1998), 531-544.

74 Plantinga defines a turp as 'the basic unit of evil, so that '1013 turps' is a name of the evil, past, present and future, the actual world ... contains,' 'The Probabilistic Argument from Evil', 2. Note that Plantinga's argument does not depend on the assumption that there is a cardinal measure of evil. Specification in terms of turps is simply to make clear that the actual amount of evil in the world (however that might be measured) is on view.

75 'The Probabilistic Argument from Evil', 2.

is improbable on E, but probable with respect to everything else a person knows. The atheologian must show, at the very least, that G is improbable on the *total* evidence that he or the theist has. This is not such an easy thing to do, as Plantinga argues:

> To do this, he would be obliged to consider all the sorts of reasons natural theologians have invoked *in favor of* theistic belief - the traditional cosmological, teleological and ontological arguments, for example. He would also have to consider more recent versions of the moral argument as developed, for example, by A. E. Taylor, and still more recently by Robert Adams, along with the broadly inductive arguments developed by F. R. Tennant, C. S. Lewis, E. L. Mascall, Basil Mitchell, and others; and he'd have to show either that these arguments don't really produce any evidence for G at all, or that, if they do, that evidence is outweighed by the evidence *against* G furnished by E. This would be a substantial and difficult project - one that no atheologian has undertaken so far.[76]

The atheologian's task is therefore a daunting one.[77] Even to show that G is improbable on E requires an argument.[78] In 'The Probabilistic Argument From Evil', Plantinga considers a number of such arguments, including one proposed by William Rowe.[79] As Plantinga understands him,[80] Rowe holds that the theist is committed to one or other of the following propositions; which are entailed by G:

(9)[81] God is omnipotent, omniscient and wholly good; and every world God could have actualized that contains less evil than the actual world, contains a less favorable overall balance of good and evil than does the actual world;

or, equivalently,

---

76   'The Probabilistic Argument from Evil', 3. Also, *WCB,* 432, 433.
77   Plantinga has, however, somewhat overstated the task facing the atheologian. An atheologian is surely not required to consider every argument which has been urged in favour of theistic belief, or even every widely influential argument. It may be sufficient for him to be aware of the existence of such arguments, and of their strength, as a factor to be kept in mind as he ponders the probability of God's existence. It may be that he has examined a representative sample of the arguments, and, given that life is short, has decided to let that sample be a sufficient guide for him. This, I think, is the approach of most of us in comparable situations.
78   'The Probabilistic Argument from Evil', 5.
79   Plantinga responds (in 'The Probabilistic Argument From Evil') to a paper by Rowe delivered at that APA Eastern Division Symposium, Dec. 1977.
80   For the remainder of this discussion, it will be Rowe's argument as reconstructed and elaborated by Plantinga that will be referred to.
81   My numbering.

(10) God is omnipotent, omniscient and wholly good; and the actual world is a better world than any world God could have actualized that contains less evil than the actual world.

(9) or (10) are, according to Rowe, entailed by G. However, again according to Rowe, (9) or (10) are improbable given the amount and variety of evil found in the world. Plantinga questions this contention, and the anti-theistic conclusion that would follow from it, arguing, in the first instance, how difficult it is to construct probabilistic arguments. Determining the exact relationship between propositions, when that relationship is one of probability, is an incredibly complex activity, as Plantinga points out:

> The nature of this relationship is ... subject to enormous dispute; this area of inquiry bristles with paradox, mystery, and confusion; it is fraught with difficulty, darkness, and despair.[82]

In the course of 'The Probabilistic Argument From Evil', and in subsequent papers, Plantinga considers a number of contemporary interpretations of probability calculus, including the logical, the statistical and personalistic interpretations. He considers how a probabilistic case against theism might be construed in terms of these various interpretations, concluding that no successful case can be so construed.[83] In the process of reaching this conclusion, Plantinga explores one further interpretation, epistemic probability,[84] which he describes as 'a guide to life, as something like *degree of rational belief.*'[85] Unlike the logical, statistical and personalist understandings, it is a normative conception:

> Probability so thought of is not a merely factual property or relation among propositions; it has to do instead with what is the (or a) right, or correct, or proper, or satisfactory way of holding one's beliefs.[86]

Plantinga elaborates his understanding of probability in terms of the proper functioning of noetic faculties:

---

82 'The Probabilistic Argument from Evil', 10.
83 'The Probabilistic Argument from Evil', 17-49. On Plantinga's dismissal of a logically construed probability case against the existence of God, along with a case construed in these terms, see Richard Swinburne, 'Does Theism Need A Theodicy?' *Canadian Journal of Philosophy*, Vol. 18, No. 2 (June, 1988), 305-311.
84 In *WPF*, Plantinga considers a number of contemporary understandings of epistemic probability before proposing his own account, 139-175.
85 'Epistemic Probability and Evil', 572.
86 'Epistemic Probability and Evil', 572.

Probability has to do, I propose, with the degree of belief that would be accorded a given proposition (relative to circumstances) by someone who was suffering from no cognitive defect or deficiency or dysfunction, *someone whose noetic faculties were functioning properly*.[87]

Plantinga notes that there are a number of factors which will influence the degree to which a rational person will believe a certain proposition. Experience, for example, will play a key role, as will a person's circumstances. One person will often be in a better position than another to judge the probability of a particular proposition simply due to their knowledge or experience of other factors relevant to the judgement being made. Also, the degree to which a person believes a proposition on which the probability of another is being judged will affect that person's degree of belief. With these complicating factors in mind, Plantinga proposes this slightly more elaborate account of epistemic probability:

The conditional epistemic probability of A on B, then, initially and to a first approximation, is the degree to which a rational person, a person whose faculties are functioning properly, would accept A given that she was certain of B, knew that she accepted B, reflectively considered A in the light of B, and had no other source of warrant or positive epistemic status for A or for its denial.[88]

Plantinga notes that the degree to which various beliefs are believed will often be quite vague, making it impossible to assign real numbers to degrees of belief in those cases. A comparative rather than a quantitative conception of epistemic probability would therefore need to be adopted. Moreover, different rational people are likely to hold their beliefs (even given the same information) with different degrees of conviction.[89]

Having proposed and refined his epistemic conception of probability,[90] Plantinga returns to the question of the probability of belief in God on the proposition that 'there are 10^{13} turps of evil' in the world.'[91] He asks how rational people would react having duly reflected on the amount and character of evil observed in the world. His answer is:

Variously. For some, belief in God is if anything strengthened by confrontation with massive evil; there is no record that Mother Teresa's faith in God was weakened by her daily work in the presence of hideous evil, and

---

87   'Epistemic Probability and Evil', 572.
88   'Epistemic Probability and Evil', 574.
89   'Epistemic Probability and Evil', 574.
90   Which, he notes, is 'close to a notion of warrant, or positive epistemic status', (573).
91   Or some equivalent proposition about evil, 'Epistemic Probability and Evil', 575.

there are many cases - including some in Auschwitz circumstances - where direct confrontation with appalling evil strengthened rather than weakened belief in God. Someone else may find the evil in question perplexing, but say to God: 'I don't know and can't imagine what reason you have for allowing this particularly heinous evil: but I know that you are perfectly good, just, wise and loving and so I know that you *have* good reason for it, even if I haven't any idea what it is.' Others will initially feel doubts - of God's goodness, or trustworthiness, or existence - but think, e.g., of the marvellous goodness involved and displayed in God's redemptive scheme and then no longer suffer doubts - or perhaps still suffer them, but still believe. Still another reaction: Job was inclined to mistrust God, to say: 'You may be magnificent and wonderful and omniscient and omnipotent and wholly good, and all that, but I don't like what you are doing, and I wish you would let me argue it out with you'. And finally, someone without much inclination to believe in God may say: a good, all-powerful, all-knowing God couldn't possibly allow *that*, so there isn't any such person.[92]

The examples illustrate the person-relative nature of probability judgements,[93] although their usefulness is somewhat limited by the fact that particular instances of horrendous evil are in view. Probabilistic arguments from evil, such as Rowe's, tend to be more global in their scope, having concern for the total quality and quantity of evil in the world. That said, Plantinga is nevertheless right to point out the person-relative nature of probability judgements. Various factors, including the total belief systems of those the atheologian is seeking to persuade, will inevitably (and often justifiably[94]) affect their judgement.

Plantinga continues by considering the kinds of evidence the person will have upon which their belief system depends. Plantinga draws attention to both propositional and non-propositional evidence. There is both propositional and non-propositional evidence for the existence of God. Both, in Plantinga's estimation, are strong. Of the propositional evidence, Plantinga writes:

---

92 'Epistemic Probability and Evil', 576.
93 A point made earlier in 'The Probabilistic Argument from Evil', 48, and also in 'Degenerate Evidence and Rowe's New Evidential Argument From Evil'. Rowe's argument is that if judged on the basis of knowledge held in common by the theist and non-theist, it will be shown that God probably does not exist. Plantinga argues that this is not the case as he affirms the illegitimacy of limiting the theist's (or atheist's) knowledge or sources of knowledge, 536-543.
94 It could be, of course, that people stubbornly go on believing that God is good, even in the face of evidence that should persuade them otherwise, as might happen analogously in the case of a person who refuses to believe her lover has committed a murder even when the evidence overwhelmingly suggests he has.

Now as a matter of fact there are very many propositions many or most of us believe with respect to which it is epistemically probable that there is such a person as God.[95]

Of the non-propositional evidence for God, Plantinga suggests:

Perhaps belief in God resembles certain perceptual beliefs, memory beliefs, certain *a priori* beliefs and others in being *properly basic* (in the right circumstances); if so, belief in God, like these others, will (under the right conditions) have non-propositional warrant.[96]

If this account is correct, the theist is in the enviable position of having non-propositional as well as propositional warrant for her belief. In Plantinga's opinion, she is doubly blessed.[97]

The non-propositional evidence may, in fact, be the source of greater warrant for a theist. It may, in some instances, be of such strength that even if no propositional evidence existed in favour of the conclusion that God exists, even if considerable propositional evidence existed against that conclusion, the theist could nevertheless still conclude (and with ample warrant[98]) that God does exist. As Plantinga puts it:

So, suppose at any rate for purposes of argument, that [G] is indeed improbable on [E],[99] or on the conjunction of [E] with some other relevant proposition about evil: that fact, if indeed it is a fact, is not taken by itself of much moment. It is only one of several facts that must be taken into account in determining the positive epistemic status enjoyed by belief in God. For all this tells us, it could be that the theist is like someone who has substantial propositional evidence against the claim that pigeons are to be found near Devil's Tower, and no propositional evidence for it; in point of fact, however, he is in full view of the tower and sees several large flocks of pigeons flying around it.[100]

---

95 'Epistemic Probability and Evil', 578. Plantinga has in mind here the arguments of natural theology, which, in his opinion, render the existence of God more probable than not.
96 'Epistemic Probability and Evil', 579.
97 'Epistemic Probability and Evil', 582.
98 Plantinga points out that a judgement as to whether a person's noetic faculties were functioning properly in coming to a basic belief in God will ultimately depend upon the metaphysical or religious stance one takes. This illustrates once again the person-relative nature of probability judgements, 'Epistemic Probability and Evil', 583, 584.
99 I have substituted G and E for Plantinga's numbering which was (1) and (2).
100 'Epistemic Probability and Evil', 583.

Plantinga's third major response to the evidential form of the problem of evil is found in a 1996 article, 'On Being Evidentially Challenged'. Here, Plantinga responds to a paper by Paul Draper, 'Pain and Pleasure: An Evidential Problem for Theists' (1989).[101] In essence, what Draper argues is that there is an hypothesis which is inconsistent with theism which explains some significant facts about evil and suffering[102] much better than theism. This is the 'Hypothesis of Indifference' (HI), which is:

> HI: Neither the nature nor the condition of sentient beings on earth is the result of benevolent or malevolent actions performed by non-human persons.[103]

The implication that Draper draws from his claim that certain facts about evil and suffering are better explained by HI is that, if this is true, 'we have a *prima facie* good epistemic reason to reject theism - that is, a reason that is sufficient for rejecting theism unless overridden by other reasons for not rejecting theism.'[104]

Plantinga responds first by objecting to the assumption underlying Draper's challenge that theistic belief ought to be judged adequate or inadequate, rational or irrational in the same manner as a scientific hypothesis is judged. Plantinga argues forcefully in these terms:

> it is an enormous and in my opinion wholly false assumption to think that belief in God, or more broadly, the larger set of Christian (or Jewish or Muslim) beliefs of which belief in God is a part, is, at any rate for most believers, relevantly like a scientific hypothesis. The evidence for these beliefs is not the fact (if it is a fact) that they properly explain some body of

---

101 P. Draper, 'Pain and Pleasure: an Evidential Problem for Theists' in *The Evidential Argument From Evil*, 12-29; reprinted from *Noûs* Vol. 23 (1989), 331-350.

102 Draper argues that '[a] statement reporting the observations and testimony upon which our knowledge about pain and pleasure is based bears a certain significant negative evidential relation to theism.' The relevant statement, which he designates as O, is 'a statement reporting both the observations one has made of humans and animals experiencing pain or pleasure and the testimony one has encountered concerning the observations others have made of sentient beings experiencing pain or pleasure,' 'Pain and Pleasure', 12, 13. O is then subdivided into three statements which Draper will argue stand in a negative evidential relation to theism: O1: moral agents experiencing pain or pleasure that we know to be biologically useful; O2: sentient beings that are not moral agents experiencing pain, or pleasure that we know to be biologically useful, and O3: sentient beings experiencing pain or pleasure that we do know to be biologically useful, 'Pain and Pleasure', 16.

103 'Pain and Pleasure', 13.

104 'Pain and Pleasure', 12.

data. For most believers, theistic belief is part of a larger whole, a Christian or Muslim or Jewish whole, and is not accepted as anything like a scientific hypothesis. That is, it is not accepted as an *explanation* of anything; and its evidence does not consist in the fact that it nicely explains some body of data.[105]

With this caveat expressed, Plantinga is nevertheless willing to entertain the possibility that the existence of evil and suffering is more consistent with HI, and that this fact may pose an evidentialist challenge to theistic belief. Working on this assumption, Plantinga asks whether HI *does* explain the facts of evil and suffering better than does theism. Draper had suggested in his paper that pain and suffering are best explained in terms of the biological purposes to which they contribute,[106] rather than in theistic terms. Plantinga responds in a number of ways. He questions the assumption that God's purposes in allowing pain and suffering can be known, and notes that certain human behaviour patterns do not conform easily to a simple biological explanation.[107] Draper suggests that the fundamental role of pleasure and pain is biological and that this fact makes best sense on HI. Plantinga questions the first of these contentions noting that much of the enormous diversity and variety of human pleasure and pain 'doesn't seem to have any direct connection at all with such biological goals as survival and reproduction.'[108] Draper suggests that if theism is true one would expect that sentient creatures would in general be happy. Plantinga again is unconvinced. Even if it is true (which would be difficult to demonstrate) that sentient creatures are not in general happy, this fact is expected rather than surprising given the teachings of a number of theistic religions including Christianity.[109]

---

105 'On Being Evidentially Challenged', 249.
106 Such as the organic goals of survival and reproduction.
107 Plantinga points out that morality, although it plays an enormously important role in human life, does not (in many instances) contribute to biological survival and reproduction. Similarly with human altruism, religion, literature, poetry, music, art, mathematics, logic, philosophy, nuclear physics, evolutionary biology, play, humour, exploration, and adventure. Biological explanations of these phenomena, in Plantinga's estimation, 'range from the dubious to the preposterous,' 'On Being Evidentially Challenged', 253.
108 'On Being Evidentially Challenged', 254. Plantinga elaborates at length in terms of friendships, accomplishments, aesthetics, music, religion, a sense of moral failure, and so on.
109 As Plantinga points out, many, perhaps most, theists believe that the world is fallen, and, because of that, characterised by brokenness and pain. As a result, one would not expect that creatures inhabiting this world would, in general, live happy lives, 'On Being Evidentially Challenged', 256.

In *WCB*, Plantinga develops his response to Draper,[110] concentrating here on the claim made by Draper in 'Pain and Pleasure' that if the total amount of pain and suffering known to exist by a person (henceforth summarised as O) is much more likely on a serious alternative hypothesis, such as HI, then a theist has a *prima facie* reason to reject theism.

Plantinga argues against Draper insisting that even if traditional Christian belief is subject to an evidential challenge (with evil being better explained by HI), this, in itself, does not provide a Christian with sufficient reason to discard Christian belief. Many beliefs can be better explained in terms of still further beliefs, but this will seldom constitute a reason to reject them, particularly if the degree of warrant enjoyed by the evidentially challenged belief is high. Plantinga believes that Christian belief, produced in the believer by the Holy Spirit, *does* have a high degree of warrant, and therefore is not threatened by being challenged evidentially.[111]

Plantinga concedes that an evidentialist challenge *may* constitute a *prima facie* defeater for theistic belief in two circumstances: first, where the believer only just believes in Christian theism, and second, where the sole reason for believing is the explanatory power of theism, and HI is judged better able to explain the evil and suffering of the world. However, even in a such a case, a theist may conclude that his theism does a better job of explaining some other relevant phenomena, and therefore retain his theism.[112]

Plantinga concludes that Draper's challenge fails to establish a case against theism.[113] He asserts that all such challenges are likely to fail.[114] Plantinga concedes, however, that unlike the logical form, the 'probabilistic argument is much more realistic and perhaps more disturbing.'[115] He does not elaborate as to why. A likely reason is that probabilistic arguments are more likely to draw attention to the extent and intensity of suffering (and because of this are more disturbing) than would be necessary for various logical forms of the argument.

Having disposed of both the logical and evidentialist forms of the problem of evil and suffering, to his satisfaction at least, Plantinga, raises the interesting possibility that evil and suffering may yet constitute a defeater to theistic belief, although not by way of argument. It could be that an

---

110   Plantinga takes into account articles by Draper written after 'Pain and Pleasure', including 'Evil and the Proper Basicality of Belief in God,' *Faith and Philosophy*, Vol. 8, No. 2 (April, 1991), 135-147; 'Probabilistic Arguments from Evil,' *Religious Studies*, Vol. 28, No. 3 (September, 1992), 303-317; and 'Evolution and the Problem of Evil,' in Louis Pojman, (ed), *Philosophy of Religion*, third edition (Belmont, CA: Wadsworth, 1997).
111   *WCB*, 478, 479.
112   *WCB*, 480, 481.
113   *WCB*, 481.
114   In 'Epistemic Probability and Evil', he claims that 'the prospects for [the probabilistic atheological argument] are bleak,' 557.
115   'Christian Philosophy at the End of the 20th Century', 38.

observation of evil and suffering (in all of its horrifying contours) produces, in a properly basic way, the belief that God does not exist. As Plantinga puts it:

> Perhaps the defeating power of these facts in no way depends upon the existence of a good antitheistic argument (deductive, inductive, abductive, probabilistic, whatever) from the facts of evil.[116]

Perhaps an encounter with evil in sufficient magnitude can have the effect of making obvious the non-existence of God. The resulting belief that God does not exist would therefore be a basic belief, arising independently of arguments or propositionally articulated evidence. One might even argue that the employment of arguments is a distraction from experiencing the full impact of evil: '... it permits the believer in God to turn his attention away, to avert his eyes from the abomination of suffering, to take refuge in antiseptic discussions of possible worlds, probability functions and other arcana. It diverts attention from the situations that in fact constitute a defeater for belief in God.'[117] Plantinga thinks that an argument along these lines holds promise of being the best version of the atheological case from evil.[118]

As an initial response to such a way of arguing, Plantinga suggests that 'the perception of evil is not a defeater for belief in God with respect to *fully rational* noetic structures.'[119] In such, the *sensus divinitatis* is fully operational, and therefore the existence of God is completely and fully obvious. Even though evil and suffering may be perplexing, their existence would not constitute a defeater of theistic belief. To the obvious objection that there are no fully rational noetic structures, as a result of damage done to the *sensus divinitatis* by the effects of sin, Plantinga responds by asserting:

> ... that damage to the *sensus divinitatis* is in principle and increasingly repaired in the process of faith and regeneration. The person of faith may be once more such that, at least on some occasions, the presence of God is completely evident to her.[120]

Plantinga goes on to argue that knowledge of divine love 'revealed in the incarnation, the unthinkable splendor of the suffering and death of Jesus Christ, himself the divine and unique son of God, on our behalf,'[121] provides a believer with additional warrant for believing in God. Although this knowledge provides an inadequate explanation for suffering, one at least has the comforting knowledge that God himself suffers and cares. It is at this point that Plantinga

---

116   *WCB*, 482.
117   *WCB*, 484.
118   *WCB*, 484.
119   *WCB*, 485.
120   *WCB*, 487.
121   *WCB*, 487.

comes closest to suggesting some possible reasons for God's allowance of evil; comes closest to a theodicy, or, at least, to considerations that may contribute to a theodicy. He makes the following suggestions:

> Perhaps our suffering is deeply connected with the possibility of salvation for human beings; perhaps we share in Christ's suffering in such a way that our suffering too is salvific, and perhaps even essential to the plan of salvation.[122]

> It is plausible to think that the best possible worlds God could have actualized contain the unthinkably great good of divine incarnation and redemption - but then of course also sin and suffering. God choses one of these worlds to be actual - and in it, humankind suffers. Still, in this world there is also the marvellous opportunity for redemption and for eternal fellowship with God, an inconceivably great good that vastly outweighs the suffering we are called upon to endure. Still further, in being offered eternal fellowship with God, we human beings are invited to join the charmed circle of the Trinity itself; and perhaps that invitation can be issued only to creatures who have fallen, suffered, and been redeemed. If so, the condition of mankind is vastly better than it would have been, had there been no sin and no suffering. *O Felix Culpa* indeed![123]

These suggestions have merit, and may even be somewhat close to the sober truth. However, as is perhaps the case with all attempts to find an explanation for evil and suffering, they raise as many questions as they answer. Whose suffering, for example, is salvific? If Plantinga means the suffering of Christians, then what of the suffering of those who are not Christian? Further, if it is the suffering of Christians which brings salvation to others, how many others? The great majority of the world's current population, not to mention the millions upon billions who have lived previously, are unlikely to benefit either from the sufferings of Christ or from the sufferings of his people, at least on a traditional and conservative understanding of the scope of Christ's salvific work.[124]

Plantinga speaks of the marvellous opportunity of redemption, and of the inestimable benefits of eternal participation in Trinitarian fellowship, but he does not mention that most people (again on a conservative estimate of the gospel's importance and effectiveness) will not have this opportunity. In fact, Plantinga's own account of how people come to believe the gospel, along with a healthy Reformed emphasis upon predestination, would suggest that human beings left to their own resources have no opportunity to believe, nor any way

---

122   *WCB*, 488, 489.
123   *WCB*, 489.
124   See my earlier discussion on Religious Pluralism (chapter three).

of knowing that the gospel is true, apart from the electing power of God and the internal instigation of the Holy Spirit.

Plantinga may, of course, wish to distance himself from such traditionally held Reformed teaching, and if so, with some reason. The problem of evil becomes more acute if propositions such as the following are added to the propositional mix one is seeking to defend:

(11) Every human creature has inherited from Adam the guilt of his primeval sin, as well as a nature which inexorably tends towards sin.

(12) God has chosen from eternity only some of Adam's race to be saved, a choice which is no way dependent on human merit or choice.

(13) All those who are unsaved will suffer eternal conscious torment in hell.

The addition of such propositions creates a complication for Plantinga in his attempts to defend Christian theism. If Plantinga distances himself from such propositions, the question is raised: which particular version of Christian theism is Plantinga defending? If it is the Reformed version, then questions are raised as to why Plantinga would distance himself from doctrines which, historically, have been characteristic of Reformed theology.[125] If Plantinga does accept the above propositions, then his suggestions as to God's possible good reasons for allowing evil are much less credible. At the very least, it is hard to see how the incarnation and costly death of Jesus, along with the election of only some human beings to salvation, is a better world than any other God could have actualised, particularly considering the horrendous cost in human suffering (both temporal and eternal) that such a version of Christianity entails. The question posed in the first half of this chapter returns with greater poignancy: is it reasonable to think that God was unable or justifiably unwilling to actualise a world populated by creatures who freely and only choose to do good, including the supreme good of living in worshipful dependence on God?[126]

---

125 There is some evidence that Plantinga has distanced himself from certain aspects of his Reformed heritage. As was noted in our discussion of religious pluralism, Plantinga is inclined to believe that human beings will have post-mortem chances to repent. Such a position certainly goes beyond traditional Reformed teaching, both in thinking that repentance is possible after death and in its apparent acceptance of chance or free choice.

126 If one takes a compatibilist view of human freedom, as is common among Reformed theologians, then one would have to say that God *could* have actualized such a world. That he did not means that some good reason (other than inability) needs to be found.

The problem of evil becomes more perplexing the more specific one becomes concerning God's nature and purposes. The potential impact of this perplexity is greater than Plantinga acknowledges. In his discussion of the evidential problem of evil, Plantinga makes the contention that Christian believers do not typically accept Christian beliefs because of their explanatory power. This may be so. However, the presence of evil and suffering, often in an experientially profound and disturbing way, does raise the question of explanations. How *can* evil and suffering, especially particularly horrific cases of it, be explained? If it is an implication of the Bible's teaching that evil and suffering will persist forever in hell, and for most of Adam's race, how can such an outcome be morally justified? The explanatory resources of Christianity are stretched to the absolute limit by such questions. The fact that there are no very good (or at least comprehensively good) answers to these questions has the potential to seriously unsettle a Christian, and to give credence to alternative hypotheses such as the Hypothesis of Indifference. It could also have the effect of undermining confidence in the truth of Scripture,[127] and, ultimately, of the gospel.[128] As already noted in chapter three, conviction, once lost, is not easily recovered.

Plantinga's defence of Christian theism against probabilistic forms of the problem of evil depends, rather crucially, on what he judges are the convictional resources of the Christian believer. A Christian believer has at her disposal (if indeed Christian theism is true, and Plantinga's description of these resources is correct) various good arguments for the existence of God as well as the *sensus divinitatis* and the internal instigation of the Holy Spirit. Together, these are designed to produce such confidence in the truth of Christian theism that contradictory evidence is unlikely to deflate that confidence, or, at least, it need not. However, Plantinga's analysis raises the interesting possibility that evil and suffering, along with our inability to explain it, may so sap a believer's confidence as to render the conditional epistemic probability of G on E so low that she no longer believes G, and thus no longer believes in the Holy Spirit, or in the *sensus divinitatis*.[129] Only slightly less seriously for an apologist like Plantinga, she may no longer believe in the Christian God, or in God as portrayed in the Bible. She may find herself unable to accept propositions such as (11) to (13) above.

---

127 Especially if there exist other reasons to doubt Scripture's truth.
128 Some such process appears to have happened in the case of John Hick who came, by stages, to doubt the truth of traditional formulations of Christian doctrine. Included in that process were questions as to whether it really could be the case that a God of love would send the majority of the human race to hell. For a brief autobiographical description of this process, see John Hick, 'A Pluralist View', in *Four Views on Salvation in a Pluralistic World,* 29-45.
129 On Plantinga's account of epistemic probability, this would seem to be an entirely rational thing to do.

The potential of the problem of evil to unsettle and even undermine the faith of a Christian is matched by an even greater potential to prevent faith in the case of a person who is not a Christian. Such a person is in a much weaker position, epistemologically. Without neither a properly functioning *sensus divinitatis*, nor the benefit of the inward instigation of the Holy Spirit, people (on Plantinga's own reckoning) are more likely to be profoundly disturbed by the presence of evil and suffering in the world. This is so much the case that an agnosticism about the existence of God and the truth of the gospel is likely to be a rational choice.

This raises the question of the extent of Plantinga's success in his efforts to provide a defence of Christian theism in the face of evidential forms of the problem of evil. As noted at the beginning of chapter two, the task of the negative apologist is two-fold: (1) to fortify the Christian in the face of various challenges to Christian belief, and (2) to demonstrate to the unbeliever that these challenges do not constitute sufficient reason for rejecting Christian belief. Plantinga has been somewhat successful in both tasks, but more so with respect to (1) than (2).

Much of what Plantinga has argued could be helpful to both Christian and non-Christian. Plantinga has rightly insisted that people take into account all the evidence when making judgements about the probability of God's existence in the light of evil and suffering. He has rightly drawn attention to explanatory power of Christian theism with respect to this total body of evidence. Significantly included in this total body of evidence is the gospel account of the suffering and death of Jesus on the cross.

However, herein lies a difficulty with Plantinga's defence. Plantinga speaks of propositional as well as non-propositional evidence for the existence of God, yet, importantly, does not suggest that there is good propositional evidence for the truth of the Christian gospel, that is, for the truth that Jesus did die on the cross (and rise again).[130] This is a serious limitation of resources, and evidence. A person who is not a Christian may well conclude on the basis of Plantinga's work on the evidential form of the problem of evil that a god of some sort may, possibly, exist, but remain entirely agnostic, and with good warrant, about whether the God of Christian theism exists. Although Plantinga could respond by arguing that such a person could become the recipient of the inward instigation of the Holy Spirit, and thus acquire non-propositional warrant for his belief in the Christian gospel, the lack of propositional warrant is nevertheless significant. Given that one is engaged in weighing up evidence both for and against the truth of Christian theism, the lack of propositional evidence is glaring. Even someone who is the recipient of the inward instigation of the Holy Spirit may be unsettled, perhaps seriously (as noted

---

130 This lack of confidence in the propositional evidence for the truth of the Christian gospel, which was described in chapter three, will be discussed further in chapter eight.

Negative Apologetics: Evil and Suffering

above), by this lack. For the person who is *not* the recipient of the inward instigation of the Holy Spirit, this lack will almost certainly, and even rightly, lead to or reinforce unbelief in the truth of the Christian gospel.

To sum up, Plantinga's defence of Christian theism in the face of evidentialist versions of the problem of evil is not without its problems and limitations. It is likely to be of most help to a Christian believer who is strongly convinced of the truth of the Christian gospel, and is of decreasing value for the wavering Christian and, even less, for the unbeliever. The source of its greatest limitation is the (claimed) lack of propositional support for the Christian gospel.

More could (and perhaps should) be said by way of critique. However, now is an appropriate point to progress from a consideration of Plantinga's contribution to negative apologetics to consider his contribution to positive apologetics.

CHAPTER 6

Plantinga and Positive Apologetics

6.1 Criticisms of Plantinga's Contribution to Positive Apologetics

Alvin Plantinga has been criticised for providing little help to those involved in positive apologetics.[1] H. A. Netland, for example, while noting with appreciation Plantinga's efforts in defusing the evidentialist challenge to Christian belief, expresses disappointment that Plantinga's work in the area of epistemology has not aided the cause of commending the Christian gospel. Most seriously, it fails to lay upon unbelievers any epistemic obligation to believe the gospel.[2] William Alston notes, in similar vein, that while Plantinga has, commendably, provided believers with an 'internal' defence, a way of justifying belief from within their own perspective, he has not sufficiently drawn upon common ground shared with those of a different perspective, thereby providing unbelievers with reasons for believing they are likely to accept.[3]

There is some warrant in the above criticisms, as will be seen.[4] However, a number of things can be said in (partial) defence of Plantinga. Further, if Plantinga's epistemology as a whole is taken into account, there is potential for Plantinga to make a significant contribution to positive apologetics.

---

1   I have voiced the criticism myself, in 'Apologetics As Dialogue: A New Way of Understanding an Old Task' in *The Reformed Theological Review*, Vol. 54, No. 2 (May-August, 1995), 58, 59.
2   H. A. Netland, 'Truth, authority and modernity: shopping for truth in a supermarket of worldviews' in P. Sampson, V. Samuel and C. Sugden, (eds), *Faith and Modernity* (Oxford: Regnum Books, 1994), 101, 102.
3   Alston's comments are made in the context of a comparison between his own position and Plantinga's. He elaborates in these terms: 'Plantinga's defence of his position is carefully crafted and very much to the point. Nevertheless, except for negative critiques, the defence is an internal one. It consists of taking one's stance within the doxastic practice in question and defying all comers to dislodge him. This is valuable, but it would also be worthwhile to have some positive reasons in support of the practice that appeal to more widely shared assumptions,' *Perceiving God: The Epistemology of Religious Experience* (Ithaca and London: Cornell University Press, 1991), 197.
4   In this chapter, and in the chapters which follow.

Serious criticisms still remain, but these need to be considered in light of the arguments of this chapter.

6.1.1 No Intention to Contribute

In defence of the charge that Plantinga's work in the area of epistemology has done little to aid the cause of positive apology, it must first be said that Plantinga never intended it to fulfil that role.

Plantinga, on a number of occasions, has had to field criticisms that his arguments in favour of viewing belief in God (and belief in the gospel) as properly basic would not persuade unbelievers, and certainly not those who are sceptical of Christian truth claims. His frequent reply has been that it was not his intention, or at least primary intention, to do this. To mention just one example, in 'Reformed Epistemology Again' (1982), Plantinga responds to a claim by Van Hook that 'unless a claim to know can be demonstrated to a sceptic, it is quite useless for the purposes of apologetics'. Plantinga's reply: '... when the Reformed epistemologist claims that one can have basic knowledge of God - knowledge independent of argument or demonstration - she's not doing apologetics and not trying to convince the sceptic.' He continues:

> There is more to the epistemology of religious belief than apologetics, just as there is more to the epistemology of perception than refuting the perceptual sceptic. In 'On Reformed epistemology' I wasn't attempting a piece of apologetics; instead, I was making an effort to see how we - that is, we Christians - should think about knowledge of God.[5]

Not that Plantinga has no interest in apologetics. As we have seen, he does, and has done throughout his career. However, Plantinga's efforts to explore the nature and status of theistic and Christian beliefs has its own intrinsic value, regardless of the implications for positive apologetics. It is therefore unfair to criticise him or depreciate his work because it does not fulfil a purpose it was not intended to fulfil in the first place.

6.1.2 A Small, but Significant Change in Attitude

A second defence of Plantinga, in the light of charges made above, is that despite what one may think about his contribution (or lack of contribution) to positive apologetics, he himself, has, from about the mid-80s, been clearly in favour of positive apologetics, insofar as it provides support for theistic belief.

---

5   A. Plantinga, 'Reformed Epistemology Again', *Reformed Journal*, Vol. 32 (July, 1982), 7.

During the mid-80s there appears to have been a change of thinking, or a softening in attitude, towards positive apologetics in Plantinga's work. If one were to rely on some of Plantinga's earlier statements, made, for example, in articles from the early 80's,[6] one could conclude that Plantinga saw little, if any, place for positive apologetics.[7] Positive apologetics was then associated, in Plantinga's thinking, with natural theology,[8] to which he had a less than positive attitude. In 'The Reformed Objection to Natural Theology', published in 1980, Plantinga outlined, with obvious approval, the traditional Reformed opposition to natural theology. One of Plantinga's key concerns, in writing this article, and the ones which followed, was to underline his support for the Reformed contention that belief in God does not need to be supported by arguments in order to be considered knowledge. Although this conviction, in itself, would not rule out the usefulness of arguments in certain contexts, Plantinga did appear to favour the Reformed belief that one need not, and even *should* not believe on the basis of argument. Speaking for Calvin, he writes:

> The Christian doesn't *need* natural theology, either as the source of his confidence or to justify his belief. Furthermore, the Christian *ought* not to believe on the basis of argument; if he does, his faith is likely to be unstable and wavering.[9]

Elsewhere Plantinga represents the Reformed tradition as holding that *the most appropriate way*,[10] or *the best way,* or *the epistemically most correct way*[11] to believe in God is 'to eschew argument and accept the belief in question as

---

6   Including 'The Reformed Objection to Natural Theology', 'On Reformed Epistemology', 'Reformed Epistemology Again', and 'The Reformed Objection Revisited', *Christian Scholars Review*, Vol. 12 (1983), 57-61.

7   Going back further into the 70's, 60's and late 50's, one would have further reason for thinking that Plantinga has a less than positive attitude to positive apologetics. Whenever he mentions apologetics, or engages in it (in his free will defence against the atheological argument from evil, for example) his consistent emphasis is upon negative apologetics, upon meeting challenges to theistic belief rather than upon using arguments to persuade people of the truth of theism or of Christianity.

8   Plantinga has had a tendency to virtually equate natural theology and positive apologetics. See, for example, 'Augustinian Christian Philosophy', 293. The likely reason for this is that Plantinga believes that natural theological arguments provide the best argumentative support for Christian beliefs.

9   'The Reformed Objection', 53. In 'Reason and Belief in God', Plantinga makes essentially the same statement, this time as representing the views of Calvin, Kuyper, Bavinck and Barth, 72.

10   'On Reformed Epistemology', 14.

11   'Objection Revisited', 57

basic.'[12] It is hard to see how Plantinga, with this understanding, could have a positive attitude (or much of a positive attitude) to positive apologetics. If the epistemically superior way to believe is to believe in a basic way, without argumentative support, then surely the best thing to do, in seeking to win an unbeliever to belief, is *not* to argue. It would be epistemically unwise, to say the least, to subject a potential convert to the uncertainty of having his faith linked with (or even founded upon) the results of some argument, when a safer and better way would be to encourage him into environments known to be conducive to basic theistic and Christian belief. For example, it would be better to take him to an evangelistic rally, or give him a Bible to read, or take him out to observe the stars, than to engage in positive apologetics. This would certainly seem to be a more natural way for Plantinga to proceed. However, as stated, Plantinga expresses his support for positive apologetics.

As far back as 1983, only months after[13] having written in favour of Reformed Epistemology, Plantinga was asked in an interview, 'What approach do you think would be most effective for a Christian thinker dealing with sceptics?' His response was that the Christian community needs to do a number of things, *including* producing arguments 'for God's existence'.[14] In 'The Foundations of Theism' (1986), Plantinga says of negative and positive apologetics, that they are *'both* [my emphasis] important disciplines'[15] In 'A Christian Life Partly Lived' (1993), he points out that Christian philosophers are involved in a common project that has a number of different sides, including 'apologetics, both positive and negative.'[16]

It is a little puzzling to work out how Plantinga can be a supporter of Reformed epistemology on the one hand, and simultaneously (or shortly later) affirm so strongly the value of positive apologetics. The way to solve the puzzle is to note two things. The first is that Plantinga has never (as far as I am aware) ruled out positive apologetics as a useful endeavour in certain circumstances. Second, he has become progressively more open to the value of positive apologetics.

These observations or suggestions can be supported and illustrated by reference to a number of statements made by Plantinga, the first appearing in

---

12   'Objection Revisited', 57. In Plantinga's early and seminal article, 'Is Belief in God Rational', he states that 'the mature theist accepts belief in God as basic, not tentatively, or hypothetically, or until something better comes along.' He 'commits himself to belief in God,' 27.
13   Or perhaps months earlier. I am unsure of the exact sequence in which the articles were written.
14   'Modern philosophy and the turn to belief in God', in R. Varghese, (ed.), *The Intellectuals Speak Out About God* (Chicago: Ill.: Regnery Gateway, 1984), 166.
15   'The Foundations of Theism: A Reply', *Faith and Philosophy,* Vol.3, No. 3 (July, 1986), 313 fn.
16   'A Christian Life', 80.

early 80's, the rest more recently. One of Plantinga's early discoveries in the area of natural theology was that the traditional arguments for (and against) the existence of God are unsuccessful, at least as measured against the high standards employed by those traditionally engaged in that enterprise. This lack of success gave impetus to Plantinga's efforts to defend theistic belief as properly basic.

An obvious question to ask, in the light of these efforts, is: is there any need for, or value in, positive apologetics? Plantinga has answered that question a number of times, sometimes directly, sometimes by way of implication. Plantinga's response has altered, subtly, but significantly over the last ten to fifteen years. To support this contention, a contrast between pronouncements made by Plantinga regarding the value of natural theology in the early 80's will be made with others made approximately a decade later. There is (at least) a noticeable change of tone from one to the other.

In 1983, in response to a number of criticisms to his apparently negative assessment of natural theology, Plantinga made several concessions to the enterprise of natural theology (or positive apologetics). After delineating the contours of Reformed epistemology, he wrote (in 'The Reformed Objection Revisited'):

> But of course none of this entails that natural theology is either impious or useless. It is impious, in the view of some reformers, to *refuse* to believe without argument; and for someone who already knows that God exists, natural theology isn't very useful - at least it isn't useful with respect to the end of enabling him to achieve knowledge of the existence of God. But all of this is entirely compatible with natural theology's being useful in *other* ways. If there were some clearly valid arguments for the existence of God from premises widely accepted by believers and unbelievers alike, these arguments could obviously serve as *confirmations* of the existence of God - for at least some believers. Further, such arguments could be useful in preparing the way for faith and in leading some people closer to it. Still further, arguments of this sort would be of great theoretical interest. I certainly didn't mean to deny any of these things, and to the extent that the Reformed thinkers I mentioned rejected natural theology *in toto* I think they were mistaken. As I see it, their real point is that natural theology is needed neither for rational justification of theistic belief, nor for the knowledge that God exists; their rejection of it, therefore, should perhaps have been more nuanced than it was. They should have insisted that the believer doesn't need natural theology in order to be within his noetic rights in believing in God ...[17]

Here Plantinga appears to be reasonably positive in his assessment of the on-going value of natural theology, yet it is worth noting the heavily qualified way in which he allows the possibility that the arguments of natural theology *could*

---

17 'Objection Revisited', 57, 58.

serve as confirmations of the existence of God, and *could* be useful in preparing the way for faith, and in leading *some* people closer to it. One probable reason for the reasonably heavy qualification is that Plantinga still considered the arguments of natural theology to be unsuccessful. He therefore goes on to nuance his already cautious acceptance of natural theology:

> In the first place, then, I agree that natural theology *could have* the uses mentioned above. But in fact I don't believe that there are any widely successful theistic arguments. At any rate there aren't any meeting the stringent conditions for success laid down by the classical Thomist natural theologian.[18]

Plantinga goes on to suggest that perhaps (a word he repeats a number of times) the standards employed by natural theologians may have been too high. *Perhaps* there are more modest standards that *could* be employed, such as those employed by A. E. Taylor, F. R. Tennant, C. S. Lewis, and Richard Swinburne.[19]

In 1983, Plantinga appears uncomfortable even with these concessions, demonstrated in his immediate qualification of his statements by suggesting a possible (negative) outcome that may result from the use of such arguments, apparently in an evangelistic or positive apologetic context.

> We must remember, however, that an argument is reversible; there is *modus tollens* as well as *modus ponens*. Some non-theists, if confronted by a valid theistic argument from premises they accept, may choose to reject the premises rather than accept the conclusion. In this way it is possible to reduce the extent of someone's knowledge by giving him a valid argument from premises he knows to be true.[20]

---

18 'Objection Revisited', 58. Plantinga goes on to note that the prospects that such an argument could be developed are not bright.
19 'Objection Revisited', 58. It is interesting to note that earlier on in Plantinga's career, he had defined natural theology as 'the attempt to infer central religious beliefs from premises that are either obvious to common sense (e.g., that some things are in motion) or logically necessary', *The Free Will Defence*, 205 fn. Clearly, by 1983 Plantinga was beginning to move beyond this traditional and limited understanding of natural theology.
20 'Objection Revisited', 58. Plantinga repeats this point in 'Reason and Belief in God' (82, 83), and in his inaugural address as the John A. O'Brien Professor of Philosophy at the University of Notre Dame, published as 'Advice to Christian Philosophers', 264. One wonders why Plantinga thought it important to state this. It is undeniably true, even expected, that people will be unwilling to accept certain conclusions, especially concerning God or his Son, Jesus. There are uncomfortable consequences that follow from such acceptance. However, this is no reason for pulling back from presenting good arguments (if there are such, and the implication of Plantinga's point is that there are, or very well may be) for the existence of God,

Plantinga, it seems, *perhaps* out of commitment to his Reformed heritage, is unwilling to concede much to natural theology or to positive apologetics. Yet this reluctance noticeably changes in the years following the writing of these articles. In 1991, for example, in a paper entitled, 'The Prospects for Natural Theology',[21] Plantinga straightforwardly endorses the use of natural theology for positive apologetic purposes. Any earlier hesitancy is gone. In response to the question of natural theology's purpose, he suggests a number of answers, including the following:

> You might be a believer in God yourself and might try to convince someone else to join you in this belief. Or you might be a wavering or troubled believer in God, and be trying to convince yourself.[22]

In a more recent paper, delivered in 1994 at the Fifth International Symposium of the Association for Calvinist Philosophy,[23] Plantinga is careful to acknowledge that those in the Reformed tradition have tended to view theistic arguments with suspicion, and have seen little (if any) value in apologetics, either positive or negative.[24] He nevertheless, and significantly in this context, comes out strongly in favour of positive apologetics, not as necessary to justify theistic belief, but for other purposes: for example, moving unbelievers towards faith, and strengthening the faith of those who already believe. In Plantinga's words:

> First, theistic arguments can obviously be of value for those who don't already believe; they can move them closer to belief, and can bring it about that belief in God is at any rate among the live options for them. Only God bestows saving faith, of course, but his way of doing so can certainly involve cooperation with his children, as in preaching and even argumentation. But

---

or for the deity of Jesus. Plantinga, fairly clearly, is wanting to minimise the importance of positive apologetics. In the immediate context of his remarks, Plantinga makes another of his 'perhaps' statements: 'Perhaps the Christian philosopher can convince the sceptic or the unbelieving philosopher that indeed there is such a person as God. Perhaps this is possible in at least some instances.' Plantinga goes on to state (or imply) that bringing about this possibility is not the most important thing a Christian philosopher should concern himself with. 'Justifying or trying to justify theistic belief in the eyes of the broader philosophical community is not the only task of the Christian philosophical community; perhaps it isn't even among its most important tasks,' 'Advice to Christian Philosophers', 264.

21 In J. Tomberlin (ed), *Philosophical Perspectives*, Vol. 5, Philosophy of Religion (Atascadero: Ridgeview Publishing Co., 1991), 287-315.
22 'Prospects', 287.
23 Held at Hoeven, the Netherlands, the conference dedicated to the memory of Herman Dooyeweerd.
24 'Christian Philosophy at the End of the 20th Century', 39, 37.

second, theistic arguments can also be useful for *believers*. Calvin notes that believers struggle constantly with doubts; in this life, he says ... 'faith is always mixed with unbelief' and '... in the believing mind certainty is mixed with doubt ...' (1536, III, ii, par. 18). At times the truth of the main lines of the Gospel seems as certain and sure as that there is such a country as the Netherlands; at other times you wake up in the middle of the night and find yourself wondering whether this whole wonderful Christian story is really anything more than just that: a wonderful story. Theistic arguments can be helpful here.[25]

Plantinga is here noticeably more open in his assessment of positive apologetics, and of natural theology, than in earlier statements.[26] A key to understanding this change lies in Plantinga's growing understanding that the standards for success traditionally employed by natural theologians were unreasonably high.[27] In a 1992 article, entitled 'Augustinian Christian Philosophy', Plantinga notes that positive apologetics has tended to be

---

25 'Christian Philosophy at the End of the 20th Century', 39, 40.
26 It is interesting to compare the above quotation from 'Christian Philosophy at the End of the 20th Century' with a similar statement made in 1983, in 'The Reformed Objection Revisited', 61. The substance of what is said is similar. The difference, more obvious in context, is that the earlier statements have more the flavour of a concession than a positive affirmation.
27 It is worth noting that Plantinga's realisation that natural theology has been wedded to unreasonably high standards of proof is not one that has dawned on him only recently. It has been a developing realisation, with implications coming to be seen more clearly as time has gone by. In 1967, for example, when Plantinga wrote *God and Other Minds*, he was apparently accepting of the high standards of natural theology, believing that standards like those traditionally accepted needed to be met for natural theology to be considered successful. It was in the light of those standards that Plantinga could announce the failure of natural theology. See for example, vii, viii, 4, 111, 115, 183, 268, 269. By 1974, in *The Nature of Necessity*, Plantinga had already begun to question those standards, perhaps as a result of having devised a version of the ontological argument he believed to be sound, and which succeeds so long as a key (and very reasonable) premise is accepted. Plantinga, in line with his earlier rejection of natural theology (a rejection he would re-iterate in his articles on natural theology in the early 80's), is careful to point out that his revised version of the ontological argument cannot be considered a 'successful piece of natural theology'. This is because 'the latter typically draws its premises from the stock of propositions accepted by nearly every sane man, or perhaps nearly every rational man.' Plantinga had not yet conceded the possibility that natural theology might itself need to be re-thought in less stringent terms. Nevertheless, the conceptual building materials were all there. See further, *The Nature of Necessity*, 221.

dominated by the assumption that a good theistic argument must be *demonstrative* to be deemed successful.[28] Then he asks:

> But why suppose a good theistic argument has to be *that* good?[29]

Plantinga proceeds to mention a number of arguments 'very much [worthy of] study and development' which he believes are *'good* arguments'.[30] The fact that not everyone is likely to accept all the premises does not discredit them as arguments.

> [It] doesn't mean that the argument in question is not a good theistic argument. It can be a fine argument, and a useful argument, even if not everyone accepts all its premises. If some do not accept its premises, then it won't be a good argument for *them*; it might nonetheless be a good argument for those who *do* accept its premises.[31]

In *WCB*, Plantinga sums up the change in his thinking with respect to argumentative standards, in these words:

> In *God and Other Minds*, I argued first that the theistic proofs or arguments do not succeed. In evaluating these arguments I employed a traditional *but wholly improper standard* [my emphasis]: I took it that these arguments are successful only if they start from propositions that compel assent from every honest and intelligent person and proceed majestically to their conclusion by way of forms of argument that can be rejected only on pain of insincerity or

---

28 'Augustinian Christian Philosophy', 291-320. This may be true. It has certainly been the case that a desire for demonstrative certainty has been a characterising impulse of modern foundationalism, and therefore of apologetic strategies attempting to meet the challenge of foundationalist evidentialism. However, there have been notable apologists who, while accepting some version of foundationalism, have been happy to advance less than demonstrative theistic arguments. Joseph Butler and William Paley come to mind, as do some of the apologists mentioned by Plantinga such as C. S. Lewis and Richard Swinburne.
29 'Augustinian Christian Philosophy', 293.
30 'Augustinian Christian Philosophy', 294. His positive assessment of them is even stronger a few lines later, when he describes them as 'extremely promising' arguments 'very much worth detailed attention and serious work'. Examples of such arguments are mentioned in 'Prospects', 312. A fuller list can be found in Plantinga's more recent 'Christian Philosophy at the End of the 20th Century'. After listing them, he concludes: 'These arguments are not apodictic or certain; nevertheless they all deserve to be developed in loving detail; and each of them will be of value both as a theistic argument, and also as a way of thinking about the relation between God and the specific sort of phenomenon in question. I believe Christian philosophers of the next century (not to mention the remainder of this one) should pay a great deal more attention to theistic argument.' 41.
31 'Augustinian Christian Philosophy', 294.

irrationality. So naturally enough, I joined the contemporary chorus in holding that none of the traditional arguments was successful. (I failed to note that no philosophical arguments of any consequence meet *that* standard; hence the fact that theistic arguments do not is of less significance than I thought.)[32]

To sum up the substance of this second point: for those who are inclined to criticise Plantinga's work for providing little by way of help to the positive apologist, it should at least be acknowledged that Plantinga himself is in favour of positive apologetics. Although his attempts to justify basic theistic belief do not (by themselves) contribute much, if anything, to the task of persuading a non-believer to believe, Plantinga commends the work of the positive apologist, and, furthermore, highlights the many good theistic arguments that such a person might employ.[33]

6.1.3 Actual and Potential Contributions

A third defence of Plantinga from the charge that his work in epistemology has done little to aid the cause of positive apology is to simply deny the charge, and to argue, as I will, that Plantinga has significantly contributed to the cause of positive apologetics, even though his contribution is less than some would like.[34] Moreover, his work in epistemology has the potential to make an even greater contribution.

Plantinga's work in epistemology, including his more recent work on warrant and proper function, is pregnant with implications for apologetics. Many of these are 'undeveloped'; some perhaps need a longer gestation period. However, if these implications are realised and exploited for the purposes of apology, the benefits for both the negative and positive apologist will be substantial.

Plantinga has contributed to the task of positive apologetics in at least three different ways. The first, rather ironically, is in his contribution to the cause of negative apologetics. It may seem strange to argue that by doing negative apologetics one is contributing to the task of positive apologetics. However, a moment's reflection will make clear how this can be, and often is, the case. A good way to consider this is through analogy. One of the things that sportspeople are often told, and which commentators love to repeat, is that defence wins games. Without a strong platform of defence, even the most talented offensive team will struggle. In other words, if the defence is good, the offence is more likely to succeed. The same is true in the area of apologetics. If

---

32 *WCB*, 69.
33 Plantinga has done some writing in this area himself, including "2 dozen (or so) good theistic arguments' unpublished manuscripts.
34 Myself included, as will become clear.

Christian apologists are able (with sensitivity and skill) to answer charges laid against Christianity, then the task of persuading a person of the truth of Christianity (which is the aim of positive apologetics) will have already begun. It will certainly be made easier. Conversely, if the non-Christian is troubled, or even persuaded, by some argument purporting to disprove Christianity, it is unlikely that she will be open to arguments designed to commend Christianity. Negative apologetics will often be needed to prepare the way for positive apologetics, the former contributing to the latter in the process of persuasion.

A second way in which Plantinga has contributed to the task of positive apology is in removing unwarranted pressure from the positive apologist. To the extent that Plantinga has been successful in resisting the evidentialist challenge to Christian belief,[35] he has removed the need for the apologist to be (unduly) defensive. Christians are not required, again on the assumption that Plantinga is correct, to stand before the bar of a hostile evidentialism and have their faith judged either rational or irrational, depending on the strength of propositional evidence in its favour. That particular pressure to perform is removed. Plantinga has even succeeded in reversing the direction of the pressure. Evidentialists themselves have been issued with the challenge to provide the necessary 'evidence' for their belief that evidence is required for theistic and Christian belief to be rational. Plantinga's evolutionary argument against naturalism has the same potential to reverse apologetic pressure.[36]

Plantinga has also helped to remove unwarranted pressure from the positive apologist by arguing that the standards by which arguments are judged are often set unrealistically high. When those standards are more modestly set, a number of very good arguments are found to exist to the conclusion that theism is true. Plantinga has also drawn attention to the importance and role of non-propositional evidence[37] in the human belief forming process. It is not only arguments which persuade us, or create beliefs within us. Various experiences can achieve this as well. Plantinga's case for the proper basicality of theistic and Christian belief, which will be examined in the next two chapters, depends upon and develops this insight.

There is a third way in which Plantinga's work in the area of epistemology has contributed, or has the potential to contribute to the enterprise of positive

---

35 I myself am not convinced that Plantinga has been wholly successful, as will become obvious in chapters seven and eight.
36 In this case, the contribution to positive apologetics of this reversal of pressure is more obvious. Given that naturalism is but one of a finite number of possible worldview choices, to the extent that naturalism (or the adoption of naturalism) is shown to be deficient, Christianity becomes an increasingly live option.
37 Plantinga mostly uses the word 'evidence' in a narrowly propositional sense, but does also use it of non-propositional 'evidence', as, for example, in *WPF*, 98, 185. See also, 'Epistemic Probability and Evil', 578.

apologetics. Plantinga has not himself elucidated the implications of his work in this direction, and although the same could be said about each of the two previously suggested contributions, it is more so the case for this third suggestion. It is a more radical suggestion, or at least it could be construed that way by those who share Plantinga's Reformed heritage. My suggestion, in brief, is that Plantinga's recently developed and articulated theory of proper function is compatible with, and has the potential to provide important resources for evidence-emphasising apologetic approaches. It could, for example, be profitably used by John Warwick Montgomery, or by William Lane Craig, to provide an epistemic rationale for their particular apologetic strategies.[38]

It may appear ironic that Plantinga's epistemology could be used by a Christian evidentialist who is inclined to emphasise (even demand) the use of evidence in defence of Christianity. After all, a large part of Plantinga's motivation in developing his theory appears to have been his desire to provide philosophical support for the Reformed contention that belief in God and in the Christian gospel does not need the support of evidence to be considered rational. That this thoroughly Reformed impulse could deliver an outcome favourable to evidentialist apologetics (often seen as the arch enemy of Reformed epistemology) is surprising, even ironic, and for many, no doubt, unwelcome.

Nevertheless, despite the apparent incongruity involved, there is no *necessary* incompatibility between the Reformed epistemology of Plantinga and an apologetic approach which intelligently makes use of both propositional and non-propositional evidence in commending the truth of Christianity.[39] It is possible, for example, for someone to agree with Plantinga that the provision of evidence is often unnecessary for warranted theistic and Christian belief, but to then to argue that sometimes it *is* necessary and desirable. At the very least, evidence can be used to increase the warrant already enjoyed by a basic belief.[40]

---

38 John Warwick Montgomery is well known as an 'evidentialist', whose almost exclusive emphasis is on the empirical evidences for Christianity. William Lane Craig is known as a 'classical apologist' because of his employment of a two-stage defence; phase one involving the employment of natural theology in defence of theism, phase two involving an examination of evidence for the truth of Christianity.

39 C. Stephen Evans, in *The Historical Christ and the Jesus of Faith* (Oxford: Clarendon Press, 1996), argues along similar lines that Reformed and Evidentialist approaches are not incompatible, but complementary.

40 Even properly basic beliefs can acquire additional warrant as a result of support from arguments, 'The Reformed Objection Revisited', 61; 'Coherentism and the Evidentialist Objection', 123. In 'Prospects', Plantinga notes that such an increase in warrant can have the effect of nudging a belief over the boundary line separating knowledge from mere true belief, thereby serving 'something like the Thomistic project of transforming belief into knowledge', 311, 312.

It is in situations like this Plantinga's developed epistemology can be of service.

It is my intention, in what follows, to draw out some implications which follow from Plantinga's epistemology, whether comfortably or not. Specifically, I want to consider how Plantinga's theory of proper function impacts upon, and provides support for, an evidentialist-type case for Christianity.

One of the more significant things that Plantinga has done, particularly in his developing epistemology of warrant, is to return the notion of knowledge to a more realistic and common-sensical level.[41] This, of course, has been one of his aims, or at least one of the acknowledged outcomes of his work. Plantinga very helpfully draws attention to the fact that if classical foundationalism is correct, then many of our common sense claims to knowledge would be invalid. According to modern versions of classical foundationalism, we can only claim to have knowledge of self-evident and incorrigible propositions, and of propositions which can be proven (to some level of probability) from this foundational level of knowledge. The great problem with this is that if we accept this epistemic standard, an enormous quantity of what we believe (including much that we would classify as knowledge) would be disallowed. As Plantinga puts it:

> One crucial lesson to be learned from the development of modern philosophy - Descartes through Hume, roughly - is just this: relative to propositions that are self-evident and incorrigible, most of the beliefs that form the stock in trade of ordinary everyday life are not probable - at any rate there is no reason to think they are probable. Consider all those propositions that entail, say, that there are enduring physical objects, or that there are persons distinct from myself, or that the world has existed for more than five minutes: none of these propositions, I think, is more probable than not with respect to what is self-evident or incorrigible for me; at any rate no one has given good reason to think any of them is.[42]

Even perceptual beliefs, such as my belief that I am now looking at a computer screen, do not pass the foundationalist test for knowledge. That I am being appeared to computerly does, but this experiential belief provides little by way of non-circular evidence for the proposition that I am, in fact, looking at a computer screen.[43] Classical foundationalism thus fails in its most cherished aim of providing a secure foundation for our ordinary beliefs about the world.

---

41 Others, along with Plantinga, have done the same, including Stephen Toulmin and Roderick Chisholm.
42 'Reason and Belief in God', 59, 60.
43 This point is well set out in 'The Foundations of Theism', 303-305 where Plantinga takes issue with Philip Quinn's contention that properly basic beliefs can

It is for this reason, among others, that Plantinga has come to reject classical foundationalism, replacing it with his own theory of warrant. In doing this, he has found a major source of inspiration in the work of Thomas Reid. One of the insurmountable problems with classical foundationalism was its tendency, following Descartes, to cast doubt upon all beliefs, treating them as 'guilty-until-proven-innocent'. The problem with this is that doubt is like an acid, which can end up being endlessly corrosive. Everything can be doubted, including a great deal of what we normally would be inclined to accept as true, such as that I am now looking at a computer screen. Plantinga, following Reid, rejects this doubting tendency, inherent within classical foundationalism, and suggests that, as a better approach, we have an initially *accepting* attitude to the beliefs we form, that we trust our cognitive faculties that they in general *do* deliver true beliefs, being aware that we can be mistaken, but not letting this fact paralyse us in our belief forming processes.[44]

One important way in which Plantinga has attempted to rescue commonsensical beliefs from the ravages of classical foundationalist doubt is by dramatically increasing the number of basic beliefs. Classical foundationalism had severely restricted these beliefs to beliefs which are self-evident or incorrigible. Plantinga adds to these memory beliefs, beliefs about other people and the self, beliefs formed on the basis of testimony, and perceptual beliefs.

Plantinga also develops a new theory about how beliefs come to qualify as knowledge, or, in his terms, how they come to have warrant. He rejects internalist accounts of knowledge, at least as a complete answer to the question of what constitutes knowledge,[45] and suggests, as a replacement, a predominantly externalist answer.[46] Armed with this understanding, Plantinga systematically explores the various segments of our epistemic 'design plan';[47] considering knowledge of self, memory, knowledge of other people, testimonial knowledge, perception, *a priori* knowledge, and knowledge acquired inductively.

The outstanding result of Plantinga's exploration is that a great many of the beliefs that could not be secured by classical foundationalism, or which were considered second or third class citizens of the epistemic kingdom, are

---

also be believed on the evidential basis of experiential beliefs without loss of epistemic justification.
44 See, for example, *WPF*, 39.
45 Plantinga does retain an internalist element in this theory. The strength with which a belief is held plays a role in determining whether a belief can be described as knowledge. Plantinga puts it this way, in *WPF*: 'When my faculties are functioning properly, a belief has warrant to the degree that I find myself inclined to accept it; and this ... will be the degree to which I do accept it,' 9.
46 Externalist theories of justification state that a person's belief can be justified even if some or all of the justifying factors for that belief are not cognitively accessible to that person, they are external to his cognitive perspective.
47 In *WPF*.

confidently accepted as respectable candidates for knowledge. Knowledge of self can now be regarded as knowledge. Memory beliefs are accepted as basic, in many cases as properly basic. Belief in other persons can happily constitute knowledge, the torturous need for argument having been removed. Testimony, 'the source of an enormously large proportion of our most important beliefs',[48] is, Plantinga believes, typically believed in a basic way, this belief frequently having sufficient warrant for knowledge. Perceptual beliefs are similarly accepted as properly basic, so long as they are 'produced by cognitive faculties successfully aimed at truth in an epistemic environment that is right for a creature of perceptual powers'.[49] Inductive beliefs are not denigrated as inferior to *a priori* knowledge. They have their own important role to play within the human cognitive design plan.

Mistakes certainly occur. We do, at times, claim knowledge, but are in error. But even this fact which has played so significant a role in the Cartesian tradition of methodical doubt, need not dampen the sort of epistemic confidence Plantinga's theory generates. We have available to us, as rational human beings, an effective defeater system[50] allowing us to correct and assess our beliefs. Our memories can deceive us, our perceptual powers can fail us, and the testimony of others can mislead us. However, from a very young age, we begin to learn ways of assessing our memories, our perceptions and the testimony of others to gauge their reliability when in doubt.

All of this, along with Plantinga's fundamental Christian assumption that God has created us with generally reliable belief-producing faculties, provides ample reason, at least from a theistic perspective, to significantly extend the borders of knowledge beyond where classical foundationalism would comfortably allow.[51] Plantinga, as a Christian, therefore believes that he can have justifiable confidence in a great many of the knowledge claims he and others make. His theory, along with the assumptions that underlie it, allows for such confidence.

Herein lies a potential problem with my suggestion that Plantinga's epistemology be pressed into the service of evidentialist apologetics. It is the problem of how an epistemological theory which depends, as Plantinga's does, upon the theistic assumption of cognitive reliability[52] can be used to commend the truth of theism, and of Christianity in particular. A perceptive critic, someone who is unwilling to accept that our belief forming faculties are reliable, could draw attention to the dependence of our evidentialist style

---

48 *WPF*, 77.
49 *WPF*, 80.
50 See, for a brief but relevant discussion, *WPF*, 41, 42.
51 Bruce Langtry notes that most classical foundationalists have tried hard, if unsuccessfully, to accommodate memory and testimony. What Plantinga's theory does is to succeed where classical foundationalism has failed.
52 Our cognitive equipment is reliable because God has designed it that way.

apology upon the assumption that God exists and has made us in a particular way. All she would need to say is, 'I cannot, as a non-theist, accept your theory. Therefore your arguments, which are so theory dependent, do not persuade me, nor should you expect them to. You have assumed God to prove God!'

This does present a problem. Plantinga has suggested a plausible and promising alternative to classical foundationalism and to the associated internalist theory of justification. However, his replacement theory is decidedly theistic in its assumptions. From Plantinga's perspective, this is not a weakness. His intention, all along, has been to understand epistemology from a Christian perspective, which he happens to think is true. The problem arises when the theory is commended to a non-theistic philosophical world,[53] and also when implications that follow from it are pressed into the service of apologetics. A non-theistic philosopher will be disinclined to accept a theory which relies so heavily on theistic assumptions. An unbelieving sceptic will likewise be reluctant to accept arguments which depend in some way for their cogency upon a theistic epistemological theory.

The problem is not insurmountable. Most of the non-theists an apologist is likely to encounter will be inclined to accept what could be referred to as the penultimate assumption of Plantinga's epistemology: that our belief forming faculties are, more often than not, reliable. Incurable sceptics aside, most people will operate (in practice, if not in theory) with a version of Thomas Reid's common sense realism. They will be inclined to accept as knowledge the varieties of basic beliefs Plantinga argues *can* be so accepted, such as that they are looking at a computer screen, or that they had breakfast that morning. One could, of course, argue that such acceptance needs to be predicated upon theism, Plantinga's *ultimate* assumption.[54] That may be so. Nevertheless, from an apologetic point of view, the acceptance of this ultimate assumption is not necessary for apologetic dialogue and persuasion to occur. It may even be the case that the person being persuaded has theistic-independent reasons for accepting the reliability and knowledge producing character of much of her cognitive apparatus. Such a conviction may even have been forged (or fortified) in reaction to Plantinga's evolutionary argument against naturalism. In such a case, the apologist will again have significant common ground from which to mount an apologetic case.

---

53 Not that Plantinga set out to do this. He was, in the first instance, mostly concerned to develop an understanding of epistemology from a Christian perspective. However, Plantinga does see that his theory of proper function may well be the best way of understanding knowledge, regardless of one's perspectives, and that this fact may in some small way constitute an argument in favour of the truth of theism.

54 And, as we have seen, Plantinga argues this way in his evolutionary argument against naturalism.

To conclude this third point, what are the implications for evidentialist apologetics that follow from Plantinga's articulated epistemological theory? The major implication (mentioned earlier, but without elaboration) is that a number of types of belief that had been banished (by some at least) to the fringes of epistemic respectability under the influence of classical foundationalism, can now be utilised by the apologist with renewed confidence. The apologist has available an epistemology which allows due weight to be given to a number of sources of belief important to the writers of the New Testament, including, in particular, memory beliefs, testimonial beliefs and inductive beliefs. The relevance of this to apology will be shown more fully in chapters eight and nine.

To conclude and sum up this chapter, the charge against Plantinga that he has done little to contribute to the cause of positive apology is unwarranted for three major reasons. First, Plantinga, in developing his theory, was not intending, at least initially, to aid the cause of positive apology. He had other admirable purposes in mind, chiefly to explore the phenomenology of Christian belief formation. Second, Plantinga, despite some possible early ambivalence, has clearly expressed his support for the enterprise of positive apologetics. Third, his epistemology is pregnant with many promising implications for positive apologetics, particularly in areas where Plantinga has not (as yet) ventured, such as commendation of the Christian gospel as true. That some of these implications have not been worked through is, as will be seen, a legitimate source of disappointment. However, to say that Plantinga has done little to aid the cause of positive apologetics is to make an unwarranted overstatement.

In the next two chapters, I will attempt a brief critique of certain key aspects of Plantinga's theory of theistic and Christian belief formation, and will also suggest a number of promising modifications.

CHAPTER 7

Plantinga's Theory of Theistic Belief Formation: A Critique

In this and the following chapter, a modest critique of Plantinga's evolving theory of properly basic theistic and Christian beliefs will be mounted. This chapter will target a number of areas where I am significantly at odds with Plantinga, or where I remain unconvinced of Plantinga's theories.

Over the years, and culminating in his recently published *WCB*, Plantinga has suggested that human beings typically, justifiably, and frequently with sufficient warrant for belief to become knowledge, form and hold,[1] in a basic way, the belief that God exists, and that the Christian gospel is true. Involved here are two claims. The first is that belief in God can be, and mostly is, formed and held in a properly (or justifiably and warrantably) basic way. The second is that belief in the Christian gospel can be, and mostly is formed and held in this way. In this chapter, I will consider the first of these claims, and, in the following chapter, the second.

Plantinga's claim that belief in God can be, and mostly is, formed and held in a properly basic way can be broken down into a number of simpler claims, including the following:

(i)   there is such a thing as basic theistic belief
(ii) theistic belief is typically formed and held in a basic way
(iii) theistic belief so formed is properly basic

The focus of this chapter will be on the second of these two claims, although some attention will be given, mostly incidentally, to (i) and (iii). All are important in Plantinga's case for the rationality and/or warrantedness of theistic belief.

---

1   Plantinga does not typically include a reference to 'holding' basic theistic and Christian belief. However, this does accurately reflect Plantinga's position. Plantinga holds that theistic and Christian belief typically remains basic, once formed, even while under pressure from potential defeaters. The experiential triggers which provide grounding for such beliefs are, in his opinion, on-goingly adequate. See, for example, 'Reason and Belief in God', 84, 85; *WCB*, 175.

7.1 Possible Instances of Basic Theistic Belief

One possible source of support for the truth of (i) and (ii), which Plantinga himself does not pursue, lies in the fact that belief in God often, perhaps most often, arises as a result of the testimony of others. People believe that God exists (in part at least) because someone, most often a parent, tells them so. In Plantinga's opinion, testimonial beliefs are typically basic.[2] If this is correct, and if what is typical for testimonial beliefs is also typical for theistic belief formed testimonially, then not only can we say that there is such a thing as basic theistic belief, we can also very plausibly suggest that theistic belief is normally formed in a basic way. This is due to the high probability that most of the people who have ever come to believe in God have done so because of the testimony of their parents and/or other significant adults.

A problem with this suggestion is that a good case can be made for the conclusion that testimonial beliefs are not typically basic. When we accept the testimony of anyone, on any matter, a whole host of other beliefs that we have are likely to influence our acceptance (or otherwise) of that testimony, so much so that they can reasonably be construed as being the basis of our acceptance. The perceived reliability (or unreliability, or presumed reliability) of the testifier, the plausibility of the testimony (measured against background beliefs), as well as the perceived reliability of the testimonial convention, will all have a bearing (albeit often unconsciously) on whether a testimony is accepted, and on the strength of this acceptance.

Suppose we concede, however, that testimonial beliefs, including theistic belief formed testimonially, can be basic. This concession, although it allows for the possibility of basic theistic belief, goes no great distance in the direction of Plantinga's contention that belief in God is typically formed and held in a basic way. Take, for example, the case of a very young child who accepts without question the testimony of a parent that God exists. It is at least conceivable that this child's resulting belief in God is not based (even subconsciously) on still further beliefs. However, very young children grow up. They quickly become discerning and critical.[3] Their other beliefs become increasingly and inevitably influential in their acceptance of testimony, with the result that a description of those beliefs as basic becomes increasingly problematic. Moreover, testimonial beliefs such as that God exists are likely to be challenged. What typically happens in such a case is that arguments and evidence become especially or manifestly important, so much so that even if a testimonial belief begins its life as basic, which we have conceded may

---

2 *WPF*, 77-80.
3 Very possibly earlier than we think, casting doubt on the possibility that their belief in testimony is ever basic.

happen,[4] it will have become non-basic in the process of critical investigation.[5]

If Plantinga's only reason for holding that belief in God is typically formed and held in a basic way were that belief in God is typically formed solely on the basis of testimony, then he would face an objection: theistic belief, if formed solely on the basis of testimony, quickly becomes (if it is not already) non-basic under pressure from the inevitable challenges facing theistic belief, certainly within contemporary Western culture.

Plantinga's contention that belief in God is typically formed and held in a basic way is not, however, dependent upon testimony as the sole belief forming mechanism. If it were, questions would quickly and inevitably arise about the justification or warrant belief in God has at the beginning of any particular testimonial chain. Belief in God at some point needs to be grounded in a non-testimonial source of belief. Testimony, as Plantinga points out, 'is ordinarily parasitic on other sources of belief so far as warrant goes.'[6]

Plantinga, in fact, does believe that there is another source or cause of basic theistic belief. This he identifies as the *sensus divinitatis*, which, as discussed in chapter four, is believed to be responsible for the production and maintenance of basic theistic beliefs. Plantinga believes that human beings have within them a God-implanted tendency to form theistic belief. This tendency is realised, most typically, in a spontaneous, non-inferential way in situations such as: beholding the starry heavens, the splendid majesty of the mountains, or the intricate, articulate beauty of a tiny flower.[7]

It is here that we arrive at the controversial heart of Plantinga's theory of properly basic theistic belief. By way of initial support for Plantinga, it does seem the case that people do form the belief, or, perhaps, more often, are re-affirmed in their belief that God exists in the sorts of circumstances he mentions. The beauty and order of nature often do have an immediate impact, and very often there is a spontaneity about a person's believing response. However, it is my contention that this process is best construed in inferential rather than non-inferential terms. Plantinga's description of the phenomenology

---

4   Robert Audi, in *Epistemology: A Contemporary Introduction to the Theory of Knowledge* (London: Routlege, 1998), 130-135, gives a credible defence of a non-inferential model of testimonial belief. For some contrary views, see Jonathan E. Adler, 'Testimony, Trust, Knowing', *The Journal of Philosophy*, Vol. 91, No. 5 (May, 1994), 264-275; Elizabeth Fricker, 'The Epistemology of Testimony', *Proceedings of the Aristotelian Society*, Supp. Vol. 61 (1987), 57-83; 'Against Gullibility', in B. Matilal and A. Chakrabarti, (eds), *Knowing With Words* (Dordrecht: Kluwer, 1994), 125-61; 'Telling and Trusting: Reductionism and Anti-Reductionism in the Epistemology of Testimony', *Mind*, Vol. 104, No. 414 (April 1995), 393-411.
5   This point will be developed further in chapter eight.
6   *WPF*, 87.
7   'The Reformed Objection to Natural Theology', 52.

of theistic belief formation is unconvincing. In order to demonstrate this, a number of frequently cited examples used by Plantinga to describe how belief in God is typically formed (including the examples mentioned above), will be considered.

7.2 Beholding the Starry Heavens

Plantinga argues that when people, 'upon beholding the starry heavens, or the splendid majesty of the mountains, or the intricate, articulate beauty of a tiny flower', form the belief that God is the creator of these, they are not doing so because of the existence of an implicit argument, such as a version of the teleological argument. I think that Plantinga is simply wrong here. Some version of the teleological argument *is* in the background to the thinking of most people.

A conscious process of thought may not always be involved. However, there is good reason to believe that an inferential process is usually or typically involved. The term inferential process is being used here to refer to a number of possible ways in which one belief is formed on the basis of other beliefs. For a belief to be based on other beliefs, something like the following condition must be met:

> Belief A is held on the basis of belief (or evidence) B, if and only if B not only causes, or forms part of the cause of A, but is a reason, or part of a person's reason, for A.[8]

The most obvious example of an inferential process is when a conclusion is arrived at on the basis of one or more beliefs which serve as premises in an argument which is deliberately and consciously elucidated. However, inferences can occur less deliberately, and at a more unconscious level. Robert Audi introduces an important distinction here, between episodically inferential beliefs and structurally inferential beliefs. *Episodically inferential beliefs* are those which arise 'from a process or episode of inferring, of explicitly drawing a conclusion from something one believes.'[9] *Structurally inferential beliefs* are beliefs which are *based* on still other beliefs, but which do not arise as a result of a conscious reasoning process.[10] Beliefs are identified as inferential if and

---

8   For this formulation, I am indebted to Dr. Bruce Langtry.
9   *Epistemology*, 155.
10 Audi gives the example of hearing a vehicle backfire, and because of familiarity with such occurrences, the belief is formed that a car has driven by. The belief that the car has driven by depends upon the belief that a car has backfired, but because of familiarity with backfires, no reasoning process of constructing premises and drawing out conclusions needs to be entered into. The belief is formed automatically and immediately. Audi argues that in the case of episodically inferential beliefs and structurally inferential beliefs 'there is an inferential structure (which is no doubt

when they are based, either consciously or unconsciously, upon other beliefs. In Stephen Wykstra's words, they are thus held 'on the basis of something that has a propositionally-codifiable information content.'[11] They can, therefore, at least to some extent, be made explicit.[12]

Thinking in terms of the scenarios mentioned by Plantinga, let us imagine that someone on a trip to the country spends a day and a night on a mountain. As he climbs it, he discovers the most intricate and articulate of mountain flowers, of such beauty that they take his breath away. On reaching the summit, he is again speechless in wonder as he surveys the majestic grandeur of the surrounding mountains. That night he is again awestruck as, from his lofty perch, he gazes into the star-studded panorama of the night sky overhead. It is easy to imagine such a person either coming to believe in God, or feeling reaffirmed in that belief as a natural conclusion from such an experience. The word 'conclusion' is deliberately chosen. Plausibly, the person has arrived at a conclusion, implying the existence of an argument (either implicit or explicit, either conscious or unconscious). That there is an argument in the vicinity is evidenced by the fact that, if questioned, awestruck mountain climbers are likely to be able to articulate a reason for their exclamation, thus fulfilling Wystra's condition of propositional codifiability.[13] The experience of mountain climbers

---

reflected in the brain) corresponding to my beliefs: I believe the conclusion *because* I believe the premise(s), even though the beliefs are related by an inferential episode in one case and by an automatic process of belief formation in the other. In the first case, I do something - I infer a conclusion. In the second, something *happens* in me - a belief arises on the basis of one or more other beliefs I hold,' *Epistemology: A Contemporary Introduction*, 156. See also, R. Audi, *The Structure of Justification* (New York: Cambridge University Press, 1993), 237-239.

11 Stephen J. Wykstra, 'Externalism, Proper Inferentially and Sensible Evidentialism', *Topoi*, Vol. 14 (1995), 117.

12 Wykstra notes that the basis for various judgements which can be thought of as inferential is not always completely specifiable. Various of the beliefs and principles that inform our judgement are likely to be tacit and not easily recoverable, 'Externalism', 117, 118.

13 This, in itself, does not prove that an inferential process was initially involved. As Plantinga, perhaps with this sort of situation in mind, puts it: 'even if I believe something in the basic way, it doesn't follow that I couldn't cite various other propositions in response to your question "Why do you believe *p*? What is your reason for believing *p*? ' 'Reason and Belief in God', 51; *WCB*, 176, fn. 11. However, the ease with which people can articulate a reasoning process is at least suggestive that such a process was initially involved. They readily observe a connection between their belief in God and the wonders and marvels of nature. Even if the connection between these is automatically perceived, as is characteristic of structurally inferential beliefs, there still remains a relationship of dependence between the beliefs which can easily be articulated.

can, I think, easily be generalised to other wonder evoking experiences, such as the birth of a child.[14]

In situations like this, where people have articulated similar expressions of belief, it is not unnatural to ask, 'Why did you just say, "There must be a God!"?' In my experience, people naturally and easily reply with a variation on the following: 'Beauty like this, or wonderful experiences like these, give credence to the idea that there is a God, someone able to create marvellous things like this.' In other words, these experiences are considered as evidence that God exists.[15] Generally, this appears to be the process of thinking. Otherwise, it is difficult to identify the nature of the connection between the experience of seeing something wonderful and the resulting exclamation of belief. Plantinga certainly does not help us here. The most he does by way of describing how the connection works is to suggest that experiences such as these 'trigger' the operation of the *sensus divinitatis*.[16] The exact nature of the connection is never spelled out. That there is a connection is clear. Moreover, the belief evoking situations mentioned by Plantinga are of a particular kind. For example, beauty (both intricate and grand) clearly plays some role in the process, as shown by Plantinga's description of the 'splendid majesty of the mountains [and] the intricate, articulate beauty of a tiny flower.' My question is: What exactly is it about this beauty which evokes belief?[17]

Plantinga seeks to avoid any process of inferential reasoning. However this seems strange, even forced. It is a simple and psychologically understandable step to move by way of inference from the beauty and grandeur of nature to a beauty-producing creator.[18] Plantinga's own wording even suggests such a movement of thought. In WCB, Plantinga elaborates on a number of his belief forming scenarios in these terms:

---

14 Not being a mountain climber myself puts me at some disadvantage to Alvin Plantinga, who is a mountain climber. However, I have had experience in the area of (witnessed) child birth!
15 Plantinga, I think, comes close to suggesting a similar line of thought in his article 'Dennett's Dangerous Idea', where he describes the experience of many people who, despite accepting Darwinian evolution in broad outline, find themselves unable, in the face of life's complexity, to resist the idea that God is needed to fully explain it, 17.
16 *WCB*, 176.
17 For a similar development of this point, see Laura L. Garcia, 'Natural Theology and the Reformed Objection', in C. Stephen Evans and Merold Westphal, (eds), *Christian Perspectives on Religious Knowledge* (Grand Rapids: Eerdmans, 1993), 118.
18 As Garcia points out, the 'inference involved need not be particularly elaborate and may even be in large part implicit.' It is, nevertheless, an argument, in her words, 'a movement of the intellect from evidence to conclusion,' 'Natural Theology and the Reformed Objection', 118, 119.

You see the blazing glory of the heavens from a mountainside at 13,000 feet; you think about those unimaginable distances; you find yourself filled with awe and wonder, and you form the belief that God must indeed be great to have created this magnificent heavenly host.[19]

This sounds so very close to a simple version of the teleological argument. The beauty and great expanse of the heavens is observed and reflected on, and a simple conclusion is reached, 'that God must indeed be great to have created this magnificent heavenly host.' The wording suggests that the person already believes in God, and is simply drawing a conclusion about what this God must be like. However, the drawing of an inference is still involved. Moreover, an inference such as this could easily be drawn by someone in the process of coming to believe. Such a person observes and marvels at nature's beauty, and then concludes that God (understood as someone of great power and wisdom) must have been responsible for it.

Plantinga resists such an inferential understanding. One reason he gives for such resistance is that if belief in God is formed inferentially, any such argument would be 'ridiculously weak':

It isn't that one beholds the night sky, notes that it is grand, and concludes that there must be such a person as God: an argument like that would be ridiculously weak.[20]

Perhaps the argument so stated is ridiculously weak. However, when people form the belief that God exists in the circumstances Plantinga envisages, the situation is often much more complicated. The grandeur of the night sky is likely to be merely one example of a host of observed (or remembered) natural 'wonders', such as Plantinga himself describes.[21] The cumulative effect of such beauty and grandeur (along with, perhaps, a host of other supportive considerations[22]) is to make quite reasonable the conclusion that 'there must be

---

19 *WCB*, 173.
20 *WCB*, 175.
21 Plantinga continues, after the passage, to describe 'the marvellous, impressive beauty of the night sky; the timeless crash and roar of the surf that resonates deep within us; the majestic grandeur of the mountains (the North Cascades, say, as viewed from Whatcom Pass); the ancient brooding presence of the Australian outback; the thunder of a great waterfall. But it isn't only grandeur and majesty that counts; [Calvin] would say the same about the subtle play of sunlight on a field in spring, or the dainty, articulate beauty of a tiny flower, or aspen leaves shimmering and dancing in the breeze..' *WCB*, 174.
22 Gary Gutting, in *Religious Belief and Religious Skepticism* (Notre Dame: University of Notre Dame Press, 1982), draws attention to multidimensional approaches to the justification of beliefs such as that God exists. Rather than depending on single arguments with clearly contained and exhaustively formulable sets of premises, multidimensional approaches seek to marshal and take account of

such a person as God.'[23] Although the specific argument to this conclusion may be a simple one, lacking conclusive weight on its own, it does not follow that the evidence upon which it is based is not good evidence, which can be supplemented and refined to produce a good teleological argument. Significantly, Plantinga considers the teleological argument to be the best of the natural theological arguments, and includes it as one of his '2 dozen (or so) good theistic arguments', which he thinks are worthy of detailed and loving development.[24]

Plantinga tries too hard to dismiss or depreciate the presence and importance of inferences. Although there are understandable reasons, given Plantinga's heritage, for his wanting to avoid resting belief upon a simple (or even a complex) teleological argument, thus taking him down the natural theology path, such an outcome has become increasingly less problematic for Plantinga given the direction of his thinking, as discussed in chapter six. Plantinga has become increasingly comfortable with natural theology. However, despite this, he continues to resist the idea that arguments (such as a teleological argument) may play an important role in the genesis of theistic belief.

To continue this critique, Plantinga's account appears to lack the sorts of reasoning controls inherent to the inferential model. Plantinga leaves unexplained the movement of thought from the beauty of nature to a beauty-producing God. In the inferential model, such movement is explained (and constrained) by the nature of the inference. One can readily and understandably move from observed beauty to a beauty-producing God. That is as far as one *can* go by way of inference, in the absence of additional information. Such an apparent control does not exist in Plantinga's model. Plantinga has stated that the outcome of properly basic theistic belief formation is belief in 'God as conceived in traditional Christianity, Judaism, and Islam: an almighty, all-knowing wholly good and loving person who has created the world and

---

'a large, diverse, and indefinitely extendible body of data, pointing as a whole to its conclusion,' 110. This way of seeing things is a promising way of understanding how people, under impact from particular evidence, come to conclusions which often appear to go beyond that evidence (narrowly considered). In chapter eight, a model for understanding how this process works with respect to Christian belief will be suggested.

23 Whether any particular mountain climber would be justified in drawing the conclusion that God exists in the sorts of circumstances Plantinga envisages would depend on a number of things, including the strength of the collaboratory evidence contributing (in his case) to the formation of this belief.

24 '2 Dozen (or so) good theistic arguments'. Plantinga defends a probabilistic form of the teleological argument in 'Dennett's Dangerous Idea', 17, 18. For further discussion by Plantinga of the teleological argument, see chapter five of *God and Other Minds*; and 'Arguments for the Existence of God', in *Routledge Encyclopedia*, Vol. 4, 89-91.

presently upholds it in being.'[25] It appears that Plantinga believes that an observation of nature is sufficient, by itself, to produce such detailed beliefs.[26] I have two problems with this: first, the exact mechanism by which such complicated beliefs are delivered is difficult to identify or imagine; second, Romans 1, an influential text in Reformed thinking, suggests that only a very limited number of beliefs about God can be known through the created order, that is: his god-ness, his power, and his distaste for evil.[27] God's kindness and providence could be added to this list by making reference to a number of Paul's recorded speeches in the Book of Acts.[28] Plausibly, each of these beliefs is a fair and understandable inference from observable aspects of the physical world.

7.3 Other Suggested Examples of Basic Theistic Belief Formation

Plantinga mentions a number of other circumstances in which belief in God is formed, some of which correspond to the beliefs referred to in Romans and Acts. A consideration of these will help to sharpen points already raised, as well as introducing a number of other major problems with Plantinga's theory. According to Plantinga, apart from an observation of the beauty and grandeur of nature, there are a number of other ways that properly basic belief in God can arise. In his words:

> Upon reading the Bible, one may be impressed with a deep sense that God is speaking to him. Upon having done what I know is cheap, or wrong, or wicked, I may feel guilty in God's sight and form the belief *God disapproves of what I have done*. Upon confession and repentance I may feel forgiven, forming the belief *God forgives me for what I have done*. A person in grave danger may turn to God, asking for his protection and help; and of course he or she then has the belief that God is indeed able to hear and help if he sees fit. When life is sweet and satisfying, a spontaneous sense of gratitude may well up within the soul; someone in this condition may thank and praise the Lord for his goodness, and will of course have the accompanying belief that indeed the Lord is to be thanked and praised.

---

25 'Reformed Epistemology', in Quinn and Taliaferro, 385.
26 Plantinga does believe that the deliverances of the *sensus divinitatis* are specific. In *WCB*, Plantinga makes the claim that a person with a properly functioning *sensus divinitatis* will have 'an intimate, detailed, vivid, and explicit knowledge of God,' 485.
27 Romans 1:20 says, 'The invisible things of God are seen through the things that have been made. These are his power and god-ness (dunami" kai qeiovth"). The word qeiovth" occurs in the New Testament only here, and is a general word for deity. This implies that what can be inferred (or spontaneously believed) from nature is quite limited. Paul includes in this context two general truths: that a powerful deity exists, and that this deity is displeased by immorality.
28 Acts 14:14-18; Acts 17:24-31.

> There are therefore many conditions and circumstances that call forth belief in God: guilt, gratitude, danger, a sense of God's presence, a sense that he speaks, perception of various parts of the universe.[29]

These examples are puzzling. As a first reaction, it strikes me that each of these beliefs is predicated on the belief (or perhaps suspicion) that a particular God exists, and that they would not have been formed in the absence of such belief. If so, it is difficult to see how they can be taken to represent part of the experiential foundations of theistic belief. Further, it is far from clear that all, or even any, of these beliefs are best understood as basic. Even if they can be so understood, other beliefs are still likely to be of crucial importance both in the formation of these beliefs and in any determination of whether they are justified or warranted. For purposes of analysis, it will be helpful to set out and number the beliefs mentioned above. These are:

(1) The belief that God is speaking to me, formed while reading the Bible.[30]

(2) The belief that God disapproves of what I have done, formed when I have done something I know to be cheap, wrong or wicked.

(3) The belief that God forgives me, formed upon confession and repentance.

(4) The belief that God is able to protect me, formed in a situation of grave danger.

(5) The belief that God is to be thanked and praised, formed when life is sweet and satisfying.

Beliefs (3) and (4) are, more so than the other examples, unlikely to be formed in the absence of already existent theistic belief. It is therefore hard to see how they provide any degree of independent warrant for the idea that God exists. Certain beliefs, including the belief that God exists, appear to be assumed, or need to be assumed, for these beliefs to even come into being.

This can be demonstrated with respect to the belief that God forgives me. There are times that I have the feeling that God forgives me in situations like the one outlined by Plantinga. It is a wonderful feeling, but the reason for its assuring strength lies in the already existing belief that God exists and is a merciful and forgiving God. It is hard to imagine someone without such beliefs coming to believe that God forgives them, on confession of sin and repentance.

---

29 'Reason and Belief in God', 80, 81.
30 I have slightly re-worded Plantinga's examples to make them more personal.

At least some level of belief or suspicion[31] would appear to be necessary. The same applies with respect to God's ability to protect. In situations of extreme danger, I am only likely to be comforted with the knowledge of God's ability to protect if I already believe that he exists and is the sort of God who is able and willing to protect. Plantinga appears to suggest that these beliefs can be formed in the very act of requesting help.[32] This is possible, although it is more likely that extreme danger simply brings to the surface an already existing belief, suspicion, or desperate hope!

With respect to the relationship between the assumed beliefs and beliefs (3) and (4), the relationship is most naturally conceived of as a relationship of inferential support. The assumed beliefs constitute reasons to believe (3) and (4), and on occasion may even be explicitly articulated in such terms:

God exists.

God is a forgiving God, forgiving those who (genuinely) ask him to forgive them.

I have (genuinely) asked God to forgive me.

Therefore, God forgives me.

Or

God has promised protection to those who love and obey him.

I love and obey God.

Therefore, he will protect me.

However, even when such a conscious articulation does not occur, it is still likely (or, at least, a most credible way of construing the situation) that an inferential process is involved; that the beliefs are, in Audi's terms, structurally inferential, and therefore non-basic. They are based on, and arise because of still further beliefs, with these beliefs being able to be construed as reasons for belief. That this is the case is suggested by the fact that if someone is challenged to explain why they believe that God has forgiven them, or why he will protect them, they, very often and naturally, will reply in terms of the

---

31 It is, I suppose, possible for someone to suspect that God might exist, and, on confession of sin to this possible God, feel such relief that suspicion graduates to belief. However, serious questions would be raised about the warrantedness of such belief, and therefore about its significance as experiential grounding for theistic belief.

32 As is suggested by his wording: 'A person in grave danger may turn to God, asking for his protection and help; and of course he or she then has the belief that God is indeed able to hear and help if he sees fit,' 'Reason and Belief in God', 80.

above premises. They are not likely to reply in terms of some experience which has occasioned their belief. Inferences do appear to be involved as essential to, or, at the very least, normally operating in the formation of (3) and (4).

The remaining three examples, (1), (2) and (5), are more complicated. They too appear, on a first reading, to assume belief in the existence of God and to provide no additional warrant for such belief. The extent to which the beliefs have warrant, if this is so, will be the extent to which belief in God, previously gained, has warrant. However, these examples could be construed slightly differently, and a case made that the experiences involved provide independent grounds for the belief that God exists. We will consider each in turn.

In the case of reading the Bible, and having a deep sense of being addressed by God, this experience could conceivably add weight to a person's conviction that God exists. It could even result in a non-theist becoming a theist. In various parts of the Bible, God does address the reader, and, even where he does not, the message often has such profound relevance that any person reading it could feel that God was speaking to them.

In the case of a person feeling guilty and, as a result, forming the belief that God disapproves of what they have done, this too could add weight to their conviction that God exists. It is, however, not quite so easy to understand how. One would think that a person would need to believe in God in the first place to think this way, and that this priorly existing belief more than adequately accounts for the belief that God disapproves of these instances of immorality. However, it is conceivable that the experience of doing wrong may make a person experientially aware of an unyielding moral dimension to existence which they identify with God, and that this experience may therefore provide additional grounds for belief that God exists.

In the case of the person who, in times of sweetness and satisfaction, forms the belief that God is to be thanked and praised, this too may provide independent support for the proposition that God exists. One can imagine even a non-theist being so overwhelmed by the sweetness of life that they cease to be a non-theist. This example, like the previous two, can therefore be understood to involve an independent grounding for the belief that God exists.

The problem, however, with these examples, even if construed in this way, is two-fold. First, (5) and (2) are better understood as non-basic, and, second, even if we accept that (1) is, or can be, basic, this does not entirely remove the need for inferentially based warrant. I will seek to justify these two contentions by looking at examples (1), (2) and (5) in inverse order.

In the case of the person who forms the belief that God is to be praised and thanked during times of sweetness and satisfaction, it is my belief that simple inferences are normally drawn in such cases. This example is similar to the earlier example of belief in God formed in the face of nature's beauty and order. It raises exactly the same question about the nature of the connection between sweetness and satisfaction and a God worthy of thanks and praise. The most natural explanation for the way in which this connection normally works is that the person *concludes* that this sweetness and satisfaction is the result of the handiwork of God, or, in the case of the converting atheist, *must be* the handiwork of a being with the ability to create such sweetness of life, which is then identified with God. Plantinga's example possibly draws on a passage from Acts 14 which it will be helpful to quote:

> In the past [God] let all nations go their own way. Yet he has not left himself without testimony: he has shown kindness by giving you rain from heaven and crops in their seasons; he provides you with plenty of food and fills your hearts with joy, (verses 16,17).

At issue between Plantinga and myself is the issue of how this testimony is intended to be received by human beings. Is it a matter of people drawing appropriate inferences, such as that the sweetness and fecundity of life is evidence of God's existence or care, or does the belief arise non-inferentially? I think the former. Although the drawing of inferences may not be done consciously, and therefore the resulting beliefs will be *structurally* rather than *episodically inferential*, they are, nevertheless, inferential. The one belief is based upon the other.

Example (2) is slightly different to the previous example. When a person feels guilty for having done something cheap, wrong, or wicked, it is conceivable that this experience will trigger an awareness of a disapproving God. The actual mechanism is not difficult to imagine. As we grow up, we are often aware when we do wrong of the disapproving presence of parents. We easily imagine them watching us, or catching us out in the act of some misdemeanour. Similarly, especially if we already believe in God and have been schooled in the Christian belief that God is all-knowing and disapproving of evil, we are likely to have a similar feeling of God's watching disapproval. Even someone not schooled in Christian belief could feel this way. As stated earlier, it could be that the person, through her experience of guilt, becomes experientially aware of an unyielding moral dimension to existence which she identifies with God (the Christian God, if she lives in the West). As to the status of the belief that God disapproves of one's actions, inferences are again likely to be involved. Various beliefs about God and about the wrongfulness of actions are the basis for the belief that God disapproves of a particular action. In the case of the person who, in an act of evil, intuits the existence of an unyielding moral order, which she then identifies as God, the process may happen simultaneously. However, even in this case, various of the person's beliefs and even suspicions are likely to be the basis upon which a belief in God's disapproval is formed.

Example (1) is the most complicated, and, in many ways, the most important. It is also Plantinga's best candidate for basicality. The example is of a person who, on reading the Bible, forms the belief that God is speaking to her. This is certainly conceivable. Moreover, it does seem possible that this could happen without any inferences being drawn (either consciously or unconsciously). The belief forms spontaneously and without being (at least obviously) based on still further beliefs. Let us assume, for the moment, that the belief is (or can be) basic.

7.4 Determining the Impact of Other Beliefs

An issue in any discussion of basic and non-basic beliefs is the influence or role of still further beliefs. A basic belief is one which is not accepted on the (evidential) basis of further beliefs.[33] A non-basic (or inferential) belief is one which *is* so accepted. This distinction, although it makes sense, and is able to be used productively in an analysis of human beliefs, leaves unanswered a number of interesting questions. For example, does basicality imply that there is *no* relationship of support between a basic belief and other beliefs within a person's noetic structure? This would hardly seem likely. Almost any belief one could imagine is supported by at least some of the other beliefs a person holds.[34] The belief that God is addressing one, for example, is likely to be supported by a range of other beliefs, such as that God exists, and that he speaks to people through the Scriptures. An important further question is: do these supportive beliefs have any influence in the acceptance of a basic belief? Quite clearly they do.

The existence of supportive as well as non-supportive beliefs will almost inevitably be influential in the process of basic belief formation. This influence is exerted in at least two different ways. First, beliefs already held by people have the potential to undercut or defeat a basic belief, and even to prevent it from being formed in the first place. As Plantinga himself recognises, basic beliefs, no less than non-basic beliefs, need to pass the coherence test in order to be accepted,[35] or accepted easily. In other words, they must be consistent, without contradicting what is already believed. Second, the other beliefs that a person has will contribute to the likelihood that a particular basic belief is formed and continues to exist. The more that a particular belief is supported by and fits in with a person's belief system, the more likely it is that it will exist and persist; alternatively, where the other beliefs that one has are not supportive, the chances are greater that the basic belief will be discarded or mistrusted.

---

33 'Rationality and Religious Belief', 259. In *WCB*, 83.
34 In other words, these other beliefs could legitimately be used as evidence for the belief in question. They are in fact supportive, irrespective of whether they play a role in any conscious or unconscious inferential process.
35 In discussing properly basic belief in the gospel, Plantinga suggests that such belief can even obtain 'some of its warrant from its coherence with a coherent system,' *WCB*, 267, 268. See also *WCB*, 112, 255.

Returning to example (1), if a person already believes in God they are more likely to believe that God is speaking to them. This likelihood is increased if they also accept that God is in the habit of speaking to people through the Scriptures. Conversely, if they do not believe that God characteristically speaks to people, or that God exists, they will be less likely to believe that God is speaking to them, or, at least, will call into question any experience suggestive of such. The implication of this is that other beliefs that a person has, even if they do not constitute the evidential basis of a particular belief, can nevertheless play a critically influential role in the formation of that belief.

Plantinga is willing to admit this. He even states that basic beliefs can 'depend' on what else a person knows or believes.[36] The exact nature and extent of this dependence is not explained in any detail.[37] However, Plantinga's admission, as well as what we have observed already about the influential role of other beliefs, raises a number of interesting and important questions. For example, given that the other beliefs a person has are often crucially influential in the formation of even basic beliefs, is it always possible to distinguish between a belief which is 'based' on further beliefs, and one which simply 'depends' in some way on further beliefs? Or, to ask the question in the terms of our previous discussion, when, and on what basis, can a supportive belief to be part of the evidential basis of another belief, and when not? I would suggest that the answer to this question is very often hard to find.

Audi's distinction between structurally and episodically inferential beliefs raises the interesting possibility that even though a person may not be conscious of his newly formed belief being based on further beliefs, it may be the case that it is, or even that it is *partly* so based. Plantinga himself admits that the distinction between a basic belief and one that is formed inferentially, but quickly and unconsciously, may be difficult to make,[38] which raises questions about the value or usefulness of the distinction, certainly with respect to the beliefs we have been considering in this chapter.[39] It also thereby calls into question Plantinga's claim that belief in God is normally or typically formed in a basic way. Such a claim is unlikely to be successfully proven.

---

36 *WCB*, 83.
37 Plantinga does no more than to give the example of a person needing to believe certain things about trucks to form the belief that a truck is bearing down on him.
38 *WCB*, 176.
39 By raising difficulties with the distinction between basic and non-basic beliefs, I am not thereby suggesting that the distinction is of no value, nor that foundationalism, which depends upon this distinction, is to be rejected. However, these and other difficulties do contribute to the case against foundationalism, such as is urged by coherentists. See, for example, L. Bonjour, *The Structure of Empirical Knowledge* (Cambridge: Massachusetts: Harvard University Press, 1985); K. Lehrer, *Theory of Knowledge* (Boulder, CO: Westview Press, 1990); E. Sosa, *Knowledge in Perspective* (Cambridge: Cambridge University Press, 1991).

There is a second interesting and important question which arises out of this discussion. Even if one grants that a particular belief is basic, what role, if any, do supportive beliefs play in conferring warrant upon such a belief? Consider the case of two people who, while reading Scripture, both form the basic belief that God is addressing them. One is a convinced theist at the time, the other a convinced atheist. I will first consider the case of the atheist.[40]

Let us assume, for the sake of argument, that the atheist is reasonably convinced of his atheism, and even more convinced that the Christian God does not exist. Influencing him in this latter conviction are pluralistic considerations, as well as his understanding of the outcome of historical Biblical criticism. Let us assume that he is also aware that people of other religions have similar experiences of (apparently) being addressed by God while reading their particular Scriptures. He has now had such an experience. Would such a person be warranted (or warranted to any great degree) in retaining his belief that God had spoken to him. I think not. Even if the experience was particularly vivid and convincing; even if we posit, with Plantinga, the existence of a reliable belief forming mechanism such as the inward instigation of the Holy Spirit, this person's (perhaps temporary) belief in the Christian God would still lack warrant. The fact that people of other religions have similar experiences, but which result in contradictory conclusions about which god exists, the fact that the atheist already has what he considers to be good reasons for not believing in the Christian God, give him more than enough reason to dismiss, or to seriously call into question, the experience he has just had. He would, in fact, be intellectually negligent to go on believing in the face of such good reasons. At the very least, he would be required to critically revisit his reasons for being atheistic. To the extent that he does not do this, his belief will lack warrant. His cognitive faculties could hardly be said to be working properly in such a way as to produce true beliefs if he failed to do this.[41]

What this example shows is how important other beliefs are in the determination of warrant, even for beliefs which are formed in a basic way. Given that the evidentialist challenge is essentially the challenge of showing how a particular belief lines up with other warrantably held beliefs, that

---

40 For a related discussion of the rationality of atheism or of unbelief, see Michael Czapkay Sudduth, 'Can Religious Unbelief Be Proper Function Rational?' *Faith and Philosophy*, Vol. 16, No. 3 (July, 1999), 297-314.

41 This point is very helpfully developed by Michael Czapkay Sudduth, in 'The internalist character and evidentialist implications of Plantingian defeaters', *International Journal for Philosophy of Religion*, Vol. 45, No. 3 (June, 1999), 167-189. Sudduth points out that when a particular belief is confronted with potential defeaters (as is the case with an atheist who has what he considers good reasons to be atheistic), internal rationality requires that some attempt be made to defeat those defeaters. A failure to make such an attempt will affect both internal and external rationality, and this because any negligence in fulfilling one's epistemic duties will constitute a failure of proper function, 170,171.

challenge isn't entirely side-stepped even by a true description of a belief as basic. The support, or otherwise, of other beliefs continues to have a bearing upon warrant. A lack of support, or, more seriously, the existence of (undefeated) defeaters, can rob even a basic belief of warrant.

We turn now to consider the case of a convinced theist who also has an experience of forming the belief that God is speaking to her while reading the Scriptures. Assume, again for the sake of argument, that this person believes in the Christian God, and also believes that God frequently speaks to people through the Scriptures. Her experience is therefore consistent with what is already believed. If we assume further that this person is a Reformed Christian, who is conversant with, and approving of, the epistemological works of Alvin Plantinga, then she may also believe that her experience has been generated within her as a result of the reliable operations of the Holy Spirit. She is thus likely to believe that her belief is entirely warranted, even to the point of constituting knowledge.

This is almost the exact opposite of the previous example. However, even in this case, evidentialist considerations intrude. Warrant, even if it exists, can very easily come under threat, and even evaporate, under pressure from sceptical thinking, both from within and without. Even on the assumption that it is the Holy Spirit who is reliably producing this belief, there is no guarantee of on-going warrantedness. Imagine, for example, that this person becomes aware of, and is disturbed by arguments against the existence of God, and, in particular, arguments against the existence of the Christian God. What might exacerbate this disturbance is the realisation that the readily formed belief that God was addressing her is duplicated, but with different content, in the experience of people from other religions, creating similar levels of confidence. This realisation may, in turn, suggest that a purely psychological explanation of her belief is possible. Her belief that God is speaking to her is, perhaps, more than adequately accounted for by the impact of previously existing beliefs such as her belief that God speaks through Scripture.

In the light of these disturbing thoughts, this person, like the atheist, is unlikely to continue being warranted in believing that God was addressing her. At the very least, her warrantedness in believing may well be diminished, as a function of any loss of confidence in her belief. A believer faced with diminishing confidence has a number of possible ways of reacting. She could, and arguably should, seek to undercut or defeat the potential defeaters of her belief. This could either take the form of showing that the potential defeaters are not actual defeaters, or of finding or drawing upon beliefs which support her belief that God is addressing her. Both are likely to involve a careful examination of evidence[42] and of its implications for her belief. In the event that this person is unable to defeat the defeaters or to marshal positive evidence in favour of her belief, her belief will cease to have warrant. What this second

---

42 Evidence in favour of the defeater and in favour of her belief.

illustration does is to once again highlight the fact that, even in the case of beliefs which begin, and continue their life as basic, evidentialist considerations are never far away, especially in a world where potential defeaters are numerous.[43]

To draw this extended discussion together, I have taken issue with Plantinga at a number of points. Reasonable doubt has been cast on Plantinga's claim that belief in God formed in the face of nature's beauty, order and bounty is typically basic. In the case of beliefs (3) and (4), these appear to assume belief in God, as well as a number of other beliefs, which, arguably, and in most conceivable cases, are the inferential basis for these beliefs. Beliefs (2) and (5) are also able to be understood, most naturally and most often, as non-basic. Example (1) is different in that it could plausibly be taken as basic, but even here the possibility of an alternative understanding is made real by the difficulties involved in determining basicality. The up-shot of this whole discussion is that Plantinga's claim that belief in God is mostly or typically formed and held in a basic way is seriously called into question.[44] At the very least, an alternative, inferential way of understanding the process is possible, even preferable.

What are some of the implications that arise out of this analysis? One is that Plantinga's attempt to immunise theistic belief from the potential ravages of the evidentialist challenge is significantly undermined. If theistic belief is *not* typically basic, then the question emerges as to whether the support undergirding inferentially formed theistic belief is sufficient to avoid the charge of irrationality. We are thus back to where Plantinga sought to leave. Given Plantinga's recent more positive attitude to natural theology, this may not be such a serious place to be, although questions still remain about the rationality of theistic belief in individual cases. For example, although it may be the case that a gifted natural theologian is justified and/or warranted in believing in God on the basis of arguments, what is one to say about the majority of less able believers?[45] It was questions such as this that Plantinga sought to avoid in proposing his inference independent model of theistic belief formation.

---

[43] M. Czapkay Sudduth's 'The internalist character and evidentialist implications of Plantingian defeaters', is again helpful here.

[44] It also undercuts Plantinga's claim, made in 'Is Belief in God Rational', 27, that this way of coming to belief is the way of the 'mature' believer. It is perhaps significant that in *WCB* Plantinga nowhere uses the term 'mature' to describe the person who comes to belief, or continues in belief in a properly basic way. As noted earlier, in chapter 6, Plantinga appears to have distanced himself from this particular designation.

[45] This is not an unanswerable question. One possible answer is along the lines that individuals and communities are warranted (to varying degrees) by virtue of accepting the testimony of those whose belief is more directly and adequately grounded.

Plantinga's contention that theistic belief which is basic is also typically properly basic (claim (iii) above), is also called into question by this chapter. Important to Plantinga's Calvinistic model of theistic belief formation is the contention that belief in God is normally formed in a basic way because of the operations of the *sensus divinitatis*. If, in fact, theistic belief is mostly formed in a non-basic way, then significant doubt is placed upon Plantinga's model as a whole.

More could be said by way of critique of Plantinga's theory of properly basic theistic belief. Various other aspects of Plantinga's theory have come under attack. Richard Grigg, Philip Quinn, Robert Audi, and Robert McKim,[46] for example, have focused their critiques on dissimilarities between theological beliefs and the paradigmatic set of properly basic beliefs while questioning the legitimacy of the proper basicality of religious beliefs. John Zeis notes that there are essentially two lines of attack involved here; the first is to propose a criterion for proper basicality which is shared by beliefs in the paradigmatic set but which theological beliefs lack, thereby denying them the status of proper basicality. The other strategy is to argue that if beliefs about God are properly basic for the theist, then the same ought to apply to religious beliefs held by others.[47] I am not persuaded that either of these strategies is successful. Criticisms have also come from various Roman Catholic scholars as to the involuntaristic nature of Plantinga's theory of theistic belief formation.[48] Some problems may exist in this area, but a discussion of (at least some of) these will be delayed until the next two chapters.

---

46 Richard Grigg, 'Theism and Proper Basicality: A Response to Plantinga,' *International Journal for Philosophy of Religion*s, Vol. 14 (1983), 123-127; Philip L. Quinn, 'On Finding the Foundations of Theism,' *Faith and Philosophy*, Vol. 2, No. 4 (October, 1985), 469-486; Robert Audi, 'Direct Justification, Evidential Dependence, and Theistic Belief, in Robert Audi and Wainwright, W., (eds), *Rationality, Religious Belief and Moral Commitment* (Ithaca and London: Cornell University Press, 1986), 139-166; Robert McKim, 'Theism and Proper Basicality,' *International Journal for Philosophy of Religion*, 26 (1989), 29-56.
47 John Zeis, 'Natural Theology: Reformed?' in Linda Zagzebski (ed), *Rational Faith: Catholic Responses to Reformed Epistemology*, 52. For a skilful development of this latter point, see Ross Ann Christian, 'Plantinga, Epistemic Permissiveness, and Metaphysical Pluralism', *Religious Studies*, Vol. 28 (1992), 553-573.
48 See, for example, Linda Zagzebski, 'Religious Knowledge'; and Laura L. Garcia, 'Natural Theology and the Reformed Objection', 121-122.

CHAPTER 8

Plantinga's Theory of Christian Belief Formation: A Critique

This chapter will continue to raise questions about Plantinga's account of properly basic belief, moving beyond mere theistic belief to specifically Christian beliefs. It is Plantinga's conviction that not only is belief in God typically basic, so also is belief in the distinctive and central teachings of Christianity. I have reservations about this which are similar to those expressed in the previous chapter. In the process of expressing them, an alternative model of Christian belief formation will be suggested, which, although at odds with Plantinga's position, is nevertheless consistent with his overall theory of knowledge.

Plantinga, although aware of definitional disputes, identifies *Christian* belief as that which 'is common to the great creeds of the main branches of the Christian church.'[1] Christian belief includes: belief in God; that God is a person; that he is all-knowing, all-powerful, perfectly good and wholly loving; that he created the world and that he constantly upholds and providentially guides it. These Plantinga identifies as the theistic components of Christian belief. There are also some uniquely Christian components, such as 'that we human beings are somehow mired in rebellion and sin, that we consequently require deliverance and salvation, and that God has arranged for that deliverance through the sacrificial suffering, death and resurrection of Jesus Christ, who was both a man and also the second member of the Trinity, the uniquely divine son of God.'[2] Plantinga uses the term 'Christian belief' to designate the combination of theistic and uniquely Christian components.

In terms of the process by which people come to Christian belief, Plantinga proposes a model that gives prominence to the role of the Holy Spirit. He argues that at the core of uniquely Christian beliefs, and also at the centre of the library of books which constitute the Bible, is the gospel, 'the stunning good news of the way of salvation God has graciously offered.'[3] It is the role of the Holy Spirit to bring about belief in this gospel.[4] The Holy Spirit's ministry

---

1   He goes on to describe it as that which 'unites Calvin and Aquinas, Luther and Augustine, Menno Simons and Karl Barth, Mother Teresa and St. Maximus the Confessor, Billy Graham and St. Gregory Palamas,' *WCB*, vii.
2   *WCB*, vii.
3   *WCB*, 243.
4   *WCB*, 244.

generates not only belief, but faith, which is a whole-hearted, and personalised believing response. The content of faith, according to Plantinga, is 'the whole magnificent scheme of salvation God has arranged', or, more specifically, 'the central teachings of the gospel'.[5]

Plantinga's proposed phenomenology of Christian belief formation has already been outlined in chapter four, but, to briefly re-iterate, he argues that beliefs constituting faith are typically taken as basic. They are not accepted by way of arguments from other propositions or on the evidential basis of other propositions. What typically happens instead is that we 'read Scripture, or something presenting Scriptural teaching, or hear the gospel preached, or are told of it by parents, or encounter a Scriptural teaching as the conclusion of an argument ... or in some other way encounter a proclamation of the Word,'[6] and find that it 'simply seems right, it seems compelling; one finds oneself saying, "Yes, that's right, that's the truth of the matter; this is indeed the word of the Lord."'[7] Plantinga notes that there are a thousand different ways in which the process might go, but suggests that common to all is 'a reading or hearing and a belief or conviction that what one reads or hears is true and a teaching of the Lord.'[8] Greater elaboration is required to fill out the details of Plantinga's theory of Christian belief formation, but this will be best done in the process of mounting a number of objections to the theory.

Plantinga believes that when people form the belief that the gospel is true, they typically do so not on the basis of arguments.

> A believer could reason as follows: I have strong historical and archaeological evidence for the reliability of the Bible (or the Church, or my parents, or some other authority); the Bible teaches the great things of the Gospel; so probably these things are true. A believer *could* reason in this way and perhaps some believers do in fact reason this way. But in the model it goes differently.[9]

I think Plantinga is partly right here. Over several years, I have surveyed theological students at the College where I teach, and have asked them how, when, and why they have come to believe that the gospel was true. In many, probably most cases, reasons and evidence were not cited, particularly in the case of people who were brought up in Christian homes. One, typical response reads: 'The gospel has always been a part of the air that I breathed.' Many cited an inner conviction of the gospel's truth, its 'just seeming right'. These responses fit well with Plantinga's description. Plantinga is also right to assert, or imply, that for many people belief in the gospel does not arise as a result of

---

5   *WCB*, 248.
6   *WCB*, 250.
7   *WCB*, 250.
8   *WCB*, 251.
9   *WCB*, 250.

a deliberate and conscious reasoning process such as outlined in the above quotation. However, none of this implies either the absence or the unimportance of arguments, or, more broadly, of inferences, in the belief forming process.

The following argument will seek to demonstrate that inferences are both present and important in the process of Christian belief formation, such that it is better to think of Christian belief as typically falling into the non-basic category. Further, the New Testament appears to support this understanding of how belief in the gospel normally arises.

8.1 The Presence and Importance of Inferences

With respect to the presence and importance of inferences, the previous chapter notes that in the acceptance of any belief, other beliefs play an inevitably influential role, more influential than Plantinga acknowledges. This requires further explanation. Plantinga does acknowledge that the existence of a potential defeater may impede or even prevent the formation of a basic belief. For example, I see what looks like a barn and would have formed the basic belief that I was being appeared to by a barn had I not also believed that in this part of the country the inhabitants love to construct facades that look like barns. Plantinga also acknowledges the importance of beliefs cohering with what is already believed.[10] He even envisages a person who has come to believe in the gospel completing the following assessment of his new-found belief:

> You have considered how it fits in with your other beliefs, have engaged in the requisite seeking of defeaters, have considered the objections that you have encountered, compared notes with the right people, and so on.[11]

Plantinga thus does acknowledge the importance of other beliefs in the broad process of Christian belief formation. He even accepts that these other beliefs may, by way of argument, contribute to acceptance of the gospel.[12] However, what Plantinga does not believe is that Christian belief is based upon, or in any way depends upon support from still further beliefs. Belief in the gospel can, and normally does arise without either conscious or unconscious dependence on still further beliefs.[13] All that is necessary and sufficient for faith is the internal instigation of the Holy Spirit (IIHS) which enables a person to accept the gospel as true.

---

10   *WCB*, 112.
11   *WCB*, 255.
12   *WCB*, 258.
13   Plantinga, as we have already seen, believes that the Christian gospel is not able to be given strong support by arguments. Faith must therefore depend for its warrant on some other warrant-creating process.

Plantinga's understanding here is deficient. The connection between belief in the gospel and the other beliefs that a person holds is both stronger and tighter than Plantinga allows. As a way of teasing this out, it will be helpful to note what Plantinga says about the explanatory power of the gospel. Plantinga argues that although the gospel does make sense of other beliefs people have, this does not typically account for gospel acceptance. Along with arguments, the explanatory power of the gospel is not what grounds Christian belief.

> According to the model, Christian belief in the typical case is not the conclusion of an argument (which is not to say arguments cannot play an important role in its acceptance), or accepted on the evidential basis of other beliefs, or accepted just because it constitutes a good explanation of phenomena of one kind or another. Specific Christian beliefs may indeed constitute excellent explanations of one or another phenomena (the Christian teaching of sin leaps to mind here), but they aren't accepted because they provide such an explanation.[14]

I simply disagree with Plantinga at this point. The explanatory power of the Christian gospel[15] often plays a crucially important role in the conversion of people, particularly of those coming to faith from a non-believing or unsympathetic background. Although it is true that the gospel frequently does just 'seem right' to people, and has a 'ring of truth' about it, a good part of the reason for that is that it lines up, often in profound and unexpected ways, with what people already believe or suspect.[16] The Christian teaching on human sin *is* likely to touch a deep chord within people when they encounter it in Scripture. The gospel story has a realism which connects deeply with our own stories. There is within Scripture a cuttingly accurate diagnosis of the human condition, combined with a confident presentation of the will of God, all of which contributes to the gospel's plausibility, giving it that 'ring of truth' when it is preached or read.

Paul Helm suggests that such characteristics, and their effect, are a key to understanding what he believes is the self-authenticating nature of Scripture.

---

14 WCB, 258. Plantinga certainly does not deny that Christian beliefs (including the belief that God exists) have explanatory potential. He says this with respect to theism: 'Theistic belief is only *one* of the things that theism can be invoked to explain. Theism has also been used to explain the fine-tuning of the universe, the existence of propositions, properties and other abstract entities, the origin of life, the nature and existence of morality, the reliability of our epistemic faculties, and much else besides,' WCB, 370.
15 Including its essential theism, which, of itself, has explanatory power.
16 As Austin Farrer points out, 'we should not find revelation intrinsically convincing if everything else made nonsense of it, and it made nonsense of everything else,' 'Revelation', in B. Mitchell (ed), *Faith and Logic* (London: George Allen and Unwin, 1957), 101.

The Bible makes claims both about itself and us which are proven true in experience:

> the Bible purports to give an analysis or diagnosis of the reader. The Scriptures offer this diagnosis as the *truth* about the reader. Now if the Scriptures are what they claim to be, the Word of God, then one would expect that careful examination and self-scrutiny would reveal that the diagnosis 'holds good' in the life of the reader.[17]

Plantinga explicitly rejects this way of understanding Scripture's self-authenticating nature.[18] However, it is characteristics such as the ones highlighted by Helm, which give to Scripture its authentic feel. It is, at least, part of the reason that people can, in Jonathan Edwards words, 'see divinity'[19] in Scripture, or, in Calvin's words, perceive its 'divine majesty'.[20]

I have been arguing thus far that the beliefs that people have when encountering the gospel play an inevitably influential role in their acceptance of the gospel. One promising way of understanding how this influence asserts itself has been suggested by Esther Meek.[21] Meek, drawing on the thinking of Michael Polanyi, notes that it is a frequent characteristic of our belief-forming practice that the beliefs we arrive at are not the result of explicit and consciously considered inductive or deductive arguments.[22] However, this does not mean that mental processes (often of a highly complicated nature) are not involved, processes which essentially take into account what is already believed or suspected. According to Polanyi, every act of knowing consists of the knower's active integration of a variety of particulars into a comprehensive whole. These acts of integration can happen instantly, and apparently automatically, or they can be the result of a long and agonising process. In either case, integration happens, although not always in a predictable way.

What is of significance for our purposes is that this integrative process is not easily identified in either inductive or deductive terms. It is difficult, if not impossible, to lay out the argument chains which may be involved. The process is a complicated one, and is often (or largely) unconscious, with a host

---

17   Paul Helm, 'Faith, Evidence, and the Scriptures' in D. A. Carson and J. D. Woodbridge (eds), *Scripture and Truth* (Grand Rapids: Baker Book House, 1992), 310.
18   For example, in *WCB*, where he resists the idea that self-authentication can be understood in 'the sense that it offers evidence *for itself* or somehow *proves* itself to be accurate or reliable,' 261.
19   *A Treatise Concerning Religious Affections*, John E. Smith, (ed), (New Haven: Yale University Press, 1959), 298.
20   *Institutes of the Christian Religion*, I, vii, 5.
21   In Esther L. Meek, 'A Polanyian Interpretation of Calvin's Sensus Divinitatis', *Presbyterion*, Vol. 23, No. 1 (1997), 8-24.
22   Robert Audi also suggests this, as we have seen.

Theory of Christian Belief Formation: A Critique 151

of different clues typically being drawn together in what Polanyi understands as a personal act of insight, or as a cognitive leap.[23] Esther Meek describes the process of discovery, and its epistemological effects in these terms:

> As a result of integration, the subsidiaries[24] appear differently from how they appeared before, and they receive fresh meaning ... The resulting focus displays a coherent shape that far outstrips the sum of the subsidiaries that we might specify. It is this feature which indicates the success of the epistemic act to the knower. Polanyi speaks of this as the ontological aspect: it brings conviction that the knower has made contact with what is real ... In anticipating the focus, preconceived notions are replaced with new standards which grow out of the impending discovery. At no point do we make a conscious choice, but when the discovery 'arrives,' we find ourselves transformed.[25]

Meek suggests that the operation of the *sensus divinitatis* can be understood in these terms:

> I would like to suggest that the universal awareness of God can be construed as a subsidiary awareness of the intimation of a hidden coherence, of a set of particulars, curious and explainable only in the light of a presently empty focus. I am putting the *sensus* in the place Polanyi accords to the problem stage in scientific discovery. Thus human awareness of God amounts to a person's perhaps still-hidden disturbance resulting from things about the universe and about himself that can only be explained in terms of God. Prior to salvation the focus remains empty. Upon salvation, which coincides with the success of the integrative feat, the puzzling particulars receive new shape and meaning as the focus fills in and overflows, explaining much more than

---

23 'A Polanyian Interpretation', 15. Note that Plantinga is aware of this aspect of human reasoning. In *WPF,* for example, he gives a broad description of induction in these terms: 'Broadly taken ... the term denotes our whole nondeductive procedure of acquiring, maintaining, and discarding beliefs about what is so far unobserved or undetected or unknown. It is a complicated, multitudinous process involving inherited ideas about the ways of the world, interlocking chains of inductions in the narrow sense, views about what is essential and what accidental and about which differences are important and which are not and judgements of initial plausibility. This process of considering, examining, and evaluating hypotheses may go on unreflectively and unselfconsciously, or by way of explicit, self-conscious reflective attention; it is guided by simplicity and in other ways by what we human beings find natural and familiar,' 123.
24 Subsidiaries are particular beliefs or awarenesses which are not being focally attended to in an act of integration.
25 'A Polanyian Interpretation', 16.

the puzzling particulars and promising all sorts of facets for us yet to explore.[26]

This is a promising suggestion. If it is the case that people, upon hearing the gospel, are already vaguely aware of God's existence and requirements, then the gospel is likely to make profound sense; it is likely (in something like the way Meek suggests) to pull together already existing beliefs and suspicions[27] in a compelling and persuasive way, and to have that 'just seems right' characteristic. What makes this Polanyian interpretation so helpful is that it accounts well for the fact that arguments and evidence, and, more broadly, other beliefs, do not appear to be obviously present, even though they are there, exercising an often unconscious influence. Other beliefs,[28] on this account, *do* play a key and determinative role in the genesis of Christian belief. They can be seen to form the inferential basis of Christian belief.

Meek's suggestion also makes good sense of what Plantinga is wanting to say about the proper basicality of Christian belief. Plantinga, at one point in *WCB*, discusses the following passage from Jonathan Edwards:

> A view of this divine glory [of the gospel] directly convinces the mind of the divinity of these things, as this glory is in itself a direct, clear and all-conquering evidence of it ... He that has his judgement thus directly convinced and assured of the divinity of the things of the gospel, by a clear view of their glory, has a reasonable conviction; his belief and assurance is altogether agreeable to reason; because the divine glory and beauty of divine things is in itself, real evidence of their divinity, and the most direct and strong evidence. He that truly sees the divine, transcendent, supreme glory of these things which are divine, does as it were know their divinity intuitively; he not only argues that they are divine, but he sees that they are divine ..[29]

Plantinga notes that Edwards can be interpreted in one of two ways:

> On the one hand, Edwards might think the believer perceives the divine glory and beauty of the things of the gospel, and then infers from that, in a quick argument, that they are indeed divine, from God, and hence are to be believed. On the other hand, the account could be that she sees the loveliness and

---

26 'A Polanyian Interpretation', 18.
27 Bruce Langtry, in private correspondence, suggests that along with beliefs and suspicions there may also be a number of unarticulated cues which are made sense of by the gospel. Bruce uses the example of someone who is vaguely aware of the presence of a tiger, and who thus cannot be said to have the belief that it is nearby, but who quickly forms that belief on being told, 'There is a tiger there!'
28 Along with various other cues and suspicions. What seems plausible is that this mix of beliefs, suspicions and cues are re-ordered and brought into some sort of coherent shape by the gospel message.
29 quoted in *WCB*, 304.

beauty - divine beauty - of the things of the gospel, and consequently *immediately* forms the belief that these things are true and that they are from God. The difference would be that in the first case there is an *inference*, perhaps so quick and inexplicit that one scarcely notices it, but an inference nonetheless.[30]

Plantinga opts for the second interpretation of Edwards,[31] which conforms to his own understanding of how things work. Plantinga rejects the theory that people (typically) see the glory and beauty of the gospel, and then infer from this that the gospel is divine, and therefore to be believed. In this, I think Plantinga is correct. Certainly, it would be unusual, particularly in today's world, for people to first come to the conclusion that the gospel is divine, and then conclude that it should be believed. However, this fact does not rule out the possibility that an inferential process, such as suggested by Meek, *is* typically involved. I would argue that frequently influential in people's acceptance of the gospel is its perceived plausibility, or, more broadly, its ability to draw together, in various profound, surprising and integrative ways, already existing beliefs, suspicions and possibilities. To the extent that this is the case, such acceptance can be understood as inferential, or as involving an inferential process. A good candidate for such a process (which, essentially, is the process Meek is describing) is 'inference to the best explanation'. Inference to the best explanation is the process by which evidence (often complex and unable to be entirely specified) is weighed up and assessed (sometimes and to some extent unconsciously), and an explanation is arrived at which appears to make best sense of the data.[32] Although this is a process which is not entirely understood, nor even easily justified in terms of its ability to arrive at the truth,[33] it does suggest promising possibilities for understanding at least one element of gospel acceptance. The important point to note, for our purposes, is that this suggestion has the implication that gospel belief, inasmuch and to the extent that it arises as a result of the (even unconsciously) perceived explanatory power of the gospel, is non-basic.

---

30   *WCB*, 304.
31   *WCB*, 305, 306.
32   For a description of this process, along with critical discussion of its epistemic legitimacy, see G. H. Harman, 'The inference to the best explanation', *Philosophical Review*, Vol. 74, No. 1 (1965), 88-95; M. Friedman, *Foundations of Space-Time Theories* (Princeton, NJ: Princeton University Press, 1983); P. Lipton, *Inference to the Best Explanation* (London: Routledge, 1991).
33   For a good brief discussion of the issues, see J. Vogel, 'Inference to the best explanation', in *Routledge Encyclopaedia*, Vol. 4, 766-769.

8.2 The Presence and Importance of Arguments in the New Testament

We turn now to consider some strong New Testament support for the idea that arguments and evidence (particularly of an historical nature) are not only important, but provide the often necessary grounding for Christian belief. Plantinga is clearly at odds with this way of thinking. In his opinion, the presence or absence of historical evidence is not something that one should be concerned about, certainly when it comes to considerations of warrant:

> My Christian belief can have warrant, and warrant sufficient for knowledge, even if I don't know of and cannot make a good historical case for the reliability of the biblical writers or for what they teach. I don't *need* a good historical case for the truth of the central teachings of the gospel in order to be warranted in accepting them. I need not be able to find a good argument, historical or otherwise, for the resurrection of Jesus Christ, or for his being the divine Son of God, or for the Christian claim that his suffering and death in fact constitutes an atoning sacrifice whereby we can be restored to the right relationship with God. On the model, the warrant for Christian belief doesn't require that I or anyone else have this kind of historical information; the warrant floats free of such questions. It doesn't require to be validated or proved by some source of belief *other* than faith, such as historical investigation.[34]

Plantinga argues that the gospel, or Scripture, is self-authenticating. It is known to be true in an immediate way as a result of the inward instigation of the Holy Spirit. The effectiveness of this supernatural belief-producing mechanism means that attempts to show the truth of the gospel by other means are unnecessary. One is completely warranted in believing without them.

Scripture is self-authenticating in the sense that for belief in the great things of the gospel to be justified, rational and warranted, no historical evidence and argument for the teaching in question, or for the veracity or reliability or divine character of Scripture (or the part of Scripture in which it is taught) is necessary. The process by which these beliefs have warrant for the believer swings free of those historical and other considerations; these beliefs have warrant in the basic way.[35]

Plantinga goes so far as to state that even if there is no evidence held by anyone, the Christian believer is warranted in believing the gospel story:

> A Christian, and indeed a well-educated, contemporary, and culturally aware Christian can be justified, so I will argue, even if she doesn't hold her beliefs

---

34   *WCB*, 259.
35   *WCB*, 262.

on the basis of arguments or evidence, even if she isn't aware of any good arguments for her beliefs, and even if indeed there aren't any.[36]

Plantinga could hardly be more clear in his dismissal of arguments and evidence. Not only is it the case that people can be justified, rational and warranted believing in the gospel without them, it does not even matter if no good arguments exist in support of the gospel. Arguments and evidence are largely unimportant. One reason for disagreeing with Plantinga lies in the fact that the New Testament writers do not appear to share this conviction.

Perhaps the clearest example of a New Testament writer who stresses the importance, even necessity, of arguments and evidence is the writer of John's Gospel. Leaving aside, for the moment, critical issues of authorship and dating, we will consider (at face value) various claims made by the Gospel writer (or writers[37]). For our purposes, it is significant that Plantinga approaches the Gospel in essentially the same way. He also takes its message at face value, although not without taking account of issues of genre and careful interpretation. This is significant because Plantinga has a principled reason for accepting what the Gospel says, including what it says about the importance and influence of arguments and evidence, that reason being that the Gospel is divine revelation. What, then, does John's Gospel say? It is clear from a careful study of John that the Gospel writer gives a very important place to arguments and evidence in the process of coming to belief, including arguments about the historical reliability of the recorded events. High claims are made, from the beginning of the Gospel, regarding the identity of Jesus. He is described as the word of God who was with God in the beginning (1:1, 2); all things were created by him (1:3); in him is life; he is light to the world (1:4); he is the Son of God (1:14, 18); he is the lamb of God, destined to take away the sins of the world (1:29). All of these claims, taken together, constitute the gospel that people, through John's Gospel, are invited to believe.

What is significant for our purposes is that within the Gospel there is no indication that people are expected to believe these various Christological claims in a basic way, without reference to, or dependence on, evidence that the claims are true. The contrary is, in fact, the case. The author, from the commencement of his Gospel, lays before his readers witness after witness to the truth about Jesus and the gospel story.[38] The contemporary legal

---

36 *WCB*, 93.
37 There are a number of indications within the Gospel that a wider Johannine community was involved in at least some way in the composition of the Gospel. See, for example, 21:24.
38 The witness theme is introduced in the Prologue with the witness of John the Baptist, and then becomes a major theme of the Gospel. The noun marturiva is used 14 times in John (as opposed to 4 times in the Synoptics); the verb marturevw is used 33 times (as opposed to 2 times in the Synoptics). A. E. Harvey, in *Jesus on Trial: A Study in the Fourth Gospel* (London: SPCK, 1976), argues, convincingly in

requirement was that at least two witnesses were required to vouch for the truth of a disputed event or claim.[39] The author brings forward seven *categories* of witness. These include John the Baptist; other human witnesses (including the apostles); the works of Jesus; God the Father (a witness that comes through the works of Jesus and the Scriptures); Jesus himself; the Scriptures, and the Holy Spirit.[40] Although the various witnesses over-lap and are mutually interdependent, they nevertheless represent an integrated, consistent and extensive witness to Jesus. And the purpose of this multi-fold witness was to persuade,[41] to engender belief,[42] to enable readers to reach the same informed conclusion about Jesus that the author (and others[43]) had reached.[44] Belief arises, in John's Gospel, as people heed the various witnesses,[45] including the witness provided by the miraculous signs of Jesus. People come to belief because of the signs,[46] or are rebuked for not so coming to belief.[47] They are urged to judge correctly; without jumping to hasty conclusions.[48] Involved in right judgement is the proper drawing of inferences, as illustrated by the following questions recorded

---

my opinion, that the witness of the witnesses was presented in John's Gospel as evidence designed to support the conclusion that Jesus was the Christ, the Son of God (Jn 20:31). In Harvey's concluding words: 'That Jesus is the Christ, the Son of God, is a proposition presented in the Fourth Gospel, not as an established fact, but as an issue on which a judgement is to be passed,' 131. Allison Trites, in *The New Testament Concept of Witness* (Cambridge: Cambridge University Press, 1977), argues to essentially the same conclusion. She too stresses the evidential character of the witness theme, both in John and throughout the New Testament.

39 See, for example, Deuteronomy 19:15.
40 Leon Morris, *The Gospel According to John*, The New International Commentary on the New Testament Series (Grand Rapids: Eerdmans Publishing Company, 1971), 90.
41 It was expected of a first-century Jewish witness that they not only pass on relevant information known to them by personal observation, but that they also persuade the court that what they claimed was true, Bernard Ramm, *The God who Makes a Difference* (Waco, Texas: Word Books, 1977), 40, 41. On some possible Biblical background to this see, *The New Testament Concept of Witness*, 84, 79.
42 The purpose of John the Baptist's testimony (which, because of its position in the Prologue, is likely to have representative status) is 'so that through him all men might believe,' 1:7. See further, Harvey, *Jesus on Trial*, 18-33.
43 It is interesting that John's Gospel concludes with what appears to be testimony of the Johannine community, or perhaps of the other apostles, identified by the 'we' sayings of 1:14 and 2:11. Whoever exactly they are, they vouch for the reliability of John's witness: 'This [ie John] is the disciple who testifies to these things and who wrote them down. We know that his testimony is true.' 21:24.
44 See, for example, 1:7; 4:42, 3:11, 10:41, 42.
45 See, for example, 1:6-8, 15; 3:11; 4:42; 5:27, 33; 10:41, 42; 15:27.
46 See, for example, 1:50; 2:11.
47 15:24.
48 See, for example, 5:16-18, 6:42; 7:24; 7:27, 41, 42; 9:16).

in the Gospel: 'When the Christ comes will he do more signs than this man has done?' (7:31); 'Could a sinner do such things?'(9:16); 'Can a demon open the eyes of the blind?' (10:21).[49] The miraculous signs are considered by the Gospel writer as evidence designed to occasion belief.[50] The fact that people do not believe is not because the evidence is unimpressive, inadequate, or irrelevant. On the contrary, the evidence is relevant, adequate and very impressive, such that those who do not believe are culpable in their unbelief. In the words of Jesus: 'If I had not done among them the works which no one else did, they would not have sin. But now they have seen and hated both me and my Father,' (15:24).

If we take what the writer of John's Gospel appears to be saying at face value, then arguments and evidence, in the form of corroborated testimony, were considered to be very important by at least one New Testament writer. A good case can be mounted for the conclusion that other New Testament writers thought likewise. Luke, for example, begins his Gospel by reminding his readers of the careful research he had carried out into the events of which he was about to inform them.[51] He begins his second volume with a reference to Jesus providing many convincing proofs[52] that he was alive.[53] He places on the lips of Peter words to the effect that God himself bore testimony to his Son by miraculous deeds done in the public sphere: 'Men of Israel, listen to this: Jesus of Nazareth was a man accredited by God to you by miracles, wonders and signs, which God did among you through him, as you yourselves know.' (2:22)

Peter appeals to the confirmatory testimony of the (Old Testament) Scriptures; and to his own status as an eye-witness, introducing themes which recur throughout the Book of Acts.[54] If we accept what we read in the New

---

49 See also 6:14; 7:40-46.
50 Harvey notes that 'in each case the result of a miraculous incident is explicitly said to be that certain persons "believe" (or, in two cases, "follow"). Moreover ... the miracles in John's Gospel (unlike the Synoptics) are called "signs", and virtually every instance of this word "sign", and every reference to the "signs" performed by Jesus, is found in the context of people "believing" (or, in one case, failing to believe) in Jesus,' *Jesus on Trial*, 97.
51 Luke 1:1-4.
52 Gk. τεκμήριον, meaning 'convincing decisive proof'; William Arndt and F. Wilbur Gingrich, *A Greek-English Lexicon of the New Testament*, Second edition (Chicago: The University of Chicago Press, 1958), 808. The exact nature of these 'convincing proofs' is not specified, although the next phrase 'being seen by him over forty days' is suggestive that the proof consisted in a number of distinct appearances during which times Jesus not only was seen, but was heard as well (1:3). Acts 10:41 refers to Jesus also eating and drinking with the apostles.
53 Acts 1:3.
54 Specifically on the concept of witness in Acts, see A. Trites, *The New Testament Concept of Witness*, 128-153; Peter Bolt, 'Mission and Witness', in I.

Testament at face value, it is hard to avoid the conclusion that the writers of the New Testament considered evidence for the truth of the gospel important. Further, they considered this evidence to be more than adequate to occasion belief, and to be the basis for a condemnation of unbelief.

The New Testament writers also appear to have believed that the provision of evidence was on-goingly important. In John's Gospel, for example, the fact that John parades before the reader a host of witnesses is an indication that he believed that his readers (who increasingly would be separated by time and space from the gospel events) needed to be persuaded to believe, and that the various witnesses could be influential in this. The story of Thomas is a relevant example. This story is often used to illustrate the superiority of believing without the aid of evidence,[55] with the suggestion that Thomas's way of believing (when confronted by the risen Lord) is in some way epistemologically inferior to believing without the aid of such undeniable evidence. This use of the Thomas story is illegitimate. If Thomas's arriving at his belief in this way is deficient, then so also is the believing of a great many of the characters of the Gospel, including the other disciples, who similarly believed when confronted with acts of exceptional power. Thomas's belief (and worship) is not censured by the writer of the Gospel. In fact, in context, it is an entirely understandable and appropriate response, in fact, the *only* appropriate response. What is implicitly censured is Thomas's reluctance to accept the testimony of his fellow disciples which he would have had every good reason to accept.

The story of Thomas, like the rest of the stories of belief formed in the face of Jesus's powerful acts, is written for the readers' benefit. The fact that the risen Jesus appeared to an incredulous Thomas is presented as good reason for the readers to also believe. The resurrection can be the basis for their belief also. That this is the intention of the writer is made plain by his words immediately following the Thomas story:

> Jesus did many other miraculous signs in the presence of his disciples which are not recorded in this book. But these are written that you may believe that Jesus is the Christ, the Son of God, and that by believing you may have life in his name. (20:30, 31)

Plantinga uses the story of Thomas to illustrate his own understanding of faith formation, according to which the drawing of inferences from evidence is downplayed to the point of irrelevance. He argues that the sort of faith being commended in the Thomas story (the believing-without-seeing variety), is faith which originates apart from 'the workings of the ordinary cognitive faculties

---

Howard Marshall and D. Peterson, *Witness to the Gospel: The Theology of Acts* (Grand Rapids: Eerdmans, 1998), 191-214.
55 As Plantinga himself does, in *WCB*, 254, 265, 266.

with which we were originally created.'[56] Belief in the truth of the gospel is produced supernaturally without dependence on ordinary belief-producing mechanisms. Plantinga's interpretation cannot be sustained by a careful look at the Thomas story, particularly when set within the wider context of John's Gospel. Taking into account this context, it is certainly the case that obedient or saving belief is a gift from God. However, as we have seen, the ordinary process of drawing inferences is very much involved, and intended to be involved, in the process of coming to belief. People are encouraged to use their ordinary reasoning faculties. That they do not do this, or do not do this responsibly, is a measure of their sin.

More can (and will) be said by way of critique. However, at this point an alternative model for understanding Christian belief formation will be suggested which I believe is superior to Plantinga's, although, at points, it is similar to his. It also draws on a number of distinctively Plantingan ideas. This model will be referred to as a warranted trust model of Christian belief formation.

8.3 A Warranted Trust Model of Christian Belief Formation

Plantinga describes his model as a 'testimonial model'.[57] According to this model, the conviction that the gospel is true:

> comes by way of the activity of the Holy Spirit. Calvin speaks ... of the internal 'testimony' and (more often) 'witness' of the Holy Spirit: Aquinas, of the divine 'instigation' and 'invitation'. On the model, there is both scripture and the divine activity leading to human belief. God himself (on the model) is the principal author of scripture. Scripture is most importantly a message, a communication from God to humankind; scripture is a word from the Lord. But then this is just a special case of the pervasive process of testimony, by which, as a matter of fact, we learn most of what we know.[58]

So Scripture is indeed testimony; even if it is testimony of a very special kind. First, the principal testifier is God. It also differs from ordinary testimony in that in this case, unlike most others, there is both a principal testifier and subordinate testifiers: the human authors. There is still another difference: it is the instigation of the Holy Spirit, on this model, that gets us to see and believe that the propositions proposed for our beliefs in Scripture really *are* a word from the Lord. This case also differs from the usual run of testimony, then, in that the Holy Spirit not only writes the letter (appropriately inspires the human authors), but also does something special

---

56   *WCB*, 265.
57   For example, *WCB*, 265, and in the heading to chapter nine, 290.
58   *WCB*, 251.

to enable you to believe and appropriate its contents. So this testimony is not the usual run of testimony; it is testimony nonetheless.[59]

This description is not disputed. However, Plantinga's insistence that the inward instigation of the Holy Spirit produces belief in the gospel in such a way as to render useless (or secondary) ordinary processes of belief formation is problematic, so much so that an alternative testimonial model will be suggested. Highlighted by the model is the place of (warranted) trust. Determining the model's fundamental characteristics, which will be drawn out in what follows, is the narrative of the gospel story:

> Beginning in the middle of the Scriptural story, Jesus comes preaching into Galilee, a region awash with messianic expectations. The flame of those expectations had already been fanned by the appearance and message of John the Baptist. Jesus, after being baptised by John, chooses a small band of disciples who accompany him throughout his ministry. They hear him teach. They witness his acts of awesome power; have their Old Testament-influenced expectations modified, and ultimately enlarged by the surprising course of Jesus's ministry which climaxes in his violent death and joyous resurrection.
>
> Between his resurrection and ascension, Jesus continues to explain the purpose and meaning of all that the disciples had witnessed. The disciples were able to draw certain true inferences from what they had seen and heard, but the teaching of Jesus (both before and after his resurrection) gave them a deeper and truer understanding of what had occurred.
>
> Armed with this understanding, which was good news indeed for those who would accept it, the disciples begin, from the Day of Pentecost, to proclaim the gospel about Jesus, in the power of the Holy Spirit.
>
> In their proclamation of this message, the disciples nowhere assume that the mere telling of the story will (necessarily) be sufficient to create belief. They provide evidence to their listeners (and readers); they appeal to established beliefs,[60] they present themselves as eye and ear witnesses to the life, death and resurrection of Jesus.[61] Arguments and evidence thus play a critical role in their gospel presentation.

---

59 *WCB*, 252.
60 About the meaning and authority of the Old Testament, for example.
61 In the choice of a successor for Judas the apostles are careful to choose someone who, with them, had been an ear and eye witness to the ministry of Jesus, from Jesus' baptism by John to his resurrection. (Acts 1:21, 22). In their evangelistic preaching, they consistently draw attention to their status as witnesses, with the implication that what they say is reliable (for example, Acts 2:31, 32).

When they came to record the story of the gospel for future generations, the writers continue to make their gospel appeal on the basis that they and their message can be trusted.[62] The fundamental call of the gospel is to trust the message, the messengers, and, ultimately, God.

When is trust in the testimony of someone justified? Trust is justified when there is no good reason to doubt either the testifier[63] or the testimony,[64] or, in cases where there *are* reasons to doubt, those reasons are not considered sufficiently strong to invalidate the testimony. In the case of the testimony of the apostles, although reasons to doubt do exist,[65] and need to be dealt with,[66] those reasons are not so strong as make belief in the gospel either irrational, unjustified or unwarranted. Acceptance of the testimony of the apostles is (or, may well be, for many) an epistemologically acceptable practice.

With respect to the warrant such belief possesses, since 'testimony is ordinarily parasitic on other sources of belief so far as warrant goes,'[67] the warrant a person has for believing the testimony of the apostles is a function of the degree of warrant enjoyed by the apostles in their belief. If a natural reading of the New Testament is accepted, the apostle's belief was warranted to a high degree, by virtue of the evidence they had seen and heard. Given their already existent theism, and their belief in the promises of the Old Testament, the spectacular career of Jesus (including his words and works) provided them with more than enough reason to believe his claims. The sorts of inferences they drew were entirely warranted. Those, both then and now, who believe the apostles' eye and ear testimony to Jesus are similarly warranted (to varying degrees)[68] in believing what they do about Jesus.

---

62 See, for example, John 19:34-35.
63 A testifier could reasonably be doubted if his competence or reliability was sufficiently in question. Things such as honesty, possession of a good track record in the past, the likelihood of the testifier being successfully in touch with the truth would all be variously relevant in justifiable decisions to trust.
64 Testimony can reasonably be doubted if it is not consistent with what is already believed, or if there are competing ways of understanding what is testified about which ought to be considered before the testimony is accepted.
65 Some of which we will shortly consider.
66 As Plantinga himself attempts to do in his discussion of Historical Biblical Criticism.
67 *WPF* 87.
68 Warrant, as Plantinga points out, comes in degrees. A twenty-first century believer's confidence in the testimony of the apostles may be affected by considerations such as the time gap between the first century and now. Further, since warrant (as Plantinga understands it) is, in part, a function of strength of belief, the degree of warrant enjoyed by twenty-first century belief may be, for that and other reasons, less than that enjoyed by believers in the first century. Among twenty-first

As for the process of coming to belief, it has been shown that arguments and evidence were employed by the apostles, indicating that they, at least, considered such a strategy necessary. In New Testament descriptions of people coming to faith, arguments and evidence are frequently cited as influential in conversion. This is not, in any way, to deny the necessary involvement of the Holy Spirit in Christian belief formation. My own opinion is that the Holy Spirit is involved in all aspects of the process of conversion. His persuasive work happens in and through arguments and evidence, and by other means as well. He does not, at least typically, by-pass the ordinary workings of human cognitive faculties. Rather, he works through and by them.

8.4 Advantages and Strengths of the Warranted Trust Model

This warranted trust model of Christian belief formation has some advantages over Plantinga's model. Plantinga acknowledges that although he considers his model to be 'rather close to the sober truth,'[69] he is willing to admit that he may be wrong. So am I. There are, perhaps, any number of problems with my own model which would disqualify it as a serious possibility, or, at least, occasion a radical reformulation. Nevertheless, I, like Plantinga, think that something like it is true. My reasons are as follows:

First, the model is personalistic. Trust is an inter-personal or inter-relational attitude. Foundationally, one trusts a person. Trust is a key to relational health. From a Biblical point of view, a loss of trust in God has been the primary cause of humankind's spiritual and moral malaise. A call to trust lies at the heart of the gospel's remedy for human failure. It is important, in any attempt to develop an epistemological theory which is true to the Scriptures, to take account of trust and of the inter-relational nature of Scriptural reality. The Scriptures are essentially about persons in (and out of) relationship. My own model is an initial attempt to delineate some implications of this.

Second, trust is the appropriate or intended response to testimony. C. A. J. Coady, in his very useful philosophical study of testimony,[70] defines testimony as a kind of evidence provided by persons,[71] and points out that trust is the fundamentally appropriate response to testimony, in the absence of reasons not to trust.[72] Ben Witherington III spells out the relevance of this with respect to the gospel story:

---

century believers, the degree of warrant is also likely to vary, depending, for example, on how responsibly they deal with potential defeaters.
69   *WCB*, 242.
70   C. A. J. Coady, *Testimony: A Philosophical Study* (Oxford: Clarendon Press, 1992).
71   *Testimony*, 27.
72   *Testimony*, 46.

We have direct access only to reports from the disciples of what they took to be extraordinary events. This means that at the primary level the question of the trustworthiness of the witnesses comes into play, and also, very importantly, what the disciples' intentions were when they conveyed the information we now find in the Gospels.[73]

Third, trust is a fundamental characteristic of faith.[74] Both the Old and the New Testaments highlight the importance of trust as the fundamentally required human response to God, in light of his kindness and grace.[75] The Reformers reaffirmed this Biblical emphasis.[76] Reacting against earlier tendencies to equate faith with credence, they insisted that faith, although including a *belief that* aspect, or *fides*, also involves, as essential to it, *fiducia* or trust.[77]

---

73 Ben Witherington III, 'Resurrection Redux', in Paul Copan (ed), *Will the Real Jesus Please Stand Up?* (Grand Rapids: Baker Book House, 1998), 132.
74 The New Testament, in fact, uses the same word (*pistis"*) for both faith and trust. It is context which determines whether a 'belief that' or a 'belief in' aspect of faith is intended, and thus whether the word is translated into English as belief, faith or trust.
75 Avery Dulles, in his useful theology of faith, *The Assurance of Things Hoped For* (New York: Oxford University Press, 1994), notes that although the Old Testament has no single term exactly corresponding to the New Testamenta term *pistis* and its cognates, a range Hebrew words are used which, in context, have the prominent meaning of trust (trust in God, trust in his word), 7-10. A short survey of the New Testament references to faith by Dulles also reveals faith's fundamentally trusting attitude. Dulles' sums up his study of both Testaments: 'In both the Old and New Testament the concept of faith is complex. It includes elements such as personal trust, assent to divinely revealed truth, fidelity, and obedience. In the Old Testament faith is depicted as the appropriate response to God's faithfulness to his covenant promises. Although the element of belief is present by implication, the emphasis falls on trust or confidence in God as Lord. Faith is tested by obedience and fidelity ... In the New Testament the cognitive element is more pronounced, partly for the reason that the hopes of Israel are held to have been surpassingly fulfilled in Christ. Salvation is linked to the memory of what God has done for his people in the death and resurrection of Jesus. But the element of trust continues to be central, especially perhaps in the Pauline letters,' 17.
76 Plantinga makes mention of trust in his description of the appropriate human response to the gospel, but underplays the role of trust as an essential element of faith; emphasising rather faith as assent; which, somewhat surprisingly, agrees more with traditional Roman Catholic teaching than with the teaching of the Reformation.
77 Luther, for example, distinguished between two types of faith; the first being a simple acceptance that what God says is true, the second being trust or confidence: 'The other way is to believe in God, as I do when I not only believe that what is said about him is true, but put my trust in Him, surrender myself to Him, and make bold to deal with Him, believing without doubt that he will do to me just what is said of Him ..' 'A Brief Explanation of the Ten Commandments, the Creed, and the Lord's

Fourth, trust is of central importance for almost everyone who comes to faith. People trust the words of their parents. People who believe the gospel as teenagers frequently do so as a result of coming to trust those who have brought the gospel to them. It is not only the Word, but the community of the Word which is often crucial in people coming to believe the gospel. It is a rare person who believes without some significant influence from a Christian individual or community who that person has come to trust.

Fifth, particularly in a fallen world, reasons often need to be given *to trust*. In a world where trust is all too frequently betrayed, it is not surprising that people more than occasionally need reassurance that their trust will be well-founded. The gospel involves a number of startling claims, and although these claims and their associated diagnosis of human life may have a degree of winning plausibility, there are still many aspects of the story that are anything but obviously true. That a man by the name of Jesus was born in Bethlehem, grew up in Nazareth, exercised a ministry in Galilee, was crucified outside of Jerusalem, seen alive within three days by his apostles and others, and is now glorified, is not something that one can be expected to believe simply on being told it. It is more than fair to ask, 'Did these things really happen, and if they did, what is the evidence of their historicity?'

Sixth, and related, a warranted trust model of Christian belief formation suggests a very sensible evidentialist principle (or perhaps a sensible sub-set of a more general principle). In the context of testimony, evidence is sensibly required when the recipient of the testimony is uncertain about whether it should be accepted. Perhaps the testifier is unknown, or not yet trusted. In situations such as this, particularly when the subject of testimony is unusual or difficult to accept (given a person's life experience), a calling for evidence, especially evidence of the testifier's reliability, is not only sensible, but very often necessary for rationality or wisdom.

Even if it is the case, as Plantinga argues, that belief in the testimony of others can (at times) be basic, in situations where doubt exists about either the testifier or the testimony, any eventuating belief will be non-basic. The doubtful testimony will have become an item of evidence which needs to be weighed against other sources of knowledge, including alternative testimony. This is typically the case in legal trials, where witnesses (often with conflicting testimony) are brought before a jury who are required to make a judgement. Evidence (including the evidence of testimony) is essential in this setting. It is also important, and often necessary, in the case of Christian belief. The writer of John's Gospel appears to have agreed. His readers are treated as a jury with the task of assessing the evidence he places before them.

Prayer' (1520) WA 7:215; *Works of Martin Luther*, Vol. 2 (Philadelphia: Muhlenburg Press, 1943), 368. Calvin also gave strong emphasis to the fiducial component of faith.

Seventh, trust is consistent with a certain amount of uncertainty. When we trust someone, and trust what they tell us, we seldom have overwhelmingly strong reasons to trust.[78] At times, there may even be evidence to suggest that we should not trust. Trust can, at times, hang on more like a thread than a rope, patiently awaiting vindication of its commitment.[79] Biblical faith, or trust, often appears to have this character. Trust, because it is an inter-personal, dynamic and historical attribute, is often not able to deliver a-temporal, or static certainty. This does not, however, necessarily count against trust.[80] In fact, it is part of the adventure of trust, numerous examples of which are paraded before us in the pages of Scripture.[81]

Trust is also important in light of the uncertainty and puzzlement created by the existence of evil and suffering in the world. A Christian, although he does not know (in detail, or even at all) what good reasons God has for allowing evil and suffering, nevertheless trusts that God does have good reasons, and that these reasons will, one day, be made clear.

Eighth, a particular attraction of the warranted trust model is that it can happily make use of Plantinga's developed theory of warrant. In both *WPF* and *WCB*, Plantinga points out that the Enlightenment 'looked askance',[82] or 'down its rationalistic nose'[83] at testimony and tradition. Coady suggests a plausible reason for this:

---

78 Richard Swinburne is wrong to suggest that trust always involves less than overwhelming reasons to trust. According to him, trust always occurs in circumstances where there is at least some evidence to suggest that trust is unwarranted, *Faith and Reason* (Oxford: Clarendon Press, 1981), 111-113. It is quite easy to imagine situations in which a person trusts another when the evidence of this person's trustworthiness is overwhelming. The trusting attitude of a child to its parent is an obvious case in point.

79 Richard Holton, in 'Deciding to Trust, Coming to Believe', in *Australasian Journal of Philosophy*, Vol. 72, No. 1 (March, 1994), suggests, I think rightly, that one can make a decision to trust, 63f. Trust is not always an involuntary attitude.

80 I say 'necessarily' because trust can, more than occasionally, be unwarranted. Lack of evidence can count against trust. There is sometimes a risk involved in trusting, a calculated risk, which does not always pay off. One of the reasons that we take this risk is that there are various non-epistemological benefits which we believe are worth securing and preserving by trust, such as the strengthening of relationship.

81 Note that this characteristic of trust, its occasional or temporary lack of groundedness in evidence provides an interesting way around the Lockean ethic of belief that regards belief as necessarily to be proportioned to internally accessible evidence. Trust operates somewhat differently to belief.

82 *WCB*, 147.

83 *WPF*, 77.

> In the post-Renaissance Western World the dominance of an individualist ideology has had a lot to do with the feeling that testimony has little or no epistemic importance. It is a commonplace that the political, social, and economic thought and practice of the West has been profoundly influenced in recent centuries by certain ideas and ideals stressing the powers, rights, dignities and autonomy of the individual person.[84]

Plantinga, as has been pointed out in chapter six, has helped to resurrect testimony (along with some other previously neglected sources of belief) from its unwarranted epistemic exile.[85] It would be useful, in the light of this resurrection, to also rehabilitate trust which is the appropriate epistemological response to testimony. Trust, like testimony, has been neglected by Western epistemologists who have concentrated their attention almost exclusively on belief.[86]

The task of rehabilitating trust to a position of epistemic respectability is, however, likely to be fraught with difficulty. Trust can easily degenerate into gullibility. It can as easily stand in the way of truth as be an avenue to truth. It is often exploited and betrayed. Beliefs formed as a result of, or within a context of trust will therefore have varying degrees of warrant. How warranted will depend on a number of factors. In what follows, I propose, as a first approximation, a model for determining the degree of warrant enjoyed by beliefs formed as a result of testimony. I have deliberately restricted myself to testimony, and to belief that arises in response to testimony, because of its obvious relevance to belief in the gospel.

Although trust in the testimony of others can lead one away from the truth, this need not be the case. Life's experiences teach us to modify our native

---

84 *Testimony: A Philosophical Study*, 13.
85 Nicholas Wolterstorff attempts a similar salvage operation in 'Evidence, Entitled Belief, and the Gospels', *Faith and Philosophy*, Vol. 6, No. 4 (October, 1989), 429-459. He comes to quite similar conclusions to my own on the role and importance of testimony in people's acceptance of the Gospels.
86 As Nicholas Wolterstorff points out in 'Epistemology of Religion' in John Greco and Ernest Sosa, (eds), *The Blackwell Guide to Epistemology* (Malden, Massachusetts: Blackwell, 1999), 303-324: 'From among the considerable diversity of propositional attitudes, epistemologists in our century have concentrated almost exclusively on beliefs. Given the fact that a good many of the truth-relevant merits present in beliefs which have been of interest to philosophers are present in other propositional attitudes as well, that limitation of focus seems groundless. It seems especially groundless in the case of epistemology of religion; for in many religious forms of life (in contrast, perhaps, to science), hoping, *trusting* [my emphasis], regretting, accepting, and so forth, are as prominent as believing,' 304. For one attempt to understand the epistemology of religious commitment in terms of one of these attitudes, see James L. Muyskens, *The Sufficiency of Hope: The Conceptual Foundations of Religion* (Philadelphia: Temple University Press, 1979).

tendency to believe what people tell us. We learn to be critically on the lookout for deception and error which can arise regardless of the best of motives. One of the benefits of the pluralistic challenge, discussed in chapter three, is that people have become increasingly aware of the need to subject their own worldview (however innocently acquired) to critical scrutiny. It may be that what they have accepted (often on the basis of testimony) is not so warranted as they had once thought.

Bearing in mind considerations such as these, when do beliefs which are (trustingly) formed as a result of testimony have warrant, and what factors determine their degree of warrant? I suggest the following:

> The degree of warrant enjoyed by a testimonial belief is a function of at least the following: (i) the degree of warrant enjoyed by that belief at the beginning of the relevant chain of testimony, (ii) whether and to what extent a person has independent reasons and/or grounds[87] either to believe or disbelieve the testimony, and (iii) whether a person has appropriately fulfilled such epistemic duties as are most likely to get them successfully in touch with the truth.[88]

This account deserves, even requires, further development, some of which will be done, incidentally, in what follows. However, having produced, in broad outline, a warranted trust model of Christian belief formation, it is important to re-engage with Plantinga. Plantinga has explicitly ruled out some of the model's key elements: chiefly the importance of evidence, but also its understanding of the role of the Holy Spirit. He gives reasons for doing so which ought to be considered in any assessment of the relative strengths of the two models. These will now be considered.

8.5 Plantinga's Defence of his Supernaturalistic Model

As I understand it, Plantinga's major reason for proposing his model of immediate, Holy Spirit produced belief which largely by-passes ordinary human processes of judgement is that any attempt to argue to the truth of the Christian gospel is likely to end up with far too tentative a conclusion. The problem with the Lockean suggestion that assent to the propositions of the gospel is made upon the credit of the proposer, is that 'it wouldn't work,'[89] for two reasons:

---

87 It may be that one has appropriately acquired a basic belief which either supports or undermines the testimony one has been given.
88 In proposing this model, I am not thereby committing myself either to externalism or internalism as a complete account of warrant. The account, however, is largely externalistic. Having some internalist constraints is important if trust is to be sufficiently critical. An awareness, by a believing community, that trust can be misplaced or poorly grounded is important in any distribution of warrant.
89 *WCB*, 268.

first, we are too 'sunk in sin'. The work of the Holy Spirit is essential to enable individual appropriation of the gospel.[90] Second, there are, additionally, two cognitive problems. First, if one tries to ascertain the truth of the gospel by ordinary historical means, utilising one's ordinary cognitive faculties, 'only a few people would acquire the knowledge in question, and then only after a great deal of effort and much time.'[91] Second, '[even these people's] belief would be both uncertain and shot through with falsehood.'[92]

Plantinga supports the second of these two claims in the following way. He argues that even without taking into account the effects of sin on our apprehension of truth, a historical case for the truth of the main lines of Christian teaching would not be sufficient to produce warranted belief.[93] That is a very strong claim. He argues for it by drawing out the weaknesses of an historical case for the truth of the Christian gospel. He suggests that such a case would typically proceed in the following way:[94]

> One would have to mount one's case without making any assumptions about the inspiration of Scripture. The Bible would need to be treated like any other ancient book. The conclusion of any such case could therefore be no stronger than that the central Christian claims are *probable*. Probability is determined by reference to a relevant body of background knowledge (either accepted by most reasonable people, or at least by the person making the probability judgement).
>
> A common way to argue (exemplified by Richard Swinburne) would be to begin by seeking to establish the existence of God as probable on the relevant background knowledge. One might then go on to argue that given the existence of God it is likely that God would reveal certain crucial truths to humankind. One could continue in similar vein 'finally winding up with some propositions with respect to which it is likely that God raised Jesus from the dead, thus authorizing and validating the message of the New Testament.'[95]
>
> The problem with such an argument chain lies in the fact that the probability of the ultimate conclusion can be no higher than the probability of the first major item; the probability that theism is true. If, as Richard Swinburne suggests in *The Existence of God*, 'on our total evidence theism is more probable than not,' then, even if all the probabilities involved in a historical

---

90   *WCB*, 268, 269.
91   *WCB*, 270.
92   *WCB*, 270.
93   *WCB*, 271.
94   What follows is a summary of Plantinga's case, 271-280. Plantinga notes that his articulated historical case for the truth of the Christian gospel is 'roughly based on Richard Swinburne's argument in his *Revelation* (Oxford: Clarendon Press, 1981), chapters 5, 7 and 8,' fn. 56, 271.
95   *WCB*, 273.

case for the truth of the Christian gospel were as high as they could be, the best we could conclude about the Christian gospel is that it is more probably true than not. But then, given such probability, one cannot rationally believe this Christian teaching. One may hope that it is true, one might think it more likely than not, but one cannot *believe* it.

The probabilities involved in the historical case are obviously not as high as they could be. Historical and scriptural scholars are involved in constant debate, for example, about what Jesus taught, with judgements of probability often very low. With respect to the key Christian belief in the resurrection, even with a fine command of the vast literature on the historicity of the resurrection, one would 'presumably think it pretty speculative and chancy',[96] its probability either very low or inscrutable. Even if one assigns generous values to the various combinations of propositions that would constitute an historical case for the truth of the Christian gospel, the resulting over-all probability (being guided by the calculus of probabilities) would, at best, be 'not ... a whole lot less likely than its denial'[97] The conclusion to be drawn, therefore, is that one's background knowledge, historical or otherwise (excluding what is known by faith or revelation) is not anywhere nearly sufficient to support serious belief in the truths of Christian theism. If this background knowledge was all that was available, the only sensible course would be agnosticism.

The main problem for an historical case for Christianity is the Principle of Dwindling Probabilities: the fact that in giving such an historical argument, the probabilities assigned to individual parts of the case must be multiplied, inevitably resulting in decreased probability.

8.6 Defence of the Warranted Trust Model

A number of points can be made in response to Plantinga's (damaging if true) dismissal of an historical case for the truth of the Christian gospel. First, Plantinga's calculation of the probability of the resurrection as either very low or inscrutable is surprising. The case for the resurrection (even the bodily resurrection) of Jesus is a good deal stronger than such a low assignment of probability would suggest.[98] Although, admittedly, it would be impossible to

---

96 *WCB*, 276.
97 *WCB*, 280.
98 For that strong case articulated, see Wolfart Pannenberg, *Jesus: God and Man*, trans. Lewis L. Wilkins and Duane, A. Priebe (Philadelphia: Westminster Press, 1968); Richard Swinburne, *The Resurrection of God Incarnate* (Oxford: Clarendon Press, 2003), W. L. Craig, *The Historical Argument for the Resurrection of Jesus* (Lewiston, NY: Edwin Mellen, 1985); W. L. Craig, *Assessing the New Testament Evidence for the Historicity of the Resurrection of Jesus*, Studies in the Bible and Early Christianity 16 (Lewiston, NY: Edwin Mellen, 1989); Gerald O'Collins, *Jesus Risen* (London: Darton, Longman and Todd, 1987); Richard Swinburne, *Revelation:*

prove by historical means that a 'resurrection' (with all of its technical and theological associations) had occurred, there is, nevertheless, strong evidence to suggest that an event of that sort of magnitude has occurred, strong evidence that Jesus, although dead, was seen alive after his death. In the absence of credible alternative explanations for these purported sightings, and, indeed, for the New Testament as a whole with its consistent (and persistent) testimony to the risen Jesus, a resurrection remains, at the very least, as a plausible possibility, certainly if judged from the standpoint of theism. I certainly would assign to the resurrection a higher probability than does Plantinga, and will further indicate why shortly.

If, however, Plantinga is correct, and the historical case for the resurrection of Jesus is as weak as he suggests, there are some serious implications. Such weakness would constitute a damaging under-cutting defeater for gospel truth claims. An unbeliever would no doubt be relieved to find that the probability of a gospel truth as central as the resurrection was 'somewhere between low and inscrutable'. The reaction of believers is likely to be more diverse. A believer *may*, following the encouragement of Plantinga, be willing to attribute his confidence in the truth of the resurrection to the inward work of the Holy Spirit, and to think it entirely unimportant that historical investigation is not able to render the resurrection probable. However, another reaction is possible. A believer could as easily be unsettled by such a low assignment of probability, and by the knowledge that there is no independent way of determining the truth of the resurrection. A believer could even begin to doubt that there is a Holy Spirit producing confidence in him, particularly now that his confidence has been shaken.

What might fuel his doubts is that in New Testament gospel presentations, the fact of the resurrection and its reliable attestation is a central theme. In the Book of Acts, for example, virtually every evangelistic address mentions the resurrection, and in most instances some reason for accepting its facticity is included. Appeals are made to the audience's prior knowledge of the miraculous ministry of Jesus, with the implication being that the resurrection is consistent with the trajectory of those powerful deeds,[99] as it is with miracles performed by the apostles.[100] Appeals are consistently made to the Old Testament,[101] as

---

From Metaphor to Analogy (Oxford: Clarendon, 1992); Stephen T. Davis, *Risen Indeed: Making Sense of the Resurrection* (Grand Rapids: Eerdmans, 1993). For a wide ranging discussion of the resurrection, including epistemological issues, see Stephen Davis, Daniel Kendall and Gerald O'Collins, (eds), *The Resurrection* (Oxford: Oxford University Press, 1997).

99 See, for example, Acts 2:22; 26:26.
100 See, for example, Acts 3:11f; 4:8f.
101 In evangelistic addresses to Jewish (or god-fearing) audiences: Acts 2:14f; 3:11f; 4:8f; 13:32f; 17:3; 11; 26:6,7, 27; 28:23.

well as to the eye and ear witness testimony of the apostles.[102] The implication of this is that the listeners (as well as those who would subsequently read the New Testament) had good reason to accept the testimony of the apostles, and to believe, on the basis of this evidence, that the resurrection of Jesus had occurred. If Plantinga is right, however, and the case for the resurrection is *not* so very good, and, if, by implication, the New Testament writers were mistaken in their belief that a good case for the resurrection could be constructed, then the problem of doubt is significantly intensified. Christians now have an additional reason (which they may not have had previously) for not accepting the testimony of Scripture. What the apostles say, or imply, about the case for the resurrection, is (to the extent that Plantinga is right) mistaken.[103]

Plantinga's argument requires closer examination. Let us assume for the moment the truth of the New Testament description of the apostolic case for the resurrection. If, as Plantinga believes, the bodily resurrection of Jesus did occur as described in the New Testament, then the apostles surely did have before them tangible and almost undeniable proof that Jesus (whose word and person they had come to trust) was alive, though he had been dead. Not only would they have been likely to believe in Jesus, they would also have been more than warranted in believing Jesus's explanation of the events (which he gave to them both before and after his resurrection). Armed with what to them was convincing proof, they bore testimony to it, arguing and debating with whoever they encountered with the purpose of persuading people to believe. They, at least, appeared to think that they had a good case to argue.

---

102 Acts 2:32; 3:15; 5:32; 22:15; 26:16. In his speech in Pisidian Antioch, Paul refers to the other apostles' status as witnesses to Jesus (13:31).

103 Plantinga, in private correspondence, has suggested that the case for the resurrection may well have been stronger in apostolic times, but is no longer so strong, thus making necessary a supernatural belief forming mechanism such as he suggests. Although it is probably true that those separated by time and space from the foundational events of the first Easter are epistemologically disadvantaged, to varying degrees, such geographical and temporal disadvantage did not appear to deter the apostles from presenting an evidential case for the resurrection (both verbally and in writing) to their own contemporaries who (in most cases) were also separated by time and space from the gospel events. In the Book of Acts, for example, the apostle Paul is depicted as involved in a ministry-long and geographically extended effort to prove (by argument) the truth of the gospel. See for example, Acts 17:2, 3: 'As his custom was, Paul went into the synagogue, and on three Sabbath days he reasoned with them from the Scriptures, explaining and proving that the Christ had to suffer and rise from the dead.' See also 18:4; 28; 19:8; 28:23. Paul's summary of his gospel in 1 Corinthians 15:3f includes both affirmations of fact as well as reasons to believe. Paul's reference to the 500 brothers, most of whom were still alive, suggests that his other references to eye-witnesses, and to the witness of the Scriptures, are intended to be taken as evidential support for the truth of the gospel.

This leads on to a second major response to Plantinga's case against an historical case for the truth of the Christian gospel. Plantinga, in his assignment of probabilities, has (or appears to have) neglected the crucially important place of testimony. He suggests that an historical case for the truth of the Christian gospel might sensibly begin (1) with the case for theism, and then progress to consider the following claims: (2) that God would make some kind of revelation to humankind; (3) that Jesus's teachings were such that they could be sensibly interpreted and extrapolated to arrive at the gospel; (4) that Jesus rose from the dead; (5) that in raising Jesus from the dead, God endorsed his teachings; and (6) that the extension and extrapolation of Jesus's teachings to the gospel is true.[104] Throughout this process, probabilities are assigned, and then, at the end of the process, multiplied to provide an overall judgement of probability. It is not surprising that on even the most generous allocation of probabilities, the over-all probability of the Christian gospel being a true expression of the mind of God is low.[105]

However, this is not the only way of constructing a case for the probable truth of the Christian gospel. Moreover, Plantinga's approach, as spelled out above, is problematic, for a number of reasons. First, it fails to take sufficient account of the mutual inter-dependency of a number of these propositions, particularly as they become influential in the actual process of making historical judgements which bear upon their truth.[106] Second, by proposing that the truth of the gospel be established through a consideration of the divinity of Scripture, Plantinga has not only guaranteed a more sceptical result, he has also suggested an approach which is significantly at odds with Scripture itself. New Testament apology is predominantly testimonial in character, with testimony being focused upon Jesus, rather than upon Scripture. This, therefore, will be the approach that I will take in what follows.

That the New Testament is a testimony to Jesus is clear. Sometimes, as in the case of John's Gospel, that testimony is deliberate and explicit. In other cases, the testimony is largely implicit and incidental to other purposes, as in the epistles. However, consistent throughout the New Testament is its overwhelming preoccupation with Jesus. He is its undeniable focus, devotion to him its *raison d'etre*. Accounting for this focus and devotion, if we take the New Testament at face value, was the career of Jesus, climaxing in his

---

[104] This argument is spelled out, in these terms, but with different numbering in *WCB*, 271-280.
[105] Richard Swinburne, in his response to Plantinga's argument, nevertheless resists such a conclusion by seeking to strengthen the probabilistic case for (1) to (6), *Plantinga on Warrant*, 210-211.
[106] On this see, Richard Swinburne, 'Natural Theology, Its "Dwindling Probabilities" and "Lack of Rapport"', *Faith and Philosophy*, Vol. 21, No. 4 (October, 2004), 540-542.

resurrection and glorification, described in fact-like fashion chiefly in the Gospels.[107]

One of the frequently noted characteristics of the Gospel narratives is their realistic nature. Commentators have been struck by the simplicity of style, the life-likeness of depiction, the lack of heroic exaggeration, and the frequent, often incidental presence of historical and geographical details.[108] The Gospels read as straightforward descriptions of fact; albeit shaped for theological and literary reasons. The historian must decide to accept, partly accept, or reject completely the fact-like testimony of the New Testament, and of the Gospels in particular. That choice depends crucially on the reliability of the witnesses. In making a decision about reliability, there are three options. First, that the apparently straightforward and fact-like narratives are a deliberate fabrication, designed to deceive. Second, that they represent sincere and honest expressions of devotion, but because of the accretion of mythical and legendary elements, or because the writers did not intend their descriptions to be taken literally, they cannot be considered factual. Third, that they are (for the most part at least) an accurate reporting of what took place. Variation on these three choices is possible. However, in broad terms, they do represent the choices facing the historian, and, indeed, the ordinary person.

In making a decision about which of these three is most probable, a person's pre-existing beliefs will have a key bearing on the choice made. If supernaturalism is ruled out in advance (as it is by Troeltschian historical Biblical critics) then options one and two will clearly be considered most probable. However, background beliefs are not always inflexible, and judgements of probability can vary over time. This is illustrated by the experience of Tony Morphett, an Australian journalist. Morphett describes himself before his conversion as 'an avowed atheist; [unwilling] to admit that there was any supernatural dimension to life.'[109] Relative to what Morphett believed at the time, theism was judged to be improbable. However, a number of events occurred in Morphett's life which had the cumulative effect of

---

107 Paul Barnett, in *Jesus and the Logic of History* (Leicester: Apollos, 1997), notes that historically valuable information about Jesus also exists in the epistles, which were written in most cases before the Gospels. Their value for historical purposes has been neglected by contemporary historians, 28. He argues that the letters of Paul ought to be the preferred point of historical entry to inquiry into Jesus and the apostolic age, 41.

108 Hans Frei, in *The Eclipse of Biblical Narrative: a study in Eighteenth and Nineteenth Century Hermeneutics* (New Haven: Yale University Press, 1974), points out that this was noted with respect to Biblical narratives as a whole, and that the major reason that these narratives increasingly ceased to be taken as factual was rejection of supernaturalism which became characteristic of critical historical scholarship, 10f.

109 Tony Morphett, *A Hole in My Ceiling* (Sydney: Hodder and Stoughton, 1985), 11.

disturbing his previously comfortable atheism. He increasingly allowed the possibility of Christian theism being true, and, at a crucial stage in his thinking, read the Gospels. To his surprise, they had the 'taste' of reporting. He came to accept them as just that, reporting, and thus came to an entirely different estimation of the probability of Christian theism. This example shows how presuppositions can change. Judgements about prior or antecedent probability can vary, sometimes considerably, under pressure from new evidence,[110] as was the case for Tony Morphett. It is also likely to have been the case for first century hearers of the gospel. They too were confronted with a message about events which, for them, would have been antecedently improbable. However, on the assumption that these events occurred, and were well attested, an acceptance of this message is likely to have been entirely justified and warranted.

A decision has to be made as to whether, in any acceptance of the apostolic testimony, arguments and evidence play a part, and whether and to what extent those arguments and evidence are sufficient to justify and to provide warrant for Christian beliefs based in any way upon them. With respect to whether they contribute to an acceptance of the apostolic testimony, my experience[111] suggests that they do. People frequently ask questions about whether the gospel is a fabrication, an exaggeration or factual. Moreover, answers to these questions are often influential in the conversion of people, particularly of those from a non-believing background. As to whether they are justified or warranted in basing their belief upon those answers, the answer is also yes.

Consider an historian who makes a careful assessment of the three possibilities. Imagine, for the sake of illustration, that she reads the New Testament for the first time (having been involved in study of another period). Imagine also that, like Tony Morphett, she has had a number of experiences which have created within her a certain openness to the Christian message. The reason for setting up the illustration in this way is not to artificially stack the decks in favour of the conclusion I'd like this person to reach, but rather to set to one side cases where metaphysical commitments are so strong and inflexible that any investigation neither would nor could yield Christian conclusions.[112]

---

110 For a skilful development of this point, as it bears on the acceptance of miracle stories, see Bruce Langtry, 'Mackie on Miracles', *Australasian Journal of Philosophy*, Vol. 66, No. 3 (1988), 368-375.

111 With significant support from the New Testament depiction of how people come to believe.

112 A convinced naturalist, for example, is unlikely to believe even the testimony of people she accepts as sincere about miraculous gospel events. She may, following Hume, even think it irrational to let relatively uncertain testimony overturn convictions which are based upon a lifetime (or even lifetimes) of experience. For two (supportive) developments of this point, see Jordan Howard Sobel, 'On the Evidence of Testimony for Miracles: A Bayesian Interpretation of David Hume's Analysis', *The Philosophical Quarterly*, Vol. 37, No. 147 (1987),

How might such an historian approach the New Testament? Thinking in terms of Plantinga's six propositions, let us imagine that she comes to her study as an agnostic with respect to belief in God. As a result of her recent experiences, she is open to the possibility that God exists, but is unwilling to assign a particular probability. She is also agnostic about whether God, if he exists, would communicate to his creatures. Much would depend on what sort of god God was. She, quite reasonably, decides to suspend judgement in the hope that her study of the New Testament might shed some light on the matter.

It is at this point that she approaches the New Testament. What does she find? She is likely to be struck (along, no doubt, with other things) by the apparently fact-like nature of the Gospel narratives. Further, she would observe the apparently sincere conviction of the writers that what they wrote about actually happened, in that Jesus was seen, heard, touched and eaten with after his death. She would fairly quickly be able to rule out deliberate and deceptive fabrication as an explanation for the New Testament, as few historians working in the area seriously countenance such a possibility. Deciding between the second and third options would be more difficult. In making this decision, she would need to carefully consider issues of genre to determine whether the writers intended their narratives to be taken literally.[113] She would need to consider issues of authorship and dating.[114] She would need to be self-consciously aware

---

166-186; David Owen, 'Hume versus Price on Miracles and Prior Probabilities: Testimony and the Bayesian Calculation', *The Philosophical Quarterly*, Vol. 37, No. 147 (1987), 187-202.

113 She could be guided in this by a number of statements within the New Testament itself; for example Luke 1:1, 2; 2 Peter 1:16; 1 John 1:1-3. How the narratives were understood in the early centuries of the church would also provide some guidance. The miracle stories, for example, were almost universally understood in realistic terms. See, for example, Harold Remus, *Pagan-Christian Conflict over Miracle in the Second Century* (Cambridge, Mass.: Philadelphia Patristic Foundation, 1983). See also Craig A. Evans, 'Life-of-Jesus Research and the Eclipse of Mythology', *Theological Studies,* 54 (1993), 3-36. Evans considers, and throws doubt upon the viability of the category of myth for understanding the miracle stories. There is a growing acceptance among New Testament scholars of the idea that Jesus was at least known as a miracle worker. Marcus Borg, a member of the Jesus Seminar, goes so far as to assert that this is 'virtually indisputable' on historical grounds, *Jesus: A New Vision* (San Francisco: Harper and Row, 1988), 61.

114 This is especially important with respect to the Gospel of John. It has been long noted that John's account of the Gospel events is distinctively different to that of the Synoptics; Matthew, Mark and Luke. The widespread assumption is that the Synoptics are earlier and therefore more useful as sources for constructing an account of the historical Jesus (that is, Jesus as he actually was). Some, such as J. A. T. Robinson, in *The Priority of John*, ed. J. F. Coakley (London: SCM, 1962) and Craig L. Blomberg, *The Historical Reliability of John's Gospel* (Leicester: Inter-Varsity Press, 2001), have argued otherwise. For a good brief discussion of the issues involved, see M. M. Thompson, 'The Historical Jesus and the Johannine

of her own metaphysical and methodological assumptions, as well as those of others working in the area. A decision would need to be made at some early stage in her research whether to even countenance the possibility of supernatural causes, given the arguments of Hume and Troeltsch, for example. This would directly bear on what scholarly method she would employ. Let us assume that she does allow herself to countenance the possibility of supernatural causes,[115] and therefore adopts something like a Spinozistic approach. Contra Plantinga, if she were to do this, she would, or could well, and with good warrant, come to the conclusion that the New Testament testimony to Jesus, and in particular to his resurrection, is largely and straightforwardly factual. She would (like other historians before her) find it difficult to account for the genesis and early success of the Christian movement (and for the emergence of the New Testament itself) without this being so, and without an event as significant as the resurrection having occurred.[116]

The historian's task of sifting through the mountain of evidence and scholarly discussion is, admittedly, a daunting one, and would, as Plantinga

---

Christ', in R. A. Culpepper and C. Clifton Black, (eds), *Exploring the Gospel of John* (Louisville, Kentucky: Westminster John Knox Press, 1996), 21-42.

115 Which she could quite reasonably do. Hume's arguments against any acceptance of testimony to supernatural events are not unanswerable. For example, Philip Dawid and Donald Gillies, in 'A Bayesian Analysis of Hume's Argument Concerning Miracles', *The Philosophical Quarterly*, Vol. 39, No. 154 (1989), point out although the sincere testimony of people ought to be discounted if the prior probability of miracles is considered sufficiently low, metaphysical commitments (or even openness to a change in one's metaphysic) can make a significant difference - so much so that Hume's argument against miracles can be circumvented, 64-65. Hume argued that 'no human testimony can have such force as to prove a miracle,' *An Enquiry Concerning Human Understanding*, (1748), ed. Tom L. Beauchamp, (Oxford: Clarendon Press, 1999), 184, but this clearly depends on the exact nature of one's prior metaphysical commitments. It also depends, as Coady points out, on what weight is given to sincere human testimony, *Testimony*, 192. See further, Richard Swinburne, *The Concept of Miracle* (London: Macmillan, 1971); Joseph Houston, *Reported Miracles: A Critique of Hume* (Cambridge: Cambridge University Press, 1994); David Johnson, *Hume, Holism, and Miracles* (Ithaca: Cornell University Press, 1999).

116 Even someone like E. P. Sanders who, for historiographical reasons, is cautious to the point of agnosticism about the resurrection, is nevertheless willing to engage in the following speculation: 'Without the resurrection, would [Jesus's] disciples have endured longer than did John the Baptist's? We can only guess, but I would guess not,' *Jesus and Judaism* (Philadelphia: Fortress, 1985), 240. For a useful development of this point, see N. T. Wright, 'Christian Origins and the Resurrection of Jesus: The Resurrection of Jesus as a Historical Problem', *Sewanee Theological Review*, Vol. 41, No. 2 (1998), 107-123; 'Early Traditions and the Origin of Christianity', *Sewanee Theological Review*, Vol. 41, No. 2 (1998), 125-140.

suggests, take much time and effort. However, despite that, I think it entirely possible (and reasonable) that an historian could conclude, at the end of or during this process, that the New Testament testimony to the resurrected Jesus is reliable and trustworthy, and, consequently, put her trust in Jesus. Note that if this happens, as it sometimes does, the probability values assigned to (1) and (2) will be affected.[117] Agnosticism with respect to (1) and (2) will be replaced by belief in the truth of (1) and (2).[118]

Supposing that the above is a plausible account of how an initially unbelieving historian might come to believe in the trustworthiness of the New Testament's testimony to Jesus, and to his resurrection, is such belief justified, or warranted? I cannot see why not. The historian has done her work meticulously and responsibly, both in her practice of history and in her determination of method. She has carefully considered the three broad possibilities of fabrication, exaggeration and accurate reporting, even to the extent, conceivably, of concluding that the probabilities are stacked in favour of the third of these. She is therefore likely to be justified in her believing. She is also likely to be warranted, on the assumption that the gospel is true, and that the writers of the New Testament enjoyed high degrees of warrant in their belief. The degree of warrant enjoyed by a testimonial belief is a function of the fulfilment of conditions such as the ones mentioned above (of epistemic responsibility and warrantedness at the beginning of the relevant chain of testimony). It is also a function of whether and to what extent a person has independent reasons for accepting the testimony.[119] It is worth noting in this regard that factors other than the testimony of the New Testament may reasonably contribute to an historian's belief in the truth of the gospel. The consistent and winsome testimony of Christian friends can be influential,[120] as can the gospel's ability to resonate within a person's life, sometimes in such a way as to integrate the various aspects of a person's experience, as Meek suggests. An historian may find a convergence happening of external and internal factors,[121] all leading to the conclusion that the New Testament witness to Jesus is true, and trustworthy.

---

117 As will, to varying degrees, the probabilities assigned to (3) to (6).
118 This illustrates the recursive nature of investigation into the truth of the Christian gospel. Judgements of probability with respect to one aspect of the case for the gospel's truth will affect other judgements, making a neat a-temporal assignment of probabilities not only difficult, but misleading.
119 This discussion depends on my suggested account of testimonial warrant outlined earlier in this chapter.
120 Giving credence to the idea that the resurrection (or the power behind the resurrection) is on-goingly influential.
121 Gerald O'Collins describes such a process in these terms: '[The] validation of Easter faith works "from the outside" and "from the inside." We need to hear and accept the historical, public testimony coming to us, ultimately from Peter, Paul, Mary Magdalene and the other original witnesses. But we also look for signs "from

The issue of trust is an important one. A potential weakness in the above account of probabilistic belief formation, one which Plantinga would no doubt exploit, is that it somewhat side-steps a point implicitly made by Plantinga in his description of a probabilistic case for the truth of the Christian gospel. To establish, as we have had our historian do, the general reliability of the New Testament witness to Jesus is not quite the same as establishing that the gospel in all its details is true. Nor does it establish that Jesus was the undiluted source of this gospel. Even after establishing the general reliability of the New Testament testimony to Jesus, there is, therefore, more to be done. Plantinga's propositions (3), (5) and (6) still need to be assessed with respect to their probability.

Yet, this is not an insurmountable problem for my account of how an historian might come to believe the truth of the gospel. Establishing the general reliability of the New Testament, particularly if that includes reliability with respect to the resurrection of Jesus, is no small achievement. It is pregnant with epistemological and metaphysical implications. If Jesus genuinely did rise from the dead, then the probability that God (his God) was endorsing both him and his teachings is significantly increased, as is the probability that this same God would ensure the reliable dissemination of those teachings. What degree of probability is assigned to (3), (5) and (6) is difficult to ascertain. They will certainly have increased as a result of the historian's scholarly work.

It is at this point that a reference to trust may be helpful. Let us assume that our imaginary historian has come to believe in the general reliability of the New Testament testimony to Jesus, and as a result has come to put her trust in God, and in Jesus as Son of God. It does not follow that all of her questions will have been answered. She is likely to have any number of questions. For example, is *everything* within the apostolic testimony to be accepted as factual? Have human errors been involved in the process of inscripturation, and if so, to what extent, and with what implications? To what extent were the New Testament writers captive to a now outmoded worldview in their description of the gospel, requiring a re-interpretation to make Christian faith relevant to those living in the twenty-first century? These are serious questions, deserving of careful attention. However, they are not questions which need to be answered (or entirely answered) before a person (even a diligent historian) can come to faith. Coming to faith, in the experience of many at least, is, essentially, an experience of coming to trust. It is seldom made with every question answered.

---

the inside," acknowledging the ways in which belief in the risen Jesus confronts our mortality and correlates existentially with our deepest experiences and with our insatiable yearning for life, meaning and love which cannot be fulfilled in this transitory life and which led William Blake to remark that "the heart is a bottomless gorge,"' *The Resurrection of Jesus Christ: Some Contemporary Issues* (Milwaukee: Marquette University Press, 1993), 34, 35.

Trust simply begins a journey of understanding. It does not begin already finished.

Is such trust warranted? Raised (again) by this whole discussion is the epistemological status of trust. Although a number of suggestions about how trust operates have already been made, and a model for determining the warrant enjoyed by beliefs (trustingly) formed in response to testimony has been proposed, it will be helpful to continue our analysis. Plantinga uses the term 'warrant' to refer to that somewhat elusive quality which, together with true belief, is able, depending upon the degree of warrant, to constitute knowledge. Warrant is a quality the presence of which bestows varying degrees of positive epistemic status, with such status being determined by whether and to what extent the epistemological practice is likely to get one in touch with what is true. The term 'warrant' can also, helpfully, be used with respect to trust. Trust can also be said to be warranted (or not warranted) in a similar sense to its application to belief. It too can be judged according to whether and to what it extent it is likely to get one in touch with what is true.[122] Plantinga's theory of warranted belief can therefore be modified and made relevant to trust, in the following way:

> a person's trust has warrant only if (1) it has been produced in him by cognitive faculties that are working properly (functioning as they ought to, subject to no cognitive dysfunction) in a cognitive environment that is appropriate for [his] kinds of cognitive faculties, (2) the segment of the design plan governing the production of such trust is aimed at getting him in touch with what is true, and (3) there is a high statistical probability that trust produced under those conditions will succeed in getting him in touch with what is true. Under these conditions, furthermore, the degree of warrant is an increasing function of degree of trust.

In any development of this model, the distinctive characteristics of trust would need to be taken into account. Given that trust is often directed towards a person (or people), issues of reliability are likely to loom large. Temporal considerations also need to be taken into account. Initial trust must be differentiated from mature trust, or trust which has had the benefit of on-going vindication. The relationship between trust and belief would need to be explored. Trust is unlikely to be formed without the existence of certain firm beliefs, with the warrantedness of those beliefs being influential in the assignment of warrant to trust. However, this need not always be the case.

---

[122] Trust, perhaps even more so than belief, has many non-alethic purposes, such as the maintenance of comfort, or of relationship. These purposes more than occasionally stand in the way of people getting in touch with what is true. Therefore, the word 'warrant', when used with respect to trust, would need to be deliberately truth oriented. The degree of warrant enjoyed by trust would need to be a function of whether and to what extent it gets one in touch with what is true.

Warranted trust can exist in the absence of firm beliefs, or where a number of beliefs which are relevant to trust are uncertain. There is, at times, a certain risk involved in trust, but risk on its own is not enough to invalidate trust, particularly when the object of trust proves trustworthy over time.

In the light of these considerations, many of which have already been mentioned, it can now be said that our imaginary historian is (on the basis of the above account) likely to be highly warranted in coming to trust in God. To trust in God is to trust in someone whose trustworthiness is unsurpassed. Although at the point of initial trust she may have had many unanswered questions, her belief in the general reliability of the New Testament is likely to be of sufficient strength to warrant such initial trust. Her cognitive faculties have been working properly (subject to no cognitive dysfunction) in a cognitive environment that is appropriate for her kinds of cognitive faculties. She has been appropriately critical in her thinking. God himself (on the assumption that God exists) is responsible for the design plan according to which trust is elicited in response to reliable testimony. The statistical likelihood that someone who thus trusts in God is successfully in touch with the truth is high. Given that trust ushers someone into a relationship with God which has its own authenticatory aspect, it is possible that our historian could come to have high levels of warranted trust, and for her trust to be highly warranted.

Plantinga's objections to an inference dependent model of Christian belief formation fail, in my opinion. It *is* possible for someone to come to warranted belief and warranted trust, simply by the use of their God-given cognitive faculties.[123] This is certainly possible for an historian. It is also possible for someone who is not an historian, or a scholar of any variety. Although it is likely that such a person will be somewhat less warranted both in their belief and trust,[124] what will preserve warrant for them is that they are part of a community of belief and trust, and, inasmuch and to the extent that the community as a whole is warranted in believing the gospel and trusting in God, they too will (or may) share in this warrant.[125] The epistemology is essentially the same as with ordinary testimony. If someone is trusted to have done the necessary research and has reliably come to a true conclusion, say about theoretical physics, a person is warranted to some lesser degree in believing in

---

123 Not being denied by this statement is the work of the Holy Spirit who, as I understand it, works in and through our ordinary belief forming faculties.

124 What will, in all likelihood, be lacking for many ordinary believers is a critical approach to belief formation. In terms of my suggested model of testimonial warrant, they will be less likely to appropriately fulfil such epistemic duties as are most likely to get them in touch with the truth (condition 3).

125 For a valuable discussion about the role of an epistemic community with particular reference to evidentialism, see Stephen Wykstra, 'Toward a Sensible Evidentialism'.

the truth of that conclusion.[126] The same applies to someone within the Christian community who is trustingly depending on the expertise and responsible scholarship of people like my imaginary historian. If the historian is warranted in her belief and trust, so also (to varying degrees) will those who rely upon her for their belief and trust. Not every person within a believing community needs to do the hard work of establishing the general reliability of the gospel. What is important is that someone has (representatively) done this.

To draw this chapter to a conclusion, one further strength of the warranted trust model of Christian belief formation will be considered, and that is that it makes good (or at least better) sense of the New Testament's condemnation of unbelief. According to Plantinga's model, the internal instigation of the Holy Spirit is sufficient for a person to form the belief that the Christian gospel is true. Moreover, this belief forming mechanism is able to deliver a level of warranted certitude that ordinary belief forming mechanisms cannot.[127] In fact, ordinary belief forming mechanisms will not (and cannot, reasonably) provide anything like the certitude that is necessary for belief, let alone knowledge.[128] Instead, they deliver uncertainty. Although simple theism is perhaps more likely than not,[129] if judged by our ordinary belief-forming mechanisms (referred to by Plantinga as the Standard Package),[130] the same cannot be said for Christian theism, with the startling possible implication that unbelief is the more reasonable option. As Plantinga puts it:

> Now perhaps from [the perspective of the Standard Package] it isn't at all clear that the rational decision would be to endorse Christian belief; perhaps the rational decision would be to give it up.[131]

The implication of this state of affairs, which Plantinga thinks *is* the way things are,[132] is that the best and most rational choice for unbelievers, who are

---

126 There generally is some diminishing of warrant in the movement down a testimonial chain.
127 '[Even though] you don't have either sensuous imagery or evidence from other things you believe to go on; the beliefs are none the worse, epistemically speaking, for that. In fact (on the model) they are all the better for that; they have (or can have) much more firmness and stability than they could sensibly have if accepted on the basis of rational argument or, as in this case, historical investigation; they can also have much more warrant,' WCB, 264.
128 WCB, 274.
129 WCB, 131.
130 Included in the Standard Package are induction, deduction, memory, sympathy and so on, WCB, 131.
131 WCB, 133.
132 Plantinga repeats a number of times his contention that the case for Christianity, on the Standard Package, is significantly weaker than the case for theism. For example: 'To show that these models are in fact true, therefore, would

not the beneficiaries of the internal instigation of the Holy Spirit (IIHS), is to withhold belief or be agnostic. To do otherwise would be to be irrational. This is both a startling and disturbing admission because, if it is true, it is hard to understand how an unbeliever can be condemned (by God or anyone) for not believing a message which, on rational grounds, he should not believe. If doing one's very best with the faculties God has given one does not lead one to the conclusion that the gospel is true, and if, furthermore, one is not the beneficiary of the IIHS, then condemnation itself would appear to be immoral.[133]

Herein lies a major problem with Plantinga's model. The warranted trust model of Christian belief formation, outlined above, is superior at this point. According to the model, the central belief forming mechanisms are testimony and trust. People encounter, in the gospel, a testimony to Jesus which is both human and divine. They are not expected to believe the testimony blindly, but are given many adequate reasons to believe. Whether those reasons to trust are compelling is another (important) question. It may be that people are warranted in trusting the testimony of the New Testament, even without the need for a supernatural belief forming mechanism. However, are they *required* to trust? Are they being epistemologically negligent, even immoral, in not trusting? My hunch, which would need much further justification, is that people are (or may well be[134]) epistemologically and morally negligent in not reasoning to a position of trust, particularly considering how existentially and eternally significant are the decisions which need to be made with respect to Jesus.

Some support for this is to be found in John's Gospel where people are clearly condemned for not heeding the witnesses, and not drawing sensible conclusions from the testimony of the witnesses. The problem is not that they were unable to believe (because a sufficiently strong case could not be mounted in favour of accepting the apostolic testimony) but because they refused to

---

also be to show that theism and Christianity are true; and I don't know how to do something one could sensibly call 'showing' that either of these *is* true. I believe there are a large number (at least a couple dozen) good arguments for the existence of God; none, however, can really be thought of as a *showing* or *demonstration*. As for classical Christianity, there is even less prospect of demonstrating its truth,' *WCB*, 170. See also, 200, 201.

133 Plantinga has suggested, in private correspondence, that, *perhaps,* all who hear the gospel are beneficiaries of the Internal Instigation of the Holy Spirit, and that by refusing the gift of faith people are culpable in their unbelief. This suggestion, if true, would alleviate the ethical problem raised. However, it has at least this disadvantage, from Plantinga's point of view: it runs counter to (or at least does not comfortably cohere with) the teaching of John Calvin who describes the Holy Spirit's ministry as a ministry of illuminating the otherwise totally darkened minds of only some human beings, that is, God's elect. See, for example, *The Institutes*, II, II, 19-21, 278-281.

134 Depending on whether and to what extent they have access to the gospel message.

Theory of Christian Belief Formation: A Critique 183

believe. It is significant that in the description of unbelief in John's Gospel, the most frequently cited reasons for unbelief are attitudinal, not cognitive. Refusal to believe has to do with a love of darkness, rather than light,[135] a preference for the praise of others rather than God,[136] and a fear of the Jews.[137] These attitudinal problems are seen as the (human[138]) reason that people arrive at illegitimate or superficial conclusions,[139] and explains their failure to accept the powerful evidence of the work of God, through Jesus, in their midst. They are, from a Johannine point of view, justly condemned. The same could be argued for people today. In what is a well-attested gospel, people, even today, have more than enough reason to accept the New Testament testimony, and to trust. People's failure to trust, and their failure to follow the evidence where it leads may, as it did in New Testament times, be the basis for just condemnation.

Sufficient has now been offered by way of critique of Plantinga's position. In the final chapter of this work, a broader assessment of Plantinga's significance with respect to apologetics, both positive and negative, will be offered. Both the criticism and praise of the preceding chapters will need to be combined to achieve this.

---

135 3:19-20; 7:7.
136 5:44; 12:42, 43.
137 7:13; 9:22; 12:44, 45; 19:38.
138 Unbelief is also seen in John as related to the electing activity of God (6:37-40; 10:14, 15, 26). Fully fledged, or obedient belief is seen, from a divine perspective, as a gift from God (1:13; 10:27-29; 17:2, 6, 9).
139 5:16-18, 6:14f; 6:42; 7:24; 7:27, 41, 42; 9:16.

CHAPTER 9

Plantinga's Significance

We now draw together the various threads of critique and appreciation that have wound their way through this work, and to make an assessment of the nature and stature of Plantinga's contribution to the enterprise of Christian apologetics.

As at least some measure of his contribution, Plantinga has been involved in the broad area of Christian defence for virtually the entire length of his long and distinguished career. Plantinga's life-long interest in apologetics has culminated (to this point at least) in the release of *Warranted Christian Belief* which has as one of its explicit aims the defence of Christian belief against the charge that such belief is irrational, or unjustified, or in some other way deficient from an intellectual point of view.[1]

There has not been one major contemporary challenge to traditional Christian belief which Plantinga has not, in some way, responded to. Included among the issues examined under the microscope of Plantinga's analytical skills are logical positivism, Freudianism, Marxism, foundationalist evidentialism, religious pluralism, subjectivism, postmodernism, theological liberalism, naturalism, historical Biblical criticism, and the perennially disturbing problem of evil. Although Plantinga does not refer to himself as an apologist, and although his academic interests are both more narrow (because of a concentrated interest in epistemology), and more broad (because of a range of interests beyond epistemology), Plantinga can certainly be classified as an apologist, and this by virtue of having wrestled with, and having provided powerful responses to each of the challenges mentioned above. Moreover, he has done this in the public arena, thereby effectively engaging the non-Christian world.

Plantinga has not cloistered himself in cosy theological isolation. Even his choice of philosophy as a career was freighted with risk. At the time of his choice, American philosophy departments, almost without exception,[2] ranged from unsympathetic to hostile in their attitude to traditional Christian faith. Yet it was within this context that Plantinga established himself both as a philosopher and as a Christian philosopher. It was within this context that Plantinga developed his unapologetic, uncompromising style of doing

---

1   *WCB*, viii.
2   The two most notable groups of exception would have been Catholic Universities and Christian liberal arts colleges.

philosophy from a Christian perspective, and also encouraged others to do likewise. He was a founding member of the Society of Christian Philosophers,[3] which, from its beginnings in 1978 as 200 member subsociety of the American Philosophical Society, has grown to a membership in excess of 1,000.[4] So noteworthy has been this growth that, as far back as 1980, *Time* magazine reported:

> In a quiet revolution in thought and arguments that hardly anyone could have foreseen only two decades ago, God is making a comeback. Most intriguingly, this is happening not among theologians or ordinary believers ... but in the crisp, intellectual circles of academic philosophers, where consensus had long banished the Almighty from fruitful discourse.[5]

Plantinga is mentioned as influential in this resurgence of interest in God, being described as 'America's leading orthodox Protestant philosopher of God'.[6] Whether this description is (or was) correct, Plantinga has certainly made a significant and enduring contribution. James Sennett describes Plantinga's impact in the areas of epistemology and the philosophy of religion as 'momentous'.[7] C. Stephen Evans makes the claim that, 'No Christian philosopher has had a bigger influence on the [North American] intellectual scene than Alvin Plantinga.'[8] Eleonore Stump, a Roman Catholic scholar from Saint Louis University, gives this assessment:

> Alvin Plantinga has had a great influence on contemporary philosophy of religion. More than anyone else in the last thirty years he has shaped the questions asked in the field, and the answers he has proposed have been at the center of everyone's discussion of the questions. He has managed to combine philosophical rigor and precision with great richness and depth, so that his work is both creative and powerful. Philosophy of religion will bear the imprint of his thought for a long time to come.[9]

This work and impact has had the effect of giving valuable resources, as well as renewed confidence, to those involved in Christian defence. A new generation of

---

3   The SCP was the brainchild of William P. Alston. Other founding members include Robert and Merilyn Adams, Arthur Holmes, and George Mavrodes.
4   As of the 29th of August, 2001, the number of members of the Society was 1,051.
5   'Modernizing the case for God,' *Time* 115, no. 14 (April 7, 1980), 65-68.
6   *Time*, 66.
7   *The Analytic Theist*, xi.
8   *The Analytic Theist*, dust jacket comment.
9   *The Analytic Theist*, dust jacket comment.

confident Christian scholars have emerged following in the footsteps of Plantinga, the fruit of whose work is already beginning to be felt.[10]

Plantinga's greatest contribution to apologetics lies in the area of negative apologetics, a fact which is reflected in the shape of this thesis. Plantinga has done considerably more *defending* than *commending*. Arguably his two greatest contributions have been his work on the problem of evil and his evolving response to the Enlightenment initiated charge that theistic and Christian belief is unjustified, irrational or unwarranted. With respect to the problem of evil, Plantinga has been a trail-blazer. In seeking to understand and respond to this the most serious of all threats to traditional Christian belief, he has broken new ground. His response to the logical form of the problem stands as an enduring obstacle to those who would attempt to prove that the existence and persistence of evil is incompatible with the existence of God. Plantinga has also been an active and significant participant in efforts to respond to the evidential form of the problem. With respect to the charge that theistic and Christian belief is unjustified, irrational, or unwarranted, Plantinga has advanced an impressive, even audacious defence. He has boldly challenged long-held evidentialist dogma, and, in the process, has developed a distinctive, idiosyncratically Reformed way of understanding how theistic and Christian beliefs are formed. This defence, along with Plantinga's skilfully crafted theory of warrant, represent a considerable challenge to all those who would urge a *de jure* objection to theistic and Christian belief.

One could elaborate further on Plantinga's achievements. They are not restricted to his work on evil and rationality, as shown throughout this thesis. However, rather than continuing to itemise his achievements, it will be more helpful to assess Plantinga's contribution and significance against the background to his work, as outlined in chapter one. There, Plantinga was described as a conservative Christian apologist possessed of various Augustinian, Calvinian, Reidian and Kuyperian convictions. Although this description is fair, Plantinga's position has evolved to become a good deal more complicated and subtle than can be neatly summarised by such labels. He is his own person in so many ways that he defies neat categorisation. Moreover, there are elements within his thinking which show promise of breaking down some of the barriers which have divided apologists, and of creating significant *rapprochement* between several major schools of Christian apology.

9.1 Plantinga and Augustinianism

To begin with the Augustinian label, Plantinga identifies himself as Augustinian, particularly in his approach to Christian scholarship. He insists

---

10 For example, in the production of book like *Reason for the Hope Within* (Grand Rapids: William B. Eerdmans, 1999), edited by Michael J. Murray with contributions from a group of mostly young Christian philosophers.

that what is known by faith should be given full scope to influence, even determine, the approach one has to intellectual endeavour. There must be no artificial sealing off of the deliverances of faith from the deliverances of reason, as has been the Thomistic tendency.[11] Plantinga also gives a primacy to faith which is consistent with the Augustinian formula 'faith seeking understanding.'[12] For Plantinga, faith very definitely precedes reason, and, in fact, renders reason[13] virtually[14] irrelevant in the process of coming to faith. Faith is a gift of God created in the mind of a Christian without the mediatorial aid of arguments or evidence. Under the influence of the internal instigation of the Holy Spirit, the gospel is known immediately to be true. Coming to faith thus happens largely independently of reason, although reason can (and does) have a role subsequent to faith.[15] This understanding of the relationship between faith and reason places Plantinga very decidedly in the camp of contemporary Augustinians. I will argue shortly that Plantinga's teaching about faith and its relationship to reason is not, in fact, true to Augustine himself. Nevertheless, Plantinga does represent a tradition which (whether we call it Augustinian or not) very definitely places faith first, and which significantly isolates faith from reason. Plantinga is true to this tradition. He is also true to Calvin in his depreciation of the value of arguments prior to faith.[16] He is true to Calvin (and to the Augustinian-Calvinian tradition in general) in his emphasis on the ruinous effects of sin, sin having both affective and cognitive consequences.[17] His understanding of faith is significantly similar to Abraham

---

11   See, for example, 'Using What We Know By Faith', *Reformed Journal*, Vol. 37 (September, 1987), 10-11; 'Augustinian Christian Philosophy'. Note that among twentieth century Thomists (or neo-Thomists) there is a range of opinions about the relationship between revelation and philosophy (or scholarship generally). Some maintain the autonomy of reason in non-theological scholarly discourse, whereas others, such as E. Gilson and J. Maritain, maintain that revelation exerts a more direct and intrinsic influence. J. A. Weisheipi, 'Scholasticism', *The New Catholic Encyclopedia* (New York: McGraw Hill, 1967), 1169.
12   It is certainly consistent with how that formula has been understood in post-Kantian times.
13   Understood as the Standard Package of induction, deduction, credulity and so on.
14   Although not completely. Reasoning is certainly occasionally necessary (in advance of faith) to deal with potential defeaters of Christian belief, and also, more basically still, to simply understand the gospel message.
15   Both in the process of seeking understanding (engaging, for example, in Christian scholarship) and in dealing with potential defeaters.
16   Calvin believed that although there was a place for arguments to the conclusion that the Scriptures were divine, these were only of value subsequent to faith and to the certifying work of the Holy Spirit. See chapters seven and eight of Book One of the *Institutes of the Christian Religion*.
17   See, for example, chapter seven of *WCB*, entitled 'Sin and its Cognitive Consequences'.

Kuyper's. Kuyper defined faith as 'that function of the soul by which it obtains certainty directly and immediately, without the aid of discursive demonstration.'[18] Plantinga, in these respects, is very clearly on the Augustinian side of the Augustinian/Thomistic fence. To represent this position as 'Augustinian', however, is a little unfortunate. Augustine himself had a significantly different understanding of the relationship between faith and reason. For example, he made use of natural theological arguments in the defence of, and as a means of commending, Christian doctrine.[19] He also believed that reason had an important place prior to faith, as well as subsequent to faith,[20] as he explains in the following letter to Consentius. Consentius had expressed the view that Christian truth was grasped more by faith than by reason. Augustine's reply:

> God forbid that He should hate in us that faculty by which he made us superior to all other living beings. Therefore, we must refuse so to believe as not to receive or seek a reason for our belief, since we could not believe at all if we did not have rational souls. So then, in some points that bear on the doctrine of salvation, which we are not yet able to grasp by reason - but we shall be able to sometime - let faith precede reason, and let the heart be cleansed by faith so as to receive and bear the great light of reason; this is indeed reasonable. Therefore the Prophet said with reason: 'If you will not believe, you will not understand'; thereby he undoubtedly made a distinction between these two things and advised us to believe first so as to be able to understand whatever we believe. It is, then, a reasonable requirement that faith precede reason, for, if this requirement is not reasonable, then it is contrary to reason, which God forbid. But, if it is reasonable that faith precede a certain great reason which cannot be grasped, there is no doubt that, however slight the reason which proves this, it does precede faith. That is why the Apostle warns

---

18 *Principles of Sacred Theology*, 182.
19 R. Douglas Geivett argues, for example, that Augustine's proof of the existence of God plays a key role in his treatise *On Free Choice of the Will*. He even describes it, somewhat controversially, as 'the cornerstone of Augustine's theodicy,' *Evil and the Evidence For God* (Philadelphia: Temple University Press, 1995), 14. Geivett takes issue with those, such as Dewey J. Hoitenga Jr. (*Faith and Reason from Plato to Plantinga*), who minimise the importance of natural theology for Augustine. For further discussion on the nature and importance of natural theology in Augustine, see Norman Kretzmann, 'Faith Seeks, Understanding Finds', in Thomas Flint, (ed), *Christian Philosophy* (Notre Dame: University of Notre Dame Press, 1990); also Paul Helm, *Faith and Understanding* (Grand Rapids: Eerdmans, 1997), 26-52. Helm has a sensible discussion of Kretzmann and Hoitenga, along with a number of other understandings of Augustine.
20 This aspect of Augustine's understanding was drawn attention to by R. C. Sproul, John Gerstner and Arthur Lindsley in *Classical Apologetics* (Grand Rapids: Academie Books, 1984), 189f. They also note the neglect of this aspect of Augustine's thought, particularly among presuppositionalists.

us that we ought to be ready to give an answer to anyone who asks us a reason for our faith and hope ...[21]

Here Augustine asserts almost the contrary of Plantinga's position that reasons should not (or need not) be sought for belief. Reasons can legitimately be sought. They even should be in the light of the apostle's 'warning' that a reason be given. One reason for seeking a reason lies in the need for people to decide which authority to place their confidence in. Augustine became convinced that in virtually all matters of belief, authority is important. In the case of religious belief, the authority of God, of the apostles, and of the church is essential to guide believers in matters which are beyond their direct experience.[22] Since various demands are made by different and often competing authorities, a decision must be made as to which authority to accept.

Authority demands belief and prepares man for reason. Reason leads to understanding and knowledge. But reason is not entirely absent from authority, for we have got to consider whom we have to believe.[23]

In making the decision about who to believe, miracles played a key role in Augustine's thinking.[24] Miracles provide people with good (certainly adequate) reason to believe.[25] Although Augustine understood that miracles, on their own, will not occasion faith, divine power being required to change a person's heart, the operation of divine power is not considered to be in any way inconsistent with the corroboratory importance of miracles, or of other types of

---

21 *Letters* Vol. 2, Sister W. Parson, (ed), The Fathers of the Church (New York: Fathers of the Church Inc., 1953), CXX, 302.
22 See further, John M. Rist, *Augustine: Ancient Thought Baptized* (Cambridge: Cambridge University Press, 1994), 56-63.
23 'Of True Religion', in J.H.S. Burleigh, (ed), *Earlier Writings*, Library of Christian Classics (Philadelphia: Westminster, 1979), XXIV, 45, 247.
24 For more on the importance of miracles, and their role of establishing authority, see 'The Usefulness of Belief', XIV, 32, 318; 'Of True Religion', XXV, 47, 248; *Letters*, CXXXVII, 18-36; *The Trinity*, tr. Stephen McKenna, C.SS.R., The Fathers of the Church (Washington: The Catholic University of America Press, 1963), IV, XIX, 25, 162, 163; *The City of God*, in Philip Schaff, (ed), Nicene and Post Nicene Fathers (Grand Rapids: Eerdmans, 1974), XXII, 5, 482; 7, 484, 485.
25 Although miracles, at least of the stature of the New Testament miracles, were restricted to the New Testament, or so Augustine believed ('Of True Religion', XXV, 47, 248), their existence and reliable attestation ('Of True Religion', XXV, 47, 248) continued to be an important reason to accept the authority of the Scriptures and the Church ('The Usefulness of Belief', XIV, 31, 317). The other major reason, for Augustine, was the success of the church, 'The Usefulness of Belief', XVI, 34, 319.

evidence.[26] All such evidence enables people to accept the authority of the Scriptures, and of the Church.

Augustine's position, when considered in isolation from the apologetic tradition which has appropriated his name, is actually closer to my own warranted trust model of Christian belief formation than it is to the tradition of Kuyper and Plantinga. Augustine believed it was important to have good reasons to trust. He also believed that at the root of faith is trust, trust in the testimony of the apostles, and ultimately of God himself.[27] Plantinga, in this respect at least, is not truly Augustinian. In fact, his position is closer to that of Thomas Aquinas, and has become closer still in recent years, as I will now seek to demonstrate.

9.2 Plantinga and Thomism

In 1974, Plantinga wrote a short tribute to Aquinas to mark the 700th anniversary of his birth.[28] Although the tribute was genuinely appreciative in tone, Plantinga, at that stage, was in no doubt about the magnitude of the differences between himself and Aquinas. In his words: 'A Protestant Calvinist may find himself obliged to differ with Aquinas at many points, some of them important. There are mountains between Rome and Geneva.'[29] The most obvious 'mountain' between Rome and Geneva (at least in the area of apologetics) has been natural theology. As an example of how polarising natural theology has been in its effects, when Plantinga first spelt out his Reformed objection to natural theology in the early 80s, the response from a number of Thomistic scholars was hostile. Henry Veatch, in a scathingly critical response to *Faith and Rationality*, was dismissive of Plantinga, and of Reformed epistemology in general. He concluded his essay with the words: 'And so, as Mark Twain might say, is not the most charitable thing that we

---

26 Not only miracles, but a range of other evidence was thought influential by Augustine in occasioning faith, as he makes clear in the very section of *The City of God* where divine power is emphasised: '[In so enlightened an age as the first century] the human mind [would] have refused to listen to or believe in the resurrection of Christ's body and its ascension into heaven, and have scouted it as an impossibility, had not the divinity of truth itself, or the truth of divinity, and corroborating miraculous signs, proved that it could happen and had happened? For the predictions of the prophets that had preceded the events were read, they were corroborated by powerful signs, and the truth was seen to be not contradictory to reason, but only different from customary ideas, so that at length the world embraced the faith it had furiously persecuted,' *The City of God*, XXII, 7, 484.
27 D. X. Burt, *Augustine's World*, 43-45.
28 Alvin Plantinga, 'Aquinas - 700 Years Later', *Reformed Journal*, Vol. 24 (April, 1974), 5-7.
29 *Aquinas - 700 Years Later*, 6.

might now do is simply 'draw the curtain' on the sorry spectacle of [Plantinga, Wolterstorff and Co.'s] proposed Calvinist-Analyst variety of epistemology.'[30]

The mountains between Geneva and Rome loomed large when those words were written. However, significant change has occurred since then. Scholars from both sides have begun to engage in constructive dialogue.[31] Plantinga himself, from his position as John A. O'Brien Professor of Philosophy at the University of Notre Dame, has been a model of conciliation, nowhere more so than in *WCB*. Here, he goes so far as to invoke the authority of Aquinas as well as Calvin in the naming of his A/C model of Christian belief formation. He describes his model as 'based on a claim made jointly by Thomas Aquinas and John Calvin.'[32] Plantinga goes out of his way to honour to Aquinas, as in the following quotation:

> Thomas Aquinas and John Calvin concur on the claim that there is a kind of natural knowledge of God (and anything on which Calvin and Aquinas are in accord is something to which we had better pay careful attention).[33]

Plantinga is even willing to describe Calvin's proposal regarding the *sensus divinitatis* as 'an interesting development' of an idea of Aquinas'.[34] Plantinga elaborates: 'Here, as in several other areas, we can usefully see Calvin's suggestion as a kind of meditation on and development of a theme suggested by Aquinas.'[35] With respect to Christian belief formation, Plantinga also enthusiastically invokes the authority and intellectual heritage of Aquinas:

> The suggestion that belief in the 'great things of the gospel' (Jonathan Edward's phrase) is the result of some special work of the Holy Spirit is often thought of as especially the teaching of such Calvinist thinkers as Edwards and John Calvin himself. It is indeed central to their teaching, and here the model follows them. On this point as on so many others, however, Calvin, despite his pugnacious noise about the pestilential papists and their colossal offences, may be seen as following out and developing a line of thought already found in Thomas Aquinas. 'The believer,' says Aquinas, 'has sufficient motive for believing, for he is moved by the authority of divine teaching confirmed by miracles and, what is more, *by the inward instigation of the divine invitation.*'[36]

---

30 Henry B. Veatch, 'Preliminary Statement', in *Thomistic Papers IV*, 58.
31 As, for example, in the volume edited by Linda Zagzebski, *Rational Faith: Catholic Responses to Reformed Epistemology*, (1993).
32 *WCB*, 168.
33 *WCB*, 170.
34 *WCB*, 170.
35 *WCB*, 170.
36 *WCB*, 249.

Plantinga is clearly seeking to reconcile Geneva and Rome, at least in the area of religious epistemology. The differences are not considered so significant as to prevent such a project. In this, I think Plantinga is correct, and in what follows will argue that Plantinga's position on the epistemology of faith is significantly similar to that of Thomas Aquinas. Moreover, in some of the areas where Plantinga and Aquinas disagree on the epistemology of faith, I myself am at odds with Plantinga.

As has been noted above, Plantinga draws attention to similarities between Aquinas and Calvin (and therefore between Aquinas and himself). Included among these similarities is the belief that there exists a natural knowledge of God, and that the inner working of the Holy Spirit is necessary for saving faith. Plantinga and Aquinas agree in other ways. They share the conviction (though not necessarily expressed in these words) that belief in God is (or can be) a deliverance of reason.[37] In Plantingan terms, belief in God is formed by cognitive faculties operating as they were designed to, in an environment conducive to such belief formation. The significant difference between Aquinas and Plantinga is that Aquinas restricted the scope of reason's competence to the workings of the Standard Package of intuition, induction, deduction and so on, whereas Plantinga does not. Despite this difference, Plantinga could, with some justification, see his own Calvinian approach as a development or refinement of Aquinas' thought.

Plantinga also shares with Aquinas a reluctance to use probabilistic arguments, particularly to argue for the truth of the Christian gospel, as opposed to simple theism. Aquinas had a place for probabilistic argumentation, but preferred, in a context of controversy with unbelievers, to use the more demonstrative arguments of natural theology.[38] Plantinga holds a remarkably similar view. He effectively recommends against an historical apology, on very

---

[37] Plantinga has been insistent that his approach to theistic belief is not fideistic. Belief in God arises as a result of the proper functioning of our God-given cognitive equipment: '... the Reformed epistemologist is not a fideist at all with respect to belief in God. He does not hold that there is any conflict between faith and reason here, and he does not even hold that we cannot attain this fundamental truth by reason; he holds instead, that it is among the deliverances of reason,' 'Reason and Belief in God', 90.

[38] In *Summa Contra Gentiles*, Aquinas recommends the use of demonstrative arguments to convince an adversary, say that God exists, but since such arguments do not exist to prove the truth of distinctive Christian beliefs, he recommends against arguing to the conclusion that Christianity is true: 'For the very inadequacy of the arguments would rather strengthen them in their error, since they would imagine that our acceptance of the truth of faith was based on such weak arguments,' *SCG*, 1, 9, 2. Probabilistic arguments nevertheless have a place. They are useful for the 'training and consolation of the faithful', *SCG*, 1, 9, 2, and are used within *SCG* to answer the objections of adversaries and to set forth the truth of faith, *SCG*, 1, 9, 3.

much the same grounds as Aquinas; the arguments involved are considered too weak.

Possibly the most surprising similarity between Plantinga and Aquinas lies in their attitude to natural theology and its role. Both agree that natural theology can be used for apologetic purposes, to challenge unbelievers as well as to strengthen believers.[39] Both are aware of the limitations of natural theology.[40] Neither is of the opinion that the pursuit of natural theology is necessary for the ordinary Christian, or that a successful natural theology provides the necessary underpinnings for revealed theology.[41] Both give precedence to faith, again in unexpectedly similar ways. Aquinas believed that the certitude created by faith is, for various reasons, and for most people, greater than that created by reason. Plantinga concurs. One of his major reasons for developing a supernaturalist model of faith is because of the lack of certitude which would be created if faith were dependent on reason. In his opinion, ordinary reasoning processes can only deliver *uncertainty* with respect to the gospel.[42] Aquinas' reasons for the same conclusion are somewhat different. For him, the greater certitude created by faith is accounted for by the reliability of faith's object, and by the relative unreliability of human reasoning processes:

> Other things being equal, sight is more certain than hearing; but if [the authority of] the person from whom we hear greatly surpasses that of the seer's sight, hearing is more certain than sight; thus a man of little science is more certain about what he hears on the authority of an expert in science; than about what is apparent to him according to his own reason; and much more is a man certain about what he hears from God, Who cannot be deceived, than about what he sees with his own reason which can be mistaken.[43]

---

39 See, for example, 'Christian Philosophy at the End of the 20th Century', 39, 40; 'The Prospects for Natural Theology', 287; and on Aquinas, Garcia, 'Natural Theology and the Reformed Objection', 125.
40 According to Aquinas, natural theology is limited in that only a small number of Christian beliefs can be established by way of natural reason; moreover, arriving at these conclusions is likely to be difficult and time consuming; with any resulting certitude being frequently deficient because of the human tendency to error. L. Garcia, 'Natural Theology and the Reformed Objection', 124. Plantinga further highlights the limitations of natural theology by pointing out that the arguments of natural theology, if measured by the standards traditionally applied to them, are unsuccessful, 'The Prospects for Natural Theology', 287-289.
41 *Aquinas, Calvin & Contemporary Protestant Thought*, 83.
42 *WCB*, 264, 265.
43 *STh*, II-II, q.4. art. 8, and 2. See also *SCG*. After pointing out the limitations of natural theology (all of which are related to human limitation), Aquinas concludes, 'That is why it was necessary that the unshakeable certitude and pure truth concerning divine things should be presented to men by way of faith,' 1, 4, 5.

One other surprising similarity between Plantinga and Aquinas is that both see very little role for reason in the process of coming to faith; or prior to faith. This is definitely true of Plantinga, but it is also true of Aquinas, the difference being that Aquinas places more emphasis upon the will than does Plantinga. For Aquinas, faith is the result of an act of the will in the absence of compelling evidence. Evidence, while not irrelevant, is not what grounds faith. According to Aquinas, the driving impetus to faith is an act of the will moved by the promise of eternal life. As he puts it:

> we are moved to believe what God says because we are promised eternal life as a reward if we believe. And this reward moves the will to assent to what is said, although the intellect is not moved by anything which it understands.[44]

For Aquinas, a desire for evidence prior to faith, far from being natural and understandable, actually diminishes the merit of faith.

> Human reasoning in support of what we believe may stand in a two-fold relation to the will of the believer. First, as preceding the act of the will, as, for instance when a man either has not the will, or not a prompt will, to believe, unless he be moved thereto by human reason; and in this way human reasoning diminishes the merit of faith ... Secondly, human reasons may be consequent to the will of the believer. For, when a man has a will ready to believe, he loves the truth he believes, he thinks out and takes to heart whatever reasons he can find in support thereof; and in this way human reasoning does not exclude the merit of faith, but is a sign of greater merit.[45]

Aquinas, as we will see, does not altogether rule out reasons and evidence in support of faith. He sometimes sees them as operating in parallel to each other.[46] However, Aquinas, cannot be accused of making faith dependent on reason, or of adopting an *understand in order to believe* stance with respect to faith and reason. If anything, Aquinas belongs more comfortably under the banner of Augustinianism (as that banner is frequently understood, particularly in Reformed circles), as the following quotation indicates:

> Faith is called a consent without inquiry in so far as the consent of faith, or assent, is not caused by an investigation of the understanding. Nonetheless, this does not prevent the understanding of one who believes from having

---

44 *The Disputed Questions on Truth*, 14, 1.
45 *STh*, II-II, 5, 2.
46 Aquinas makes the point this way, in *The Disputed Questions on Truth*, 14, 1: 'in faith, the assent and discursive thought are more or less parallel. For the assent is not caused by the thought, but by the will.'

some discursive thought or comparison about those things which he believes.[47]

Ironically, Aquinas is more 'Augustinian' than Augustine himself, at least with respect to the role of reason prior to faith. The same is true of Plantinga. In this respect, he is closer to Aquinas than he is to Augustine.

There is one final significant similarity between Plantinga and Aquinas, and it has to do with the purpose of natural theology. According to Aquinas, natural theology serves to advance the goal of human happiness, which consists in 'seeing' (by intellectual vision) truths about God. To the extent that knowledge about God is attained, this goal is (imperfectly) achieved. Faith, which is formed in the absence of compelling evidence, can be converted into sight. What we simply believe can achieve the lofty status of knowledge. Plantinga argues, similarly, that what people believe as Christians (as a result of the operations of the *sensus divinitatis* or the internal instigation of the Holy Spirit) can be given extra warrant by way of the deliverances of reason.[48] On occasion, this extra warrant can be enough to convert mere belief into knowledge. Plantinga is in agreement with the spirit of medieval natural theology, at least.[49]

The similarities between Plantinga and Aquinas are remarkable considering that Reformed epistemology (tracing this heritage through Abraham Kuyper to Calvin himself) has had, as its *raison d'etre,* a principled repudiation of the natural theology tradition of Thomas Aquinas. Plantinga has not only (effectively) down played the differences between these two traditions, he has invoked the authority of Aquinas in developing his own theory of theistic and Christian belief formation. This is surely a matter of some significance. As is becoming clear, the differences between Plantinga and Aquinas are not as large

---

47   *The Disputed Questions on Truth*, q.14, a.1 ad 2m. Another passage inviting a similar conclusion is: 'Since the understanding does not in this way have its action terminated at one thing so that it is conducted to its proper term, which is the sight of some intelligible object, it follows that its movement is not yet brought to rest. Rather, it sill thinks discursively and inquires about the things which it believes, even though its assent to them is unwavering. For, in so far as it depends on itself alone, the understanding is not satisfied and is not limited to one thing; instead, its action is terminated only from without. Because of this, the understanding of the believer is said to be "held captive," since, in place of its own proper determinations, those of something else are imposed on it: "bringing into captivity every understanding,"' *The Disputed Questions on Truth*, 14, 1.

48   See, for example, 'Coherentism and the evidentialist objection to belief in God', 123. Note that Plantinga believes that the *sensus divinitatis* is itself a rational faculty possessed by all humans, such that the beliefs that it produces are *among* the deliverances of reason.

49   'The Prospects for Natural Theology', 311, 312.

as one might have expected. If anything, they have diminished in light of Plantinga's reinstatement of natural theology to a position of some value.

Thus far, attention has been drawn attention to the similarities between Plantinga and Aquinas. However, a number of significant dissimilarities also exist, three of which are particularly significant. The first is that Aquinas, unlike Plantinga, places almost exclusive emphasis upon discursive reason when discussing reason and its role. Although Aquinas does raise the possibility of an immediate or intuitive grasp of such truths as that God exists, he considers it more likely that discursive reason will be the means by which these truths are arrived at.[50]

A second significant difference between Plantinga and Aquinas lies in Plantinga's unwillingness to give to miracles the same evidential importance as does Aquinas. Although Aquinas cannot (because of his emphasis on the will) be accused of being rationalistic or evidentialist in his approach to faith; although his is certainly not an *understanding seeking faith* stance, he does, nevertheless, suggest a confirmatory role for miracles, as indicated by the following quotation:

> The believer has sufficient motive for believing, for he is moved by the authority of divine teaching confirmed by miracles and, what is more, by the inward instigation of the divine invitation.[51]

Plantinga quotes this passage (see above), but only to highlight the Holy Spirit's importance. He neglects the reference to miracles. Aquinas, like Augustine, gives to miracles the role of confirming the authority of divine teaching.[52] As he puts it in *Summa Contra Gentiles*:

> [Divine Wisdom] reveals its own presence, as well as the truth of its teaching and inspiration, by fitting arguments; and in order to confirm those truths that exceed natural knowledge, it gives visible manifestation to works that surpass the ability of all nature. Thus, there are the wonderful cures of illnesses, there is the raising of the dead, and the wonderful immutation in the heavenly bodies; and what is more wonderful, there is the inspiration given to human minds, so that simple and untutored persons, filled with the gift of the Holy Spirit, come to possess instantaneously the highest wisdom and the readiest eloquence ...[53]

---

50 See, for example, *SCG*, 3, 38, 1.
51 *STh*, II-II, q.2, art.9, ad 3.
52 Miracles have this role, as does the Holy Spirit. L. Garcia, in 'Natural Theology and the Reformed Objection', notes that in answer to the question of how we can know that it is God who is speaking in Scripture, Aquinas gives two answers: firstly, by the outward evidence of miracles, and, secondly, by the 'inward instinct of the Divine invitation.' [*STh*, II-II, q.2, a.9], 128.
53 *SCG*, I, 6, 1.

The exact role miracles are thought to play in individual cases of Christian belief formation is unclear. They are certainly not considered as a *necessary* foundation for faith. However, according to Aquinas, they have at least this role: they rescue faith from the charge of foolishness or irresponsibility.[54] They may also aid in producing faith in some people. That they played this role in apostolic and post-apostolic eras is recognised by Aquinas.[55] It is possible that he expected this role to continue.[56] Whether he did or not, Aquinas certainly gave to miracles (and to other confirmatory evidence) a greater importance than does Plantinga.

A third significant area of difference between Plantinga and Aquinas is Aquinas' emphasis on the role of the will in theistic and Christian belief formation. Plantinga, by contrast, is neglective of the will. It is both interesting and significant that the reason that Aquinas emphasises the will is the same reason Plantinga has for ignoring the importance of probabilistic evidence: the evidence for the truth of the Christian gospel is inconclusive. Linda Garcia explains the effect of this with respect to Aquinas's voluntarism:

---

54 Aquinas begins chapter six of Book One of *SCG* with these words: 'Those who place their faith in this truth, however, "for which the human reason offers no experimental evidence," do not believe foolishly, as though "following artificial fables" (2 Peter 1:16),' 1, 6, 1. Aquinas goes on, later in the same chapter, to contrast Christian belief, which has the support of miracles (along with other confirmatory signs) with Islamic faith, which, in his opinion, lacks these supports: 'As for proofs of the truth of [Mohammed's] doctrine, he brought forward only such as could be grasped by the natural ability of anyone with a very modest wisdom. Indeed, the truths that he taught he mingled with fables and with doctrines of the greatest falsity. He did not bring forth any signs produced in a supernatural way, which alone fittingly gives witness to divine inspiration; for a visible action that can be only divine reveals an invisibly inspired teacher of truth,' 1, 6, 4.

55 Aquinas recognized that miracles (and arguments from miracles) were influential in the conversion of people in the early church. He states: 'When these arguments were examined, through the efficacy of the above mentioned proof [of miracles], and not the violent assault of arms or the promise of pleasures, and (what is most wonderful of all) in the midst of the tyranny of the persecutors, an innumerable throng of people, both simple and learned, flocked to the Christian faith,' *SCG*, I, 6, 1. Aquinas mentions a number of other indications of the divine truth of the gospel. These include the miracle of faith itself, the fact that people under the under the influence of the gospel spurn visible things for the invisible, the testimony of the ancient prophets, and, most wonderfully of all, the conversion of the world, *SCG*, I, 6, 1.

56 Aquinas concludes his discussion of the evidence for the truth of the Christian gospel with a reference to the witness of contemporary miracles: 'Yet it is also a fact that, even in our own time, God does not cease to work miracles through His saints for the confirmation of the faith,' *SCG*, I, 6, 3. Aquinas may have seen it as possible that these contemporary miracles might occasion faith in the same way as was evidenced in the early eras of the church.

Aquinas holds that most believers accept the mysteries of faith by an act of faith, that is, by taking them on God's authority. In this act of faith it is the intellect that assents, but always moved by the will, since the evidence or grounds are in themselves insufficient to cause the mind to assent to what is revealed, and since the claim that the proposed revelation is from God is similarly incapable of proof.[57]

Aquinas argues that the will must take up the slack between what the evidence can ascertain and what faith demands. Plantinga, alternatively, suggests a supernatural belief producing mechanism which entirely crosses that chasm (a chasm which he thinks is deeper than even Aquinas had thought). Both Aquinas and Plantinga think it important that the chasm be crossed, and a high level of certitude achieved for faith. They have simply proposed different ways of achieving that certitude. For Aquinas, certitude is created by an act of the will; for Plantinga, certitude is produced entirely by the Holy Spirit.[58]

I have argued in chapter eight that some unfortunate consequences result from an acceptance of Plantinga's non-voluntaristic model. To briefly re-iterate, it is difficult to accept that people can be condemned for not having a belief which, when not formed as a result the internal instigation of the Holy Spirit, is unwarranted given the evidence. A serious issue of justice is involved here, if people are condemned for sensibly withholding belief. However, instead of pursuing it, I will draw attention to a problem which appears to beset the theories of both Aquinas and Plantinga. It has to do with certitude. Both Aquinas and Plantinga attempt to preserve for faith a high level of certitude. Aquinas does this by giving a key role to the will; Plantinga by way of the internal instigation of the Holy Spirit. Each of these suggestions is considered necessary because, for both Aquinas and Plantinga, ordinary belief producing mechanisms are unable (by themselves) to deliver the sort of certitude which is necessary for faith.

Two problems arise. First, Aquinas and Plantinga have over-inflated the value of certitude. Second, faith does not require, and, indeed, often does not have the high level of certitude that Aquinas and Plantinga consider essential. Both Aquinas and Plantinga have, arguably, been overly influenced by the long-standing Western preoccupation with (and pursuit of) certitude. Certainty (creating certitude[59]) has been a much cherished ideal among Western epistemologists, evidenced by the tendency to prefer deductive over inductive arguments, and to relegate probabilistic knowledge to second class status. This over-valuation of certainty is exemplified in Aquinas' suggestion that probabilistic arguments not be used in apologetic dialogue; as it is in

---

57 Natural Theology and the Reformed Objection', 133.
58 Note that Aquinas does not neglect the role of the Holy Spirit, but, unlike Plantinga, locates the effect of the Holy Spirit's ministry in an act of the will, whereas Plantinga locates it in a gift of insight.
59 Certitude is used here to refer to the psychological state of feeling certain.

Plantinga's avoidance of such arguments, certainly earlier in his career, but also more recently in his reluctance to argue a case for the Christian gospel.[60] Such avoidance of the probabilistic is unnecessary. Not only is probabilistic knowledge often the only knowledge available, it is also an entirely adequate base from which to negotiate life. It is, as well, an entirely adequate basis for trust, for negotiating one's relational life, including one's relationship with God.[61]

The second (and related) problem with Aquinas' and Plantinga's attempts to preserve a high level of certitude for faith is that Christian faith does not require, and very often does not achieve, the high level of certitude that Aquinas and Plantinga think it must. What matters with faith, from a New Testament point of view, is not so much its strength, but its object. Jesus taught that faith the size of a mustard seed was sufficient to move mountains (Matthew 17:20, 21). Largeness of faith, although certainly an ideal in the New Testament, is often not the reality. All too frequently, human faith is of the kind possessed by the man who cried: 'I believe; help my unbelief'.[62] William Alston suggests that this is the experience of many Christians. In his opinion, 'a significant proportion of contemporary sincere, committed, devout Christians are accepters rather than believers.'[63] They don't quite 'believe' that the gospel is true, in the sense of thinking it unquestionably true,[64] but they 'accept' it as true, with occasional, or even frequent feelings of doubt.[65] Alston describes the situation in these terms:

> Some Christians have firm *beliefs* that, for example, Jesus of Nazareth was an incarnation of the second person of the Trinity, that he was resurrected after being crucified and buried, and that he is alive today and in personal

---

60 To be fair, Plantinga has become increasingly comfortable with probabilistic argumentation. Moreover, his reluctance to argue for the truth of the Christian gospel stems not so much from any discomfort with probabilistic argumentation as it does from his belief that the relevant arguments are too weak to support reasonable belief. Having said that, my suspicion is that Plantinga's Dutch rationalistic background has prejudiced him somewhat against probabilistic argumentation, a prejudice certainly evident in his earlier writings.
61 As was seen in the previous chapter, trust has a complex and variable relationship with belief. It can (and does) exist with low levels of belief, and this occasionally with warrant.
62 Mark 9:23.
63 William Alston, 'Belief, Acceptance, and Religious Faith', in J. Jordan, D. Howard-Snyder, *Faith, Freedom and Rationality* (Lanham: Rowman and Littlefield, 19960, 18.
64 'Belief, Acceptance, and Religious Faith', 6.
65 For a detailed analysis of the difference between belief and acceptance, see L. Jonathan Cohen, *An Essay on Belief and Acceptance* (Oxford: Clarendon Press, 1992).

relationship with the faithful. For them these are facts about which they have no more doubts than they do about their physical surroundings and the existence of family and friends. Even if they can see how one *could* doubt or deny these doctrines, they are not themselves touched by this. Perhaps this has been part of their repertoire of constant belief for as long as they can remember, and nothing has come along to shake it.

But not all sincere, active, committed, devout Christians are like this, especially in these secular, scientific, intellectually unsettled times. Many committed Christians do not find themselves with such an assurance. A sense of the obvious truth of these articles does not well up within them when they consider the matter. They *are* troubled by doubts; they ask themselves or others what reasons there are to believe that all this has really happened. They take it as a live possibility that all or some central Christian doctrines are false.[66]

If this description is correct, which I think it is, there are a number of implications with respect to faith, and faith's certitude. My suggestion (following Alston) is that faith's certitude is varied, and variable. For some, such as those who have been brought up in strong Christian homes, certitude is often high. For others it is low. In almost all cases, certitude varies throughout life, depending on circumstances and age. From the point of view of the warranted trust model presented in this thesis, it is significant that levels of certitude appear to be proportional to the perceived trustworthiness of the those from whom the gospel is heard. Those with a strong Christian heritage are often not plagued by doubt or uncertainty. There are strong emotional, psychological and sociological reasons for this. Trust and belief is relatively easy. This is less so for those whose parents and social circumstances are not so encouraging of Christian belief. My informal surveying of theological students suggests that those who become Christians as adults, or who come to faith from an unsympathetic background, are more likely to question and doubt; are more likely to seek reassurance that the gospel message (and the community of that gospel) is trustworthy. That is, they are more inclined to require reasons to trust. The degree of strength required of these reasons will also vary. Some, because of their background and religious beliefs, will require the development of a strong case. Others will be satisfied simply by hearing that such a case has been mounted. In almost all cases, the reliability and expertise of the person or group commending Christian faith (from the apostles to the contemporary Christian community) will be the decisive issue. The important question is: 'Can I trust what they are telling me?'

Once a person decides to trust, various factors will determine the level of certitude from that point: the on-going reliability of the Christian group; an increasing understanding of the gospel; answers to prayer; and the person's own

---

66 'Belief, Acceptance, and Religious Faith', 16.

disposition, circumstances, and level of commitment. Plantinga discusses the probabilistic case for Christianity in the abstract, measuring probability in a static way against background beliefs. As he himself observes, this is not how people normally think.[67] The process is more dynamic, fluid and variable than that. Often, all that is required is *some* reason to trust;[68] some reason to begin what is a *lifetime* of trust.

Plantinga neglects the fiduciary aspect of faith. He almost exclusively identifies faith with *fides*. What is significantly missing in Plantinga's account is reference to the inter-personal or relational, and temporally unfolding nature of faith. A relationship, even with God, is something which grows and develops. It has a history. Levels of certitude are therefore likely to change over time. Laura Garcia suggests that in this relational process trust is the key to certitude. When assailed by doubts, believers 'feel that God should be given the benefit of the doubt, quite literally.'[69] Garcia appeals to Aquinas to develop her point:

> Aquinas says that faith is a virtue which is perfected by charity, so that one who believes God comes to know God, and in knowing him comes to love him. Many believers seem to be convinced of their faith, not so much because of the reasons that led them to embrace it in the first place, but because of the many confirmations they have received in their lives of the truth that it teaches, especially what they take to be their own experiences of the one whom they believe. That is, it seems to them as though God has proved worthy of their trust. That is why the assurance of faith often seems like folly to those who do not believe, since the kind of knowledge and love of God that sustains it cannot be made available to them.[70]

Garcia's account has the advantage of making certitude a function of a developing relationship. It ties certitude to history, including personal history. Certitude will thus vary from person to person and from time to time. It is the product of a dynamic, developing, and sometimes stagnating relationship of trust. An understanding of certitude in these terms renders unnecessary a supernatural gift of direct insight. The actual way in which people believe, with

---

67 For example, when confronted with evil and suffering, *WCB*, 488.
68 In *Faith and Reason* (Oxford: At the Clarendon Press, 1981), Richard Swinburne argues that the faith which is needed for a religion is basically a commitment to seek a particular goal, and that this commitment can exist even without the belief that the goal is there to be attained, or that the chosen way will achieve that goal. All that is required of religious faith is that the person concerned thinks that there is some good chance that the goal is there, and that the chosen way will realise that goal. As a Christian, one sets out assuming, but not necessarily believing the claims of the Creed.
69 'Natural Theology and the Reformed Objection', 130.
70 'Natural Theology and the Reformed Objection', 131.

all of its variation and uncertainty (occasional or chronic), is explained well enough by normal belief forming and maintaining processes, at least at the cognitive level.

To conclude, we have been considering areas of similarity and dissimilarity between Plantinga and Aquinas, and have noted that Plantinga is remarkably similar to Aquinas in various ways. He has also taken a number of deliberate steps in a Thomistic direction. Most significantly, perhaps, natural theology has come to assume a place of increased importance in Plantinga's thinking, which is very similar to that of Aquinas. Plantinga has also sought to build bridges between Aquinas and his own Kuyperian-inspired Reformed epistemology. This too is remarkable, considering that, until recently, the mountains standing between these two positions would have been considered too large to cross. It is hard to estimate the likely future effects of this movement of *rapprochement*. One key to continued progress could lie in the vicinity of Aquinas' appeal to the confirmatory role of miracles. Plantinga neglects this aspect of Aquinas' religious epistemology, and shows no immediate signs of any change. However, as was argued in chapter six, Plantinga's theory of proper function contains yet untapped resources for the development of an apology which gives to miracles the prominence awarded them in the New Testament. Although this takes apologetics into the admittedly uncertain and risky waters of history, which was problematic for Aquinas, and still is for Plantinga, it need not be such a problem, as I have argued, and will further.

The implications for apologetics of Plantinga's move in a Thomistic direction are, again, difficult to determine. It is, however, likely that an on-going process of mutual enrichment, understanding and cooperation will be encouraged. The formerly sharp divide between Thomism and Augustinianism-Calvinianism is likely to begin to blur, and perhaps evaporate altogether. Time will tell.

Time will also tell what impact Plantinga's work will have in bringing together a number of other formerly divided positions. Under the broad umbrellas of Thomism and Augustinianism-Calvinianism are some smaller umbrellas. Two, which have been influential in recent times, are presuppositionalism and evidentialism, the first drawing inspiration from Abraham Kuyper, the second from B. B. Warfield and others.

9.3 Plantinga and the Presuppositionalist/Evidentialist Divide

Plantinga continues to be Kuyperian in some of his most fundamental convictions. His understanding of faith, for example, is decidedly Kuyperian. Kuyper's definition of faith as 'that function of the soul by which it obtains certainty directly and immediately, without the aid of discursive demonstration,'[71] could easily be Plantinga's definition. However, despite their agreement on faith, Plantinga differs with Kuyper in a number of ways. He now accepts natural theology as a legitimate and useful enterprise. He believes that a place for apologetics, both positive and negative, exists. In these respects, Plantinga has moved away from Kuyper and toward Warfield. Warfield, although stronger than Plantinga about the need for positive apologetics, was willing to accept belief in God as a first principle,[72] or, in Plantingan terms, as properly basic. The differences between Plantinga and Warfield are less considerable than one may have had reason to expect.[73]

Plantinga's work, once again, shows promise of initiating significant *rapprochement* between two formerly polarised positions. Differences between Kuyper and Warfield have tended to crystallise into hard and unyielding positions, no more so than in the passionate debates following the development of Cornelius Van Til's pre-suppositionalism. This apologetic system was devised in conscious reaction to all previous apologetic approaches, including Thomism and the Reformed evidentialism of Warfield and others. Much of the heat of these earlier debates has subsided, and various conciliatory efforts have been made.[74] Nevertheless, differences still remain.

Plantinga, despite his own struggle with evidentialism, has mostly declined to enter the apologetic battle created by Van Til. However, Plantinga's increasingly influential writings are likely to accelerate the reconciliation of these previously divided positions. As in the case of the Thomistic/Calvinian divide (which in many ways reflects the evidentialist/presuppositionalist divide), Plantinga represents a mediating position, although leaning somewhat in a presuppositional direction. His understanding of faith as a supernaturally created response to the self-authenticating gospel or Scripture is essentially the same as Van Til's.[75] He believes with Van Til that Scripturally revealed truths constitute 'a proper *starting point* for thought'[76] (in Van Til's case, the *only* legitimate starting point for thought). Plantinga and Van Til also agree that these Scriptural truths should be allowed to exert maximum influence on all thought and scholarship.

---

71 *Principles of Sacred Theology*, 182.
72 'Bi-Level Evidentialism', 382.
73 Perhaps the major difference lies in Warfield's more ready acceptance of the need to provide evidence in support of Christian claims.
74 See, for example, R. Mayers, *Both/And: A Balanced Apologetic* (Chicago: Moody Press, 1984).
75 See, for example, Cornelius Van Til, 'My Credo' in E.R. Geehan (ed), *Jerusalem and Athens* (Phillipsburg: Presbyterian and Reformed Publishing Co., 1971), 15-19; *Christian Apologetics* (Phillipsburg: Presbyterian and Reformed Publishing Co., 1976), 65f.
76 *WCB*, 343; 'My Credo', 21.

Plantinga and Van Til are similar in one other significant way. Van Til was convinced that unaided and unregenerate human reason is unable to secure the truth *about anything*. Non-Christian systems of thought must inevitably self-destruct, or lead to irrationality. Only by assuming the truth of Christianity could knowledge and truth be secured.[77] In his evolutionary argument against naturalism, and against Humean scepticism, Plantinga argues along similar lines that to be a naturalist or a sceptic puts one in a position of potential (and, under certain circumstances, real) irrationality.[78] By developing these arguments, Plantinga has placed some very valuable (one might say explosive) ammunition in the hands of contemporary presuppositionalists.[79] The presuppositional method of apology employs essentially the same strategy of drawing out the (hopefully unwelcome) implications of non-Christian ways of thinking.

Plantinga, by the provision of these arguments, has become a powerful ally of presuppositionalists.[80] He is, however, no more than an ally. Plantinga certainly has not endorsed a narrowly presuppositional approach to apology. He has been much more willing to engage the non-Christian world on its own terms, without insisting on the ultimacy of Christian presuppositions. One of the purposes of apologetics, as Plantinga understands it, is to persuade unbelievers that certain implications follow from what they already believe which are supportive of Christian belief,[81] and not simply destructive of their

---

77 Van Til did not believe that non-Christians were incapable of knowledge. He simply believed that such knowledge was inadequately grounded in non-Christian assumptions. See, for example, *The Defense of the Faith* (Philadelphia: Presbyterian and Reformed Publishing Company, 1955), 102, 396; *Why I Believe in God* (Philadelphia: Presbyterian and Reformed Publishing Company, n.d.), 20.

78 For Plantinga's evolutionary argument against naturalism see chapter three. Plantinga's case against Humean scepticism is spelled out in *WCB*. His basic assertion is 'that one who displays a certain kind of agnosticism with respect to his origin and place in the universe, and also grasps a certain cogent argument, will not, in fact, know anything at all; nothing he believes will have warrant sufficient for knowledge,' 218. For the argument in full, 222-227.

79 Plantinga, unlike Van Til, actually develops the arguments. Van Til had a habit of making unsubstantiated assertions, and of providing illustrations rather than arguments, John Frame, *Apologetics to the Glory of God* (Phillipsburg: P&R Publishing, 1994), 69-75.

80 The recent very positive review of *WCB* by K. Scott Oliphint (Associate Professor of Apologetics at Westminster Theological Seminary) is some small evidence that Plantinga is considered a valuable ally by contemporary presuppositionalists, 'Epistemology and Christian Belief', *Westminster Theological Review*, Vol. 63 (2001), 151-182.

81 And not simply destructive of non-Christian belief. Plantinga points out, for example, that 'as a matter of fact there are very many propositions many or most of us believe with respect to which it is epistemically probable that there is such a person as God,' 'Epistemic Probability and Evil', 578.

own belief systems. Significant epistemological common ground therefore does exist between believers and unbelievers which an apologist can exploit; a point denied by Van Til.[82]

Although Plantinga is not a Van Tillian presuppositionalist, he is also not an evidentialist. He stands between the two positions, and therefore has the potential to be an agent of *rapprochement* between them. He is, however, also likely to be a source of disappointment. This is certainly the case for evidentialists, and particularly for those involved in seeking to commend the truth of the Christian gospel by way of an historical apology. As we have seen, Plantinga argues that the existence of God is (perhaps) more probable than not (if judged by the Standard Package, minus the *sensus divinitatis*). However, he thinks the same cannot be said for specifically Christian beliefs such as that 'God's love was revealed among us in this way: God sent his only Son into the world so that we might live through him,' (1 John 4:9).[83] Plantinga is therefore forced to concede that the Reformed epistemologist does not know by way of argument that Christianity is true. He is dependent on the inward instigation of the Holy Spirit for his knowledge. However, whether or not such instigation is actual is entirely dependent on whether Christianity is true. In Plantinga's words:

> the Reformed epistemologist (*this* Reformed epistemologist) doesn't claim as part of his philosophical position that belief in God and the deliverances of IIHS *do* have warrant. This is because in all likelihood they have warrant only if they are true, and I am not arguing that these beliefs are in fact true. No doubt the Reformed epistemologist does in fact believe they *are* true, and is prepared to *claim* that they are, even if he doesn't propose to argue for this claim.[84]

This seems an odd position. Plantinga is unwilling to argue for the truth of Christianity. He *is* willing to argue for theism, and, to this extent, to provide support for at least some Christian beliefs, beliefs shared by Muslims and Jews. Yet, he does not believe that he can argue that Christianity is true, because of his belief that such arguments are too weak. For those who consider that good arguments do exist to the conclusion that Christianity is true, such a stance is likely to be disappointing. Harold Netland's criticism of Plantinga, mentioned in chapter six, that Plantinga has done little to aid the cause of commending the Christian gospel, can be seen to have real warrant. Netland is critical of

---

82 See, for example, *The Defense of the Faith*, 115, 116. Van Til denied the usefulness of building a case for Christian theism from beliefs held in common by believers and unbelievers; restricting significant common ground to the sense of deity which exists within every human person.
83 Alvin Plantinga, 'What's the Question?' *Journal of Philosophical Research*, Vol. 20 (1995), 38.
84 *WCB*, 347.

Plantinga for not helping the cause of persuading an unbeliever that she too ought to believe. This is not entirely fair, as we have seen. Plantinga's extensive work in negative apologetics, which contribute indirectly to positive apology, as well as his increasingly less cautious endorsement of positive apologetics need to be acknowledged.[85] However, there is still likely to be disappointment that Plantinga has done relatively little (by example or encouragement) to commend the truth of the Christian gospel.

It is difficult to ascertain the extent to which Plantinga will be an agent of *rapprochement* between presuppositionalists and evidentialists. Perhaps the most likely way is by encouraging a more positive attitude to natural theology among presuppositionalists, and to religious experience among evidentialists. Both presuppositionalists and evidentialists, under the influence of Plantinga, could increase their repertoire of apologetic options.

So far, Plantinga's contribution (and potential contribution) to apologetic theory and practice has been discussed by noting where Plantinga stands in relation to the traditions of Augustinianism, Thomism, Calvinianism, Kuyperianism and evidentialism. An adequate assessment of Plantinga's contribution to apologetics must also incorporate an evaluation of his interaction with the Enlightenment, including postmodern developments.

9.4 Plantinga and Postmodernism

Plantinga has contributed to what is a widespread reaction to various characteristically modern ways of thinking, chiefly by way of his repudiation of classical foundationalism and foundationalist evidentialism. Thomas Oden includes Plantinga in a long list of 'mod-surviving' evangelicals who are involved in a robust and widespread critique of Enlightenment methods and convictions.[86] One could argue, however, that Plantinga is not, as yet, sufficiently postmodern. He has not taken as full account as he could Thomas Reid's reaction to the modernism of Hume and his successors. Reid resisted attempts to construct knowledge on a sceptical and non-theistic foundation, and to begin the quest for knowledge with doubt as opposed to trust. Plantinga,

---

85 As recently as 2001, Plantinga has said about the arguments of positive apologetics that they are 'extremely useful', and this in at least four different ways: 'They can confirm and support belief reached in other ways; they may move fence-sitters closer to Christian belief; they can function as defeater-defeaters; and they can reveal interesting and important connections,' 'Rationality and Public evidence: a reply to Richard Swinburne', *Religious Studies*, Vol. 37, No. 2 (June, 2001), 217.

86 Thomas C. Oden, 'So What Happens after Modernity? A Postmodern Agenda for Evangelical Theology', in David S. Dockery, (ed), *The Challenge of Postmodernism: An Evangelical Engagement* (Wheaton: BridgePoint, 1995), 399, 404.

following the lead of Thomas Reid, has developed an epistemology which has re-instated trust as the ultimate basis of epistemology.[87] However, Plantinga has not yet fully explored the implications of this with respect to the role of testimony and trust as centrally important belief forming mechanisms. He has, for this reason and others, been dismissive of efforts to show the reliability of the New Testament testimony to Jesus. This is unfortunate in the light of efforts by scholars, including himself, to debunk the methodology of those who cast doubt on that reliability. Thomas Oden compiles an impressive list of New Testament scholars who have sought to defend the reliability of the New Testament account of gospel events, including Wolfart Pannenberg, Karl Braaten, Antony Thistelton, Gerald O'Collins, Richard B. Hays and Ben Witherington III. With respect to biblical hermeneutics, he notes:

> The postmodern evangelical critique of *hermeneutical criticism* (as seen in Peter Stuhlmacher, Martin Hengel, Eta Linnemann, and Brevard Childs) stands poised to speak of the normative canon and the plain sense of Scripture, resisting speculative fashions of redaction and form-criticism and reader-response theories and socio-pragmatic contextualizations that tyrannize and nonchalantly rape the text.[88]

Oden continues by asking:

> Does modern historical criticism represent a devastating challenge to the principle of apostolicity? Briefly answered, no. When criticism is working well, so that an orthodox skepticism places in question the speculations of the historical critics, there is nothing to fear from solid historical inquiry into the tradition of transmission of apostolic testimony. There is only the task of improving historical inquiry and bringing it ever closer to the datum of the incarnate, risen Lord and His body, the church.[89]

Plantinga has not fully discarded the legacy of Immanuel Kant. Although Plantinga has contributed to the rehabilitation of natural theology, thereby taking one step back towards a more traditional apology, he has not taken the next (to me) logical step of rehabilitating historical apology. There are various reasons for this, including his own well argued convictions, and also, perhaps, the influence of a long, Western, and rationalistic tendency to depreciate probabilistic knowledge. One further explanation for Plantinga's reluctance to seriously countenance an historical apology may lie in the abiding influence of Abraham Kuyper's Kantian influenced understanding of faith. Kuyper, following Kant, drove a wedge between faith and reason. Apologetics was

---

[87] Underlying Plantinga's (and Reid's) epistemology is a theistically grounded trust in the general reliability of human belief forming faculties.
[88] 'So What Happens after Modernity', 401.
[89] 'So What Happens after Modernity', 401, 402.

repudiated. Reason was considered incapable of bridging the gap between the phenomenal and the noumenal. Faith, understood as a direct apprehension of truth independent of discursive processes, was required. The effect of this understanding of faith, which Plantinga shares, is that trust, or personal appropriation of the gospel, is set adrift from reasons to trust; the 'belief in' aspect of faith is divorced from the 'belief because' aspect of faith. The New Testament insistence on giving reasons for faith is entirely neglected, largely due to the unnecessary wedge driven between faith and reason by Immanuel Kant.

There are three further unfortunate consequences which follow from Plantinga's unwillingness to bring faith and historical reasoning into relationship. The first is that positive apologetics is effectively disconnected from the heart of the Christian message, which is the gospel. The energy of the positive apologist is exclusively expended in the service of conclusions which are as readily accepted by Muslims and Jews as by Christians. Reasons for believing the gospel are never given. Indeed, this is considered wise as such reasons are considered weak.

A second unfortunate consequence of Plantinga's unwillingness to bring faith and historical reasoning into relationship (other than in a negative apologetic way) is that Christian conviction is denied the benefit of important collaboratory support. It may be the case that the gospel is often believed without there being any conscious reliance on arguments or evidence. However, certainly for people coming to faith from outside the Christian community, this is not the case. Reasons to trust are sought. Moreover, under pressure from problems created, for example, by religious plurality and the issue of suffering, doubts as to the truth of the gospel are frequently raised. In these contexts, evidence that the gospel is true (and not merely not demonstrably false) is important, even crucial. If Plantinga is right and the evidence for the truth of Christianity is slender, then people (with good warrant) may decide to withhold belief. Further, Christian conviction (which is so important to Plantinga's Christian epistemology) may, in this context, begin to weaken, even to the point of being lost.

The third unfortunate consequence of Plantinga's unwillingness to bring faith and historical reasoning into relationship is that Christianity begins to take on a certain gnostic flavour. The gospel, in effect, becomes a body of timeless truths unable to be known by ordinary means (historical or otherwise). A special endowment of the Holy Spirit, reserved only for some,[90] is required. Those who are not part of this group cannot know unless they receive the gift of enlightenment. This framework of understanding Christianity is problematic

---

90 According to traditional Reformed doctrine, this would be the elect, who, through the ministry of the Holy Spirit come to know that the gospel is true. According to a suggestion by Plantinga, the few would be those who accept the gift of faith by taking heed to the internal instigation of the Holy Spirit.

in the light of the New Testament insistence on the tangible, public and accessible nature of the incarnation. 'What we have heard, what we have seen with our eyes, what we have looked at and touched with our hands, concerning the Word of life - we declare to you'[91] are the introductory words of a New Testament letter written to guard against first century tendencies to gnosticism.

This is not to suggest that Plantinga is wanting to actively cast doubt on the factual or historical nature of the incarnation and resurrection.[92] However, the effect of his conviction that historical investigation will not provide sufficient support for the truth of the gospel is to create a gospel epistemologically severed from its historical roots. The Jesus of history is lost, or, at least, is considered irretrievable by ordinary historical means. All that is left, epistemologically, is the Christ of faith.

9.5 A Final Assessment

These are significant problems for Plantinga's position. However, rather than conclude this thesis with criticism, it is better (and fairer to Plantinga) that a more positive evaluation be given by way of conclusion. Plantinga has made, and, no doubt will continue to make, an outstanding contribution both to the theory and practice of apologetics. Throughout his long and distinguished career as a Christian philosopher, he has responded with outstanding vigour and skill to many of the most serious challenges to traditional Christian faith, including most notably the evidentialist challenge and the problem(s) of evil and suffering. He has wrestled with, and provided his own counter-challenge to the challenges of naturalism and skepticism. He has fearlessly and confidently engaged the philosophical community of the United States and beyond. In line with his Augustinian and Kuyperian convictions, he has theorised from a confident and self-consciously Christian point of view, making him post-modern even before the movement by that name became fashionable.

Plantinga has been an outstandingly apologist. He has also developed an epistemological theory to undergird his apologetic efforts. He has even ventured into the area of theology in seeking to understand how a Christian can be said to know that the gospel is true. Although I am not persuaded that Plantinga has been successful, his work on the role of the Holy Spirit in Christian belief formation represents a thoughtful and thought-provoking excursus into an area which has been largely neglected by Christian epistemologists.[93] It is likely that Plantinga's efforts will stimulate much useful future discussion.

---

91 1 John 1:1-3.
92 As noted in chapter three, Plantinga happily acknowledges that it has this character.
93 As pointed out, for example, by William J. Abraham, in 'The Epistemological Significance of the Inner Witness of the Holy Spirit', *Faith and Philosophy*, Vol. 7, No. 4 (October, 1990), 434-450.

In 'Christian Philosophy at the End of the 20th Century', Plantinga mentions, as one of the roles of the negative apologist, the removal of obstacles 'to the spiritual peace and wholeness of the Christian community.'[94] Plantinga, in my opinion, has admirably fulfilled that role. He has been something of an apologetic watchman, not allowing any significant threat to Christian faith to pass without being challenged, and, in some cases, made to defend itself. His is a significant and extensive contribution to the peace and wholeness of the Christian community.

---

94 'Christian Philosophy at the End of the 20th Century', 37.

BIBLIOGRAPHY

1. Primary Works - Books

2. Primary Works - Articles

3. Secondary Works - Books

4. Secondary Works - Articles

1. Primary Works - Books

Plantinga, A., (ed), *Faith and Philosophy: Philosophical Studies in Religion and Ethics*, Grand Rapids: William B. Eerdmans, 1964.

Plantinga, A., (ed), *The Ontological Argument: from St. Anselm to Contemporary Philosophers*, Grand Rapids: William B. Eerdmans, 1965.

Plantinga, A., *God and Other Minds: a study of the rational justification of belief in God*, Ithaca: Cornell University Press, 1967.

_ *The Nature of Necessity*, Oxford: Oxford University Press, 1974.

_ *God, Freedom and Evil*, New York: Harper Torchbook, 1974.

Plantinga, A. and Wolterstorff, N., (eds), *Faith and Rationality: Reason and Belief in God*, Notre Dame: University of Notre Dame Press, 1983.

Plantinga, A, *The Twin Pillars of Christian Scholarship*, [pamphlet] Grand Rapids: The Stob Lectures Endowment, 1990.

_ *Warrant: The Current Debate*, Oxford: Oxford University Press, 1993.

_ *Warrant and Proper Function*, Oxford: Oxford University Press, 1993.

_ *Warranted Christian Belief*, Oxford: Oxford University Press, 2000.

2. Primary Works - Articles

Plantinga, A., 'Dooyeweerd on Meaning and Being', *Reformed Journal*, Vol. 8 (October, 1958), 10-15.

_ 'An Existentialist's Ethics', *Review of Metaphysics*, Vol. 12 (1958), 235-56.

_ 'A Valid Ontological Argument?' *Philosophical Review*, Vol. 70 (1961), 93-101.

_ 'The Perfect Goodness of God', *Australasian Journal of Philosophy*, Vol. 40 (May, 1962), 70-75.

_ 'Analytic Philosophy and Christianity', *Christianity Today*, Vol. 8 (October 25, 1963), 17-20.

_ 'On Being Honest to God', *Reformed Journal*, Vol. 14 (April, 1964), 11-15.

- 'The Skeptic's Strategy', in J. Hick, (ed), *Faith and the Philosophers*, New York: St. Martin's Press, 1965, 226-227.
- 'The Free Will Defense', in M. Black, (ed), *Philosophy in America*, Ithaca, NY: Cornell University Press, 1965, 204-220.
- 'Comments' (on Paul Ziff's 'The Simplicity of Other Minds') *Journal of Philosophy*, Vol. 62 (1965), 585-587.
- 'Induction and other Minds', *Review of Metaphysics*, Vol. 19 (March, 1966), 441-461.
- 'Kant's Objection to the Ontological Argument', *Journal of Philosophy*, Vol. 63 (1966), 537-546.
- 'Radical Theology', *Reformed Journal*, Vol. 17 (May/June, 1967), 7-10.
- 'Why Climb Mountains?' *Reformed Journal*, Vol. 20 (November, 1969), 8.
- 'The Incompatibility of Freedom and Determinism', *Philosophical Forum*, Vol. 2 (1970), 141-148.
- 'Christians, Scholars and Christian Scholars', *The Banner*, Vol. 106 (June, 1971), 4-7.
- 'Which Worlds Could God Have Created?', *Journal of Philosophy*, Vol. 70 (1973), 539-552.
- 'Transworld Identity or Worldbound Individuals?', in M. Munitz, (ed), *Logic and Ontology*, New York: New York University Press, 1973, 193-212.
- 'God and Rationality', *Reformed Journal*, Vol. 24 (January, 1974), 28-29.
- 'Aquinas - 700 Years Later', *Reformed Journal*, Vol. 24 (April, 1974), 5-7.
- 'Our Reasonable Service', *The Banner*, Vol. 109 (October, 1974), 6-8.
- 'Aquinas on Anselm', in C. Orlebeke and L. Smedes, (eds), *God and the Good: Essays in Honor of Henry Stob,* Grand Rapids: Eerdmans Press, 1975, 122-139.
- 'Actualism and Possible Worlds', *Theoria*, Vol. 42 (1976), 139-160.
- 'The Boethian Compromise', *American Philosophical Quarterly*, Vol. 15 (April, 1978), 129-138.
- 'The Probabalistic Argument from Evil', *Philosophical Studies*, Vol. 35 (1979), 1-53.
- 'Is belief in God rational?', in C. Delaney, (ed), *Rationality and Religious Belief,* South Bend: University of Notre Dame Press, 1979, 7-27.
- 'The Reformed Objection to Natural Theology', *Proceedings of the American Catholic Philosophical Association*, Vol. 54 (1980), 49-62.
- 'Is Belief in God Properly Basic?', *Nous*, Vol. 15 (1981), 41-51.
- 'The Case of Kant: A Contemporary Response', in J. Rogers, (ed), *Introduction to Philosophy*, San Francisco: Harper and Row, 1981, 117-119.
- 'Rationality and Religious Belief', in S. Cahn and D. Shatz, (eds), *Contemporary Philosophy of Religion*, New York: Oxford University Press, 1982, 255-277.
- 'On Reformed Epistemology', *Reformed Journal*, Vol. 32 (January, 1982), 13-17.

- 'Tooley and Evil: A Reply', *Australasian Journal of Philosophy*, Vol. 60, No. 1 (March, 1982), 66-75.
- 'How To Be an Anti-Realist', *Proceedings of the American Philosophical Association*, Vol. 56 (1982), 47-70.
- 'Reformed Epistemology Again', *Reformed Journal*, Vol. 32 (July, 1982), 7-8.
- 'The Reformed Objection Revisited', *Christian Scholars Review*, Vol. 12 (1983), 57-61.
- 'Reason and Belief in God', in A. Plantinga, N. Wolterstorff, (eds), *Faith and Rationality: Reason and Belief in God*, Notre Dame: University of Notre Dame Press, 1983, 16-93.
- 'Modern philosophy and the turn to belief in God', in R. Varghese, (ed), *The Intellectuals Speak Out About God*, Chicago: Ill.: Regnery Gateway, 1984, 165-167.
- 'Advice to Christian Philosophers', *Faith and Philosophy*, Vol. 1, No. 3 (July, 1984), 253-271.
- 'Self-profile', in J. Tomberlin and P. Van Inwagen, (eds), *Alvin Plantinga*, D. Reidel Publishing Company, 1985, 3-97.
- 'Replies to Articles', in J. Tomberlin and P. Van Inwagen, (eds), *Alvin Plantinga*, D. Reidel Publishing Company, 1985, 313-96.
- 'On taking belief in God as basic', in J. Runzo and C. K. Ihara, Lanham, MD: University Press of America, 1986, 1-17.
- 'Coherentism and the evidentialist objection to belief in God', in R. Audi, (ed), *Rationality, Religious Belief, and Moral Commitment: New Essays in the Philosophy of Religion*, Ithaca: Cornell University Press, 1986, 109-138.
- 'Is theism really a miracle?' *Faith and Philosophy*, Vol. 3, No. 2 (April, 1986), 109-134.
- 'The Foundations of Theism: A Reply', *Faith and Philosophy*, Vol. 3, No. 3 (July, 1986), 298-318.
- 'On Ockham's Way Out', *Faith and Philosophy*, Vol. 3, No. 3 (July, 1986), 235-269.
- 'Sheehan's shenanigans: how theology becomes tomfoolery', *Reformed Journal*, Vol. 37 (April, 1987), 19-25.
- 'Justification and theism', *Faith and Philosophy*, Vol. 4, (October, 1987), 403-426.
- 'Using What We Know By Faith', *Reformed Journal*, Vol. 37 (September, 1987), 10-11.
- 'Method in Christian Philosophy: A Reply', *Faith and Philosophy*, Vol. 5, (1988): 159-164.
- 'Epistemic Probability and Evil', *Archivio di Filosophia*, Vol. 56, No. 1-3 (1988), 557-584.

- 'The Problems of Evil and the Free-will Defense', *Reformed Journal*, Vol. 38 (September, 1988), 8-9.
- 'Positive Epistemic Status and Proper Function', in J. Tomberlin, (ed), *Philosophical Perspectives, 2, Epistemology*, Atascadero, CA: Ridgeview Publishing, 1988, 1-50.
- 'Chisholmian Internalism', in D. Austin, (ed), *Philosophical Analysis: a Defense by Example,* Dordrecht: D. Reidel, 1988, 127-151.
- 'Ad de Vries', *Christian Scholar's Review*, Vol. 19 (1989), 171-178.
- 'On Christian Philosophy' (Reply to Robbins), *Journal of the American Academy of Religion*, Vol. 57, No. 3 (Fall, 1989), 617-623.
- 'Justification in the 20th Century', *Philosophy and Pnenomenological Research*, Vol. 50 (1990) Supplement, 45-71.
- 'Ad Walls', *Philosophy and Phenomenological Research*, Vol. 51, No. 3 (September, 1991), 621-624.
- 'When faith and reason clash: evolution and the Bible', *Christian Scholar's Review* , Vol. 21, No. 1 (1991), 8-32.
- 'Evolution, neutrality, and antecedent probability: a reply to McMullin and Van Till', *Christian Scholar's Review*, Vol. 21, No. 1 (1991), 80-109.
- 'Warrant and Designing Agents: A Reply to James Taylor', *Philosophical Studies* Vol. 64 (1991), 203-215.
- 'The Prospects for Natural Theology', in J. Tomberlin, (ed), *Philosophical Perspectives, Vol. 5, Philosophy of Religion,* Atascadero, CAL: Ridgeview Publishing Co., 1991, 287-315.
- 'Augustinian Christian Philosophy', *The Monist,* Vol. 75, No. 3 (July, 1992), 291-320.
- 'Agnosticism,' 'Dogmatism' and 'Epistemology of religious belief', in J. Dancy and A. Sosa, (eds), *A Companion to Epistemology*, Oxford: Basil Blackwell, 1992.
- 'Divine Knowledge', in C.S. Evans and M. Westphal, (eds), *Christian Perspectives on Religious Knowledge,* Grand Rapids: William B. Eerdmans Publishing Company, 1993, 40-65.
- 'Why we need proper function', *Nous* Vol. 27, No. 1 (1993), 66-82.
- 'An Evolutionary Argument Against Naturalism', in E.S. Radcliffe, and C.J. White, (eds), *Faith in Theory and Practice: Essays on Justifying Religious Belief,* Chicago and La Salle: Open Court, 1993, 35-65.
- 'Plantinga: A Christian Life Partly Lived', in J.C. Kelly, (ed), *Philosophers Who Believe,* Downers Grove, InterVarsity Press, 1993, 45-82.
- 'On Christian Scholarship', in Theodore Hesburgh, (ed), *The Challenge and Promise of a Catholic University,* Notre Dame: University of Notre Dame Press, 1994, 267-295.
- 'Naturalism Defeated' 1994, unpublished manuscript.

- 'Pantheism', 'Essence and Essentialism', 'Haecceity', 'Natural Theology', in E. Sosa, J. Kim, (eds), *A Companion to Metaphysics,* Oxford: Blackwell Ltd., 1995.
- 'What's the Question?' *Journal of Philosophical Research,* Vol. 20 (1995), 19-43.
- 'Precis of Warrant: The Current Debate and Warrant and Proper Function', *Philosophy and Phenomenological Research,* Vol. 55, No. 2 (1995), 393-396.
- 'Reliabilism, Analyses and Defeaters', in *Philosophy and Phenomenological Research,* Vol. 55, No. 2 (June, 1995), 427-464.
- 'Pluralism: A Defense of Religious Exclusivism', in Thomas Senor (ed), *The Rationality of Belief and the Plurality of Faith:Essays in Honor of William P. Alston,* Ithaca, New Haven: Cornell University Press, 1995, 191-215.
- 'Christian Philosophy at the End of the 20th Century', in Sander Griffioen and Bert Balk, (eds), *Chrisitan Philosophy at the Close of the 20th Century,* Kampen: Uitgeverij Kok, 1995, 29-53.
- 'Methodological Naturalism?' in J. van der Meer, (ed), *Facets of Faith and Science,* Lanham, Md.: University Press of America, 1996, 177-221.
- 'On Being Evidentially Challenged', in Daniel Howard-Snyder, (ed),*The Evidential Argument from Evil,* Bloomington and Indianapolis: Indiana University Press, 1996, 244-261.
- 'Science: Augustinian or Duhemian?' *Faith and Philosophy,* Vol. 13, No. 3 (1996), 368-94.
- 'Dennett's Dangerous Idea', *Books and Culture,* (May/June, 1996), 16-18, 35.
- 'Respondeo', in *Warrant in Contemporary Epistemology: Essays in Honor of Plantinga's Theory of Knowledge,* Lanham: Rowman and Littlefield, 1996, 307-378.
- 'Ad Hick', *Faith and Philosophy,* Vol. 14, No. 3 (July, 1997), 295-298.
- 'Warrant and Accidentally True Belief', *Analysis,* Vol. 57, No. 2 (April, 1997), 140-145.
- 'Reformed Epistemology', in Philip L. Quinn and Charles Taliaferro, (eds), *A Companion to Philosophy of Religion,* Oxford: Blackwell Publishers, 1997, 383-389.
- 'Two (or more) Kinds of Scriptural Scholarship', *Modern Theology,* Vol. 14, No. 2 (April, 1998), 243-278.
- 'Afterword', in James Sennett, (ed), *The Analytical Theist: A Collection of Alvin Plantinga's Works in Philosophy of Religion,* Grand Rapids: Eerdmans, 1998, 253-258.
- 'Arguments for the existence of God', in Edward Craig, (ed), *Routledge Encyclopedia of Philosophy,* Vol. 4, New York: Routledge, 1998, 85-93.

- 'Religion and Epistemology' in Edward Craig, (ed), *Routledge Encyclopedia of Philosophy*, Vol. 8, New York: Routledge, 1998, 209-218.
- 'Twenty Years Worth of the SCP', *Faith and Philosophy*, Vol. 15, No. 2 (April, 1998), 151-155.
- 'Degenerate Evidence and Rowe's New Evidential Argument from Evil', *Noûs*, Vol. 32, No. 4 (1998), 531-544.
- 'On Heresy, Mind, and the Truth', *Faith and Philosophy*, Vol. 16, No. 2 (April, 1999), 182-193.
- 'Warranted Christian Belief: the Aquinas/Calvin Model', in G. Bruntrup and R. Tacelli, (eds), *The Rationality of Theism*, Boston: Kluwer Publishers, 1999.
- 'Pluralism: A Defence of Religious Exclusivism', in Philip L. Quinn and Kevin Meeker, (eds), *The Philosophical Challenge of Religious Diversity*, New York: Oxford University Press, 2000.
- 'Direct Aquaintance?', *Resurrecting Old-Fashioned Foundationalism*, M. DePaul, (ed), Lanham: Rowman and Littlefield, 2001.
- 'Reid, Hume and God', unpublished manuscript.
- 'Creation and Evolution: a Modest Proposal', given at the Eastern Division Meetings of the American Philosophical Association, Dec. 1998, unpublished manuscript.
- 'Reply to Beilby's Cohorts' in James Beilby, (ed), *Naturalism Defeated: Essays on Plantinga's Evolutionary Argument Against Naturalism*, Ithaca: Cornell University Press, 2002, 204-275.
- 'Rationality and public evidence: a reply to Richard Swinburne', *Religious Studies*, Vol. 37, No. 2 (June, 2001), 215-222.
- 'Swinburne and Plantinga on Internal Rationality', *Religious Studies*, Vol. 37, No. 3 (September, 2001), 357-358.
- '2 dozen (or so) good theistic arguments' unpublished manuscripts.

3. Secondary Works - Books

Adams, R.M., *The Virtue of Faith,* Oxford: Oxford University Press, 1987.
Alston, W.P., *Epistemic Justification*, Ithaca and London: Cornell Universty Press, 1989.
- *Perceiving God: The Epistemology of Religious Experience,* Ithaca and London: Cornell University Press, 1991.
Aquinas, T., *Summa Contra Gentiles*, trans. A.C. Pegis, Notre Dame: Notre Dame Press, 1975.
- *Summa Theologiae*, trans. Thomas Gilby et al, 61 vols, New York: McGraw-Hill, 1964-81.
- 'Commentary on Boethius' De Trinitate', in *The Trinity and the Unicity of the Intellect*, trans. Sister Rose Emmanuella Brennan, St. Louis: Herder, 1946.

_ *The Disputed Questions on Truth*, trans. J.V. McGlynn, S.J., Chicago: Henry Regnery, 1953.
Audi, R. and Wainwright, W., (eds), *Rationality, Religious Belief and Moral Commitment,* Ithaca and London: Cornell University Press, 1986.
Audi, R., *The Structure of Justification*, New York: Cambridge University Press, 1993.
_ *Epistemology: A Contemporary Introduction to the Theory of Knowledge*, London: Routlege, 1998.
Augustine, 'On Free Will', *Earlier Writings*, J.H.S. Burleigh, (ed), The Library of Christian Classics, Philadelphia: Westminster, 1979.
_ 'Of True Religion', *Earlier Writings*, J.H.S. Burleigh, (ed), The Library of Christian Classics, Philadelphia: Westminster, 1979.
_ 'The Usefulness of Belief', *Earlier Writings*, J.H.S. Burleigh, (ed), The Library of Christian Classics, Philadelphia: Westminster, 1979.
_ 'On the Predestination of the Saints', *Saint Augustin's Anti-Pelagian Works*, tr. P. Holmes, R. E. Wallis, Nicene and Post-Nicene Fathers, Grand Rapids: Eerdmans, 1971.
_ *Letters,* 5 vols, tr. Sister W. Parsons,The Fathers of the Church, New York: Fathers of the Church Inc., 1953.
_ *Expositions on the Book of Psalms*, A. Cleveland Coxe, (ed), Nicene and Post-Nicene Fathers, Grand Rapids: Eerdmans, 1974.
_ *Sermons*, John E. Rotelle, (ed), The Works of Saint Augustine, Brooklyn, New York: New City Press, 1992.
_ *Tractates on the Gospel of John*, tr. J. W. Retting, The Fathers of the Church, Washington: The Catholic University of America Press, 1988.
_ *The Trinity*, tr. Stephen McKenna, C.SS.R., The Fathers of the Church (Washington: The Catholic University of America Press, 1963.
_ *The City of God*, in Nicene and Post Nicene Fathers, Grand Rapids: Eerdmans, 1974.
Bahnsen, G.L., *Van Til's Apologetic: Readings and Analysis,* Phillipsburg: P&R Publishing, 1998.
Banner, M.C., *The Justification of Science and the Rationality of Religious Belief,* Oxford: Oxford University Press, 1990.
Barbour, I., *Religion in an Age of Science*, New York: Harper and Row, 1990.
Barnett, P., *The Truth about Jesus: the challenge of the evidence*, Sydney: Aquila Press, 1994.
_ *Jesus and the Logic of History*, Leicester: Apollos, 1997.
Bartholomew, D.J., *Uncertain Belief: Is it Rational to be a Christian?* Oxford: Clarendon Press, 1996.
Beatty, M.D., *Christian Theism and the Problems of Philosophy,* Notre Dame: University of Notre Dame, 1990.
Beilby, J., (ed), *Metaphysical Naturalism and Rationalism: Essays on Plantinga's Evolutionary Argument Against Naturalism*, forthcoming.

Berkhof, L., *Systematic Theology*, London: The Banner of Truth Trust, 1939.
Bloesch, D.G., *Holy Scripture: revelation, inspiration and interpretation*, Downers Grove, Ill.: InterVarsity Press, 1994.
Blomberg, C.L., *The Historical Reliability of John's Gospel*, Leicester: InterVarsity Press, 2001.
Borg, M., *Jesus: A New Vision*, San Francisco: Harper and Row, 1988.
Brown, C., *Faith and History: A Personal Exploration*, Grand Rapids: Academie Books, 1987.
Burt, D.X., *Augustine's World: An Introduction to his Speculative Philosophy,* Lantham, Maryland: University Press of America, 1996.
Bush, L.R., *Readings in Christian Apologetics*, Grand Rapids: Academie Books, 1983.
Calvin, J., *Institutes of the Christian Religion*, trans. F. L. Battles, John T. McNeill, (ed), The Library of Christian Classics, Vols. 20, 21, Philadelphia: The Westminster Press, 1960.
Clark, D.K., *Dialogical Apologetics*, Grand Rapids: Baker Book House, 1993.
Clark, K.J., (ed), *Philosophers Who Believe*, Downers Grove, Ill.: InterVarsity Press, 1993.
Coady, C.A.J., *Testimony: A Philosophical Study,* Oxford: Clarendon Press, 1992.
Cohen, L.J., *An Essay on Belief and Acceptance*, Oxford: Clarendon Press, 1992.
Craig, W.L., *The Historical Argument for the Resurrection of Jesus,* Lewiston, NY: Edwin Mellen, 1985.
_ *Assessing the New Testament Evidence for the Historicty of the Resurrection of Jesus*, Studiesin the Bible and Early Christianity 16, Lewiston, NY: Edwin Mellen, 1989.
Dancy, J., *Introduction to Contemporary Epistemology*, Oxford: Basil Blackwell, 1985.
Dancy, J. and Sosa, A., *A Companion to Epistemology*, Oxford: Basil Blackwell, 1992.
Davis, C.F.,*The Evidential Force of Religious Experience*, Oxford: Clarendon Press, 1989.
Davis, S.T., *Logic and the Nature of God*, Grand Rapids: Eerdmans, 1983.
Davis, S.T., *Risen Indeed: Making Sense of the Resurrection*, Grand Rapids: Eerdmans, 1993.
Davis, S.T., Kendall, D. *The Resurrection*, Oxford: Oxford University Press, and O'Collins, G., (eds), 1997.
Delaney, C., (ed), *Rationality and Religious Belief*, South Bend: University of Notre Dame Press, 1979.
Devine, P.E., *Relativism, Nihilism and God*, Notre Dame: University of Notre Dame Press, 1989.

Dowey, E., *The Knowledge of God in Calvin's Theology*, New York: Columbia University Press, 1952.
Dyrness, W., *Christian Apologetics in a World Community*, Downers Grove: Inter-Varsity Press, 1983.
Dulles, A., *A History of Apologetics*, London: Hutchinson and Co Ltd, 1971.
_ *The Assurance of Things Hoped For: A Theology of Christian Faith*, Oxford: Oxford University Press, 1994.
Evans, C.S. and M. Westphal, (eds), *Christian Perspectives on Religious Knowledge*, Grand Rapids: William B. Eerdmans Publishing Company, 1993.
Evans, C.S., *The Historical Christ and the Jesus of Faith: The Incarnational Narrative as History*, Oxford: Oxford University Press, 1996.
Fiorenza, F.S., *Foundational Theology: Jesus and the Church*, New York: Crossroad, 1984.
Flint, T., (ed), *Christian Philosophy*, Notre Dame: University of Notre Dame Press, 1990.
Flint, T., *Divine Providence: The Molinist Account*, Ithaca: Cornell University Press, 1998.
Frame, J., *Apologetics to the Glory of God*, Phillipsburg: P&R Publishing, 1994.
Frei, H., *The Eclipse of Biblical Narrative: a study in Eighteenth and Nineteenth Century Hermeneutics*, New Haven: Yale University Press, 1974.
Geisler, N.L., *Thomas Aquinas: An Evangelical Appraisal*, Grand Rapids: Baker Book House, 1991.
_ *Baker Encyclopedia of Christian Apologetics*, Grand Rapids: Baker Books, 1999.
Geivett, R.D. and Sweetman, B., (eds), *Contemporary Perspectives on Religious Epistemology*, Oxford: Oxford University Press, 1992.
Geivett, R.D., *Evil and the Evidence for God*, Philadelphia: Temple University Press, 1995.
Gill, J.H., *Faith in Dialogue: A Christian Apologetic*, Waco, Texas: Jarrell, 1985.
Green, J., and Turner, M., (eds), *Jesus of Nazareth: Lord and Christ*, Grand Rapids: W.B. Eerdmans, 1994.
Gutting, G., *Religious Belief and Religious Scepticism*, Notre Dame: University of Notre Dame Press, 1982.
Gutting, G., (ed), *Pragmatic Liberalism and the Critique of Modernity*, New York: Cambridge University Press, 1999.
Hart, H., Van Der Hoeven, J. and Wolterstorff, N., (eds), *Rationality in the Calvinian Tradition*, Lanham: University Press of America, 1983.
Harvey, A.E., *Jesus on Trial: A Study in the Fourth Gospel*, London: SPCK, 1976.
Helm, P., *Faith and Understanding*, Grand Rapids: Eerdmans, 1997.

Hoitenga, D.J., *Faith and Reason From Plato to Plantinga: An Introduction to Reformed Epistemology*, Albany: State University of New York Press, 1991.

Houston, J., *Reported Miracles: A Critique of Hume*, Cambridge: Cambridge University Press, 1994.

Hume, D., *An Enquiry Concerning Human Understanding*, (1748), Tom L. Beauchamp, (ed), Oxford: Clarendon Press, 1999.

Johnson, D., *Hume, Holism, and Miracles*, Ithaca: Cornell University Press, 1999.

Kelly, J.C., (ed), *Philosophers Who Believe*, Downers Grove, InterVarsity Press, 1993.

Kenny, A., *Faith and Reason*, New York: Columbia University Press, 1983.

_ *What is Faith? Essays in the Philosophy of Religion*, New York: Oxford University Press, 1992.

Kuyper, A., *Encyclopaedie der heilige Godgeleerdheid*, 3 vols., Amsterdam: J.A. Wormser, 1894; ET, *Principles of Sacred Theology*, 1898, reprinted Grand Rapids: Baker Books, 1980.

Kvanvig, J.L., (ed), *Warrant in Contemporary Epistemology: Essays in Honor of Plantinga's Theory of Knowledge*, Lanham: Rowman and Littlefield, 1996.

Lindbeck, G., *The Nature of Doctrine: Religion and Theology in a Postliberal Age*, Philadelphia: Westminster Press, 1984.

Lipton, P., *Inference to the Best Explanation*, London: Routledge, 1991.

Locke, J., *An Essay Concerning Human Understanding*, New York: Dover Publications, 1959.

Mascall, E.L., *The Openness of Being: Natural Theology Today*, London: Darton, Longman and Todd, 1971.

Mayers, R., *Both/And: A Balanced Apologetic*, Chicago: Moody Press, 1984.

McCool, G.A., *The Neo-Thomists*, Milwaukee: Marquette University Press, 1994.

McCord Adams, M., *Horrendous Evils and the Goodness of God*, Carlton South: Melbourne University Press, 1999.

McCullagh, C.B., *Justifying Historical Descriptions*, Cambridge: Cambridge University Press, 1984.

McLeod, M.S., *Rationality and Theistic Belief: An Essay on Reformed Epistemology*, New York: P. Lang, 1992.

Mitchell, B., (ed), *Faith and Logic*, Boston: Beacon Press, 1957.

Mitchell, B., *The Justification of Religious Belief,* NY: Seabury Press, 1974.

Morphett, T., *A Hole in My Ceiling*, Sydney: Hodder and Stoughton, 1985.

Morris, L., *The Gospel According to John*, The New International Commentary on the New Testament Series, Grand Rapids: Eerdmans Publishing Company, 1971.

Morris, T.V., (ed), *Philosophy and the Christian Faith*, Notre Dame: University of Notre Dame Press, 1988.
Murphy, N., *Beyond Liberalism and Fundamentalism*, Valley Forge: Trinity Press International, 1996.
Murray, M.J., (ed), *Reason for the Hope Within*, Grand Rapids: William B. Eerdmans, 1999.
Muyskens, J.L., *The Sufficiency of Hope: The Conceptual Foundations of Religion*, Philadelphia: Temple University Press, 1979.
Newell, R.W., *Objectivity, Empiricism and Truth*, London: Routledge and Kegan Paul, 1986.
Noll, M.A., *The Scandal of the Evangelical Mind*, Grand Rapids: William B. Eerdmans, 1994.
O'Connor, D., *God and Insrutable Evil: In Defense of Theism and Atheism*, London: Rowman and Littlefield, 1998.
O'Collins, G., *Jesus Risen*, London: Darton, Longman and Todd, 1987.
_ *The Resurrection of Jesus Christ: Some Contemporary Issue*, Milwaukee: Marquette University Press, 1993.
Okholm, D.L. and Phillips, T.R., (eds), *Four Views on Salvation in a Pluralistic World*, Grand Rapids: Zondervan, 1995.
O'Meara, T.F., *Thomas Aquinas: Theologian*, Notre Dame: University of Notre Dame Press, 1997.
Pannenberg, W., *Jesus - God and Man*, trans. Lewis L. Wilkins and Duane.A. Priebe, Philadephia: Westminster Press, 1968.
Parsons, K., *God and the Burden of Proof*, Buffalo, New York: Prometheus Books, 1989.
Pinnock, C., *A Wideness in God's Mercy*, Grand Rapids: Zondervan, 1992.
Ramm, B., *A Christian Appeal to Reason*, Waco: Word Books, 1972.
_ *Varieties of Christian Apologetics*, Grand Rapids: Baker Book House, 1973.
_ *The God Who Makes a Difference*, Waco: Word Books, 1977.
Reid, T., *An Inquiry into the Human Mind on the Principles of Common Sense,* Edinburgh: Printed for A Millar, London, and A. Kincaid and J. Bell, Edinburgh, 1764.
Rist, J.M., *Augustine: Ancient Thought Baptized*, Cambridge: Cambridge University Press, 1994.
Rorty, R., *Philosophy and the Mirror of Nature*, Princeton: Princeton University Press, 1979.
_ *Contingency, Irony and Solidarity*, New York: Cambridge University Press, 1989.
Rowe, W. and Wainwright, W., (eds), *Philosophy of Religion*, New York: Hartcourt Brace Jovanovich, 1989.
Sanders, E.P., *Jesus and Judaism*, Philadelphia: Fortress Press, 1985.
Schaeffer, F., *Escape From Reason*, Downers Grove, Ill.: InterVarsity Press, 1968.

_ *The God Who is There*, Downers Grove, Ill: InterVarsity Press, 1968.
Sennett, J.F., *Modality, Probability, and Rationality: A Critical Examination of Alvin Plantinga's Philosophy*, New York: Peter Lang Publishing, 1992.
Sennett, J.F., (ed), *The Analytical Theist: A Collection of Alvin Plantinga's Works in Philosophy of Religion*, Grand Rapids: Eerdmans, 1998.
Seymour, C., *A Theodicy of Hell*, Dordrecht: Kluwer Academic Publications, 2000.
Sproul, R.C., Gerstner, J. and Lindsley, A., *Classical Apologetics*, Grand Rapids: Academie Books, 1984.
Stump, E., (ed), *Reasoned Faith,* Ithaca: Cornell University Press, 1993.
Swinburne, R., (ed), *Revelation*, Oxford: Clarendon Press, 1981.
Swinburne, R., *Faith and Reason*, Oxford: At the Clarendon Press, 1981.
_ *Miracles*, New York: Macmillan, 1989.
_ *Revelation: From Metaphor to Analogy*, Oxford: Clarendon, 1992.
_ *Providence and the Problem of Evil*, Oxford: Oxford University Press, 1998.
_ *The Resurrection of God Incarnate,* Oxford: Clarendon Press, 2003.
_ *The Existence of God,* Oxford: Clarendon Press, 2003.
Tomberlin, J.E. and Van Inwagen, P., (eds), *Alvin Plantinga*. Dordrecht: D. Reidel Publishing Company, 1985.
Trites, A., *The New Testament Concept of Witness*, Cambridge: Cambridge University Press, 1977.
Van Til, C., *The Defense of the Faith*, Phillipsburg: Presbyterian and Reformed Publishing Co., 1955.
_ *Christian Apologetics*, Phillipsburg: Presbyterian and Reformed Publishing Co., 1976.
_ *Why I Believe in God*, Philadelphia: Presbyterian and Reformed Publishing Company, n.d..
Vos, A., *Aquinas, Calvin, and Contemporary Protestant Thought: A Critique of Protestant Views on the Thought of Thomas Aquinas*, Washington: Christian University Press, 1985.
Westphal, M., *Suspicion and Faith: the religious uses of atheism*, Grand Rapids: W.B. Eerdmans, 1993.
Wood, W.J., *Epistemology: Becoming Intellectually Virtuous*, Leicester: Apollos, 1998.
Yandell, K.E., *The Epistemology of Religious Experience,* Cambridge: Cambridge University Press, 1993.
Zagzebski, L., (ed), *Rational Faith: Catholic Responses to Reformed Epistemology*, Notre Dame: University of Notre Dame Press, 1993.

4. Secondary Works - Articles

Abraham, W.J., 'The Epistemological Significance of the Inner Witness of the Holy Spirit', *Faith and Philosophy,* Vol. 7, No. 4 (October, 1990), 434-450.
Adams, R., 'Middle Knowledge and the Problem of Evil', *American Philosophical Quarterly,* Vol. 14, No. 2 (April, 1977), 109-117.
_ 'Plantinga on the Problem of Evil', in J. E. Tomberlin, P. van Inwagen, (eds), *Alvin Plantinga,* Dordrecht: D. Reidel Publishing Company, 1985, 224-255.
_ 'An anti-Molinist argument', in J. E. Tomberlin, (ed), *Philosophical Perspectives,* 5, Philosophy of Religion, Atascadero: Ridgeview Publishing Co., 1991, 343-353.
Adler, J.E., 'Testimony, Trust, Knowing', *The Journal of Philosophy,* Vol. 91, No. 5 (May, 1994), 264-275.
Alston, W.P., 'Plantinga's Epistemology of Religious Belief', in J. E. Tomberlin and P. van Inwagen, (eds), *Alvin Plantinga,* Dordrecht: D. Reidel Publishing Company, 1985, 289-311.
_ 'Religious Experience as a Ground of Religious Belief', in J. Runzo and C. K. Ihara, Lanham, MD: University Press of America, 1986, 31-51.
_ 'Belief, Acceptance, and Religious Faith', in J. Jordan, D. Howard-Snyder, *Faith, Freedom and Rationality,* Lanham: Rowman and Littlefield, 1996, 3-27.
Ameriks, K., 'Plantinga and Other Minds', *Southern Journal of Philosophy,* Vol. 16 (1978), 285-291.
_ 'Kant', in R. Audi, (ed), *The Cambridge Dictionary of Philosophy,* Cambridge: Cambridge University Press, 1995, 398-404.
Appleby, P.C., 'Reformed epistemology, rationality and belief in God', *International Journal for Philosophy of Religion,* Vol. 24 (1988), 129-141.
Askew, R., 'On fideism and Alvin Plantinga', *International Journal for Philosophy of Religion,* Vol. 23 (1988), 3-16.
Audi, R., 'Direct Justification, Evidential Dependence, and Theistic Belief', in R. Audi. and W. Wainwright, (eds), *Rationality, Religious Belief and Moral Commitment,* Ithaca and London: Cornell University Press, 1986, 139-166.
_ 'Faith, Belief, and Rationality', in J. E. Tomberlin, (ed), *Philosophical Perspectives,* 5, Philosophy of Religion, Atascadero: Ridgeview Publishing Co., 1991, 213-239.
_ 'The Place of Testimony in the Fabric of Knowledge and Justification', *American Philosophical Quarterly,* Vol. 34 (1997), 405-422.
Bagger, M.C., 'The Miracle of Minimal Foundationalism: Religious Experience and Justified Belief', *Religions Studies,* Vol. 29 (1993), 297-312.
Baier, A., 'Trust and Antitrust', *Ethics,* Vol. 96 (1986), 231-260.

Baldwin, A., De Boer, J. and Losin, P., 'Reformed Epistemology: Three Replies', *Reformed Journal*, Vol. 32 (April, 1982), 21-25.

Bassinger, D., 'Plantinga, Pluralism and Religious Belief', *Faith and Philosophy*, Vol. 8, No. 1 (1991), 67-80.

Bergmann, M., 'Might-Counterfactuals, Transworld Untrustworthiness and Plantinga's Free Will Defence,' *Faith and Philosophy*, Vol. 16, No. 3 (July, 1999), 336-351.

Beversluis, J., 'Reforming the "Reformed" Objection to Natural Theology', *Faith and Philosophy*, Vol. 12, No. 2 (1995), 189-206.

Bishop, J., 'Compatibilism and the Free Will Defence', *Australasian Journal of Philosophy*, Vol. 71, No. 2 (June, 1993), 104-120.

Bolt, P., 'Mission and Witness', in I. Howard Marshall and D. Peterson, *Witness to the Gospel: The Theology of Acts*, Grand Rapids: Eerdmans, 1998, 191-214.

BonJour, L, 'Plantinga on Knowledge and Proper Function', in J. L. Kvanvig, (ed), *Warrant in Contemporary Epistemology: Essays in Honor of Plantinga's Theory of Knowledge*, Lanham: Rowman and Littlefield, 1996, 47-71.

Boyle, J., Hubbard, J. and Sullivan, T., 'The Reformed Objection to Natural Theology: A Catholic Perspective', *Christian Scholars Review*, Vol. 11 (1982), 199-211.

Boyle, J.M., 'Is "God Exists" a Properly Basic Belief?': A consideration of Alvin Plantinga's Argument', in L. A. Kennedy, (ed), *Thomaistic Papers IV*, Houston, Texas: Center for Thomistic Studies, 1988, 169-184.

Bratt, J.D., 'The Dutch Schools', in David F. Wells, (ed), *Dutch Reformed Theology*, Grand Rapids: Baker Book House, 1989, 13-32.

Brown, H., 'Alvin Plantinga and natural theology', *International Journal for Philosophy of Relgion*, Vol. 30 (1991), 1-19.

Buckhout, R., 'Eyewitness Testimony', *Scientific American*, Vol. 231, No. 6 (December, 1974), 23-31.

Byrne, P., 'Warranted Christian Belief: a Review', *Journal of Theological Studies*, Vol. 52, No. 2 (2001), 990-93.

Christensen, W. and King-Farlow, J., 'Gambling on Other Minds - Human and Divine', *Sophia*, Vol. 10 (1971), 1-6.

Christian, R.A., 'Plantinga, Epistemic Permissiveness, and Metaphysical Pluralism', *Religious Studies*, Vol. 28 (1992), 553-573.

Clifford, W.K., 'The Ethics of Belief', in *Lectures and Essays*, Leslie Stephen and Frederick Pollock, (eds), 2nd ed. London and New York: Macmillan, 1886, 342-46.

Craig, W.L., 'The Teleological Argument And The Anthropic Principle', in W. L. Craig and M. S. McLeod, (eds), *The Logic of Rational Theism: Exporatory Essays*, Lewiston, The Edwin Mellen Press, 1990, 127-153.

Czapkay Sudduth, M.L., 'Bi-level Evidentialism and Reformed Apologetics', *Faith and Philosophy*, Vol. 11, No. 3 (July, 1994), 379-396.
- 'The Prospects for "Mediate" Natural Theology in John Calvin', *Religious Studies*, Vol. 31 (1995), 53-68.
- 'Alstonian foundationalism and higher-level theistic evidentialism', *International Journal for Philosophy of Religion*, Vol. 37 (February, 1995), 25-44.
- 'Calvin, Plantinga, and the Natural Knowledge of God: A Response to Beversluis', *Faith and Philosophy*, Vol. 15, No. 1 (January, 1998), 92-103.
- 'The internalist character and evidentialist implications of Plantingian defeaters', *International Journal for Philosophy of Religion*, Vol. 45, No. 3 (June, 1999), 167-189.
- 'Can Religious Unbelief Be Proper Function Rational?' *Faith and Philosophy*, Vol. 16, No. 3 (July, 1999), 297-314.

Davis, S.T., 'Is it possible to know that Jesus was raised from the dead?' *Faith and Philosophy*, Vol. 1, No. 2 (April, 1984), 147-159.

Dawid, P., and Gillies, D., 'A Bayesian Analysis of Hume's Argument Concerning Miracles', *The Philosophical Quarterly*, Vol. 39, No. 154 (1989), 57-65.

de Broglie, G., 'La vraie notion thomiste des "preambula fidei"', *Gregorianum*, Vol. 34 (1953), 341-389.

Depaul, M., 'The Rationality of Belief in God', *Religious Studies*, Vol. 17 (1981), 343-356.

Draper, P., 'Pain and Pleasure: an Evidential Problem for Theists', *Noûs*, Vol. 23 (1989), 331-350.
- 'Evil and the Proper Basicality of Belief in God,' *Faith and Philosophy*, Vol. 8, No. 2 (April, 1991), 135-147.
- 'Probabilistic Arguments from Evil,' *Religious Studies*, Vol. 28, No. 3 (September, 1992), 303-317.
- 'Evolution and the Problem of Evil,' in Louis Pojman, (ed), *Philosophy of Religion*, third edition, Belmont, CA: Wadsworth, 1997.

Dulac, H., 'An Incredulous First Reaction to *Faith and Rationality*', in L. A. Kennedy, (ed), *Thomaistic Papers IV*, Houston, Texas: Center for Thomistic Studies, 1988, 65-72.

Evans, C.A., 'Life-of-Jesus Research and the Eclipse of Mythology', *Theological Studies*, Vol. 54 (1993), 3-36.

Evans, C. S., 'Apologetics in a New Key: Relieving Protestant Anxieties Over Natural Theology', in W. L. Craig and M. S. McLeod, (eds), *The Logic of Rational Theism: Exporatory Essays*, Lewiston, The Edwin Mellen Press, 1990, 65-75.
- 'Critical Historical Judgement', *Faith and Philosophy*, Vol. 11, No. 2 (April, 1994), 184-206.

Fales, E., 'Should God Not Have Created Adam?' *Faith and Philosophy*, Vol. 9, No. 2 (April, 1992), 193-209.

_ 'Plantinga's case against naturalistic epistemology', *Philosophy of Science*, Vol. 63 (1996), 432-451.

_ 'Darwin's Doubt, Calvin's Calvary', and W. J. Talbott, 'The Illusion of Defeat', in *Metaphysical Naturalism* (forthcoming)

Farrar, A., 'Revelation', in B. Mitchell, (ed), *Faith and Logic*, London: George Allen and Unwin Ltd., 1957, 84-107.

Flew, A., Divine Omnipotence and Human Freedom', in *New Essays in Philosophical Theology*, A. Flew and A. MacIntyre, (eds) (London: SCM Press, 1955), 144-169.

Frame, J., 'Scripture and the Apologetic Task', *The Journal of Biblical Counselling,* Vol. 13, No. 2 (Winter, 1995), 9-12.

Fricker, E., 'The Epistemology of Testimony', *Proceedings of the Aristotelian Society*, Supp., Vol. 61 (1987), 57-83.

_ 'Against Gullibility', in B. Matilal and A. Chakrabarti, (eds), *Knowing With Words* (Dordrecht: Kluwer, 1994), 125-61.

_ 'Telling and Trusting: Reductionism and Anti-Reductionism in the Epistemology of Testimony', *Mind*, Vol. 104, No. 414 (April, 1995), 393-411.

Friguegnon, M., 'God and Other Programs', *Religious Studies*, Vol. 15 (1979), 83-89.

Fuller, D. and Gardiner, R., 'Reformed Theology at Princeton and Amsterdam in the Late Nineteenth Century: A Reappraisal', *Presbyterion*, Vol. 21, No. 2 (Fall, 1995), 89-117.

Garcia, L.L., 'Natural Theology and the Reformed Objection', in C. Stephen Evans and Merold Westphal, (eds), *Christian Perspectives on Religious Knowledge*, Grand Rapids: Eerdmans, 1993, 112-133.

Gettier, E.L., 'Is Justified True Belief Knowledge?' *Analysis*, Vol. 23, No. 6 (June, 1963), 121-123.

Gill, J.H., 'The Possibility of Apologetics', *Scottish Journal of Theology*, Vol. 16 (1963), 136-150.

Goetz, S.C., 'Belief in God Is Not Properly Basic', *Religious Studies*, Vol. 19, No. 4 (December, 1983), 475-484.

Gowen, J., 'Foundationalism and the justification of religious belief', *Religious Studies*, Vol. 19 (1983), 393-406.

Griffiths, P., 'An Apology For Apologetics', *Faith and Philosophy*, Vol. 5, No. 4 (October, 1988), 399-420.

Grigg, R., 'Theism and Proper Basicality: A Response to Plantinga', *International Journal for Philosophy of Religion*, Vol. 14 (1983), 123-127.

_ 'The Crucial Disanalogies Between Properly Basic Belief and Belief in God', *Religious Studies,* Vol. 26 (1983), 389-401.

Groothius, D., 'Proofs, Pride, and Incarnation: Is Natural Theology Theologically Taboo?' *Journal of the Evangelical Theological Society*, Vol. 38, No. 1 (March, 1995), 67-76.

_ Review of Warranted Christian Belief, *Journal of the Evangelical Theological Society,* Vol. 45, No. 1 (March, 20020, 178-182.

Haldane, J., 'Thomism', in Edward Craig, (ed), *Routledge Encyclopaedia*, Vol. 9, London: Routledge, 1998, 380-388.

Harman, G.H., 'The inference to the best explanation', *Philosophical Review*, Vol. 74, No. 1 (1965), 88-95.

Harvey, V.A., 'New Testament Scholarship and Christian Belief', in R. Joseph Hoffman and Gerald A. Larue, (eds), *Jesus in History and Myth,* Buffalo: Prometheus Books, 1986, 193-200.

Hasker, W., 'A Refutation of Middle Knowledge', *Noûs*, Vol. 20 (December, 1986), 545-557.

_ 'Plantinga on Warranted Beliefs: Does his theory function properly?' *Christian Scholars Review*, Vol. 35, No. 1 (1996), 350-355.

_ 'The Foundations of Theism: Scoring the Quinn-Plantinga Debate', *Faith and Philosophy*, Vol. 15, No. 1 (January, 1998), 52-67.

Helm, P., 'Faith, Evidence, and the Scriptures', in D. A. Carson and J. D. Woodbridge, (eds), *Scripture and Truth* (Grand Rapids: Baker Book House, 1992), 303-320.

_ 'John Calvin, the *sensus divinitatis*, and the noetic effects of sin', *International Journal for Philosophy of Religion*, Vol. 43 (1998), 87-107.

Hester, M., 'Foundationalism and Peter's Confession', *Religious Studies*, Vol. 26, No. 3 (September, 1990), 403-413.

Hick, J., 'The Epistemological Challenge of Religious Pluralism', *Faith and Philosophy*, Vol. 14, No. 3 (July, 1997), 277-286.

Hobbs, J., 'Religious and Scientific Uses of Anecdotal Evidence', in E. S. Radcliffe, and C. J. White, (eds), *Faith in Theory and Practice: Essays on Justifying Religious Belief,* Chicago and La Salle: Open Court, 1993, 141-169.

Holton, R., 'Deciding to Trust, Coming to Believe', *Australasian Journal of Philosophy*, Vol. 72, No. 1 (March, 1994), 63-76.

Howard-Snyder, D. and O'Leary-Hawthorne, J., 'Transworld sanctity and Plantinga's Free Will Defense', *International Journal for Philosophy of Religion*, Vol. 44 (1998), 1-21.

Iseminger, G., 'Successful Argument and Rational Belief', *Philosophy and Rhetoric*, Vol. 7 (1974), 47-57.

James, W., 'The Will to Believe', in W. James, *The Will To Believe and Other Essays*, New York: Longeman's and Green, 1896.

Jones, K., 'Trust', in Edward Craig, (ed), *Routledge Encyclopaedia*, Vol. 9, London: Routledge, 1998, 466-470.

Kamitsuka, D.G., 'The Justification of Religious Belief in the Pluralistic Public Realm: Another Look at Postliberal Apologetics', *Journal of Religion*, Vol. 76, No. 4 (October, 1996),588-606.

Kasemann, E., 'The Problem of the Historical Jesus', in *Essays on New Testament Themes*, Napersville, Ill.: Alec R. Allenson, 1964, 15-47.

Kaufman, G.D., '"Evidentialism": A Theologian's Response', *Faith and Philosophy*, Vol. 6, No. 1 (January, 1989), 35-45.

Keller, J.A., 'Reflections on a Methodology for Christian Philosophers', *Faith and Philosophy,* Vol. 5, No. 2 (April, 1988), 144-155.

Konyndyk, K., 'Faith and Evidentialism', in R. Audi., and W. Wainwright, (eds) *Rationality, Religious Belief and Moral Commitment,* Ithaca and London: Cornell University Press, 1986, 82-108.

_ 'The return of the Christian philosopher', *The Reformed Journal*, Vol. 38 (September, 1988), 6-7.

Kretzmann, N., 'Faith Seeks, Understanding Finds: Augustine's Charter for Christian Philosophy', in Thomas Flint, (ed), *Christian Philosophy*, Notre Dame: University of Notre Dame Press, 1990, 1-36.

_ 'Evidence Against Anti-Evidentialism', in James Clark Kelly, (ed), *Our Knowledge of God*, Dordrecht: Kluwer Academic Publishers, 1992, 17-38.

Kretzmann, N., and Stump, E., 'Thomas Aquinas', *Routledge Encyclopedia of Philosophy*, Vol. 1, London: Routledge, 1998, 326-350.

Lackey, J., 'Testimonial Knowledge and Transmission', *Philosophical Quarterly*, Vol. 49, No. 197 (October, 1999), 471-490.

Langtry, B., 'Mackie on Miracles', *Australasian Journal of Philosophy*, Vol. 66, No. 3 (1988), 368-375.

_ 'Properly unargued belief in God', *International Journal for Philosophy of Religion*, Vol. 26 (1989), 129-154.

Levin, M., 'Plantinga on Functions and the Theory of Evolution', *Australasian Journal of Philosophy*, Vol. 75, No. 1 (March, 1997), 83-98.

Lewis, D., 'Evil For Freedom's Sake?', *Philosophical Papers*, Vol. 22, No. 3 (1993), 149-172.

Losin, P., Baldwin, A. and de Boer, J., 'Reformed epistemology: three replies', *Reformed Journal,* Vol. 32 (April, 1982), 21-25.

Luther, M., 'A Brief Explanation of the Ten Commandments, the Creed, and the Lord's Prayer' (1520) WA 7:215; *Works of Martin Luther*, Vol. 2, Philadelphia: Muhlenburg Press, 1943.

J. L. Mackie, 'Evil and Omnipotence', *Mind,* Vol. 64, No. 254 (April, 1955), 200-212.

_ 'Miracles and Testimony', in Richard Swinburne, (ed), *Miracles*, New York: Macmillan, 1989, 85-96.

McCafferty, A., 'Calvin and Insignifying Grounds', *Faith and Philosophy*, Vol. 11, No. 1 (January, 1994), 109-116.

McCord Adams, M., 'The Problem of Evil', in Edward Craig, (ed), *Routledge Encyclopaedia*, Vol. 3, London: Routledge, 1998, 466-472.

McInerny, R., 'On Behalf of Natural Theology', *Proceedings of the American Catholic Philosophical Association*, Vol. 54 (1980), 63-73.

McKim, R., 'Theism and Proper Basicality', *International Journal for Philosophy of Religion*, Vol. 26 (1989), 29-56.

McLeod, M., 'Can Belief In God Be Confirmed?' *Religious Studies*, Vol. 24 (1988), 311-323.

_ 'Passionate Religion: Toward a Theory of Epistemic Commitment For Theistic Belief', in W .L. Craig and M. S. McLeod, (eds), *The Logic of Rational Theism: Exporatory Essays*, Lewiston, The Edwin Mellen Press, 1990, 17-40.

Mascord, K., 'Apologetics as Dialogue: A New Way Of Understanding An Old Task', *Reformed Theological Review*, Vol. 54, No. 2 (May-August, 1995), 49-64.

_ 'An Apology for Hope for the New Era', *Explorations 13* (forthcoming)

Matthews, G. B., 'Augustine', in Edward Craig, (ed), *Routledge Encyclopaedia*, Vol. 1, London: Routledge, 1998, 541- 559.

Meek, E.L., 'A Polanyian Interpretation of Calvin's Sensus Divinitatis', *Presbyterion*, Vol. 23, No. 1 (1997), 8-24.

Nathan, N. M. L., 'Naturalism and Self-Defeat', *Religious Studies*, Vol. 33, No. 2 (June, 1997), 135-142.

Netland, H.A., 'Truth, authority and modernity: shopping for truth in a supermarket of worldviews', in P. Sampson, V. Samuel and C. Sugden, (eds), *Faith and Modernity*, Oxford: Regnum Books, 1994, 89-115.

Noll, M., 'Warfield, Benjamin Breckinridge', in Walter A. Elwell, (ed) *Evangelical Dictionary of Theology*, Grand Rapids: Baker Book House, 1984, 1156.

O'Connor, D., 'A Reformed Problem of Evil and the Free Will Defense', *International Journal for Philosophy of Religion*, Vol. 1 (February, 1996), 33-63.

O'Daly, G., 'Augustine', in David Furley, (ed), *From Aristotle to Augustine*, Routledge History of Philosophy, Vol. 2, London: Routledge, 1999, 388-425.

Oden, T.C., 'So What Happens after Modernity? A Postmodern Agenda for Evangelical Theology', in David S. Dockery, (ed), *The Challenge of Postmodernism: An Evangelical Engagement*, Wheaton: BridgePoint, 1995, 392-406.

Oliphint, K.S., 'Epistemology and Christian Belief', *Westminster Theological Journal*, Vol. 63 (2001), 151-182.

Ostien, P., 'God and Other Minds, and Inference to the Best Explanation', *Canadian Journal of Philosophy*, Vol. 4 (1974), 149-162.

Owen, D., 'Hume versus Price on Miracles and Prior Probabilities: Testimony and the Bayesian Calculation', *The Philosophical Quarterly*, Vol. 37, No. 147 (1987), 187-202.

Pargetter, R., 'Experience, proper basicality and belief in God', *International Journal for Philosophy of Religion*, Vol. 27 (1990), 141-163.

Peressini, A., 'Naturalism, evolution, and self-defeat', *International Journal for Philosophy of Religion*, Vol. 44 (1998), 41-51.

Perszyk, K.J., 'Free will defence with and without Molinism', *International Journal for Philosophy of Religion*, Vol. 43 (1998), 29-64.

_ 'Molinism and Theodicy', *International Journal for Philosophy of Religion*, Vol. 44 (1998), 163-184.

_ 'Compatibilism and the Free Will Defence: A Reply to Bishop,' *Australasian Journal of Philosophy*, Vol. 77, No. 1 (March, 1999), 92-105.

_ 'Stump's Theodicy of Redemptive Suffering and Molinism', *Religious Studies*, Vol. 35 (1999), 191-211.

Pestana, M., 'Radical Freedom, Radical Evil and the Possibility of Eternal Damnation', *Faith and Philosophy*, Vol. 9, No. 4 (October, 1992), 500-507.

Pinnock, C., 'Cultural Apologetics: an evangelical perspective', *Bibliotheca Sacra*, Vol. 127 (January-March, 1970), 58-63.

Purtill, R.L., 'Miracles: What If They Happen?' in Richard Swinburne, (ed), *Miracles*, New York: Macmillan, 1989, 189-205.

Quinn, P., 'On Finding the Foundations of Theism', *Faith and Philosophy*, Vol. 2, No. 4 (October, 1985), 469-486.

Reiter, D., 'Calvin's "Sense of Divinity" and Externalist Knowledge of God', *Faith and Philosophy*, Vol. 15, No. 3 (July, 1998), 253-270.

Richman, R., 'Plantinga, God, and (Yet) Other Minds', *Australasian Journal of Philosophy*, Vol. 50 (1972), 40-54.

Robbins, J.W., 'Is Belief in God Properly Basic?' *International Journal for Philosophy of Religion*, Vol. 14, No. 4 (1983), 246-247.

_ 'Does Belief in God Need Proof?' *Faith and Philosophy*, Vol. 2, No. 3 (July, 1985), 272-286.

_ 'Is Naturalism Irrational?' *Faith and Philosophy*, Vol. 11, No. 2 (April, 1994), 255-259.

Rowe, W.L., 'The Problem of Evil and Some Varieties of Atheism', *American Philosophical Quarterly*, Vol. 16 (1979), 335-341.

_ 'Evil and the Theistic Hypothesis: A Response to Wykstra', *International Journal for Philosophy of Religion*, Vol. 16 (1984), 95-100.

_ 'The Empirical Argument from Evil', in R. Audi, and W. Wainwright, (eds), *Rationality, Religious Belief and Moral Commitment*, Ithaca and London: Cornell University Press, 1986, 227-247.

_ 'Ruminations about Evil', *Philosophical Perspectives* 5, Philosophy of Religion, (1991), 69-88.

— 'In Defense of "The Free Will Defense"', *International Journal for Philosophy of Religion*, Vol. 44 (1998), 115-120.
Rudinow, J., 'Gambling on Other Minds', *Sophia*, Vol. 10 (1971), 27-29.
Russell, R.P., 'Augustinianism', in *The New Catholic Encyclopedia*, Vol. 1, New York: McGraw Hill, 1967, 1063-1069.
Russman, T.A., '"Reformed" Epistemology', in L.A. Kennedy, (ed), *Thomaistic Papers IV*, Houston, Texas: Center for Thomistic Studies, 1988, 185-207.
Saunders, J., 'Persons, Criteria, and Skepticism', *Metaphilosophy*, Vol. 20 (1973), 95-123.
Sennett, J.F., 'Reformed Epistemology and Epistemic Duty', in E. S. Radcliffe, and C. J. White, (ed), *Faith in Theory and Practice: Essays on Justifying Religious Belief*, Chicago and La Salle: Open Court, 1993, 189-207.
— 'Is There Freedom in Heaven?' *Faith and Philosophy*, Vol. 16, No. 1 (January, 1999), 69-82.
Sessions, W.L., 'Plantinga's Box', *Faith and Philosophy*, Vol. 8, No. 1 (January, 1991), 51-66.
— 'The Certainty of Faith', in E. S. Radcliffe, and C. J. White, (ed), *Faith in Theory and Practice: Essays on Justifying Religious Belief*, Chicago and La Salle: Open Court, 1993, 76-89.
Shermer, M., 'Why People Believe in God', *The Humanist*, Vol. 59, No. 6 (November/December 1999), 20-26.
Sobel, J.H., 'On the Evidence of Testimony for Miracles: A Bayesian Interpretation of David Hume's Analysis', *The Philosophical Quarterly*, Vol. 37, No. 147 (1987), 166-186.
Stump, E. and Kretzmann, N., 'Thomas Aquinas', in Edward Craig, (ed), *Routledge Encyclopaedia*, Vol. 1, London: Routledge, 1998, 326- 350.
Sullivan, T., 'Adequate Evidence for Religious Assent', in L.A. Kennedy, (ed), *Thomaistic Papers IV*, Houston, Texas: Center for Thomistic Studies, 1988, 73-99.
Sweet, W. and O'Connell, C., 'Empiricism, Fideism and the Nature of Religious Belief', *Sophia*, Vol. 31, No. 3 (1992), 1-15.
Swinburne, R., 'A Theodicy of Heaven and Hell', in A. Freddosco, (ed), *The Existence and Nature of God*, Notre Dame: Notre Dame Press, 1983, 37-54.
— 'Historical Evidence', in R. Swinburne, (ed), *Miracles*, New York: Macmillan, 1989, 133-151.
— 'Does Theism Need A Theodicy?' *Canadian Journal of Philosophy*, Vol. 18, No. 2 (June, 1988), 287-312.
— 'Plantinga on Warrant', *Religious Studies*, Vol. 37, No. 2 (June, 2001),203-214.
— 'Swinburne and Plantinga on Internal Rationality', *Religious Studies*, Vol. 37, No. 3 (September, 2001), 357-358.

— 'Natural Theology, Its "Dwindling Probabilities" and "Lack of Rapport"', *Faith and Philosophy*, Vol. 21, No. 4 (October, 2004), 533-546.
Talbott, T., 'The Doctrine of Everlasting Punishment', *Faith and Philosophy*, Vol. 7 No. 1 (January, 1990), 19-42.
Taliaferro, C., 'A Hundred Years with the Giants and the Gods: Christians and Twentieth Century Philosophy', *Christian Scholars Review*, Vol. 24, No. 4 (Summer, 2000), 694-712.
Taylor, J.E., 'Plantinga's Proper Functioning Analysis of Epistemic Warrant', *Philosophical Studies*, Vol. 64 (1991), 185-202.
Thompson, M.M., 'The Historical Jesus and the Johannine Christ', in R. Alan Culpepper and C. Clifton Black, (eds), *Exploring the Gospel of John*, Louisville, Kentucky: Westminster John Knox Press, 1996, 21-42.
Tilley, T.W., Review of Warranted Christian Belief, *Theological Studies*, Vol. 62, No. 2 (June, 2001), 388-90.
Tomberlin, J., 'Is Belief in God Justified?' *Journal of Philosophy*, Vol. 67 (1970), 31-38.
Tooley, M., 'The Argument from Evil', *Philosophical Perspectives* 5, Philosophy of Religion, 1991, 89-134.
Van Hook, J.M., 'Knowledge, belief, and Reformed epistemology', *The Reformed Journal*, Vol. 31 (July, 1981), 12-17.
— '"Knowledge" in quotes', *The Reformed Journal*, Vol. 32 (June, 1982), 8-9.
Van Til, C., 'My Credo', in E. R. Geehan (ed), *Jerusalem and Athens*, Presbyterian and Reformed Publishing Co., 1971, 3-21.
Veatch, H.B., 'Preliminary Statement of Apology, Analysis, and Critique', in L. A. Kennedy, (ed), *Thomaistic Papers IV*, Houston, Texas: Center for Thomistic Studies, 1988, 5-63.
Vogel, J., 'Inference to the best explanation', in *Routledge Encyclopaedia*, Vol. 4, London: Routledge, 1998, 766-769.
Walls, J. L., 'Is Molinism As Bad As Calvinism?' *Faith and Philosophy*, Vol. 7, No. 1 (January, 1990), 85-98.
Warfield, B.B., 'Apologetics', in S. M. Jackson, (ed), *The New Schaff-Herzog Encyclopedia of Religious Knowledge*, Grand Rapids: Baker Book House, 1960, 232-238.
Weisheipl, J.A., 'Scholasticism', *The New Catholic Encyclopedia*, New York: McGraw Hill, 1967, 1153-1170.
Westphal, M., Review of Warranted Christian Belief, *Modern Theology*, Vol. 17, No. 1 (January, 2001), 99-100.
Wierenga, E., 'Review of Alvin Plantinga', in *Faith and Philosophy*, Vol. 5, No. 2 (April, 1988), 214-219.
Wisdo, D., 'The Fragility of Faith: Toward a Critique of Reformed Epistemology', *Religious Studies*, Vol. 24, No. 3 (September, 1988), 265-374.

Witherington, B., 'Resurrection Redux', in P. Copan (ed), *Will the Real Jesus Please Stand Up?* Grand Rapids: Baker Book House, 1998, 129-145.
Wolters, A., 'Dutch Neo-Calvinism: Worldview, Philosophy and Rationality', in H. Hart, J. Van der Hoeven, N. Wolterstorff, (eds), *Rationality in the Calvinian Tradition*, Boston: University Press of America, 1983, 113-131.
Wolterstorff, N., 'The Migration of the Theistic Arguments: From Natural Theology to Evidentialist Apologetics', in R. Audi,, and W. Wainwright, (eds), *Rationality, Religious Belief and Moral Commitment*, Ithaca and London: Cornell University Press, 1986, 38-81.
_ 'Evidence, Entitled Belief, and the Gospels', *Faith and Philosophy*, Vol. 6, No. 4 (October, 1989), 429-459.
_ 'Tradition, Insight and Constraint', *Proceedings and Addresses of the American Philosophical Association*, Vol. 66, No. 3 (November, 1992), 43-57.
_ 'Epistemology of Religion', in J. Greco and E. Sosa, (eds), *The Blackwell Guide to Epistemology*, Malden, Massachusetts: Blackwell, 1999, 303-324.
Wood, W.J., 'The Justification of Doctrinal Beliefs', in W. L. Craig and M. S. McLeod, (eds), *The Logic of Rational Theism: Exploratory Essays*, Lewiston, The Edwin Mellen Press, 1990, 41-63.
Wright, N.T., 'Christian Origins and the Resurrection of Jesus: The Resurrection of Jesus as a Historical Problem', *Sewanee Theological Review*, Vol. 41, No. 2 (1998), 107-123.
_ 'Early Traditions and the Origin of Christianity', *Sewanee Theological Review*, Vol. 41, No. 2 (1998), 125-140.
Wykstra, S., 'The Humean Obstacle to Evidential Arguments from Suffering: On Avoiding the Evils of "Appearance,"' *International Journal for the Philosophy of Religion*, Vol. 16 (1984), 73-93.
_ 'Toward a sensible evidentialism: On the notion of needing evidence', in W. Rowe and W. Wainwright, *Philosophy of Religion*, New York: Hartcourt Brace Jovanovich, 1989, 426-437.
_ 'Externalism, Proper Inferentiality and Sensible Evidentialism', *Topoi*, Vol. 14 (1995), 107-121.
Zagzebski, L., 'Religious Knowledge and the Virtues', in *Rational Faith: Catholic Responses to Reformed Epistemology*, Notre Dame: University of Notre Dame Press, 1993, 199-225.
Zeis, J., 'A critique of Plantinga's theological foundationalism', *International Journal for Philosophy of Religion*, Vol. 28 (1990), 173-189.
_ 'Natural Theology: Reformed?' in Linda Zagzebski (ed), *Rational Faith: Catholic Responses to Reformed Epistemology*, Notre Dame: University of Notre Dame Press, 1993, 48-78.
_ 'Plantinga's Theory of Warrant: Religious Beliefs and Higher Level Epistemic Judgements', *American Catholic Philosophical Quarterly*, Vol. 72, No. 1 (1998), 23-38.

General Index

Augustinianism, 2-4, 6-8, 186-190

Basic beliefs, 29, 59-60, 128-29
Belief in God as properly basic, 29, 61-62, Chapter 7
Belief in the gospel as properly basic, Chapter 8

Calvin, John, 8-9

De facto objections, 69, 76-78
De jure objections, 69, 70-78

Enlightenment, 10-11
Evidentialism, 11, 58-59, 202-206

Foundationalism, 60-61, 122-126
Free will defence, 84-85

Historical Biblical Criticism, 53-57
Holy Spirit, 74, 146, 192

Jellema, William Harry, 27-28

Kant, Immanuel, 13, 207-208
Kuyper, Abraham, 17-19, 23-24, 26, 202-203

Logical Positivism, 33-34

Mackie, J.L., 86
Middle Knowledge, 86 (fn)
Molina, Luis de, 86 (fn)

Naturalism, 41-47
Natural theology, 6, 12, 58, 112-13
Negative Apologetics, 21, Chapters 2-5

Positive Apologetics, 21, Chapter 6
Postmodernism, 47-52, 206-209
Presuppositionalism, 202-206
Problem of evil, 79-80, Chapter 5, logical form, 81-95; evidential form, 95-109
Properly basic beliefs, 29, 62

Rationality, 58-59, 71-72
Reformed apologetics, 9-10, 23-24
Reid, Thomas, 11-13, 123-25
Religious Pluralism, 34-41, 77

Schleiermacher, Friedrich, 1, 14-15
Sensus divinitatis, 74-75, 129, 132, 151

Thomism, 4-8, 190-202
Transworld depravity, 87-88

Van Til, Cornelius, 19-20

Warfield, Benjamin, 15-17
Warrant, 65-66, 122
Warranted trust, 159-167, 169-83

Paternoster Biblical Monographs

(All titles uniform with this volume)
Dates in bold are of projected publication

Joseph Abraham
Eve: Accused or Acquitted?
A Reconsideration of Feminist Readings of the Creation Narrative Texts in Genesis 1–3
Two contrary views dominate contemporary feminist biblical scholarship. One finds in the Bible an unequivocal equality between the sexes from the very creation of humanity, whilst the other sees the biblical text as irredeemably patriarchal and androcentric. Dr Abraham enters into dialogue with both camps as well as introducing his own method of approach. An invaluable tool for any one who is interested in this contemporary debate.
2002 / 0-85364-971-5 / xxiv + 272pp

Octavian D. Baban
Mimesis and Luke's on the Road Encounters in Luke-Acts
Luke's Theology of the Way and its Literary Representation
The book argues on theological and literary (mimetic) grounds that Luke's on-the-road encounters, especially those belonging to the post-Easter period, are part of his complex theology of the Way. Jesus' teaching and that of the apostles is presented by Luke as a challenging answer to the Hellenistic reader's thirst for adventure, good literature, and existential paradigms.
2005 */ 1-84227-253-5 / approx. 374pp*

Paul Barker
The Triumph of Grace in Deuteronomy
This book is a textual and theological analysis of the interaction between the sin and faithlessness of Israel and the grace of Yahweh in response, looking especially at Deuteronomy chapters 1–3, 8–10 and 29–30. The author argues that the grace of Yahweh is determinative for the ongoing relationship between Yahweh and Israel and that Deuteronomy anticipates and fully expects Israel to be faithless.
2004 / 1-84227-226-8 / xxii + 270pp

Jonathan F. Bayes
The Weakness of the Law
God's Law and the Christian in New Testament Perspective
A study of the four New Testament books which refer to the law as weak (Acts, Romans, Galatians, Hebrews) leads to a defence of the third use in the Reformed debate about the law in the life of the believer.
2000 / 0-85364-957-X / xii + 244pp

Mark Bonnington
The Antioch Episode of Galatians 2:11-14 in Historical and Cultural Context

The Galatians 2 'incident' in Antioch over table-fellowship suggests significant disagreement between the leading apostles. This book analyses the background to the disagreement by locating the incident within the dynamics of social interaction between Jews and Gentiles. It proposes a new way of understanding the relationship between the individuals and issues involved.

2005 / 1-84227-050-8 / approx. 350pp

David Bostock
A Portrayal of Trust
The Theme of Faith in the Hezekiah Narratives

This study provides detailed and sensitive readings of the Hezekiah narratives (2 Kings 18–20 and Isaiah 36–39) from a theological perspective. It concentrates on the theme of faith, using narrative criticism as its methodology. Attention is paid especially to setting, plot, point of view and characterization within the narratives. A largely positive portrayal of Hezekiah emerges that underlines the importance and relevance of scripture.

2005 / 1-84227-314-0 / approx. 300pp

Mark Bredin
Jesus, Revolutionary of Peace
A Non-violent Christology in the Book of Revelation

This book aims to demonstrate that the figure of Jesus in the Book of Revelation can best be understood as an active non-violent revolutionary.

2003 / 1-84227-153-9 / xviii + 262pp

Robinson Butarbutar
Paul and Conflict Resolution
An Exegetical Study of Paul's Apostolic Paradigm in 1 Corinthians 9

The author sees the apostolic paradigm in 1 Corinthians 9 as part of Paul's unified arguments in 1 Corinthians 8–10 in which he seeks to mediate in the dispute over the issue of food offered to idols. The book also sees its relevance for dispute-resolution today, taking the conflict within the author's church as an example.

2006 / 1-84227-315-9 / approx. 280pp

Daniel J-S Chae
Paul as Apostle to the Gentiles
His Apostolic Self-awareness and its Influence on the Soteriological Argument in Romans
Opposing 'the post-Holocaust interpretation of Romans', Daniel Chae competently demonstrates that Paul argues for the equality of Jew and Gentile in Romans. Chae's fresh exegetical interpretation is academically outstanding and spiritually encouraging.
1997 / 0-85364-829-8 / xiv + 378pp

Luke L. Cheung
The Genre, Composition and Hermeneutics of the Epistle of James
The present work examines the employment of the wisdom genre with a certain compositional structure and the interpretation of the law through the Jesus tradition of the double love command by the author of the Epistle of James to serve his purpose in promoting perfection and warning against doubleness among the eschatologically renewed people of God in the Diaspora.
2003 / 1-84227-062-1 / xvi + 372pp

Youngmo Cho
Spirit and Kingdom in the Writings of Luke and Paul
The relationship between Spirit and Kingdom is a relatively unexplored area in Lukan and Pauline studies. This book offers a fresh perspective of two biblical writers on the subject. It explores the difference between Luke's and Paul's understanding of the Spirit by examining the specific question of the relationship of the concept of the Spirit to the concept of the Kingdom of God in each writer.
2005 / 1-84227-316-7 / approx. 270pp

Andrew C. Clark
Parallel Lives
The Relation of Paul to the Apostles in the Lucan Perspective
This study of the Peter-Paul parallels in Acts argues that their purpose was to emphasize the themes of continuity in salvation history and the unity of the Jewish and Gentile missions. New light is shed on Luke's literary techniques, partly through a comparison with Plutarch.
2001 / 1-84227-035-4 / xviii + 386pp

Andrew D. Clarke
Secular and Christian Leadership in Corinth
A Socio-Historical and Exegetical Study of 1 Corinthians 1–6

This volume is an investigation into the leadership structures and dynamics of first-century Roman Corinth. These are compared with the practice of leadership in the Corinthian Christian community which are reflected in 1 Corinthians 1–6, and contrasted with Paul's own principles of Christian leadership.

2005 / 1-84227-229-2 / 200pp

Stephen Finamore
God, Order and Chaos
René Girard and the Apocalypse

Readers are often disturbed by the images of destruction in the book of Revelation and unsure why they are unleashed after the exaltation of Jesus. This book examines past approaches to these texts and uses René Girard's theories to revive some old ideas and propose some new ones.

2005 / 1-84227-197-0 / approx. 344pp

David G. Firth
Surrendering Retribution in the Psalms
Responses to Violence in the Individual Complaints

In *Surrendering Retribution in the Psalms*, David Firth examines the ways in which the book of Psalms inculcates a model response to violence through the repetition of standard patterns of prayer. Rather than seeking justification for retributive violence, Psalms encourages not only a surrender of the right of retribution to Yahweh, but also sets limits on the retribution that can be sought in imprecations. Arising initially from the author's experience in South Africa, the possibilities of this model to a particular context of violence is then briefly explored.

2005 / 1-84227-337-X / xviii + 154pp

Scott J. Hafemann
Suffering and Ministry in the Spirit
Paul's Defence of His Ministry in II Corinthians 2:14–3:3

Shedding new light on the way Paul defended his apostleship, the author offers a careful, detailed study of 2 Corinthians 2:14–3:3 linked with other key passages throughout 1 and 2 Corinthians. Demonstrating the unity and coherence of Paul's argument in this passage, the author shows that Paul's suffering served as the vehicle for revealing God's power and glory through the Spirit.

2000 / 0-85364-967-7 / xiv + 262pp

Scott J. Hafemann
Paul, Moses and the History of Israel
The Letter/Spirit Contrast and the Argument from Scripture in 2 Corinthians 3
An exegetical study of the call of Moses, the second giving of the Law (Exodus 32–34), the new covenant, and the prophetic understanding of the history of Israel in 2 Corinthians 3. Hafemann's work demonstrates Paul's contextual use of the Old Testament and the essential unity between the Law and the Gospel within the context of the distinctive ministries of Moses and Paul.
2005 / 1-84227-317-5 / xii + 498pp

Douglas S. McComiskey
Lukan Theology in the Light of the Gospel's Literary Structure
Luke's Gospel was purposefully written with theology embedded in its patterned literary structure. A critical analysis of this cyclical structure provides new windows into Luke's interpretation of the individual pericopes comprising the Gospel and illuminates several of his theological interests.
2004 / 1-84227-148-2 / xviii + 388pp

Stephen Motyer
Your Father the Devil?
A New Approach to John and 'The Jews'
Who are 'the Jews' in John's Gospel? Defending John against the charge of antisemitism, Motyer argues that, far from demonising the Jews, the Gospel seeks to present Jesus as 'Good News for Jews' in a late first century setting.
1997 / 0-85364-832-8 / xiv + 260pp

Esther Ng
Reconstructing Christian Origins?
The Feminist Theology of Elizabeth Schüssler Fiorenza: An Evaluation
In a detailed evaluation, the author challenges Elizabeth Schüssler Fiorenza's reconstruction of early Christian origins and her underlying presuppositions. The author also presents her own views on women's roles both then and now.
2002 / 1-84227-055-9 / xxiv + 468pp

Robin Parry
Old Testament Story and Christian Ethics
The Rape of Dinah as a Case Study
What is the role of story in ethics and, more particularly, what is the role of Old Testament story in Christian ethics? This book, drawing on the work of contemporary philosophers, argues that narrative is crucial in the ethical shaping of people and, drawing on the work of contemporary Old Testament scholars, that story plays a key role in Old Testament ethics. Parry then argues that when situated in canonical context Old Testament stories can be reappropriated by Christian readers in their own ethical formation. The shocking story of the rape of Dinah and the massacre of the Shechemites provides a fascinating case study for exploring the parameters within which Christian ethical appropriations of Old Testament stories can live.
2004 / 1-84227-210-1 / xx + 350pp

Ian Paul
Power to See the World Anew
The Value of Paul Ricoeur's Hermeneutic of Metaphor in Interpreting the Symbolism of Revelation 12 and 13
This book is a study of the hermeneutics of metaphor of Paul Ricoeur, one of the most important writers on hermeneutics and metaphor of the last century. It sets out the key points of his theory, important criticisms of his work, and how his approach, modified in the light of these criticisms, offers a methodological framework for reading apocalyptic texts.
2006 / 1-84227-056-7 / approx. 350pp

Robert L. Plummer
Paul's Understanding of the Church's Mission
Did the Apostle Paul Expect the Early Christian Communities to Evangelize?
This book engages in a careful study of Paul's letters to determine if the apostle expected the communities to which he wrote to engage in missionary activity. It helpfully summarizes the discussion on this debated issue, judiciously handling contested texts, and provides a way forward in addressing this critical question. While admitting that Paul rarely explicitly commands the communities he founded to evangelize, Plummer amasses significant incidental data to provide a convincing case that Paul did indeed expect his churches to engage in mission activity. Throughout the study, Plummer progressively builds a theological basis for the church's mission that is both distinctively Pauline and compelling.
2006 / 1-84227-333-7 / approx. 324pp

David Powys
'Hell': A Hard Look at a Hard Question
The Fate of the Unrighteous in New Testament Thought
This comprehensive treatment seeks to unlock the original meaning of terms and phrases long thought to support the traditional doctrine of hell. It concludes that there is an alternative—one which is more biblical, and which can positively revive the rationale for Christian mission.
1997 / 0-85364-831-X / xxii + 478pp

Sorin Sabou
Between Horror and Hope
Paul's Metaphorical Language of Death in Romans 6.1-11
This book argues that Paul's metaphorical language of death in Romans 6.1-11 conveys two aspects: horror and hope. The 'horror' aspect is conveyed by the 'crucifixion' language, and the 'hope' aspect by 'burial' language. The life of the Christian believer is understood, as relationship with sin is concerned ('death to sin'), between these two realities: horror and hope.
2005 / 1-84227-322-1 / approx. 224pp

Rosalind Selby
The Comical Doctrine
The Epistemology of New Testament Hermeneutics
This book argues that the gospel breaks through postmodernity's critique of truth and the referential possibilities of textuality with its gift of grace. With a rigorous, philosophical challenge to modernist and postmodernist assumptions, Selby offers an alternative epistemology to all who would still read with faith *and* with academic credibility.
2005 / 1-84227-212-8 / approx. 350pp

Kiwoong Son
Zion Symbolism in Hebrews
Hebrews 12.18-24 as a Hermeneutical Key to the Epistle
This book challenges the general tendency of understanding the Epistle to the Hebrews against a Hellenistic background and suggests that the Epistle should be understood in the light of the Jewish apocalyptic tradition. The author especially argues for the importance of the theological symbolism of Sinai and Zion (Heb. 12:18-24) as it provides the Epistle's theological background as well as the rhetorical basis of the superiority motif of Jesus throughout the Epistle.
2005 / 1-84227-368-X / approx. 280pp

Kevin Walton
Thou Traveller Unknown
The Presence and Absence of God in the Jacob Narrative
The author offers a fresh reading of the story of Jacob in the book of Genesis through the paradox of divine presence and absence. The work also seeks to make a contribution to Pentateuchal studies by bringing together a close reading of the final text with historical critical insights, doing justice to the text's historical depth, final form and canonical status.
2003 / 1-84227-059-1 / xvi + 238pp

George M. Wieland
The Significance of Salvation
A Study of Salvation Language in the Pastoral Epistles
The language and ideas of salvation pervade the three Pastoral Epistles. This study offers a close examination of their soteriological statements. In all three letters the idea of salvation is found to play a vital paraenetic role, but each also exhibits distinctive soteriological emphases. The results challenge common assumptions about the Pastoral Epistles as a corpus.
2005 / 1-84227-257-8 / approx. 324pp

Alistair Wilson
When Will These Things Happen?
A Study of Jesus as Judge in Matthew 21–25
This study seeks to allow Matthew's carefully constructed presentation of Jesus to be given full weight in the modern evaluation of Jesus' eschatology. Careful analysis of the text of Matthew 21–25 reveals Jesus to be standing firmly in the Jewish prophetic and wisdom traditions as he proclaims and enacts imminent judgement on the Jewish authorities then boldly claims the central role in the final and universal judgement.
2004 / 1-84227-146-6 / xxii + 272pp

Lindsay Wilson
Joseph Wise and Otherwise
The Intersection of Covenant and Wisdom in Genesis 37–50
This book offers a careful literary reading of Genesis 37–50 that argues that the Joseph story contains both strong covenant themes and many wisdom-like elements. The connections between the two helps to explore how covenant and wisdom might intersect in an integrated biblical theology.
2004 / 1-84227-140-7 / xvi + 340pp

Stephen I. Wright
The Voice of Jesus
Studies in the Interpretation of Six Gospel Parables
This literary study considers how the 'voice' of Jesus has been heard in different periods of parable interpretation, and how the categories of figure and trope may help us towards a sensitive reading of the parables today.
2000 / 0-85364-975-8 / xiv + 280pp

Paternoster
9 Holdom Avenue,
Bletchley,
Milton Keynes MK1 1QR,
United Kingdom
Web: www.authenticmedia.co.uk/paternoster

Paternoster Theological Monographs
(All titles uniform with this volume)
Dates in bold are of projected publication

Emil Bartos
Deification in Eastern Orthodox Theology
An Evaluation and Critique of the Theology of Dumitru Staniloae
Bartos studies a fundamental yet neglected aspect of Orthodox theology: deification. By examining the doctrines of anthropology, christology, soteriology and ecclesiology as they relate to deification, he provides an important contribution to contemporary dialogue between Eastern and Western theologians.
1999 / 0-85364-956-1 / xii + 370pp

Graham Buxton
The Trinity, Creation and Pastoral Ministry
Imaging the Perichoretic God
In this book the author proposes a three-way conversation between theology, science and pastoral ministry. His approach draws on a Trinitarian understanding of God as a relational being of love, whose life 'spills over' into all created reality, human and non-human. By locating human meaning and purpose within God's 'creation-community' this book offers the possibility of a transforming engagement between those in pastoral ministry and the scientific community.
2005 */ 1-84227-369-8 / approx. 380 pp*

Iain D. Campbell
Fixing the Indemnity
The Life and Work of George Adam Smith
When Old Testament scholar George Adam Smith (1856–1942) delivered the Lyman Beecher lectures at Yale University in 1899, he confidently declared that 'modern criticism has won its war against traditional theories. It only remains to fix the amount of the indemnity.' In this biography, Iain D. Campbell assesses Smith's critical approach to the Old Testament and evaluates its consequences, showing that Smith's life and work still raises questions about the relationship between biblical scholarship and evangelical faith.
2004 / 1-84227-228-4 / xx + 256pp

Tim Chester
Mission and the Coming of God
Eschatology, the Trinity and Mission in the Theology of Jürgen Moltmann
This book explores the theology and missiology of the influential contemporary theologian, Jürgen Moltmann. It highlights the important contribution Moltmann has made while offering a critique of his thought from an evangelical perspective. In so doing, it touches on pertinent issues for evangelical missiology. The conclusion takes Calvin as a starting point, proposing 'an eschatology of the cross' which offers a critique of the over-realised eschatologies in liberation theology and certain forms of evangelicalism.
2006 / 1-84227-320-5 / approx. 224pp

Sylvia Wilkey Collinson
Making Disciples
The Significance of Jesus' Educational Strategy for Today's Church
This study examines the biblical practice of discipling, formulates a definition, and makes comparisons with modern models of education. A recommendation is made for greater attention to its practice today.
2004 / 1-84227-116-4 / xiv + 278pp

Darrell Cosden
A Theology of Work
Work and the New Creation
Through dialogue with Moltmann, Pope John Paul II and others, this book develops a genitive 'theology of work', presenting a theological definition of work and a model for a theological ethics of work that shows work's nature, value and meaning now and eschatologically. Work is shown to be a transformative activity consisting of three dynamically inter-related dimensions: the instrumental, relational and ontological.
2005 / 1-84227-332-9 / xvi + 208pp

Stephen M. Dunning
The Crisis and the Quest
A Kierkegaardian Reading of Charles Williams
Employing Kierkegaardian categories and analysis, this study investigates both the central crisis in Charles Williams's authorship between hermetism and Christianity (Kierkegaard's Religions A and B), and the quest to resolve this crisis, a quest that ultimately presses the bounds of orthodoxy.
2000 / 0-85364-985-5 / xxiv + 254pp

Keith Ferdinando
The Triumph of Christ in African Perspective
A Study of Demonology and Redemption in the African Context
The book explores the implications of the gospel for traditional African fears of occult aggression. It analyses such traditional approaches to suffering and biblical responses to fears of demonic evil, concluding with an evaluation of African beliefs from the perspective of the gospel.
1999 / 0-85364-830-1 / xviii + 450pp

Andrew Goddard
Living the Word, Resisting the World
The Life and Thought of Jacques Ellul
This work offers a definitive study of both the life and thought of the French Reformed thinker Jacques Ellul (1912-1994). It will prove an indispensable resource for those interested in this influential theologian and sociologist and for Christian ethics and political thought generally.
2002 / 1-84227-053-2 / xxiv + 378pp

David Hilborn
The Words of our Lips
Language-Use in Free Church Worship
Studies of liturgical language have tended to focus on the written canons of Roman Catholic and Anglican communities. By contrast, David Hilborn analyses the more extemporary approach of English Nonconformity. Drawing on recent developments in linguistic pragmatics, he explores similarities and differences between 'fixed' and 'free' worship, and argues for the interdependence of each.
2006 / 0-85364-977-4 / approx. 350pp

Roger Hitching
The Church and Deaf People
A Study of Identity, Communication and Relationships with Special Reference to the Ecclesiology of Jürgen Moltmann
In *The Church and Deaf People* Roger Hitching sensitively examines the history and present experience of deaf people and finds similarities between aspects of sign language and Moltmann's theological method that 'open up' new ways of understanding theological concepts.
2003 / 1-84227-222-5 / xxii + 236pp

John G. Kelly
One God, One People
The Differentiated Unity of the People of God in the Theology of Jürgen Moltmann
The author expounds and critiques Moltmann's doctrine of God and highlights the systematic connections between it and Moltmann's influential discussion of Israel. He then proposes a fresh approach to Jewish–Christian relations building on Moltmann's work using insights from Habermas and Rawls.
2005 / 0-85346-969-3 / approx. 350pp

Mark F.W. Lovatt
Confronting the Will-to-Power
A Reconsideration of the Theology of Reinhold Niebuhr
Confronting the Will-to-Power is an analysis of the theology of Reinhold Niebuhr, arguing that his work is an attempt to identify, and provide a practical theological answer to, the existence and nature of human evil.
2001 / 1-84227-054-0 / xviii + 216pp

Neil B. MacDonald
Karl Barth and the Strange New World within the Bible
Barth, Wittgenstein, and the Metadilemmas of the Enlightenment
Barth's discovery of the strange new world within the Bible is examined in the context of Kant, Hume, Overbeck, and, most importantly, Wittgenstein. MacDonald covers some fundamental issues in theology today: epistemology, the final form of the text and biblical truth-claims.
2000 / 0-85364-970-7 / xxvi + 374pp

Keith A. Mascord
Alvin Plantinga and Christian Apologetics
This book draws together the contributions of the philosopher Alvin Plantinga to the major contemporary challenges to Christian belief, highlighting in particular his ground-breaking work in epistemology and the problem of evil. Plantinga's theory that both theistic and Christian belief is warrantedly basic is explored and critiqued, and an assessment offered as to the significance of his work for apologetic theory and practice.
2005 / 1-84227-256-X / approx. 304pp

Gillian McCulloch
The Deconstruction of Dualism in Theology
With Reference to Ecofeminist Theology and New Age Spirituality
This book challenges eco-theological anti-dualism in Christian theology, arguing that dualism has a twofold function in Christian religious discourse. Firstly, it enables us to express the discontinuities and divisions that are part of the process of reality. Secondly, dualistic language allows us to express the mysteries of divine transcendence/immanence and the survival of the soul without collapsing into monism and materialism, both of which are problematic for Christian epistemology.
2002 / 1-84227-044-3 / xii + 282pp

Leslie McCurdy
Attributes and Atonement
The Holy Love of God in the Theology of P.T. Forsyth
Attributes and Atonement is an intriguing full-length study of P.T. Forsyth's doctrine of the cross as it relates particularly to God's holy love. It includes an unparalleled bibliography of both primary and secondary material relating to Forsyth.
1999 / 0-85364-833-6 / xiv + 328pp

Nozomu Miyahira
Towards a Theology of the Concord of God
A Japanese Perspective on the Trinity
This book introduces a new Japanese theology and a unique Trinitarian formula based on the Japanese intellectual climate: three betweennesses and one concord. It also presents a new interpretation of the Trinity, a co-subordinationism, which is in line with orthodox Trinitarianism; each single person of the Trinity is eternally and equally subordinate (or serviceable) to the other persons, so that they retain the mutual dynamic equality.
2000 / 0-85364-863-8 / xiv + 256pp

Eddy José Muskus
The Origins and Early Development of Liberation Theology in Latin America
With Particular Reference to Gustavo Gutiérrez
This work challenges the fundamental premise of Liberation Theology, 'opting for the poor', and its claim that Christ is found in them. It also argues that Liberation Theology emerged as a direct result of the failure of the Roman Catholic Church in Latin America.
2002 / 0-85364-974-X / xiv + 296pp

Jim Purves
The Triune God and the Charismatic Movement
A Critical Appraisal from a Scottish Perspective
All emotion and no theology? Or a fundamental challenge to reappraise and realign our trinitarian theology in the light of Christian experience? This study of charismatic renewal as it found expression within Scotland at the end of the twentieth century evaluates the use of Patristic, Reformed and contemporary models of the Trinity in explaining the workings of the Holy Spirit.
2004 / 1-84227-321-3 / xxiv + 246pp

Anna Robbins
Methods in the Madness
Diversity in Twentieth-Century Christian Social Ethics
The author compares the ethical methods of Walter Rauschenbusch, Reinhold Niebuhr and others. She argues that unless Christians are clear about the ways that theology and philosophy are expressed practically they may lose the ability to discuss social ethics across contexts, let alone reach effective agreements.
2004 / 1-84227-211-X / xx + 294pp

Ed Rybarczyk
Beyond Salvation
Eastern Orthodoxy and Classical Pentecostalism on Becoming Like Christ
At first glance eastern Orthodoxy and classical Pentecostalism seem quite distinct. This ground-breaking study shows they share much in common, especially as it concerns the experiential elements of following Christ. Both traditions assert that authentic Christianity transcends the wooden categories of modernism.
2004 / 1-84227-144-X / xii + 356pp

Signe Sandsmark
Is World View Neutral Education Possible and Desirable?
A Christian Response to Liberal Arguments
(Published jointly with The Stapleford Centre)
This book discusses reasons for belief in world view neutrality, and argues that 'neutral' education will have a hidden, but strong world view influence. It discusses the place for Christian education in the common school.
2000 / 0-85364-973-1 / xiv + 182pp

Hazel Sherman
Reading Zechariah
The Allegorical Tradition of Biblical Interpretation through the Commentary of Didymus the Blind and Theodore of Mopsuestia
A close reading of the commentary on Zechariah by Didymus the Blind alongside that of Theodore of Mopsuestia suggests that popular categorising of Antiochene and Alexandrian biblical exegesis as 'historical' or 'allegorical' is inadequate and misleading.
2005 / 1-84227-213-6 / approx. 280pp

Andrew Sloane
On Being a Christian in the Academy
Nicholas Wolterstorff and the Practice of Christian Scholarship
An exposition and critical appraisal of Nicholas Wolterstorff's epistemology in the light of the philosophy of science, and an application of his thought to the practice of Christian scholarship.
2003 / 1-84227-058-3 / xvi + 274pp

Damon W.K. So
Jesus' Revelation of His Father
A Narrative-Conceptual Study of the Trinity with Special Reference to Karl Barth
This book explores the trinitarian dynamics in the context of Jesus' revelation of his Father in his earthly ministry with references to key passages in Matthew's Gospel. It develops from the exegeses of these passages a non-linear concept of revelation which links Jesus' communion with his Father to his revelatory words and actions through a nuanced understanding of the Holy Spirit, with references to K. Barth, G.W.H. Lampe, J.D.G. Dunn and E. Irving.
2005 / 1-84227-323-X / approx. 380pp

Daniel Strange
The Possibility of Salvation Among the Unevangelised
An Analysis of Inclusivism in Recent Evangelical Theology
For evangelical theologians the 'fate of the unevangelised' impinges upon fundamental tenets of evangelical identity. The position known as 'inclusivism', defined by the belief that the unevangelised can be ontologically saved by Christ whilst being epistemologically unaware of him, has been defended most vigorously by the Canadian evangelical Clark H. Pinnock. Through a detailed analysis and critique of Pinnock's work, this book examines a cluster of issues surrounding the unevangelised and its implications for christology, soteriology and the doctrine of revelation.
2002 / 1-84227-047-8 / xviii + 362pp

Scott Swain
God According to the Gospel
Biblical Narrative and the Identity of God in the Theology of Robert W. Jenson
Robert W. Jenson is one of the leading voices in contemporary Trinitarian theology. His boldest contribution in this area concerns his use of biblical narrative both to ground and explicate the Christian doctrine of God. *God According to the Gospel* critically examines Jenson's proposal and suggests an alternative way of reading the biblical portrayal of the triune God.
2006 / 1-84227-258-6 / approx. 180pp

Justyn Terry
The Justifying Judgement of God
A Reassessment of the Place of Judgement in the Saving Work of Christ
The argument of this book is that judgement, understood as the whole process of bringing justice, is the primary metaphor of atonement, with others, such as victory, redemption and sacrifice, subordinate to it. Judgement also provides the proper context for understanding penal substitution and the call to repentance, baptism, eucharist and holiness.
2005 / 1-84227-370-1 / approx. 274 pp

Graham Tomlin
The Power of the Cross
Theology and the Death of Christ in Paul, Luther and Pascal
This book explores the theology of the cross in St Paul, Luther and Pascal. It offers new perspectives on the theology of each, and some implications for the nature of power, apologetics, theology and church life in a postmodern context.
1999 / 0-85364-984-7 / xiv + 344pp

Adonis Vidu
Postliberal Theological Method
A Critical Study
The postliberal theology of Hans Frei, George Lindbeck, Ronald Thiemann, John Milbank and others is one of the more influential contemporary options. This book focuses on several aspects pertaining to its theological method, specifically its understanding of background, hermeneutics, epistemic justification, ontology, the nature of doctrine and, finally, Christological method.
2005 / 1-84227-395-7 / approx. 324pp

Graham J. Watts
Revelation and the Spirit
A Comparative Study of the Relationship between the Doctrine of Revelation and Pneumatology in the Theology of Eberhard Jüngel and of Wolfhart Pannenberg

The relationship between revelation and pneumatology is relatively unexplored. This approach offers a fresh angle on two important twentieth century theologians and raises pneumatological questions which are theologically crucial and relevant to mission in a postmodern culture.

2005 / 1-84227-104-0 / xxii + 232pp

Nigel G. Wright
Disavowing Constantine
Mission, Church and the Social Order in the Theologies of John Howard Yoder and Jürgen Moltmann

This book is a timely restatement of a radical theology of church and state in the Anabaptist and Baptist tradition. Dr Wright constructs his argument in dialogue and debate with Yoder and Moltmann, major contributors to a free church perspective.

2000 / 0-85364-978-2 / xvi + 252pp

Paternoster
9 Holdom Avenue,
Bletchley,
Milton Keynes MK1 1QR,
United Kingdom
Web: www.authenticmedia.co.uk/paternoster

www.ingramcontent.com/pod-product-compliance
Lightning Source LLC
Chambersburg PA
CBHW050435240426
43661CB00055B/2393